WESTMAR COLLEGE LIBRARY

W9-AEB-325

MAN AND CULTURE

Contributors

J. R. FIRTH

RAYMOND FIRTH

MEYER FORTES

H. IAN HOGBIN

PHYLLIS KABERRY

E. R. LEACH

LUCY MAIR

S. F. NADEL

TALCOTT PARSONS

RALPH PIDDINGTON

AUDREY I. RICHARDS

I. SCHAPERA

At the Annual Meeting of the American Anthropological
Association in 1939 at Chicago

Photograph by Leslie A. White

Man and Culture

AN EVALUATION OF THE WORK
OF BRONISLAW MALINOWSKI

EDITED BY RAYMOND FIRTH

Routledge & Kegan Paul
LONDON

GN
8
.F5

572.04
F527m

52159

First published 1957
by Routledge & Kegan Paul Limited
Broadway House, 68-74 Carter Lane
London, E.C.4

© *Routledge & Kegan Paul Limited 1957*

Printed in Great Britain
by Lowe & Brydone (Printers) Limited
London, N.W.10

Second impression 1959
Second impression with corrections 1960

Contents

The Authors

J. R. FIRTH is Emeritus Professor of General Linguistics in the University of London.

RAYMOND FIRTH is Professor of Anthropology in the University of London.

MEYER FORTES is William Wyse Professor of Social Anthropology in the University of Cambridge; Fellow of King's College, Cambridge.

H. IAN HOGBIN is Reader in Anthropology in the University of Sydney.

PHYLLIS KABERRY is Reader in Anthropology in the University of London.

E. R. LEACH is Reader in Anthropology in the University of Cambridge.

LUCY MAIR is Reader in Applied Anthropology, University of London.

S. F. NADEL (died 1956) was Professor of Anthropology and Sociology in the Australian National University.

TALCOTT PARSONS is Professor of Sociology, Harvard University.

RALPH PIDDINGTON is Professor of Anthropology, Auckland University College, University of New Zealand.

AUDREY I. RICHARDS is Vice-Principal, Newnham College, Cambridge.

I. SCHAPERA is Professor of Anthropology in the University of London.

Editor's Note

THE plan for this volume arose from discussions in the Department of Anthropology of the London School of Economics, where Malinowski was for so long a distinguished student, teacher, and leader. As a result of these discussions I was given responsibility for collecting and editing the essays which here appear. I am grateful to all my collaborators, whose names are in the Table of Contents, for the patience and good humour with which they have complied with editorial demands and borne with delays. I am especially indebted to Audrey I. Richards and to I. Schapera for their help and counsel.

The essays here are not eulogies but evaluations. Their viewpoints are essentially personal and therefore by no means all the same. Their intention is to try and give, after a lapse of much more than a decade since Malinowski's death, a clear notion of his contribution to his chosen subject, in terms of its meaning for a student today. This subject, the science of man as seen in the regularities and significance of man's social behaviour, has of necessity been split up rather arbitrarily by the originators of this volume into a number of themes. Not every major aspect of Malinowski's work has been thus separately treated. For example, his concept of function and his use of psycho-analytical theory are mentioned, though somewhat briefly, under other heads. But it will probably be agreed that the essays as a set do give a synoptic view of the main strength and weakness of Malinowski's contribution and its modern relevance.

In the selection of authors, the intention of the originators of the volume was to obtain the opinions of a representative set of Malinowski's former students and colleagues who came under his influence in London. This meant giving primarily, though not exclusively, a British viewpoint. It has also meant severe limitation on the number of contributors and on the space allotted to them. Yet even though some who were invited to contribute were unable to accept, a substantial book has still been put together. It is regretted that various other colleagues with full entitlement to appear are not here represented. But it is hoped that they will approve the spirit of the volume.

Acknowledgements

For assistance with the Introduction acknowledgement is gratefully made to Sĕnora Valetta Swann (Mme Valetta Malinowska) for permission to quote from various letters by Bronislaw Malinowski to Raymond Firth and for much helpful information; to Mrs. B. Z. Seligman for permission to quote from letters of Malinowski to C. G. Seligman; and to the Association of Polish University Professors and Lecturers in Great Britain for permission to reproduce passages from an Address by Raymond Firth printed in their memorial publication in honour of Malinowski (see Bibliography).

Gratitude is also due to Malinowski's daughters Jozefa (Mrs. Walker Stuart), Wanda (Mrs. Donald Allen), and Helena (Mrs. Donald Burke) for their help in reading and commenting upon the Introduction; and to Mrs. Burke and to Leslie A. White for photographs of Malinowski. To Mrs. Sheila Patterson thanks are also due for her help in verifying and abstracting Polish items in the Bibliography of Malinowski's works.

References

For uniformity and to save space, references in the text are usually given to Malinowski's works by date and page only: where page alone is given, the reference is to the work cited immediately before. References to works of other authors are given usually by name, date and page. Details are to be found in the Selected Bibliography at the end of the volume—a distinction being drawn between works by Malinowski, works primarily about Malinowski, and works by other authors cited.

R. F.

London School of Economics and Political Science
June, 1956

Introduction: Malinowski as Scientist and as Man

RAYMOND FIRTH

THIS book has been written because some of us have thought for a long while that too little attention has been paid to the work of Bronislaw Malinowski. He has been one of the outstanding influences in shaping modern British social anthropology. More than ten years have passed since his death and the time has come for a fresh estimate of his contribution. His achievement has indubitably suffered from his early death. If he had lived for another decade his dialectical skill, let alone the richness of his creative mind, would have found many answers to his critics and derived profit from their comment. Much of this comment has been justified, but by no means all, and sometimes his work has been passed over where credit was due.

Three factors in particular seem to be responsible for this. One is that the climate of opinion, particularly in British social anthropology, changed radically in the decade and a half after Malinowski left England. This was partly due to the influence of Radcliffe-Brown, and partly to the growing realization of the need for a clearer structural approach to give more precision to many anthropological generalizations. Malinowski was not a structuralist in the narrow sense, and appreciation of his work suffered by comparison. Secondly, Malinowski's analytical contributions to anthropology were much stronger than his systematic contributions. He did not develop his concept of function very far. And in his attempts to create a system which would take full account of his concept of culture he landed himself with a difficult, unwieldy and to some extent unprofitable theoretical construction. The third reason was that Malinowski's personal qualities made for him 'unfriends' as well as friends. His intolerance of what he considered sham or insincerity, his impatience with criticism that he did not think was based on loyalty, his tenderness towards personal slights and his relative insensitivity to the effects of his exuberance towards others all tended to arouse hostility. Some criticisms of Malinowski's work, however justified, could hardly be expected therefore to have been made with entire detachment.

One result was that Malinowski has become something of a legend to those who never knew him. He has continued to be a great name in anthropology. But while his reputation as a superb field-worker has been maintained, his fame as a really great teacher in the Socratic tradition has been allowed to fade, and his achievement in creating a new and enduring approach to anthropology has not been properly understood. Without him, the aridities of the *Kulturkreislehre* and the fantasies of pan-Egyptianism would doubtless have in due course been corrected and overcome. But for the younger generation of anthropologists in Europe, at least, he fought that battle and won it by the end of the 'twenties'. And though now this is dim history, those who were students at that time know what formidable opponents were to be encountered in Elliot Smith, Pater Schmidt, and their adherents. Yet this was merely by the way. It was incidental to the main task Malinowski had set himself—a dynamic interpretation of human behaviour in the widest range of cultural circumstances, in terms which were at once more theoretically sophisticated, and more realistic, than any then current. At that time, the tradition was that an anthropologist was primarily either a theoretician or an ethnographer, and that the theory should be kept separate from the facts. It was part of Malinowski's contribution, not only to combine them, but to show how fact was meaningless without theory and how each could gain in significance by being consciously brought into relation.[1] The main theoretical apparatus which he constructed over a decade and a half has proved unable, in the end, to bear the systematic weight he wished to put upon it. But much of it is still usable, and it has given many ideas to others, often unacknowledged by them.

The Malinowski legend sometimes takes an extreme form—as expressed in this student's examination answer: 'Because of his views Malinowski did not make abstractions and was at best a misguided theorist.' Such a distortion of his theoretical position ignores his keen preoccupation with methodology—and indeed his general interest in philosophical issues. Moreover it misses one important point. The great question is of course—why, if his theory was so inadequate, was his influence upon his pupils so profound? The contributions to this book will help to show where the answers lie.

Bronislaw Kaspar Malinowski was born on April 7th, 1884, in Cracow, and died on May 16th, 1942, in New Haven. The events of his life need be recapitulated only briefly here, since they have been referred to in various notices (see Bibliography ii. at the end of this volume).

[1] His separation of inference from observation, for which he gave credit to Haddon, Rivers and Seligman (1922*a*, p. 3n.), was assisted by his theoretical insight into the meaning of 'facts' (see especially 1916, pp. 418-19).

Malinowski was educated in Cracow, first in the King Jan Sobieski public school and then in 'the oldest University in eastern Europe', where he took his Ph.D. (*summa cum laude*) in 1908. This degree was in physics and mathematics, but he was prevented by illness from continuing these studies. At this time he was allowed to read the *Golden Bough*. Powerfully attracted on this 'first attempt to read an English masterpiece in the original' (then only three volumes), he turned to anthropology. He also acquired an admiration for Frazer which, despite a fundamental difference in their viewpoints, lasted throughout his career and is expressed in the perceptive essay (1944, pp. 179–221) published posthumously. After a period at Leipzig, working under Karl Bücher and Wilhelm Wundt, Malinowski came to England in 1910. He became a postgraduate student at the London School of Economics, from which he obtained his D.Sc. degree in 1916, with two printed works on the Australian Aborigines and on the Mailu (1913*a* and 1915*a*). In 1913–14 he was one of the 'Lecturers in Special Subjects' at the London School of Economics. He taught in the department of Sociology, giving short courses on 'Primitive Religion and Social Differentiation' and on 'Social Psychology'. In 1914, largely through the help of C. G. Seligman, he was awarded a Robert Mond Travelling Studentship (University of London) and a Constance Hutchinson Scholarship of the London School of Economics, and went out to undertake field research in New Guinea. He travelled via Australia, with other anthropologists going out for the British Association meeting in Melbourne. It was at this time that he first met Radcliffe-Brown (then A. R. Brown) and received from him what he later spoke of as valuable hints about field-work. Arriving in New Guinea in September 1914, he spent about four weeks waiting in Port Moresby for a boat to the eastwards, and took advantage of this period to work with Ahuia Ova, Seligman's earlier informant. After some months with the Mailu, Malinowski returned to Australia in February 1915, making a call at Woodlark island on the way. A financial stringency having been overcome through Seligman's help, he returned to New Guinea in May 1915 with assistance from the Commonwealth Department of External Affairs, Melbourne. He meant to go to Mambare, and to Dobu, as well as to Rossel island, which Seligman had wanted him to investigate. But he stopped in the Trobriands, since apparently the people with whom he had made arrangements in those other places had moved elsewhere. His field experiences in the Trobriands, on his two expeditions, have been examined elsewhere in this volume (pp. 77–80).

After his final return to Australia from the Trobriand field, in October 1918, Malinowski lived for a while in Melbourne, where he married Elsie Masson, daughter of Sir David Orme Masson, then Professor of Chemistry at Melbourne University. Threatened by tuberculosis on his return to Europe, Malinowski lived for a year or so with his wife on

3

Tenerife, in the Canary islands, where, in April 1921, the preface to his *Argonauts of the Western Pacific* was signed. He again took up a post as occasional lecturer at the London School of Economics in 1921–2, this time in Ethnology, giving eighteen lectures on 'The Sociology and Economics of Some Island Communities' (i.e. the Trobriands). This was in the Summer Term, i.e. mid-1922—though he seems to have given a similar course on an *ad hoc* basis in the summer of 1920. He was appointed lecturer in Social Anthropology for 1922–3, and gave short courses in the Summer Term on 'Early Beliefs and Social Differentiation', 'Social Organization of Australian Aborigines', and 'Economics of Primitive Peoples'. He also, in collaboration with Morris Ginsberg, led a seminar on 'Primitive Mentality'. From 1922, for nearly twenty years, London was his academic home, though he travelled widely from it, especially during the summer months. On the Continent, he lectured in Geneva, Vienna, Rome, and Oslo; he visited other European capital cities; he lived for a time (during sabbatical leave in 1931–2) at Tamaris in the south of France. He maintained for many years, until his death, a villa at Oberbozen (Soprabolzano) in the South Tyrol, looking out on the Dolomites, on the mountains of Rosengarten, Latemar, and Schlern —on to what he declared was the finest scenery in Europe. In 1924 Malinowski was appointed to a Readership in Anthropology in the University of London (tenable at the London School of Economics), and in 1927 to the first Chair in Anthropology in the University. (Seligman held the Chair in Ethnology.) In May 1934 Malinowski went to South Africa to participate in the New Education Fellowship Conference, and from July till October he toured in South and East Africa, visiting his students in the field and doing anthropological survey work among the Swazi, Bemba, Chagga, Masai, Kikuyu, and Maragoli peoples.

In 1926 he had visited the United States for the first time at the invitation of the Laura Spelman Rockefeller Memorial. (He then took the opportunity to visit some of the Pueblo Indians, coming back with the confession that at last he had found languages that were really difficult even for him to learn!) He returned to the United States in 1933 to deliver the Messenger Lectures at Cornell University, and again in 1936 as a delegate of the University of London to the Harvard Tercentenary celebrations, when he received an Honorary D.Sc. from Harvard. He went back again in 1938 on sabbatical leave. This time he remained in North America for three-and-a-half years—until his death. In the early part of this last stay he lived in Tucson, Arizona, to fortify his health, which had continued for years to be somewhat delicate. He was appointed Visiting Professor at Yale for the year October 1939–June 1940, and then, from September 1940, he became for a year the Bishop Museum Visiting Professor at Yale—an appointment made by an arrangement between Yale and the Bernice P. Bishop Museum at Honolulu. (A school-friend of his youngest daughter asked at this time, to his delight, if it were true that he was a 'Yale Professor Visiting Bishop at Honolulu'!) This appointment was renewed for the following year. In the summer vacations of 1940 and 1941 he carried out field-trips (totalling nearly eight months in all) to the Zapotec of Oaxaca, in Mexico, and studied their peasant marketing system. At the beginning of 1942 he was appointed permanently as a Professor at Yale as from October 1942; he died before this appointment became effective.

In this volume specific mention should be made of Malinowski's position in British anthropology, in which he was a brilliant figure for a quarter of a century. Arriving in London as a pale, bespectacled student with a high forehead and a difficult Slavonic name, he was at first looked on as a somewhat alien figure. But his English was good, and able to express his ideas easily, he was speedily recognized as an anthropologist of great intellectual gifts and exceeding promise. He worked in the beginning mainly with C. G. Seligman and with Westermarck. To Seligman in particular Malinowski owed a great deal for anthropological training and for friendly encouragement and assistance both in and out of the field. In later years they grew apart, in large degree owing to their very different conceptions of the scope and aims of anthropology. But their earlier relations were close. In correspondence when Malinowski was in New Guinea (in 1914) he half-jokingly referred to Seligman on one occasion as *kakagu* ('my elder brother' in Motu) in the classificatory sense, and he wrote in 1941 after Seligman's death of the 'very, very warm memories of him' in the early period, and how 'he was an extremely kind, pleasant and in many ways stimulating personality and mind'. Malinowski's debt to Seligman for support in his field research was expressed in various contexts (e.g. 1915*a*, p. 496; 1916, p. 354; 1922*a*, p. xix). It appears characteristically in one of his letters at a time when he had already been a month in New Guinea, working with Ahuia Ova, and he was threatened with shortage of funds: 'I hope that this idyll will not find an untimely end through want of money and that the School of Economics will not prove a barren rock, or at least that you will prove the Moïse who is able to tap this rock. . . . I must say the work has got hold of me already and I would be loath not to bring it to a successful end. . . .'

With Westermarck in particular Malinowski felt an intellectual kinship. Though often prolific in acknowledgement, when a quarter of a century later he remembered 'Edward Westermarck, to whose personal teaching and to whose work I owe more than to any other scientific influence' (1937*a*), these were no empty words. Malinowski's first substantial essay in English (1912*a*), a contribution on primitive Australian economics, appeared in the commemorative volume to mark Westermarck's fiftieth birthday, and Westermarck (1913) reviewed Malinowski's book on *The Family among the Australian Aborigines* with enthusiasm, as from a methodological point of view, 'a model which ought to be imitated in all future inquiries of a similar kind'.

In a few years after his arrival in London Malinowski had extended his relations with British anthropologists widely. He became well known to C. G. Seligman and B. Z. Seligman, Frazer, Haddon, Rivers, and Marett. He exchanged ideas with G. C. Wheeler (a fellow contributor to the Westermarck *Festskrift* and a helper with the book on the *Family among the Australian Aborigines*), with Marie Czaplicka (a brilliant co-national authoress of a book on the aboriginal peoples of Siberia, who died in tragic circumstances), and with Barbara Freire-Marreco (Mrs. B. W. Aitken, of Oxford, who had already done field-work among the Pueblo Indians). At that period, anthropology was still treated primarily as a general, all-embracing discipline. Malinowski did no physical anthropology or archaeology. But then as later he was prepared to undertake observation and description of technological processes if this seemed in any way to advance the analysis and understanding of social relationships. This is shown in his Mailu and his Trobriand work, in the house-measurements he made for Audrey Richards among the Bemba in 1934 (Richards, 1950b, p. 88), and in his paper on stone implements in the commemorative volume for Seligman (1934b)—though this was rather in the nature of a *défi*. Yet it was always to social anthropology that his interests turned. Hence the work of W. H. R. Rivers tended to have a considerable influence upon him, though he viewed it critically. Rivers's acknowledgement to suggestions made by Malinowski is given in the introduction to his *Kinship and Social Organization*, dated November 1913. After Malinowski had returned from the field, having studied the realities of a kinship system at close quarters, he began increasingly to react against Rivers's views and to measure himself against Rivers's reputation. At that time the works of another great expatriate Pole, Joseph Conrad, had a considerable vogue. I have been told by Mrs. B. Z. Seligman that Malinowski once said proudly, 'Rivers is the Rider Haggard of anthropology; I shall be the Conrad.' Yet shortly after Rivers's death Malinowski, who earlier had praised his introduction of the genealogical method and his systematic study of the functions of kin, still cited him (1922b, p. 218) as one of the best modern writers, who more consistently and explicitly than anyone else had tended to shift the main weight of scientific attention from isolated, curious detail to comprehensive groups of fundamental ideas.

For a long time, in the field of British social anthropology, Malinowski was one of the men best equipped in Continental scientific scholarship. His early wide reading of ethnological source materials, his linguistic mastery of both the spoken and the written word, and his considerable travel, combined with his theoretical penetration, gave him a very great range of knowledge. Though in later years he himself read little, it was his practice to have works read to and discussed with him, and the early

6

scholarly discipline remained. His references to Cunow, Schurtz, E. Grosse, Graebner, Hahn, Van Gennep, Ehrenreich, Nieboer, K. T. Preuss and others now almost forgotten were tokens of theoretical grasp of content, not a mere parade of learning.

Malinowski has stated in various contexts (e.g. 1913a, pp. vii–ix; 1913b, p. 531; 1916, p. 423n.; 1925a, p. 23; 1933, p. 154; 1944, pp. 19, 25, 26) his recognition of Durkheim and Steinmetz, with Westermarck, as founders and leaders of sociology, especially as 'an empirical, i.e. real' science. The impression made upon him by Karl Bücher and Wilhelm Wundt, and later, by Marcel Mauss and by Richard Thurnwald, is fairly well known. So also is the counter-reaction he had to the work of Wilhelm Schmidt and others of the *Kulturhistorische Schule*, as well as to that of Lévy-Bruhl. He had also known of Max Weber (e.g. 1925b, p. 930), though he made little use of his work. Among other condition-ing elements of his thought were the influences of L. T. Hobhouse, James B. Watson and W. McDougall, and notably, A. F. Shand. At the time I first knew Malinowski, Shand's *Foundations of Character*, con-taining the theory of the three orders of systems—impulses, emotions and sentiments—was one of his household books, and contributed much to the formation of his views on family and kinship, and the nature of institutions. As time went on, he developed a large personal acquaint-ance with scholars in various fields all over the world—aided in this by his ability to converse with most of them in their own vernaculars. In Britain alone he co-operated with or was influenced by a range of men including Richard Gregory, Havelock Ellis, A. H. Gardiner, Julian Huxley, C. K. Ogden, Cyril Burt, C. S. Myers, J. C. Flugel, W. Powys Mathers, G. H. L.-F. Pitt-Rivers, J. H. Oldham—all of whom were interested from different angles in the wider human implications of his science. He was closely in touch for a considerable time with the work of the British Social Hygiene Council, he gave wise advice to the founders of Mass Observation, he was responsible for the first anthropo-logical field training programme of the International African Institute. He looked upon his subject as a science, its rôle being 'first hand-maiden to a general theory of human society'; but he saw it also in its bearings upon human affairs—'a theory trying to achieve a deeper grasp of human nature and human history', perhaps capable of being used to influence the makers of policy but above all 'useful in creating a saner attitude, finer and wider ideals in the minds of men' (1922b, pp. 218–19).

These essays are concerned as a whole with Malinowski's scientific work, and it is not for me here to go over the same ground. But Malin-owski's influence in his science was also due to the impact of his person-ality. In this introduction it is therefore appropriate to round off the commentary by saying something of Malinowski as a man.

Malinowski was a complex personality, highly intelligent, cultured, and gifted in most things with a fine degree of sensitivity. In the

RAYMOND FIRTH

academic field, quite apart from his writings, it was his contribution
as a teacher that was important. I think I cannot do better in what
follows than to quote from a few of his letters to me, as well as from
a tribute which I paid to him shortly after his death.[1] These give a
fresher impression of the personality of the man than an evaluation
after long retrospect. I wrote in 1942:

'. . . Almost more than anything else, Malinowski was a great teacher.
He drew to him students from all over the world, and from a variety of
branches of knowledge.

'What was the secret of his attraction? Of course, it is not easy to
describe. Primarily, I think, it lay in his real love of teaching, in the
vitality he put into his classes and the pains he took with his students.
Not that he gave many ordinary lectures—he could use the rostrum
brilliantly, on formal occasions, but what he really liked was the seminar,
the informal discussion group, with someone else giving the paper.
Bending over his sheaf of notes at the head of the table or sunk in his
deep armchair, nothing would escape him—no loose phrase, no shoddy
thinking, no subtle point of emphasis. With a suave question, a caustic
word, or a flash of wit, he would expose a fallacy, probe for further
explanation, or throw new light on something said. At the end, after
inviting opinion from all sides, he would draw together the threads in
a masterly way, lifting the whole discussion to a higher theoretical level,
and putting it in a perspective of still wider problems. He was always
constructive. One of his gifts was so to transform what had been said
as to bring out its value as a contribution to the discussion. He made
each member of the seminar feel that, fumbling and inept as the words
had been, Malinowski perceived the ideas and gave them all or more
than they deserved. He inspired, too, by the way he spoke. He rarely
laid down the law; he talked as one who was also seeking knowledge, as
a fellow-worker asking the co-operation of his pupils in a common task.
Always, too, he insisted on laying bare the roots of the matter. His constant question was: "Where does the real problem lie?" And he saw it
always not in terms of fine-spun academic theories, but arising out of
the behaviour of ordinary human beings. It was the same whether the
subject under discussion was the initiation rites of the Kikuyu, the
agricultural magic of the Trobrianders, or the basis of faith and morals
in Europe. He wrote much of savages—many of his books have that

---

[1] This is taken from a pamphlet published after a memorial meeting convened
by the Association of Polish University Professors and Lecturers in Great
Britain, and held under the auspices of the London School of Economics and
Political Science, the Royal Anthropological Institute, the Institute of Sociology,
the International Institute of African Languages and Cultures, the School of
Slavonic and East European Studies, and the Association of Polish Professors
and Lecturers in Great Britain. The speakers were R. E. Marett, M. Ginsberg,
H. J. Braunholtz, Raymond Firth, and A. Jurasz, with Sir William H. Beveridge
(Lord Beveridge) in the Chair.

word in their title—but he thought always of the Man in the savage, of those impulses and emotions which are common to savage and civilized alike. So his teaching was never remote from reality. In whatever part of the world the discussion might begin, and with whatever strange customs it might deal, the relevance of its problems to fundamental human situations was brought home to us. Anthropology to Malinowski was not simply the study of the savage, but the study through which by understanding the savage we might come to a better understanding of ourselves. This "coefficient of reality", as he once jokingly called it, was one of the reasons for his superb work in the field.'

It was also one of the reasons for his influence in helping to make anthropology a subject more accessible to non-specialists interested in social questions of a theoretical as well as a practical order. As contributors to this volume show, his generalizing viewpoint was a source of weakness in his attempt to develop more rigorous propositions about social phenomena. Too easily he sought universal, not specific comparison. But it did help to give people in other disciplines the sense that anthropology shared with them a common purpose, a common field of human behaviour, a similar kind of generalization; that they could latch into it at a number of points in a significant, dynamic way. But to return to his relations with his students, to whom, above all, he opened the doors of the mind.

'To his pupils, Malinowski's stimulus lay in a combination of many qualities: his subtle power of analysis, his sincerity in facing problems, his sense of reality, his scholarly command of the literature, his capacity for integrating detail into general ideas, his brilliance and wit in handling discussion. But it was due to something more, to his liberal interpretation of the rôle of a teacher. A Chinese student of ours once said to me: "Malinowski is like an Oriental teacher—he is a father to his pupils. He has us to his home; he gets us to run messages for him; sometimes we even cook for him. And we like to do these things for him." He took a personal interest in each of his pupils; he talked over with them not only their academic problems but their own human problems as well. As with any father, he and his students did not always see eye to eye. But one felt that he had a great store of wise advice, which he expressed in his own inimitably shrewd fashion. Whether he gave it soberly or flippantly, one knew that he was sympathetic, that he felt the trouble as his own. And if a crisis arose—because one could argue fiercely with him at times—he had a most disarming way of suddenly putting aside all emotion, and spreading the whole thing out on the table, as it were, for analysis of his own motives as well as those of the other person. It was this capacity for friendship and sympathy, going beyond the relations of a teacher to pupil, that helped to strengthen his attraction.'

Part of Malinowski's success as a teacher lay in the way in which he was able to draw his pupils either in the formal capacity of research assistants, or informally as helpers, into the orbit of his own work. He was a great believer in well-formulated plans on paper for a book or even an article, and they were of great theoretical value in exploring and defining relationships and concepts. Malinowski rarely wrote out his own manuscripts—he could not type—but dictated them, and these outlines helped to give control and direction to the process. Such plans generated elaborate discussion and reshaping. In a way it was partly this zeal for order in argument which was responsible for Malinowski's failure to produce a single synoptic account of Trobriand culture; a failure for which he has been often criticised. It was not of course only this. In a letter to me shortly after my return from the field in 1929, he gave a few words of advice about the working up of my material: 'I would start with the working out of the "documents" such as magical Formulae, Genealogies, Maps and Charts, Statistical data, etc. You have, no doubt by now, already a general plan of your future work. I wonder whether you will procced at once to a full straightforward account of the Tikopean [*sic*] culture or whether you will do what I did —that is write it up piecemeal. I hope you will do the former, as I would do now, if I could go back ten years. I had, of course, my good reasons for proceeding as I did. One of them was, as you know, the poor health with which I had to fight at that time, and which prevented me from really taking in hand the difficult task of handling my full material. The other reason was that, at the time when I started my work, it was rather urgent to present the theoretical point of view which we now label "functional", and which I could only do by presenting some fragments of my stuff, well placed in an extensive theoretical setting.'

Another quotation from his correspondence with me in the field brings up the point of his aesthetic interest in his field-work. 'I got quite a bit of Sehnsucht when reading about the surf [he wrote "serf"] beating on the beach, the piping of mosquitoes and the moths fluttering round the hurricane lamp. I wish I had been on your island instead of on the beastly coral pan of Boyowa. I always loved the direct proximity of the sea and in the Trobriands I could get it only from time to time, or else in the unpalatable form of the lagoon. On the other hand, I expect that you must be rather stinted for physical exercise.' Exercise was one of Malinowski's fetishes. Various of his pupils will remember having been taken for long walks through the pinewoods of the Ritten Plateau, from his villa in the South Tyrol, being caught at supper time by the sound of the evening bell, and having to run down the hillsides in order not to be late.

One of the most difficult things to swallow in Malinowski for those who were not prepared to surrender themselves to him was his particular sense of humour. He delighted in playing with words. He infuriated some of his colleagues by the statement (often quoted against him) in the Special Foreword to *The Sexual Life of Savages* that 'the magnificent title of the Functional School of Anthropology has been bestowed by myself, in a way on myself, and to a large extent out of my own sense of irresponsibility'. This, like his mention of himself as 'the Arch-Functionalist' (1938*a*, p. xxxvi), was his idea of a joke. It revealed, indeed paraded, his own egocentricity, his own belief in his intellectual achievement. Yet it also reveals what he was never hesitant to show, the comic rather pathetic human figure on the stage of destiny. Harlequin was always to Malinowski a sympathetic image.

In April, 1935 I received a postcard from Chicago, with the following message, in Malinowski's handwriting: 'Greeting from the classical Functional School (A. R.-B. & B. M.)—see lower picture on verso—To the London Functionalist (R. F.)—see on top.' The message is signed 'B. M.' The postcard is in colour and is from the Lincoln Park Zoo. On the top verso is a solemn-looking orang-outang sitting in a chair and gazing into space; in the lower picture, two orang-outangs sit in straw, side by side, holding, and sucking from, what appear to be identical bottles of milk. The postcard is completed by a sedate message: 'Best greetings from Rex' (i.e. Radcliffe-Brown).

The following was his reply on one occasion to an At Home invitation:

'Professor B. Malinowski (functionalist in Partibus Infidelium) begs to transmit his obsequious obeisance to Mrs..............

$$\left. \begin{array}{l} \text{hyper} \\ \text{epi} \\ \text{meta} \end{array} \right\} \text{functionalist-in-law} \Big)$$

and advise her of the imminent contingency of a potential incursion by the first-mentioned at her At Home (30.vi.38)

　　To Contribute towards the Persistance of the Social System of that Party

adding (contributing)

to its
　　Eunomia—or Disnomia?
its
　　Euphoria—or Disphoria?
its
　　Eulalia—or Dislalia?
　　　($\lambda \alpha \lambda \epsilon \iota \nu$ to babble)
its
　　Eubolia—or Disbolia?
its
　　Eukretia—or Diskretia?
etc. etc.'

In such messages, guying both himself and others, he usually managed to poke fun at some current movement or piece of jargon; pomposity in particular attracted his shafts.

In public speaking Malinowski could be most witty, and complimentary or provocative, as he chose. But his gift was not always sure; at times also he could be most laboriously unfunny. But unlike Radcliffe-Brown, who always had to have around him a protective shell, Malinowski was not afraid to reveal himself. Yet each in his own way was much in need of affection.

I quote again from 1942: 'Wherever he went, he left the impact of a powerful personality. Whether it was at an academic gathering or at a party—and he loved parties—he stood out, by his appearance, his manner, his clear intelligence and his brilliance of conversation. Like any man of marked individuality, of course, he had his foibles, but they served only to accentuate his distinction. . . .

'And then behind these foibles lay another side of the personality. Perhaps as a reflex of his keen scientific penetration he had a great emotional sensitivity. Sometimes this took on almost a melancholic form. Ever since his boyhood he had a continual struggle against illness—but a struggle during which he still managed to do more work than most ordinary men. And then there was the tragedy of illness in his family. This helped to arouse in him the feeling that he was fighting against Fate itself, which in giving him the cup of success to drink, had filled it with a bitter draught. At such times he needed friendship badly, and all the comfort his friends could give.'

The illness in particular which overshadowed nearly ten years of his life was that of his wife, who had contracted an incurable spinal complaint, but who maintained her composure and her intellect with great courage. She died in 1935. In his trouble he wrote at times almost with despair. In a letter of March 1929 he said: '. . . From this you can see that as far as I am concerned things have changed notably. The times, full of hope and anticipation, and of that new start which my early teaching gave me—all this seems ages ago. It is a different world in which I live now, at best hopelessly grey and meaningless, at worst a nightmare beyond endurance. Of course I *do* work, and even amuse myself and pursue my ambitions, hates, etc.—but it all is a thin surface, threadbare and unpleasant to touch, and beneath a horrible void.'

In someone else this might be thought histrionic, but Malinowski was always conscious of the possibility of self-deception, and regarded intellectual honesty as a supreme value. In a little-known essay on primitive religion and science (1931*b*), there are passages about his agnosticism and his feeling for religion which express his deep sense of the tragedy of his world. 'Is the modern world, with its devastating wars, its racial, national and class hatreds, with its mean rapacities and wholesale exploitations—is our world really governed by this inner and universal revelation of truth and harmony to all men alike? I see no trace of such control. I feel far nearer to the established, traditional creeds, which appeal to me aesthetically and morally—and for them I have a deep reverence. Is there any hope of bridging this deepest gulf, that between tragic agnosticism and belief? I do not know. Is there any remedy? I cannot answer this either. What can help us, perhaps, is more and more honesty, more outspokenness and more sincerity.'

But Malinowski's domestic circumstances did not remain the same. In 1938 he went on sabbatical leave to the United States and remained there till his death. By temperament he could never be a completely happy person. But as the memory of his earlier sorrow faded, especially in the last five years of his life he found family happiness once again, through his growing daughters, and through his re-marriage—to Valetta Swann the artist.

Yet now he was disturbed by war. Malinowski was never a very patriotic person in the conventional sense of the term. War—at least in the civilized sphere—seemed to him a negation of cultured behaviour, destructive of the finest flowering of the creative arts. The first World War was a shock to him, both in personal and international terms. He was worried about its effects on his mother, who was then living in Cracow, he disapproved of the crusading spirit of both sides, and he had his own troubles about his political status. In 1914 Seligman had become concerned about Malinowski's future (Malinowski was then in Australia), because he had discovered that Malinowski was an Austrian subject and therefore technically an enemy alien. (Fortunately, treatment was not very rigorous in those days, and Malinowski was allowed by the authorities to continue his anthropological work.) Seligman wrote to Malinowski that from the latter's general views of Teutons, Seligman had put him down as coming from Russian Poland. Malinowski replied, 'You are astonished I am an Austrian subject because I used abusive language even before the war about the b——y Germans. But you must know that Poles who are German subjects are avowedly Russophile, whereas Russian Poles are apt to overlook the intensity of the Teutonic danger. There is *no* such blooming thing as an "Austrian"—it is a pure fiction. We had the best treatment in Austria and as a confederation of fairly autonomous peoples, A. was one of the most possible [*sic*] states. Once A. fights for Germany, A. becomes stupidly and clumsily odious. This is my *confession de foi*.' As a result of all this, Malinowski when in New Guinea found it difficult to work when disturbed by war news, and so in his own phrase 'shrouded himself in a beastly selfish stoicism'.

But well before the second World War Malinowski had acquired British nationality. His attitude here was very different. While he still regarded a world war as destructive of the fundamental values for which civilization stood, he saw in totalitarianism an even more deadly and immediate danger. From its outset he had been a determined, outspoken opponent of National Socialism, and his books had been banned in

Germany.[1] His attitude in part is expressed by a typical letter to me of 1941: 'From the safe distance at which I am sheltered, I feel that I would give anything to be in the thick of it. This probably is an illusion. . . . If by a miracle Adolf gets his pants torn soon and there *is* a chance f. Anthropology in England, I would infinitely prefer to return. . . . In spite of all poses and affectations, I feel *au fond* rather miserable ab. my exile here and most prospects. I am trying to do as much "propaganda" as possible. Probably every little helps. . . .'

At the time of his death Malinowski was President of the Polish Institute of Arts and Science in the United States. While he always retained a sentimental affection for Poland and a benevolent interest in Polish doings, Malinowski had not seemed to be particularly conscious of himself as a Pole in any politically nationalist sense. But the brutal effects of the second World War seemed to rouse in him a new interest, stimulated in all probability by the apparent identity of Polish interests with those of the world at large. His wife has commented that the invasion of Poland touched him closely, and seemed to re-awake his sense of nationality and his feeling of solidarity with Poles. He took an active part in the preliminary organization of the Polish Institute and was active in assisting exiled Polish scholars. This was one way in which he could forward what he felt to be the cause of freedom and of civilization.

One may fittingly conclude this introduction by a quotation from the judgement of one of our American colleagues: 'Because I respect Malinowski and his work, I have criticized him severely, against an almost absolute standard. He eloquently preached an intellectual faith. There are few of us living who can rise to the passionate sincerity of his finest moments.' [2]

[1] See the preface by his wife, Mme Valetta Malinowska, to his posthumous book (1947). Also see the chapter by H. Ian Hogbin, p. 265.

[2] Kluckhohn, 1943, p. 219.

The Concept of Culture in Malinowski's Work

AUDREY I. RICHARDS

MALINOWSKI'S concept of culture, as he first developed it, was one of his most stimulating contributions to the anthropological thought of his day. The term 'culture' stood for the set of ideas to which he himself attached the most importance and which enabled him to make some of his most original hypotheses. His schemes for analysing culture into its different aspects formed a basis for the field-work methods which he taught to his students.

This contribution to anthropological theory seems to me to have been considerably under-valued since his death, and the rather extreme intellectual and emotional reactions to his work which then took place.[1] It is therefore important to trace the growth of this concept in his work, more especially since the later formulations of his views, as presented in a posthumously published book (Malinowski, 1944), are more confused and diffuse than the earlier, and give little idea of the impact of his work on his students.

I shall try first to examine Malinowski's views on culture in relation to the anthropological and psychological theory of the 'twenties in which he developed them; secondly I shall ask how far this concept actually provided a basis for his own hypotheses or stimulated theoretical work in others; and lastly I shall endeavour to account for the reactions to Malinowski's work that have taken place since his death and shall also venture on some prophecies as to future developments which seem to me to be likely to take place along the lines he laid down.

A term such as 'culture' or 'structure', as used in sociological work,

---

[1] For instance a recent American book on the use of the term culture (Kroeber and Kluckhohn, 1952) gives scant reference to his general hypotheses and none to his quite important work on culture and language, and culture and technology. Yet Malinowski was selected to write the article on 'Culture' in the American *Encyclopedia of Social Sciences* in 1931 and hence must have been considered a leading authority on the subject then.

is inevitably a heuristic device, or a way of looking at facts, and hence its meaning can best be grasped by a study of its use in the analysis of data. The neat definition may mean very little in itself, as is shown by the summary of definitions collected in the book by Kroeber and Kluckhohn cited above. It would be as easy or as fruitful to judge Darwin's contribution to science on his definition of the term 'evolution', as it is to attempt to understand, by a comparison of definitions, the revolution that took place in social anthropology with the introduction of the concept of culture in the second quarter of this century.

Malinowski's own definition given in 1931 states that 'culture, comprises inherited artefacts, goods, technical processes, ideas, habits and values'. Social organization is also included since he states that this 'cannot be really understood except as part of culture'(Malinowski, 1931a). It thus differs very little from Tylor's famous definition of 1871 stating that culture 'is that complex whole which includes knowledge, belief, art, law, morals, customs, and all other capabilities and habits acquired by man as a member of society'.[1]

To analyse Malinowski's use of the term more closely it is necessary to distinguish between a number of different intellectual preoccupations which were all subsumed for him under this one word. First there is his concept of culture as the tribal microcosm, the functioning whole, which, as Fortes (1953b) has pointed out, was a new and stimulating idea when it was first propounded by Malinowski and Radcliffe-Brown in the early 'twenties.[2]

With this idea went Malinowski's emphasis on the need to study the 'use' or 'function' of the customs, institutions and beliefs which formed part of each culture, with all the different shades of meaning he gave to the word 'use'. Thirdly, Malinowski, in common with other sociologists and psychologists of his day, was preoccupied with the difference between man's biological and sociological heritage, and he identified the latter with the term culture right from the start. He also attempted from the first to analyse culture into a number of distinct aspects which could be used as a scheme for empirical research.

The concept of culture as a nicely balanced system of separate parts is to be found in both those famous monographs published in 1922— Radcliffe-Brown's *The Andaman Islanders* and Malinowski's *Argonauts*

---

[1] The difference between Malinowski's definition and that of most British anthropologists of the present day is that he always included social organization or social structure in his analysis of culture, whereas Evans-Pritchard and his followers would exclude it. The latter's description of the 'general social system' is however very similar to Malinowski's use of culture, i.e. oecologies, economics, legal and political institutions, their (i.e. primitive societies) family and kinship organization, their religions, their technologies, their arts (Evans-Pritchard, 1951a, p. 11).

[2] Tylor spoke of culture as being 'a complex whole', but the emphasis was rather on the complexity than on the wholeness.

of the Western Pacific. Radcliffe-Brown then used the word culture in somewhat the same way as Malinowski did, and his later definitions of social structure included much that Malinowski did under culture except material culture, language, systems of knowledge, and education—the latter two of which seem never to have interested him particularly. Both worked in small islands where the holistic conception of culture must seem more obvious than it does in an inland area with a great deal of movement of peoples and tribal admixture. Both were influenced by Durkheim—Radcliffe-Brown permanently and Malinowski temporarily. In the work of both there is the tacit assumption that it is essential that cultures should continue to survive [1] and that they must be maintained, as Fortes puts it (1953*b*, p. 4), 'in a steady state'.

It is true that Malinowski recognized quite early (1929*e*) that there were conflicts within cultures and it is to his credit that he did so. He distinguished in Trobriand society conflicting rôles, rivalries expressed in reciprocal obligations, self-interest and fights for power, whereas the Andaman islanders were represented as being a united group earnestly engaged in expressing their cohesion. Yet Malinowski as well as Radcliffe-Brown seems to have believed that culture had to be maintained as a whole, and one of his definitions of the function of a custom or institution is in terms of the part it plays in relation to the culture as a whole. In 1926 for instance, he wrote that anthropological facts were to be explained 'by their function, by the part which they play in an integral system of culture' (1926*a*, p. 132).[2]

Many critics have pointed out that Malinowski never actually did describe a culture as a whole, but instead presented most of his work in the form of very detailed accounts of particular aspects. The 'whole-ness' in the treatment consisted of the study of one institution against the background of the whole culture. It would be equally true to say that Radcliffe-Brown has often bidden us study and compare 'total social structures' but has never actually described one. Both 'culture' and 'total social structure' were used as devices for the analysis of data, and both were new and stimulating concepts in British anthropology when first introduced; they still remain valuable for teaching purposes.

It must be remembered that there were emotional as well as philo-sophical reasons for Malinowski's presentation of the order of the tribal cosmos. Being a gifted field-worker, he had achieved a great measure of

---

[1] E.g. Malinowski, 1931*a*. 'The cultural need is the body of conditions, which must be fulfilled, if the community is to survive and its culture to continue'.

[2] For some reason or other this view is rarely attributed to Malinowski nowa-days. In fact, some recent writers have categorically stated that Radcliffe-Brown viewed the function of an institution as the part it plays in the maintenance of the tribal structure, whereas Malinowski examined its functions only in relation to needs and mainly biological needs. In fact the statements on function made by Malinowski (1929*e*) and Radcliffe-Brown (1935) were almost identical.

personal identification with the people he lived with. Like most anthropologists who have struggled to understand the meaning of tribal activities to the people concerned, he saw Trobriand society as a system which was admirably balanced and poised. He resented, almost passionately, attempts to change primitive customs by force and felt, as have many of us, a protective feeling towards the people with whom he had lived so closely for the best part of four years. His interest in practical anthropology, which was voiced as early as 1926 in his first *Encyclopaedia Britannica* article, warned administrators against the sudden disturbance of primitive custom, on intellectual, but also I think on emotional, grounds (p. 133).

It is difficult to tell whether the idea of the whole culture preceded Malinowski's interest in the relations between different aspects of the culture, or whether it followed from it. In his 1926 statement, repeated in 1929, both these preoccupations appear. The explanation of anthropological facts lies not only in the part they play within an integral system of culture, but also in the manner in which they are related to each other within the system, and in which the system is related to the physical surroundings. From the first, however, an interest in the usefulness of the apparently senseless antics of what we then called 'savages' was paramount in his work. His first published article set out to show that the Intichiuma ceremonies of Australian aborigines, with their wild dances, their painted bodies and their symbolically carved shields, actually performed a function in their economic life (Malinowski, 1912*a*). After his field trip to the Trobriands he published his first major article on the economic life of the islanders, which showed the same determination to prove that what seemed to the European to be useless ceremonial exchanges of goods actually played an important part in their economic organization (Malinowski, 1920*a*).

The idea that rites, beliefs, and customs, however extraordinary they appear to an observer, actually fill 'needs', biological, psychological, and social, became commonplace in anthropological teaching. It is difficult now to believe that Malinowski's teaching on this point could ever have struck his students as being brilliantly new. The changed outlook was probably due to the fact that discussions of the function of aspects or institutions of tribal life led directly into field-work material, either Malinowski's own extraordinarily rich collection of field notes or those of his first students. Those who listened to his lectures on the Trobriand islanders will remember his intense absorption in the activities of the people he described and his stress on what actually happened as distinct from what anthropologists guessed had happened in the past. This gave the work a vividness which the existing text-books, and even the best contemporary missionary or anthropological monographs, lacked. Were kinship terms a survival of past stages in history? The answer lay, Malinowski would tell us, in the empirical material. How were the terms used? What was the index of emotional content? Or again, what was the function of myth or folk tale? The answer lay in a description of how these stories were actually recited; the occasions on which they were recited, and the manner of those who spoke, whether it was bragging, serious or light-hearted. In comparison with works such as those of Frazer, Crawley, Westermarck, or Durkheim which we read at the time, or with the ethnographic work produced by observers paying short visits to different tribes, such as that of Rivers or Seligman, the work seemed lively and stimulating, and we began actually to visualize ourselves 'in the field'.[1]

The interest of the students was also partly due to the fascination of a game for which the *chose donnée* was the necessity of the custom or institution under discussion to the individual, the group or the society. If the Trobriand islanders did it, or had it, it must be assumed to be a necessary thing for them to do or to have. Thus their sorcery, condemned by the missionary and the administrator, was shown to be a conservative force supporting their political and legal system. Pre-nuptial licence, also frowned upon by Europeans, was described as supporting marriage institutions and allowing for sex selection. The *couvade* was no longer a laughable eccentricity but a social mechanism for the public assumption of the father's duties towards the child.

We now accept the fact that it is only as a working model that we can describe societies as perfectly balanced wholes, and agree that there is no need for them to survive in the particular form in which the anthropologist happens to find them. Leach's recent book on Northern Burma is an essay on this theme (Leach, 1954b). Yet at a time when social anthropology was struggling to establish itself as an empirical science the concept of the wholeness of culture had important practical effects. Its drawbacks were some far-fetched explanations reached in the effort to explain and even to idealize primitive institutions. If sex licence existed, for instance, it must be proved to be sociologically or biologically useful; yet no-one has checked Malinowski's hypothesis that pre-nuptial licence provides the best way of selecting a satisfactory mate and leads to the most enduring marriages. Again, the belief in the importance of every institution within a culture to the continued existence of that culture led to the charge, often made by administrators, that functional anthropologists were not prepared to allow for any change in the tribes they were studying. Field-workers were even suspected of supporting ritual murders or cannibalism on the ground that in some way or other they contributed to 'tribal integration'.

But the positive side of Malinowski's view of the wholeness of culture

[1] The change in the type of observation was widely remarked on. Vide Frazer's preface to *Argonauts of the Western Pacific* where he describes the work as the study of human nature in the round rather than the flat (Malinowski, 1922a, p. ix).

far outweighed the drawbacks of these initial crudities, for it gave rise to a continuous study of the relationship between the different aspects and institutions of a tribal society. From this systematic examination of relationships sprang the most fruitful hypotheses which he developed at an empirical level—the linking of the political with the religious or magical, or the political with the economic or the technological, for instance. Such correlations afterwards developed into the systematic schemes for the analysis of cultures which I shall describe.

I do not know whether the vehement protests Malinowski made against evolutionary, diffusionist and pseudo-historical reconstructions were developed on theoretical grounds before he went to the field, or whether they grew out of the sheer weight of first-hand observation made in what was then the longest period of field-work an anthropologist had undertaken, and by a man with unusual linguistic gifts, lively powers of personal contact and terrific energy. Certainly the culture concept and the field experience supported each other.

Many protests have now been made against the notion that evolutionary stages or historical survivals can account for anomalies in kinship usages or forms of marriage, or for religious or magic rites. The entirely imaginary reconstructions of history to explain present-day customs— the 'just-so stories' of anthropology as Malinowski described them— have now given place to the careful collection of historical facts. It is difficult therefore to recapture the intensity of the opposition there was in London in the early 'thirties between the diffusionists and those whom Malinowski was already beginning to call 'functionalists'. Students of the London School of Economics and University College, London, then the centre of diffusion studies, argued in refectories and 'pubs'. Malinowski debated with Elliot Smith and Perry on public platforms. Journals produced symposia by the protagonists of the two English schools (Malinowski, 1926g, 1926i, 1928a).

Malinowski was a man whose expressions became more extreme with opposition and the language he used in controversy was bound to provoke opposition. The polemic tone of some of the current writings now seems extreme, yet it is doubtful whether social anthropology would so soon have established itself as a separate discipline, apart from archaeology, technology, or physical anthropology, without Malinowski's efforts, and certainly we students felt at the time that we were crusading for our right to use the term 'science' for our studies.

Malinowski also used his culture theory to protest against the study of isolated cultural traits in order to establish connections between one area and another. Objects were not to be studied *in vacuo* but against the setting of the whole culture in which they were found. The stick was not to be relegated to the museum, but to be studied in use as a digging stick, a ceremonial stick, a walking stick, a sceptre or a wand. Kluckhohn and Kroeber, writing in 1952, say, 'The greatest advance in contemporary anthropological theory is probably the increasing recognition that there is something more to culture than artefacts, linguistic texts and lists of atomized traits' (p. 52). This advance, in England, was largely due to Malinowski's work.

Gluckman (Bib. ii, 1949, pp. 2–5) and later Evans-Pritchard (1951a, p. 58) evidently consider that an anti-historical bias is an essential part of Malinowski's type of functionalism. Gluckman suggests that he opposed scientific historical work as well as unscientific; but in fact his earliest protests were merely against a conjectural history 'invented *ad hoc* in order to account for actual and observable fact, in which therefore the known and the empirical is explained by the imaginary and the unknowable' (Malinowski, 1926a, p. 132). He returns to this position in his posthumous book. Malinowski indeed instructed his students to include a column for history in their field-work charts.

The fact, however, remains that he was much more interested in a people's own concept of their history than in their actual history. There was little documentary history to be examined in the case of the Trobriand society, but the sociological importance of the people's myths and legends in maintaining their system of clan structure, their land tenure and their magic struck him forcibly. It was the basis of his formulation of the concept of the charter of an institution which has since, as Leach says (1954b, p. 211), become an anthropological commonplace. There have been considerable developments in our knowledge of the sociological functions of current historical traditions since his day and many anthropologists have described the significance of a people's own view of their past, the genealogies they invent to account for their political institutions, or the migration tales which act as charters for their rights of ownership.[1] But this functional concept of history was first implanted in the mind of Malinowski's students by his teaching on the functions of primitive myths.

We can conveniently pause here to consider the second use Malinowski made of the term 'culture', that is to say as the 'social heritage', or the set of forces impinging on the individual born into each society. The concept of culture considered as the traditional institutions, activities, social groupings and beliefs of a tribe differs somewhat from the same term considered as the sum total of the forces conditioning the child born into the same tribe, although the two are obviously closely connected; in fact the one is reflected in the other. The latter use of the word, that is to say culture considered as the traditional influences bearing on the individual in the society, conforms very nearly to the most common American usage, as seen in the work of Linton and others. It is the underlying concept behind the numerous culture and personality

[1] Cf. Fortes's term 'counterfeit history' (1945, p. 26) and Nadel's term 'ideological history' (1942, p. 72).

studies which have appeared in the United States in the last twenty years.

It must be remembered, however, that the difference between man's biological and cultural heritage was still being hotly debated in the 'twenties and early 'thirties. The psychology of instincts was still in the ascendant. Behaviourism had not established the full grip on psychological and anthropological thought which it later achieved. The full implications of Gestalt psychology and psycho-analysis had not been realized by the main body of the social sciences. William McDougall's book (1908) giving a list of the human instincts had reached its twenty-first edition by 1932, and instincts, for instance, of acquisitiveness, aggression, sex, gregariousness or hoarding were considered to account for most forms of human behaviour. Lecturers in industrial psychology (e.g. Ordway Tead, 1918) explained labour problems in terms of instincts, and experts in juvenile delinquency were content to account for problems of crime in this way.[1]

The tide was, however, turning. J. B. Watson's first book on behaviourism appeared in 1919, and his second in 1924. Pavlov's dog became a famous figure in our discussions from the translation of his lectures on 'Conditioned Reflexes' in 1927. Graham Wallas's *Our Social Heritage* (1921) was still considered a stimulating and controversial book. Shand's theory of the sentiments impressed both Radcliffe-Brown and Malinowski and the former used his definition of 'sentiment' in *The Andaman Islanders* (1922, p. 234). Freud's *Interpretation of Dreams* was translated into English in 1910, but the full impact of his teaching was only apparent in England after the translation of his *Collected Papers* beginning in 1924-5. The conditioned reflex, the habit, the sentiment, the character and personality as formed by social influences, these are all familiar ideas to us now; they have passed into the accepted framework of first-year lecture courses. But twenty to twenty-five years ago behaviourism in its first crude form seemed to us a stirring idea. Even a novelist voiced his alarm and excitement at the new point of view in a book he entitled *Brave New World*.[2]

Malinowski was, I think, the first British anthropologist to apply the new knowledge of conditioning processes to the study of tribal societies. He did not do so by turning his mind to the type of work which has now become known as culture and personality research. There are passages in his 1929 article which show that he might have done so. From the first he studied social structure from the biographical point of view, that is to say social ties as they developed for the growing child (Malinowski, 1930a). However, his interests were too firmly wedded to the institutional type of analysis for him to undertake a systematic study of conditioning; nor had he collected very detailed information on the early

---

[1] L. Bernard (1925) gives a numerical analysis of the references to different instincts in scientific and popular books.   [2] Aldous Huxley, 1932.

training of Trobriand children. What he did was to split the forces constituting the social heritage under their different headings, such as language, material culture, activities and values—his 'aspects' of culture in fact—and to suggest how these might 'condition' a child. Material culture, for instance, he described as 'a laboratory in which the reflexes, the impulses, the emotional tendencies of the organism are formed. The hands, the arms, the legs and eyes are adjusted by the use of implements to the proper technical skill necessary in a culture' (1931*a*, p. 622). Language was described as acting on the larynx, forming speech habits and so enabling human co-operation to take place. Even in the early years of this type of study he was writing about cultural conditioning acting on the human organism to transform innate impulses and to produce 'inner constraints'.

Malinowski did not use these ideas further in his teaching of field-method, but the notion of using the different aspects of culture for the basis of a systematic study of the whole learning process could have been developed very fruitfully in this way. It would have been a useful corrective to studies which concentrate exclusively on the importance of infantile experiences in the life of the child, with a corresponding neglect of the social structure in which the child has to fulfil a series of social rôles, as well as the major institutions of his tribe. A systematic study of this sort could have been made by one of Malinowski's own observational charts. The full implications of his biographical method have never, to my mind, been realized, and his work in this field must be numbered among the many intuitive and stimulating ideas which he never put to the proof.

Instead, behaviourism led Malinowski to new developments of his ideas on culture which he equated constantly with the idea of the social heritage. 'The social heritage', he wrote (1931*a*, p. 621), 'is the key concept of cultural anthropology.' In *Sex and Repression in Savage Society*, published in 1927, he contrasted the instinctive basis of mating and propagation among animals with the forms of social grouping, the legal rules, the beliefs and rites which surround this biological process in man.[1] In his 1931 article he argued in effect that there was no sex instinct which could account for the great variety of human customs, laws and ideas which we describe under the heading of courting and marriage, parenthood and the family. The fulfilment of basic human needs by traditional human institutions was a constant theme in his work, and it has been described elsewhere in this book. Such ideas may have seemed commonplace when his posthumous work was published in 1944,[2] but they were new in the 'thirties, and his elaboration of the theme of social heritage remained one of the most popular topics for

[1] I made the same sort of analysis of the cultural conditions in which nutrition is secured in human society (A. I. Richards, 1932).

[2] Cf. Gluckman's criticism (1949).

his lectures to teachers and to the general public. The concept led to his notion of secondary needs. If man could not fulfil even such biological processes as mating and procreation, nutrition or defence, without the aid of traditional rules and ideas and equipment, then culture must be considered as an 'artificial or secondary environment' which was absolutely essential for human survival.

Hence Malinowski's analysis of culture into *imperatives*, that is to say 'conditions which must be fulfilled if the community is to survive', and his suggestion that economic organization, law, and education be described as 'instrumental imperatives', and magic, religion, knowledge, and art, also necessary, he thought, for man's survival, be called 'integrative imperatives'. Hence also his conception of the institution, which was to form such an integral part of his work.

The division into integral, integrative, and derived needs has not proved a very fruitful one as a basis either for the collection and analysis of field data or for further developments of sociological theory. There is too much overlapping of the different imperatives and the division is hard to handle. But Malinowski's concept of the institution which was directly derived from his needs approach, does not suffer from these defects and it has proved an exceedingly useful tool for collecting and analysing data. In fact Gluckman, in an article which is otherwise very critical, describes it as 'a significant and enduring contribution' (1949, p. 24). It is largely responsible for the new type of field observation which is associated with Malinowski's name. As early as 1929 he was describing basic institutions as consisting of groups attached to a certain part of the environment and endowed with material equipment, the knowledge of how to use this environment and equipment, linguistic usages enabling them to co-operate, rules and laws governing their behaviour and a body of beliefs and values shared in common. Put like this there is nothing startlingly original in the idea, but as applied to field data it was an invaluable stimulus to analysis. The canoe was described in relation to the group of men who built it, and used it, the technique of its construction, the magic used over it, the laws as to the handling of the boat and the catch and the linguistics of boat-making and sailing. Modern changes were analysed in terms of changes in one of these sets of factors which might or might not make it impossible for the institution to function. Malinowski's account of the Trobriand granary, and the social grouping, rules and beliefs surrounding it (1935, Chap. VIII), exceeds in detail any description I have seen by an expert in technology just because he used this technique.

The concept of the institution was afterwards used as a basis for a series of teaching schemes which were in fact devices for ensuring the collection of data in the field, and prodding the field-worker to make correlations between different aspects of society. This was done to secure two results—a deeper knowledge of the functioning of the particular activity considered, and also an understanding of its relation to the activities of the tribe as a whole.

These schemes grew in complexity with the years. Malinowski's own field scheme, used from 1912 onwards, consisted of files dealing with what were then usual headings in most conventional monographs, e.g. religion, magic, fishing, hunting, and so forth. In 1922 he advocated the use of synoptic charts for analysing data in a fascinating account of his field-work method given in the first chapter of *Argonauts of the Western Pacific* (1922a, pp. 83-4).

His later schemes of analysis were elaborate. The first was constructed by means of a series of vertical columns with comprehensive headings such as environment, history, knowledge, linguistics, social organization, activities (economic, political, ritual), norms including law, religion, magic, and education. This scheme could be read vertically and horizontally. Thus for instance it was possible to take the social grouping column vertically and see at a glance all the major social groupings in the tribe, its 'social structure' in fact; but it was also possible to take the family as one of these groups and to analyse horizontally and thus to relate it to the material culture (house and furniture); to the environment (farm or family holding); to the activities (agriculture, fishing, hunting, domestic); to the kinship terminologies and linguistic usages classifying relatives; to the religious and magic beliefs supporting the family or the ritual carried out by it; and to the dogma as to descent, hereditary and ancestral worship which were connected with it. The horizontal reading gave the institution of family and marriage in Malinowski's series. So also the economic activities could be considered vertically, when the field-worker would get a picture of the major tribal activities taking place at different seasons or months of the year; but it could be considered horizontally, when the emphasis would be on a particular economic institution, such as gardening, when the chart could be used to correlate the groups which carried out the particular activity, the knowledge of the environment and gardening activities, the magic associated with agriculture, land-tenure and other rules of gardening behaviour and language.

This major chart would form the basis of a cultural outline if this were wanted. More characteristic was his treatment of special institutions on the same lines, that is to say, personnel, material culture, knowledge, rules, beliefs and charter. Further correlations were used in such institutional studies and were described as second and third layer schemes. The importance of such work in the training of field-students probably lay in the fact that this type of correlation became almost second nature. It was a habit that could not easily be forgotten and I have found myself working in this way in a social survey in Glasgow done for a practical purpose in the War, or later in a study of juvenile delinquency in the Colonies.

The value of the method is in fact its wide applicability to all social situations whereas the type of 'model' now used by the field-worker specializing in the study of social relations can, from its very nature, only deal with a narrow range of phenomena, mainly kinship relationships, and is only serviceable, to my mind, in primitive and isolated and therefore rather static societies. The field-work scheme also leads to a consideration of the same data consecutively from a number of points of view, such as the environmental, the structural, the normative, the technological and the dogmatic, and hence it forces the field-worker to a fuller collection of field material and also results in new hypotheses which spring out of the empirical data. It is this type of analytical work which Fortes probably had in mind when he spoke of a new type of ethnography—'functionalist ethnography' (1953b, p. 1).

In his later work Malinowski suggested that institutions, as he defined them, would prove the ideal isolates for making comparisons between tribe and tribe. This suggestion does not seem to me to have been a happy one. The institution is too large a unit for comparative purposes and it has too many variables for it to be handled successfully.[1] Moreover, in his posthumous book Malinowski seems to have become confused between major institutions such as the family or chieftainship, and associations of people grouped for a common purpose such as a church or a trade union, and this made a programme of comparative work even harder.

But the criterion of comparability is in any case irrelevant in the case of a field monograph on a new tribe. We do not judge a historian's study of the working of the manorial system in some part of thirteenth-century England on the basis of the concepts it provides for comparison with some other European country. We judge it by the institutional framework used, the analysis of the data, and the sense of social problem behind the work.[2] The historian perhaps hopes by the accumulation of many such studies to see some general trends in economic and legal processes, but he proceeds a step at a time. Anthropologists have been too impatient to build up their generalizations in such a steady and systematic way. They have been influenced perhaps by the large-scale comparisons of epochs, stages, and moral systems in which their apical ancestors indulged; and they have certainly been afraid of producing accounts of primitive societies which would be mere catalogues of customs without theoretical problems behind them—what is now described as 'mere ethnography'.

Whatever may be the reasons for the search for social typologies which

[1] Vide M. Fortes (1953b, pp. 3, 4) and M. Gluckman (1949, p. 24) for further criticisms of Malinowski's views on this point.
[2] Cf. M. M. Postan (1939) for a number of stimulating comparisons between the methodology of the economist and that of the economic historian, which bear on this point.

characterized some schools of British anthropology in the 'forties, the assumptions behind the search now appear optimistic in the extreme. Radcliffe-Brown advocated for many years the duty of anthropologists to work out a social taxonomy similar to those of the botanist or the zoologist. He urged students to compare 'total social structures', but except where it has been possible to limit the structure to a kinship system with a very formalized classification of relatives into different categories—as in the case of his analysis of the kinship structure of Australian tribes (1931)—he was not able to do comparative work on these lines. Evans-Pritchard (1940b) has done one such study on the Nilo-Hamites of Kenya but he now seems to have abandoned this type of work. We must, I think, be much more modest. There are very few cultural areas of the world of which we have sufficient knowledge of the social structure and major institutions of the component tribes to make comparative work possible. In these areas the total social structure is not the unit of comparison, but some special aspect with a limited number of clearly defined variables, and these will be most easily revealed by institutional studies of the type Malinowski advocated and not through the comparison of models of a highly abstract type which tend to prevent the field-worker looking for new data and new correlations rather than encouraging him to do so.[1]

There has been in fact a failure to recognize the difference between an empirical field-scheme of analysis, a synoptic chart in Malinowski's terms, and a final presentation of the data in relation to a particular theoretical problem. In the latter case the exclusion of irrelevant data may be invaluable. But for a young field-worker, engaged as he must be in the first instance on empirical research, the abstract model prepared for a final analysis of data is usually a hampering way of setting to work, if indeed it does not prove a lethal endowment.

The reaction to Malinowski's work began before his death in 1942, but owing to the war new types of teaching did not make themselves felt till much later. The reaction was partly a personal one and partly the result of the fact that his field-work methods as well as his presentation of the data had brought British anthropology to a cross-road. *Coral Gardens and Their Magic*, a book which is often decried, but evidently not often read, had gone to the furthest limit of institutional study by means of correlating one set of activities, in this case agricultural institutions, with the whole. Every aspect of the culture was included, the family and kinship system, political organization, land tenure, technical processes, religious and magic beliefs, and the language of magic used

---

[1] In recent work done at the East African Institute of Social Research, we have found it difficult even to compare the political systems of the Inter-lacustrine Bantu as a whole. We are proceeding gradually on a series of pieces of comparative research, taking in the first instance the basis of selection of chiefs in ten tribes, in relation to the whole political structure.

in gardening. It was a *tour de force* but it was not practical politics to repeat such an experiment.

Moreover, besides extending the field of observation by a methodical process of correlations, Malinowski gave data on individuals as well as groups, on variations in behaviour as well as conformities.[1] His islanders strained at society's rules, fell in love, committed adultery, jumped off palm trees, bragged, cheated, quarrelled, and were subject to the romantic call of dangerous overseas 'Argonauts'. They kept incest rules but with varying degrees of intensity within the lineage, the sub-clan and the clan. They said one thing and did another; and shouted in the heat of quarrels accusations they would not have made to the ethnographer in answer to questions. Malinowski's students found that the mass of 'concrete documentation', to use his phrase, grew alarmingly. Once individual variation in human behaviour was admitted, and it had to be admitted, then anthropologists found they had fallen into the worn groove of the case-history method and were bound to the use of quantitative data.[2] The field-worker seemed to be becoming a person who tried to find out more and more about more and more.

The complexity of primitive institutions that was revealed by such methods and their wide limits of variation began to strike with alarm those who were optimistic enough to believe that social typologies could be immediately constructed, and by those who hoped to reduce their material to a few simple abstract postulates. Malinowski and his pupils were considered to have collected too many facts of too many kinds to make simple comparative work possible. Gluckman described Malinowski's data as 'too complex for comparative work' and he and Evans-Pritchard have constantly criticized it as being 'overloaded with (cultural) reality' (Gluckman, 1949, p. 15; Evans-Pritchard, 1951a, pp. 18, 40). They did not come to the conclusion that the comparisons they had in mind were too ambitious for the existing state of our knowledge, but decided instead that it would be better to have fewer facts, so as to make the comparisons easier.

A group of British anthropologists began to insist that the field of social anthropology be limited to the study of social relationships or 'social structure', a term which was first used by Evans-Pritchard in a particularly narrow sense to describe only groups which had a 'high degree of consistency and constancy' (1940a, p. 262).[3] The use of abstract

---

[1] He was interested, as Firth has pointed out, in 'the qualities of social relations' as well as the existence of such relationships (Raymond Firth, 1951b, p. 483).

[2] Raymond Firth used quantitative data from the first (see in particular Firth, 1939; 1946). I did an amateurish village census (Richards, 1935). Cf. also statements made on the necessity of quantitative work by I. Schapera (1949a, p. 106) and M. Fortes (1949b, p. 59).

[3] 'Social structure' in this sense corresponds quite closely with 'social organization' used as a heading for a vertical column in Malinowski's synoptic scheme.

models, chiefly of kinship structure, was substituted for descriptions of the workings of the institution of family and marriage in particular tribes.[1] For a time it seemed as though the retreat from *Coral Gardens and Their Magic*, and all it stood for, was going to lead to the exclusion of much data formerly considered the subject matter of social anthropology, such as economics, material culture or mythology. It was argued that social structure should be clearly separated from the other aspects of man's social heritage. These came to be subsumed under the title 'culture', a word which has often been used in the post-war years almost in a pejorative sense to describe a sort of rag-bag of odds and ends in which to thrust all facts and ideas in which the social anthropologist was not at the moment interested.

This type of work, stimulating as it was, is now seen to have been a passing stage in British anthropology from which even some of its protagonists have been gradually retreating. Social groups with a high degree of constancy and consistency are few, and to look for highly formalized kinship groups where these do not exist has often cramped observations and led to cumbrous and even distorted expressions of the facts. Evans-Pritchard's first definition of 'social structure' has in fact only proved a useful concept in the study of very simple and static societies and he has himself widened it recently to include other types of social relation.[2]

It has also proved quite impossible either to study or to describe social structure apart from culture for the obvious reason that social groups do not exist *in vacuo* apart from their environmental background, their material culture, their laws of land tenure and other rules governing settlement patterns, their beliefs and above all their activities and the reasons for which they exist. Such a separation is impossible, that is to say, if a really fruitful analysis of an unfamiliar institution is to be made or new hypotheses thrown up for testing on a comparative basis. It is often in the correlation of one aspect of an institution with another that those variables which make the most interesting subject for comparative work become apparent. In fact what seemed at one time to be a split or a division of British anthropologists into two groups, sometimes described as structuralists and functionalists, seems now to represent nothing but a difference in priorities, emphasis, and presentation.[3]

[1] See Lévi Strauss (1953*a*), E. Leach (1954*b*) and Raymond Firth (1954) for discussion and criticism of the value of models in anthropological observation.

[2] E. E. Evans-Pritchard (1951*a*, p. 16). Radcliffe-Brown's concept of social structure was always wider and Firth has long emphasized the importance of including institutionalized person-to-person relationships under social structure (Firth, 1951*a*, p. 32).

[3] Evans-Pritchard sees a marked distinction between such books as his own *Witchcraft, Oracles and Magic among the Azande* (1937) and Raymond Firth's *We, the Tikopia* (1936) or the work of Schapera and others. He considers the first to be structurally oriented and the second he describes as mere ethnography

Firth describes culture and structure as two ways of looking at the same data (Raymond Firth, 1951a, chap. I; and 1951b). I still find it more convenient to describe structure as one aspect of culture and hope that anthropologists will now concentrate on the examination of other aspects of culture such as ritual or economic organization with the same detail, so that we may see the development of new typologies in these fields. This would be a natural development of the work started by Malinowski's type of cultural analysis.

The reaction to Malinowski's view of culture has been a stimulating and instructive one because it has led to a number of advances in anthropological concepts and field methods. The attempt to isolate social structure may have failed in its original objective but it has led to much greater clarity and precision in the use of kinship and political terms in the hands of Evans-Pritchard, Fortes, Gluckman and some of their pupils. New concepts have been introduced such as Raymond Firth's use of the term 'social organization'.

It is true that some anthropologists have turned from the mass of descriptive data produced by Malinowski's field techniques to the use of abstract models, and we may well see the evolution of a separate branch of our work—the study of primitive concepts and classifications which will of necessity be closely allied to philosophy and psychology since it will concern itself so largely with cultural differences in ideas, concepts and symbols. On the other hand other British anthropologists have stuck to Malinowski's tradition of field-work but have made great advances in the intractable problem of the handling of empirical data largely through the use of statistical methods borrowed from sociologists. Malinowski's descriptions of pieces of individual behaviour and character, then hailed as a new type of work, now seem naïve in the face of the quite sophisticated techniques used for the study of individual variations from the norm and the processes of cultural change, by means of different kinds of sampling and the analysis of life histories.

There has also been a growing recognition of the need for recognizing well-marked stages in the study of an unfamiliar culture. For the field-worker in a new area there seems to be no alternative as fruitful as a 'functional' study of the major social groups, activities and values of a tribe and a systematic examination of their correlated features, and this is the type of work for which anthropologists have specialized. But such an outline is viewed now as a preface to a more detailed study of a particular institution or community, again leading to quantitative survey when a particular hypothesis seems to need testing in this way.[1] Individual variations could be studied on such a basis by those specially

'on the level of cultural realism'. Outside critics, and in particular our American colleagues, do not seem to see this distinction.

[1] Cf. the practical proposals made on similar lines by I. Schapera (1953).

interested. Finally will come the time for the selection of a modest number of isolates for comparative work, preferably in one region when the variables affecting, say the forms of marriage or chieftainship, have become clear. For if there is one thing which the experience of the past fifteen years has taught us it is the need for caution and humility in comparative work.

Thus Malinowski's conception of culture, with all the advances in anthropological method to which it has led, still seems to me to be a useful tool for the field-worker starting his observations in a new society and also for the theoretician analysing the data he has collected by this means.

Malinowski's Theory of Needs[1]

RALPH PIDDINGTON

Introduction

MANY contemporary anthropologists would appraise Bronislaw Malinowski's contribution to anthropology primarily in terms of his field-work and his unquestioned capacity to train other field-workers. But his work as a theorist, less widely recognized, was probably a more significant contribution to the development of anthropology. The two phases of his work were, of course, essentially and explicitly interconnected. His observations in the Trobriand islands were transmuted into a general theory for the comparative study of human cultures. And this theory, applied in lectures, seminars, and published works to other cultures, influenced, directly or indirectly, those field-workers who have set new standards of field-work over the past two or three decades. It is necessary to emphasize this fact, because it is often assumed that the standard of Malinowski's own field-work was due to some mystical insight which, by a sort of laying-on of hands, he was able to transmit to his students. Actually it was his theoretical framework for the study of culture, and the training which his students received in it, which accounted for the revolution in standards of field-work mentioned above.

Another essay in the present volume deals with Malinowski's general interpretation of culture. We are here concerned with what is perhaps the most significant, the most contentious, and certainly the most neglected aspect of that interpretation. A commentary on this statement is provided by certain recently published works on general problems of anthropology. Herskovits (1948, pp. 234–6) in summarizing the theory, on the whole favourably, makes no reference to integrative imperatives, Nadel (1951, p. 378–9) dismisses the theory in a single paragraph, while Bidney (1953a, p. 68) fails to deal with it in any detail and compares it

[1] I would like to express my gratitude to Dr. J. C. Trevor, and to my colleagues, Dr. W. R. Geddes, Mr. B. G. Biggs, Mr. R. A. Scobie, and Mr. Jack Golson, for valuable criticisms on various sections of this paper; also to the members of my graduate seminar for a stimulating discussion on it.

33

with Wissler's much more superficial statement (1923, chap. XII) of the relationship between the individual human organism and the phenomena of culture. On the other hand it is possible that Malinowski's theory of needs has had a more significant influence than is explicitly recognized. For example Warner's concept of 'species behaviour' (1952, pp. 42, 50-1, 143-4) canalized by society and providing its dynamic basis, is cognate with Malinowski's conception, as are Clyde Kluckhohn's observations, to be cited later, on the biological foundations of values.[1]

The theory of needs itself is set forth in Malinowski's own publications, and particularly in his posthumous *A Scientific Theory of Culture*. A brief summary will therefore be sufficient for our present purpose.

Essentials of the Theory

It will be well to start with Malinowski's definition: 'By need, then, I understand the system of conditions in the human organism, in the cultural setting, and in the relation of both to the natural environment, which are sufficient and necessary for the survival of group and organism. A need, therefore, is the limiting set of facts. Habits and their motivations, the learned responses and the foundations of organization, must be so arranged as to allow the basic needs to be satisfied' (1944, p. 90).

Taking first the 'system of conditions in the human organism', this involves the satisfaction of certain biologically determined impulses in a series of 'vital sequences'. These Malinowski lists as follows (1944, p. 77).

Permanent Vital Sequences Incorporated in all Cultures

(A) *Impulse* →	(B) *Act* →	(C) *Satisfaction*
Drive to breathe; gasping for air	intake of oxygen	elimination of CO_2 in tissues
hunger	ingestion of food	satiation
thirst	absorption of liquid	quenching
sex appetite	conjugation	detumescence
fatigue	rest	restoration of muscular and nervous energy
restlessness	activity	satisfaction of fatigue
somnolence	sleep	awakening with restored energy
bladder pressure	micturition	removal of tension
colon pressure	defecation	abdominal relaxation
fright	escape from danger	relaxation
pain	avoidance by effective act	return to normal state

---

[1] Cf. also the emphasis which Kluckhohn and Mowrer place on biological, social, and cultural determinants of 'personality in culture' (Kluckhohn and Mowrer, 1944, p. 4).

This table, it must be emphasized, refers merely to the satisfaction of the impulses of an individual. It stresses the dynamic basis of 'human nature', conceived as pertaining to an individual organism.[1] But this list of impulses corresponds only indirectly to the basic needs of man as an animal species, because at this level the concept of individual and group survival is added to that of individual impulse. The two are, of course, inter-related, since individual impulses, on the whole, conduce to survival. But it is possible, indeed necessary, to distinguish between them. An individual, under the stress of hunger or thirst, may eat a poisonous plant or drink sea water and so die: the behaviour of individuals giving way to fright, as in a panic, may lead to the decimation or extermination of the group; not so long ago publicists talked of the threat of 'race suicide' alleged to be entailed in the widespread practice of contraception; individuals can and occasionally do neglect their children with fatal results for the latter, and it is possible to imagine, under conditions of 'social pathology', such practices becoming so widespread that the group would become extinct. It was therefore necessary for Malinowski to construct a table of 'basic needs' which laid stress on the total conditions necessary to individual and group survival, and not merely on individual impulses. The table (1944, p. 91) is as follows:

	A		B
	Basic Needs		*Cultural Responses*
1	Metabolism	1	Commissariat
2	Reproduction	2	Kinship
3	Bodily Comforts	3	Shelter
4	Safety	4	Protection
5	Movement	5	Activities
6	Growth	6	Training
7	Health	7	Hygiene

What has been said about individual impulses and basic needs would apply also to other animals, including the sub-human primates. But man is a very particular kind of primate, and the special characteristics which he has acquired in the course of evolution make possible the development of that specifically human form of biological adjustment which we call culture. Man is endowed with certain crucial physical characteristics —the upright posture, allowing for the emancipation of the hands and their specialization as organs of manipulation; the development of vision, muscular co-ordination and the association areas of the cerebral cortex; and the nervous and muscular equipment which confers on man the power of articulate speech. To these anatomical and physiological

---

[1] 'The most important thing for the student, in my opinion, is never to forget the living, palpitating flesh and blood organism of man which remains somewhere in the heart of every institution' (Malinowski, 1934a, p. xxxi).

characteristics can be related some of the universal and fundamental *differentiae* of human culture, such as technology, activities implying collective forethought and planning, and the various forms of symbolism, particularly those which are concerned with normative behaviour and which make possible the emergence of values.

The anatomical and physiological developments to which we have referred not only made possible the development of culture. They made it necessary. The specialization of the extremities of the limbs for locomotion and manipulation respectively meant that man could not so readily take to the trees for protection as could his arboreal ancestors, nor so easily gather food there; life on the ground brought new dangers from predatory animals; and the much longer time taken by the young to reach maturity meant a more prolonged period of parental care, and more detailed training of the growing organism in the activities necessary to survival. But perhaps the greatest potential danger to the evolving genus *Homo* was the development of his cerebral cortex. Increase in the size and complexity of the association areas meant a greater capacity to profit from experience, to plan for the future and to satisfy individual impulses. Among the social sub-human primates which have been adequately studied such impulses include pre-eminently greed, lust and jealousy, the organizing principle of the group usually being a system of competitive dominance among adult males. It is hard to imagine what would happen to a group so organized if its members were endowed with man's superior intelligence—perhaps the process of mutual extermination among gang leaders and South American politicians provides some sort of illustration. Certainly a group of this kind would be less viable biologically than one in which individual impulses are controlled by mechanisms other than mere physical force.

Culture, then, has biological survival value. Its adaptive character is in part due to the fact that though the basic needs, shared with other animals, provide the 'primary determinism' [1] the conditions of man's life as a social animal impose a secondary determinism. This Malinowski defines in terms of 'derived needs' or 'imperatives' (1944, p. 125). These relate to the requirements of maintenance of cultural apparatus, regulation of human behaviour, socialization, and exercise of authority. The 'responses' to them comprise those of economics, social control, education, and political organization. (The list is presented in detail elsewhere in this volume—p. 65.)

This scheme, superimposed upon the list of basic needs, does not yet exhaust the imperatives imposed on man. With slight verbal alterations and in a limited range of situations, something like it could be predicated for many sub-human organisms with a fairly high degree of cortical development. The young of various animal species can be trained to

---

[1] 'Man does not live by bread alone, but primarily by bread' (Malinowski, 1944, p. 72).

co-operate with man and with one another in seeking food, and to refrain from devouring it when it is obtained. They can be conditioned not to attack other members of their group, so that something like social regulation of behaviour replaces the 'peck order' behaviour which characterizes so many of the activities of sub-human species. In one American experiment, the investigators were able to train a chimpanzee, up to a certain point, to live together with their children as members of a domestic family, and presumably adult apes could be taught, also up to a certain point, to train their young along specified lines—to reward them for certain actions and to punish them for others. Finally, groups of animals can learn to defer to the wishes of a leader, human or otherwise, as we see in a troupe of performing animals at a circus.

But all this implies nothing more than a process of individual habit formation. The female lion learns to respond in specified ways to the trainer's commands, but she cannot transmit such behaviour patterns to her cub, which has to learn them afresh by human instruction; the sub-human primate can acquire, either by trial and error or by deliberate instruction, the capacity to use artefacts, but this again is achieved individually by each organism, and cannot be transmitted. An essential characteristic of human social life is that, through what Malinowski calls the 'integrative imperatives', habit becomes transmuted into custom, parental care into the deliberate training of the rising generation, and impulses into values. And the key to this whole process is symbolism, which Malinowski held must have been present at the birth of culture. When 'Eolithic' man first recognized standards of right and wrong—in technology, in hunting techniques, or in interpersonal relations—and began to inculcate these into the younger generation, the transition to human, that is cultural, existence was effected.[1]

To the sphere of integrative imperatives, then, belong the phenomena subsumed under such terms as tradition (including a culturally recognized and transmitted social structure), normative standards or values, religion, art and ceremonial, as well as language and other forms of symbolism. The comprehensiveness of Malinowski's scheme thus becomes apparent, since under it can be subsumed the views of those who hold that the essence of human culture is to be found in symbolism or in values,[2] as well as the important concept of social

[1] It has been argued that no such point of transition can be postulated, since mother apes can and do punish their young for acts which are displeasing to them. Undoubtedly there is some continuity of species behaviour between the sub-human primates and man. But with the emergence of symbolism and values, a new set of determinants of behaviour arises. The mother chimpanzee may smack her offspring, but it would be straining the imagination too far to think that she might look across at a more complaisant mother chimpanzee in the next tree and think: 'Fancy bringing up a child like that!'

[2] There is, incidentally, no difference between these two conceptions of the essence of culture. If we accept Clyde Kluckhohn's definition of values as implying

structure. Contrast, for example, the behaviour of groups of baboons, as described by Zuckerman, with that of any human group. The former is determined by adventitious acts of individual or collective behaviour, in which the impulses of individuals such as hunger, sexual desire, or protection of self or offspring, determine stability or change in the relations between organisms, mainly on a basis of physical dominance. Corresponding behaviour in a human group is determined by a fixed system of values which defines how individuals should or should not behave; these values are crystallized in a system of symbols which enables individuals to evaluate the behaviour of others, irrespective of whether they are or are not themselves affected or involved; [1] and, finally, the relations between individuals are given permanence (recognized by the group as a whole) through such structural principles as kinship, age, and rank.

The specific contribution of the theory of needs is that it emphasizes, at all levels, the biological determinants of cultural activities and so provides a principle of analysis and comparison of universal validity. Merely to draw attention to the fact that culture involves symbolism provides us with nothing more than a catalogue of different symbolic systems unless we recognize the universal instrumental function of symbolism as a mechanism of integration, co-operation and transmission; to stress the importance and diversity of values leads to a similar catalogue unless we recognize their dynamic basis in biological impulses, canalized by cultural mechanisms into value systems; and the study of social structure, particularly when explicitly conceived as a mere chronicling of social systems,[2] gives us no indication why social systems persist other than by some inner mystical tendency to do so. But this is not the case if we recognize social structure as one of the cultural instruments by which man's needs—primary, derived and integrative—are satisfied.

The Hierarchy of Needs

A criticism often levelled at the theory of needs is that to establish a hierarchy of basic, derived and integrative needs contributes nothing to our understanding. Granted, it is said, that a community satisfies its

'oughtness' and not merely 'desiredness' (Kluckhohn, 1951, p. 397), then that 'oughtness' can only be expressed symbolically, and particularly through language; conversely symbolism, so far as the referent is the object of affective attitudes, implies values: to use the verbal symbol 'coward' implies a positive evaluation of bravery, and *vice versa*.

[1] A crucial illustration of this principle is found in legal or quasi-legal procedure when a judge or arbitrator is expected to act 'without fear or favour'. Cf. Godfrey Wilson's definition of legal action as implying basically the intervention of individuals not interested in the issue at stake (G. Wilson, 1937, p. 25).

[2] As by Evans-Pritchard (1951a). Cf. his article in *Man* (1950).

PLATE I.—Malinowski as a student

PLATE II.—At Yale in 1942 shortly before his death

Photograph by John Phillips, ' Life ' Magazine

hunger by the consumption of certain foods, well and good; granted that it has an economic system to provide for this and other material wants, well and good; and granted that this system is validated by normative standards and religious beliefs, well and good. Let us plunge straightway into an empirical description and analysis of the cultural facts we observe, without bothering about 'needs', much less about whether they can be divided into a threefold hierarchy. This, in fact, is what is done in the vast majority of ethnographic monographs, and rightly so. The ethnographer describing a feast can give an adequate account of it without adding a section or even a footnote to state that the participants are satisfying their hunger—this is implied and understood. Just as the chemist need not constantly refer to the periodic classification of the elements or the psychologist to the organization of the central nervous system, so the ethnographer does not find it necessary constantly to harp on 'needs'. But in none of these cases is it true that the basic conceptual scheme is irrelevant to scientific research.

The contribution of the theory of needs to our understanding of human culture, and therefore of any particular culture, lies not only in the fact that it provides a dynamic explanatory principle which, whether explicitly stated or not, underlies all good field records. The recognition of a hierarchy of needs—even if the classification be somewhat arbitrary —stresses the difference in specificity in the forms of responses through which they may be satisfied. The impulse to breathe can be satisfied only by the intake of oxygen; the sex impulse, apart perhaps from certain perversions and sublimations, can be satisfied only by detumescence. The possible ways of satisfying hunger are more varied, but here too there are limits to the range of possible responses. Turning to the need for the training of the young during the process of growth we see, particularly in recent studies of 'child-rearing techniques', a varied selection of forms of response. Finally, the integrative imperatives are the most flexible of all in the responses which they produce. Indeed one might almost conclude from a survey of the variety of forms of religions and value systems that it does not matter very much what members of a community believe or value so long as they all believe and value the same things. A case could in fact be made out for a more elaborate classification of needs based on different orders of specificity in the forms of responses by which they can be satisfied. A rough classification, however, is better than none, and for the moment Malinowski's seems adequate.

The point which we have made is relevant to the question of the diversity of cultures. Why, it is sometimes argued, if all cultures are to be regarded as responses to the same needs, should there be any variation between them, subject to obvious limitations and determinants such as natural environment and food supply, density of population and level of technological achievement? The answer is to be found in the variety of ways in which the less specific needs may be satisfied. And the anthropologist is not called upon to account for this variety, any more than the palaeontologist is always expected to say why from a common ancestral type, different species have evolved in different directions. Indeed, the anthropologist can hardly ever give even a descriptive account of what has occurred for, unlike the palaeontologist, he has nothing equivalent to fossils.[1] Assuming that all human cultures have a common origin (admittedly a questionable assumption, though its validity cannot be discussed here) the anthropologist cannot give an account of the historical processes which have led to the differences which exist between the cultures of Dobu, of the Eskimo or of the Kwakiutl, apart from the obvious limitations and determinants mentioned previously. All he can do is to list generically the factors which have demonstrably produced change and differentiation among cultures such as technological advance, environmental and demographic factors, migrations, relations (peaceful or hostile) with other communities, the influence of outstanding personalities and such general processes of 'drift' as cultural efflorescence, cultural degeneration, and cultural lag. He should also add, as a postulate, the suggestion that where any of these influences leads to a wholesale frustration of basic needs, either the culture will change or the group will become extinct. Revolutionary situations, the fate of dictatorships, and cases of wholesale depopulation, provide illustrations.[2]

The Cultural Standard of Living

A key concept in Malinowski's theory of needs is that of the *cultural standard of living*, which 'means that new needs appear and new imperatives or determinants are imposed on human behaviour' (1944, p. 37). It is unfortunate that Malinowski did not elaborate this concept more thoroughly, though it is of course implicit in the whole of his analysis of derived and integrative needs. At the purely material level, the modern European or American feels a requirement for knives, forks and spoons with which to eat most of his food, and is acutely uncomfortable if called upon to eat otherwise. The Australian aborigine is equally uncomfortable if called upon to use artificial equipment to

---

[1] Apart, that is, from the limited time span covered by the recorded history of civilized, and therefore specialized, societies and the limited evidence provided by prehistoric archaeology.

[2] A suggestive commentary is provided by archaeological studies of mortuary practices. These often undergo a process of efflorescence (particularly in regard to their material paraphernalia), reach a peak, and thence degenerate. It is as though there were a general tendency for such practices to effloresce until a point is reached where the 'social price', in terms of the frustration of basic needs, becomes too high (see Childe, 1944, p. 97).

convey food to the mouth. The cultural standards of living of the two cultures are different.

But the anthropological concept of the cultural standard of living is far more than a material one. The African turns to beliefs in witchcraft to explain and cope with illness; the European does not recognize any requirement for this specific form of cultural equipment but he *does* need some cultural mechanism to satisfy (actually or putatively) the universal need for health. As we have seen, many needs are generic and not specific in relation to the cultural responses which they produce. It is true that the forms of these responses are felt as 'needs' in particular cultures, but their imperative character derives secondarily from the cultural standard of living of the community concerned.

Recognition of this fact disposes of criticisms such as that of Dorothy Lee, that, since people in different cultures value different things, there can be no universal 'list' of needs; for this concept she would substitute cultural values conceived as a totality, as a 'way of life'. This of course perpetuates the two major fallacies of Ruth Benedict's theoretical system —the belief that cultures cannot be analysed but can only be conceived in terms of a total pattern or configuration, which negates the possibility of any universal basis for cross-cultural comparison; and the implication that the human personality is a *tabula rasa* upon which each culture imposes whatever value system it has arbitrarily developed. Lee illustrates her thesis with reference to a particular value in our society—that of individual privacy. The modern mother wishes to secure a measure of privacy and feels 'free to substitute a bottle for the breast and a mechanical bottle-holder for the mother's arms. . . . We withdraw ourselves, thus forcing the child to strive for emotional response and security' (Lee, 1948, p. 394). But if arbitrary cultural values are the ultimate determinants of behaviour, why should the child not be indifferent to whether it gains an emotional response or not? Clearly the modern child's protest is a reflection of some universal need, to the definition of which we shall return later. For the moment we will only point out that our desire for privacy is part of our cultural standard of living, of the particular institutions through which we satisfy our basic needs. To review these institutions in any detail would mean a lengthy digression, but we may mention that, for example, our reproductive needs are satisfied by a kinship system in which rights and obligations outside the individual family are of little importance, hence the requirement of family privacy; the specific taboos by which we regulate sexual behaviour impose a measure of segregation during sleep; the competitive nature of our economic system entails private negotiations between those engaged in running it, hence the private office, which also becomes a status symbol within the class system which largely regulates our technological exploitation of the environment. Thus universal needs produce a pattern of institutions embodying our cultural standard of living. And this pattern makes us conscious of certain *desiderata* (such as privacy) which are not viewed in the same way in other cultures.

A somewhat similar criticism of Dorothy Lee's position is advanced by Clyde Kluckhohn who points out (1951, p. 428) that 'values *both* rise from and create needs. A value serves several needs partially, inhibits others partially, half meets and half blocks still others.' In another passage Kluckhohn shows that certain universal values are immutably linked with certain biological facts, though he does not elaborate the point. He writes (1951, p. 418):

'Contrary to the statements of Ruth Benedict and other exponents of extreme cultural relativity, standards and values are not completely relative to the cultures from which they derive. Some values are as much given in human life as the fact that bodies of certain densities fall under specified conditions. These are founded, in part, upon the fundamental biological similarities of all human beings. They arise also out of the circumstance that human existence is invariably a social existence. No society has ever approved suffering as a good thing in itself. As a means to an end (purification or self-discipline), yes; as punishment—as a means to the ends of society, yes. But for itself—no.'

This statement is perhaps somewhat limited, because the term 'suffering' as usually employed refers primarily to physical pain and only secondarily to certain forms of mental distress. But what Kluckhohn has said about it could with equal truth be said of the frustration of any of the other vital impulses (hunger, sex appetite, fatigue and so on) which form the psychological and physiological core of the basic needs of man. Where a positive value is placed upon such frustrations, it emerges from the specific cultural standard of living of the community concerned.

This brings us to a final and very important point in Malinowski's theory, namely that 'certain devices, forms of organization, customs or ideas enlarge the range of human potentialities on the one hand, and impose certain restrictions on human behaviour on the other' (Malinowski, 1944, p. 116; cf. p. 119). Though this is obvious enough from the nature of derived and integrative needs, which impose organization, that is, control, on the activities of individuals, it requires emphasis. Criticisms of the theory of needs sometimes suggest that it implies a complete range of satisfactions, that 'all social institutions appear right and good by definition', and that, in every culture, all is for the best in the best of all possible worlds (Gregg and Williams, 1948, p. 597). A moment's reflection will reveal the absurdity of such an implication—it is certainly not to be found anywhere in Malinowski's writings. There must always be a measure of conflict between the needs of the individual and of society, between those of different factions or groups within the community, and between the demands of different needs within the individual personality.[1] And these, it must be noted, always occur within

[1] Cf. Raymond Firth, 1953, p. 152.

an existing matrix of cultural knowledge, attitudes and values. Efforts, conscious or unconscious, to resolve such conflicts through myriads of acts of individual choice lie at the core of the vital process of social organization, as this concept has been defined by Raymond Firth (1951a, pp. 35–40). In spite of occasional and transient situations which Malinowski and others have called manifestations of 'social pathology', there does seem to be a tendency for societies to approximate to a condition in which the maximum satisfaction of needs is achieved. This is because of the general human agreement that, subject to the reservations specified by Kluckhohn, the satisfaction of basic needs is desirable, though obviously some limitation must be placed upon it by the demands of community life, while unnecessary frustrations also arise in the process of social organization—a chief or leader may choose to exercise his power despotically and to his own advantage or a fanatical religious movement may for a time impose extreme asceticism on a community. But, if the group does not become extinct, such situations sooner or later resolve themselves. A clear understanding of the instrumental function of social institutions may help to expedite the process. The theory of needs thus opens up, if not a road to Utopia, at least a starting point for the resolution of some of the conflicts and tensions of modern civilization.

Some Contentious Points

Since the theory of needs as formulated by Malinowski claims to provide a general basis for the understanding of human behaviour in all cultures, as well as a conceptual instrument for the observation and recording of ethnographic data, it would be surprising indeed if it were not open to question on several important points. The first is terminological. Malinowski was often inconsistent, even uncritical, in his selection and use of terms. For the needs which are called 'basic' in his posthumous work, he variously used in earlier expositions the terms 'biological' and 'primary'. The last of these seems the most satisfactory. If Malinowski is correct in his contention that the derived and integrative imperatives are just as necessary to the survival of human groups as man's individual physiological requirements, then in a sense the former are just as 'basic'. Malinowski is again inconsistent in the terms which he applies in elaborating his three categories. He speaks of 'basic needs', of derived 'needs' or 'imperatives' but always of 'integrative imperatives'. Here it seems better to use the term 'needs' throughout.[1]

Another difficult question concerns the precise definition of different needs and the minimal conditions necessary to their satisfaction. But we should not be pessimistic about the future of the definition of needs. Some fifty years ago it might have been said that it is impossible to define precisely what is meant by the need for food. Today the dietician

[1] Cf. Piddington, 1950, Chapter VI, Section 2.

can tell, practically down to the last calorie or milligram of iodine, just what dietetic components are necessary for the healthy functioning of the human organism. Less precise, but nevertheless impressive, is the information gathered in recent years on the sexual impulse. For our own society numerous investigators, from Havelock Ellis to Kinsey, have produced a body of data which may be matched against research on sexual behaviour in sub-human animals on the one hand and studies in comparative ethnography on the other. Though much of this information may be superficial or unreliable, it is nevertheless true that we know a great deal more than we did fifty years ago of the various cultural mechanisms by which the sexual impulse is at the same time given expression and forced to conform with moral and aesthetic standards. Similarly in regard to the training of the young, modern educationalists and child psychologists have shed much light on the working of our educational system, both in its formal and informal aspects; and this again is paralleled in the comparative ethnography of exotic cultures, both under indigenous conditions and in situations of cultural contact.

The proper course today, then, is not to abandon the concept of needs because of difficulties in definition, but to seek to define them with the greatest precision which our present knowledge permits.

A more serious criticism concerns Malinowski's failure to state clearly the relation of certain needs to the biological survival of individuals and groups. So far as the primary needs are concerned, this is obvious enough. In regard to derived needs, Malinowski points out that the disruption of any of the delicately balanced systems of organization found in human cultures militates against survival. He cites as an example the fact that modern war-making involves not merely attempts to kill or starve the enemy. Propaganda, fifth-column activity and other forms of psychological warfare are largely aimed at disorganization. 'Here, if we want to test our principle of stringency and derived needs, we could well refer to the dramatic demonstration thereof in the present historical world situation. The integral world wars are not waged merely by implements of destruction. Here, obviously, the ultimate aim of this instrumental approach is also biological; the extermination of human organisms. Indirectly, however, here also the victorious army often achieves its ends by disorganizing and confusing the opponents, and thus forcing them to surrender. The integral war, however, has its concomitants in economic battles, in the contest of nerves, and in propaganda. Here we see that if in an economic war a large modern nation can impose conditions of starvation or even malnutrition, surrender will be achieved by the break-down of an instrumental apparatus of organized food production or food import. If, through economic warfare, the supply of raw materials for industrial production can be cut off, destroyed or labour subverted, we see once more how indirectly and through many relays, the destruction of one of the instrumental, large

44

scale devices will affect the biological efficiency of a large modern community. By sapping or undermining the organization, the morale, and the symbolically implemented relation between people, one organized state can, under conditions of war, defeat another. Propaganda, through fifth-column tactics, sometimes introduces what might be called a sociologically disoriented symbolism. When in the overwhelming of Norway, treacherous orders were given to Norwegian units by German agents, these were correctly formulated symbolic orders placed in the wrong, that is, falsely apprehended, position of authority' (Malinowski, 1944, pp. 123-4).

From this it is clear that established forms of organization, generally understood by the members of the community, are necessary to survival. Furthermore, morale, that is the readiness to accept and act according to established value orientations, may likewise be postulated as necessary. But when we turn to other phases of human culture mentioned by Malinowski in dealing with 'integrative imperatives', the position is not so clear. Indeed, it could be argued that though forms of art, ceremonial and recreation are in fact found in all societies, they are not necessary to biological survival in the same way as nutritional or reproductive systems, though they have, of course, a physiological basis in the enjoyment of certain patterns of sense impressions—visual, auditory, kinaesthetic, and even gustatory and olfactory.

The last two of these brings us back to what was said about the need for food, which can today be accurately defined in terms of the minimal dietetic requirements necessary to health and survival. But man desires not merely to eat, but to eat well. The cross-cultural study of food preferences—determined partly by universal psycho-physical responses and partly by cultural standards—is a field of research in which anthropologists, psychologists, and physiologists might well co-operate. Such research might form the starting point for the definition of universal human *potentialities* which would supplement the list of needs necessary to biological survival. This question is obviously closely related to the process of cultural efflorescence mentioned previously.

Malinowski's theory of needs has also been criticized on the ground that it does not include the human tendency or tendencies which have been loosely subsumed under the term 'the social appetite'. Perhaps this omission was part of Malinowski's protest against those vague, even mystical, explanatory concepts which have militated against searching enquiry into the complexities of human motivation. One recalls his strictures on such concepts as 'social solidarity', 'group sentiment', and 'primitive communism'. Indeed, one of his greatest contributions in this field was his insistence upon the empirical study of individualistic or egotistic elements in human motivation, and above all of the social institutions through which they operate in specific cultures studied by the field-worker. But on this point at least Malinowski may be accused

RALPH PIDDINGTON

of pouring out the baby with the bath water. In all cultures human
beings demonstrably seek association with their fellows; they strive for
material and social rewards (esteem, affection or prestige) through that
association. Moreover it is impossible to envisage the biological survival
of a group from which such behaviour was absent, if only because of the
initial dependence of the young upon the adult generation. We therefore
clearly have here a need or group of needs, as the term is defined by
Malinowski.

This position has been argued by Ashley-Montagu (1950, p. 53) who,
in presenting Malinowski's table of vital sequences in a slightly amended
form, adds the following basic needs:

Satisfaction

Physiological Tension	$=\begin{cases} Urge\ or \\ Need\ to \end{cases}$	$\xrightarrow{}$	*Which Leads to the Act of*	$\xrightarrow{}$ *Homeostasis*
Feeling of non-dependency or aloneness	$=\begin{cases} be\ with \\ others \end{cases}$	$\xrightarrow{}$	physical contact or association	$\xrightarrow{}$ feeling of security or interdependency
General need or tension	$=\{$ expression	$\xrightarrow{}$ communication	$\xrightarrow{}$ social recognition	

Two important questions arise in connection with this suggested
elaboration of Malinowski's theory. Firstly, is what might be provision-
ally termed the *need for association* an innate characteristic of the individual organism? Or is it developed by an inevitable process of conditioning through the satisfaction of other needs provided by human
association, initially in the act of suckling? Ashley-Montagu argues
cogently for the former view, and adduces biological and psychological
evidence in support of his contention.[1] On the other hand, in the
absence of an experimental situation like that envisaged in Aldous
Huxley's *Brave New World*, the second possibility cannot be completely
ruled out. In any case, the only point at issue is whether the need in
question should be classified, as by Ashley-Montagu, as basic or primary,
or whether it should be grouped with the derived needs as emerging

[1] Ashley-Montagu 1950, *passim*. The suggested biological basis of social
behaviour is summarized in his following passage: 'Whatever the nature of the
factors involved in the co-operation of cells cohering to form functioning many-
celled organisms, such co-operation does exhibit the elements of a social act. The
suggestion is that such acts originally represent the expression of a drive which
has its origin in the nature of the reproductive-dependency relationship, further
that the tendency of living things to form societies is coeval with life itself, and
finally, that human society represents the culmination of this tendency, and that
in virtue of what seems to be the accident of the development of man's remarkable mental potentialities, his great plasticity, and freedom from biologically
predetermined forms of behaviour, human society has assumed a unique form,
it has become culturalized' (p. 36).

46

secondarily from the conditions of human social life. Its universality and survival value cannot be disputed.

A more difficult question concerns the denotation of the term. In view of the infinite variety of inter-personal relations, both structured and unstructured, and of satisfactions arising therefrom, the universal characteristics of the need are hard to disentangle from specific cultural and individual responses. Dorothy Lee (1948, p. 391) is justified in criticizing the tendency arbitrarily to invent new needs as explanatory principles of universal validity and applicability: 'When we found that the original list of basic needs or drives was inadequate, we, like the psychologists, tried to solve the difficulty by adding on a list of *social and psychic needs*; and, from here on, I use the term *need* in a broad sense to cover the stimulus-response phrasing of behaviour. When the list proved faulty, all we had to do was to add to the list. We have now such needs as that for novelty, for escape from reality, for security, for emotional response.' Obviously some of these needs do not accord at all with Malinowski's conception of the term. The 'need for novelty' is absent from conservative, static societies, while the 'need' to escape from reality depends largely on how unpleasant reality happens to be at any given time or place, or for any particular individual. Clearly these vague and spurious 'needs' are invented *ad hoc* in an effort to elucidate some of the psychological and sociological problems peculiar to our own society.

This complex issue is one for interdisciplinary research, and cannot be pursued here. We can only affirm that what is required is a more searching analysis (such as that attempted by Ashley-Montagu) rather than a discarding of the concept of needs in favour of the less fundamental, though more easily studied, category of 'values'.

A point on which Malinowski has been extensively criticized is his contention that elements of culture do not survive unless they subserve some need, in other words, that there is no such thing as 'cultural lag' (1944, pp. 28–9, 141–2). The issue here really concerns the time span involved. Clearly, when a culture changes, as in contemporary culture contact, elements in it neither disappear overnight nor change their function immediately to accord with new conditions. But Malinowski was thinking in terms of a much longer time span. He was criticizing the views of certain evolutionary schools that elements of culture could survive through sheer inertia for centuries, long after they had ceased to serve any function. In this criticism he was undoubtedly correct. For example the soldier's breastplate once served a protective function. As worn by Life Guards today, it has assumed a purely ceremonial function. If Great Britain were ever to become a republic, it might disappear altogether. But what is certain is that it would not survive indefinitely after it has ceased to satisfy any need, primary, derived or integrative.

This should be obvious enough, and the real task is to define empirically in terms of specific situations of social change how long elements of culture persist through cultural lag, how quickly they assume new functions or how soon they disappear.

The Theory of Needs and Contemporary Anthropology

The importance of Malinowski's theory of needs for contemporary anthropology rests on several bases. The first is operational, and concerns the work of anthropological field-workers. Apart from a few general 'surveys' of cultures, which in the nature of the case can never be comprehensive or profound on any given topic, it is not true to say that modern ethnographers study 'cultures as wholes'. They deal with specific problems against the total cultural background. These problems are variable in their nature. An ethnographer may describe a particular system of human activity (for example, the *kula*) or aspects of culture such as economics, religion, law, or social organization. Such studies are, in effect, concerned with describing cultural responses to various derived and integrative needs. But the same can, and should, be done with primary needs, particularly those for food and sex. This aspect of Malinowski's theory has been naïvely criticized by Gluckman in the following terms (1949, p. 23): 'There appears to me to be little point in sending an anthropologist trained expensively and living at some cost in the field, to Africa to find out that some Bantu tribe has a complex organization to satisfy the need of its members for food, just as we have a complex organization for this purpose.' The obvious comment is that neither is there any point in financing a field-worker to discover that a Bantu tribe has a social structure. The task is always to describe in detail a defined system of human activities and inter-relationships. And the system connected with the satisfaction of primary needs is just as valuable a subject for study as any other, as has been demonstrated in the work of Malinowski (1929a) and Audrey Richards (1932). These studies show how different cultures not only satisfy, but also regulate and limit, the vital sequences underlying basic needs. Apart from their purely anthropological importance as one way of arranging and analysing cultural data, they are of profound importance to psychologists as demonstrating the different ways in which the raw material of 'human nature' can be handled by different cultures.

This brings us to the second justification for the theory of needs, that it provides a basis for co-operation between psychologists and anthropologists. Not that the concept of needs is identical with such psychological concepts as 'drives' or 'instincts', which refer to individual motivation in particular situations or series of situations and not to the total system of organization of a human group. 'Human beings under their conditions of culture wake up with their morning appetite ready, and also with a breakfast waiting for them or ready to be prepared' (Malinowski, 1944, p. 94). From the psychological point of view this situation is produced by a complex set of heterogeneous drives or motives of many individuals, such as the farmer who produced the food, the tradesman who sold it and the housewife who cooked it. Broadly speaking the psychologist is primarily concerned with the drives or motives of individuals, whether common to a group (social psychology) or idiosyncratic (individual psychology). To a large extent he must take the context of institutions within which these drives or motives operate as given. The social anthropologist, on the other hand, is primarily interested in the organization of these institutions themselves, in the 'organized routine of satisfactions' and, it should be added, partial frustrations. Furthermore, the anthropological concept of needs is a biological as well as a psychological one—as pointed out earlier, needs are not co-terminous with individual impulses.

For these reasons Malinowski is careful to point out the difference between the task of the psychologist and that of the anthropologist (1944, pp. 89-90). But he insists that at certain points their interests converge. The neglect of the theory of needs, in fact, has in part been due to 'resistance of British social anthropologists to psychological concepts' (Geddes, 1953, p. 417).[1] How far this resistance has been due to the survival of Durkheimian dogmas, and how far to a too exclusive preoccupation with issues related to 'practical' problems (such as economics, law, and political organization), is a question which cannot be discussed here.

Finally, the theory of needs may help to preserve what was of value in the original conception of 'anthropology' as distinct from the specialized branches into which it is today divided. It is true that, because of accumulating knowledge and specialized techniques, no-one can today be a Tylor or a Boas. And classical anthropology did involve all sorts of assumptions and conclusions which would not be accepted by modern social anthropologists.[2] The British trend toward specialization has therefore had a stimulating effect on ethnograhpic research. Social anthropologists no longer clutter up their minds with information about

[1] Cf. the following: 'Of recent years psychology has become rather a scare-word for social anthropologists in this country, and we have tended to practise a ritual avoidance of it. But I think we have created unnecessary difficulties for ourselves. It seems to be held that psychology is the study of individuals, rather than of thoughts, feelings and emotions of men in the mass, or in generalized form' (Raymond Firth, 1954, p. 12).

[2] In fact Malinowski was the first to revolt, and to revolt vigorously, against osteophily and the older type of museum anthropology. But in his posthumous work he makes clear the contributions which prehistory and technology properly conceived can, together with social anthropology, make to our common understanding of man (1944, Chapter III); and the whole theory of needs clearly relates social to physical anthropology so far as the latter is concerned with the physical basis of specifically human behaviour, and primate behaviour generally.

skulls and potsherds but look instead to cognate social sciences (such as economics, jurisprudence, and psychology) for a stimulus in extending and deepening their research interests. The results of this speak for themselves.

But specialization has also had its disadvantages. Firstly there has been the tendency to isolate social relations and social structure from their organic basis in the psychological and biological constitution of the human organism. As we have seen, for most research projects this is a legitimate procedure; but it has led to a neglect of certain important interdisciplinary problems which have received far more attention in America. Furthermore, anthropology is more than a set of techniques for field research. During the past decade in particular it has become increasingly recognized as a subject for undergraduate teaching as part of a liberal education. Here the classical approach of Tylor or of Boas provides a better charter for the teacher than the more limited goal of describing 'societies'. It fills in some of the gaps in the traditional framework of an Arts degree, where history, the study of modern languages and the humanities are almost exclusively concerned with European languages and cultures, past and present, while the biological basis of man's behaviour receives hardly any attention. For this purpose a broad grounding in physical anthropology, prehistory, social anthropology, and some aspects of comparative linguistics should be the objective, at least in the first year of undergraduate study.[1] For such studies the theory of needs is a valuable focal point, emphasizing as it does the significance for the satisfaction of human needs of man's biological constitution and origins; of the technological and social experiments in prehistoric times and in 'pre-Hellenic' civilizations by which a variety of adaptive mechanisms were developed; and of the range of heterogeneous cultures, particularly primitive cultures, which have been studied in recent times. Of course a student so trained is not qualified to carry out ethnographic research, but in the overwhelming majority of cases he never will. For the rare exceptions, specialization can come later.[2]

To summarize, the theory of needs is essential to a broad conception of the biological and cultural determinants of human behaviour; to certain important phases of ethnographic research; and to the adequate development of social anthropology as a teaching discipline. Furthermore, it provides one avenue by which some of the vital social problems

[1] I recall, with gratitude and affection, the intellectual stimulus of Radcliffe-Brown's course in Anthropology I at Sydney University, which was organized in the way described.

[2] It should be emphasized that this plea for the teaching of general anthropology does not rule out different types of integration of social anthropology with other teaching disciplines, as in the degree in Social Relations at Harvard University.

facing humanity today may be approached. It attempts to answer some of the important questions which people who are not anthropologists insist on asking.

Ralph Linton once criticized British social anthropology in the following terms: 'The integration dealt with by the Functionalists is primarily a matter of the mutual adaptation and working interdependence of behaviour patterns. . . . The picture that emerges is that of a mass of gears all turning and grinding each other' (1939, p. viii). Until the significance of the theory of needs is explicitly and generally recognized, Linton's criticism will continue to be very largely justified.

Malinowski and the Theory of Social Systems

TALCOTT PARSONS

THE phase of Malinowski's work to be discussed in this paper is his relation to the development of the theory of social systems, a principal common interest of sociology and social anthropology. It seems to me that the most adequate way to approach the problem is to recognize that there are two relatively distinct levels on which such theorizing may be attempted. The first is the level closest to the ethnographic facts, the immediate conceptual framework in terms of which observed activities are described and interpreted. The second is the level of general theory where such facts serve illustrative and demonstrative purposes, since the main concern of the theorist is to discern general lines and patterns of order in his subject-matter.

The first level of theorizing is so close to the treatment of concrete anthropological subject-matters that in Malinowski's case it has been rather fully discussed in the other contributions to this volume. It is directly involved in his concrete discussions of kinship, of gardening, of chieftainship, of magic, of funeral ceremonies and a variety of other topics. I therefore take it that my task is to discuss Malinowski's theory in the second sense.

I would, however, like to say a few words about the former since it is so typical of the man and so important to his place in the history of social science. Indeed, at one remove as it were, it can be said of Malinowski as he himself said (1944) of Frazer that his anthropological work as a whole is of far higher quality than his explicit general theory. Indeed the latter is, in my opinion, far from being the strongest part of his work. His 'clinical' theory is in general of a higher order of excellence.

Perhaps the most distinguishing characteristic of Malinowski's 'clinical' theory is his intense interest in human motivation, and the very high level of insight which he displayed in describing and interpreting it. He was at his best in his analytical descriptions (if I may use

53

such an expression) of his Trobrianders in their regular lives, at work in their gardens or on their canoes, participating in a funeral ceremony, on the occasion when the chief's son was forced to leave the village, and in many other similar cases. And he was at his best as a theorist when he tried to give humanly understandable meaning to behaviour which the reader would otherwise find bizarre and unfathomable.

Indeed, if anything like a general agreement about Malinowski's place in the history of social anthropology were to be sought among the professionals of that field, it would probably centre more than anything in the high quality of his field observation and his contribution to the development of field techniques and the training of a whole generation of students as field-workers. It should, however, be clear that anything like this level of field-work could not be attained without at least implicit theory, and on this level Malinowski was undoubtedly a theorist of considerable stature.

What were the main lines of his theoretical thinking on this level? They were, I think, characterized by a strong effort to remain close to the relatively direct interpretation of the motives of the individual, to carry a psychological emphasis in this sense. But at the same time it was a 'psychologism' strongly tempered by keen awareness of the social and cultural context in which the individual lived. How far this empirical tempering of a psychological tendency was worked out on the level of more general and formal theory will have to be discussed later.

The main lines of Malinowski's interpretation of motivation were, I think, laid down in the duality of the conceptual scheme he formulated in *Magic, Science and Religion*.[1] The gist of his position may be said to have been that, in interpreting the 'mind of primitive man' it was not legitimate to accept either the rationalism of Tylor and Spencer, or the irrationalism of Lévy-Bruhl. Within certain spheres the 'savage', as Malinowski liked to call him, was as matter-of-fact and rational as any modern European, he possessed considerable empirical knowledge of the world he lived in and applied it in an entirely rational way to meet his needs. But at the same time his serious belief in the efficacy of ritual, in the necessity of performing magical rites in certain contexts, and in the rightness of religious rituals, including the myths behind them, was a cardinal tenet for Malinowski. One had to accept the reality and importance of *both* aspects of primitive behaviour.

There is a sense then in which Malinowski's central problem was to make both types of behaviour humanly understandable to the modern European through a theory of function of some sort. Above all an adequate theory had to account for the fact that both types of behaviour

---

[1] It is perhaps pertinent to note that my first acquaintance with Malinowski's work was a course of lectures (London School of Economics, Michaelmas term, 1924) based on the manuscript of this justly famous essay (then as yet unpublished) given under the title, 'The Psychology of Primitive Peoples'.

characterized the same people under different circumstances. It would not do, to characterize 'primitive man' as in essence the one *or* the other. This seems to be one primary focus for the genesis of the concept of functionalism as Malinowski used it.

A second focus derives from his objections to 'trait' theory as this had been used by other schools of anthropology, and among his own contemporaries, particularly by the 'diffusionists'. There seem to have been two main bases of his objection to trait theory. One was the assertion of the independence of traits which then allegedly could be arbitrarily shuffled and reshuffled in the course of historical processes. This violated what Malinowski felt to be a cardinal principle, that of the interconnectedness of all the elements of a contemporary culture.[1]

The second principal object of his attack in this connection was the doctrine of 'survivals', the view that many traits present in a contemporary culture could be interpreted as having originated in connection with a function in some situation of the past, and then have survived into the present without reference to their connection with other traits or their functions.[2]

The primary starting points of Malinowski's theorizing, then, may be said to be, first the making of any given mode of behaviour humanly understandable in terms of the motivation of individuals, second the inclusion within this requirement both of rational, 'scientifically' validated, behaviour and of 'irrational', ritual, magical, or religious, behaviour on the part of the same persons, third the recognition of the interconnectedness of the different items which constituted a 'culture' to form some kind of system, and fourth the reference of the particular item to some kind of function in the current contemporary operation of this culture, as a basis of its understandability.

All of these starting points are in themselves fully acceptable to the contemporary, theoretically interested, social scientist. It can furthermore be conceded that they are justified in critical terms, in the sense that one or more of these requirements was violated by an important part of the literature available to Malinowski especially in the early stages of his career. But the question which interests us is what he did on the basis of this platform. In what direction did he go, and how far? Did he reach a point which is satisfactory for the theoretical needs of our generation?

It is now necessary to set up a frame of reference within which some

[1] A typical statement is 'I am deeply convinced that there is a fundamental misunderstanding in any attempt at isolation of separate traits' (Malinowski, 1944, p. 34).
[2] His concept with the relation of theory to field-work is illustrated by the following quotation: 'The real harm done by this concept (survivals) was to retard effective field-work. Instead of searching for the present-day function of any cultural fact, the observer was merely satisfied in reaching a rigid, self-contained entity' (1944, p. 31).

analysis of the problem can be carried out, and on which Malinowski's views can be projected. The development of thought which covered Malinowski's career span, and periods before and since, has involved a process of differentiation as between the types of system within which the factors which can be said to play a part in the determination of human behaviour can conveniently be analysed. In one sense perhaps one of the greatest accomplishments of anthropology before and during Malinowski's time was to establish a clear distinction between man as a biological organism and man as the creator, bearer, and transmitter of culture. The importance of this distinction can be considered to be common ground between the functional school and its trait or diffusionist or other predecessors. Perhaps it can be said that Malinowski's greatest theoretical effort was devoted to re-establishing the connection which this process of differentiation had made precarious and in many respects unclear.

In the sense of full establishment in the field of professional common sense, the next stage of differentiation can hardly be said even yet to have been completed, but there are many signs that this is the main trend of theoretical development in the area. What I refer to is the further differentiation of the cultural system, which has been considered to be independent of man as organism, into two categories, first of culture in the narrower sense, and second, social systems, as analytically distinct references for theoretical analysis. Concomitantly the older conception of 'the individual' as primarily a biological organism has tended to become differentiated into the organism in the physiological sense, and the *personality* as the system of behaviour emanating from that organism.

It has been noted that, wherever this type of theoretical differentiation occurs, there arises a new problem of integration. When, as in the older anthropological sense, the organism came to be differentiated from culture, the problem arose of what is the relation between them, since living human beings are obviously both organisms and culture-bearers at the same time. Similarly, when the more refined differentiation of theoretical analysis to which we have referred occurs, again the problem arises of how social system, residual culture, organism and personality are related to each other, and how they all together fit into a larger entity, the scientific analysis of the human being, as individual and as related to others in the species and its various sub-categories.

It seems to me that the theory of human behaviour has now reached a stage where it is not possible to deal adequately with most concrete problem areas within it without carefully discriminating these four system-types or levels from each other, namely the organism, (1) as physiological system and (2) as behaving system or personality, (3) the systems constituted by the interaction of a plurality of behaving organisms, i.e. social systems, and finally (4) the systems of cultural pattern which are generated in concrete social interaction, but which survive the lifetime of particular living organisms and can be transmitted or diffused from one social system to another.

I would like to suggest that Malinowski thought primarily in terms of the first level of differentiation of system-references, between that of the organism and of the 'culture' in the less differentiated sense of the term, and within this dual frame of reference his main concern was to establish an integration between them by working out a theory of motivation which was adequate to the facts of cultural behaviour, as he knew it from the literature, but above all from his own field-work experience. There is much in his work which foreshadows a later technical theory of social systems, but he did not even take full advantage of what was available in the literature at the time,[1] and his most valuable personal contributions to it are on the 'clinical' level already referred to rather than in his attempts at more generalized formulation.

Given these principal preoccupations, it seems probable that Malinowski, in the rôle of general theorist, was a somewhat unfortunate victim of the stage of development of theoretical thinking at the time of his most active professional life. It seems probable, that is to say, that this attempt of a synthesis between cultural and psychological considerations was, given the theoretical materials he had to work with, or choose from in the literature, premature. Neither a satisfactory psychology for his purposes, nor a satisfactory theory of social systems, could be developed without a further process of theoretical differentiation which discriminated four and not merely two system-levels and which established the requisite relationships between them. Though he did not achieve the high synthesis to which he aimed, Malinowski's experience may be considered to have constituted a notable attempt and to be very instructive for our own generation with respect to the difficulties in which he became involved as well as to the positive accomplishments.

The justification for treating Malinowski as operating mainly on the less differentiated of the two levels of theoretical discrimination we have discussed, is to be found on the one hand in his concept of culture and the way he relates it to that of institutions, and on the other hand in his concept of needs. I shall discuss each of them in turn.

The feature of Malinowski's use of the concept of culture which is most striking is its encyclopedic inclusiveness. 'It obviously [sic!] is the integral whole consisting of implements and consumers' goods, of constitutional charters for the various social groupings, of human ideas and crafts, beliefs and customs. Whether we consider a very simple or primitive culture or an extremely complex and developed one, we are confronted by a vast apparatus, partly material, partly human and partly spiritual by which man is able to cope with the concrete specific problems that face him' (1944, p. 36).

[1] See p. 69.

In the first place it seems clear that, in accord with much anthropological usage, particularly perhaps in the United States, Malinowski's definition includes what otherwise are three quite disparate categories, namely, 'material culture', i.e. in his definition implements and consumers' goods, which are artefacts, i.e. physical objects, the products of human activities, or instrumental to the satisfaction of human wants; secondly, concrete categories of human activity, particularly under the term 'custom'; and third, constitutional charters for the various social groupings and beliefs, the last being what in a narrower sense we might call specifically cultural objects. Social organization is not singled out even as a specific category within culture but is most obviously included under the term customs, and less directly under the charters for social groupings.

Essentially it can be said that Malinowski follows anthropological tradition in treating culture as everything pertaining to human life and action which cannot be treated as a property of the human organism as a physiological system, in the somatic sense, or the genetic, i.e. as a direct manifestation of biologically inherited patterns of behaviour. Culture is that aspect of behaviour which is learned by the individual, and which hence may to a greater or less extent be 'held in common' by pluralities of individuals, and transmitted to other individuals, together with the physical objects associated with such learned patterns and activities.

The essential point is that Malinowski makes no attempt, in discussing culture as such, to draw any theoretical lines of distinction within this encyclopedic category. The only line which is at all clear cut, though it is not strongly emphasized, is between material objects which function as implements and consumers' goods on the one hand, and those aspects of culture like customs, beliefs and social groupings which are properties of behaving human beings or pluralities of them.[1]

To be sure Malinowski does not treat culture as simply undifferentiated. The essential point I am making is that he does not, in his differentiation of it, directly or indirectly pay primary attention to the kinds of line of analysis which would be involved in a discrimination of the three types of systems discussed above which do not belong to the organism in a physiological sense. He introduces two cross-cutting classifications which are both employed in connection with his concept of *institution*, one a classification of the elements or components which go

---

[1] Though he explicitly includes material objects on the one hand, and beliefs and values on the other, there seems to be a sense in which Malinowski *tends* to identify culture and society or social systems. Thus we find him, perhaps inadvertently, speaking of the 'members of a culture' (1944, p. 89). A human being can be a member of a social group, but certainly not of a category of consumers' goods or of a belief or value.

to make up an institution, the other of the different types of institutions themselves. Let us therefore turn to this concept.

Malinowski treats institutions as 'the concrete isolates of organized behaviour'. Since such behaviour always involves a plurality of persons, an institution in Malinowski's sense is thus a social system, not a society but a 'partial' social system which is in some sense a sub-system of a society.[1]

An institution in this sense is, though functionally differentiated from others, a segmentary cross-section of culture in that it involves *all* the components which Malinowski has included in his definition of culture. Thus he enumerates charter, norms, material apparatus, activities, and in addition function (1944, p. 53). To be sure he did not say directly that personnel and function were part of culture, but all the other elements of an institution are, by his formal definition, and it is quite clear from Malinowski's discussion that every type of component of culture is involved in every institution.

The distinctive features of Malinowski's conception of institutions within this framework are the concepts of charter and of function. Function will be taken up presently, but it is noteworthy that Malinowski, in his conception of the charter of an institution, was well in line with developing sociological theory in that he treated as the central feature of the charter 'the system of values for the pursuit of which human beings organize, or enter organizations already existing' (1944, p. 52). Closely related to this is his clear conception of the normative control of behaviour—on a certain level—and hence of the relations between norms and activities as, in his terminology, components of culture. In these respects, and in spite of the late influence on his thinking of the Yale school of behaviourism, Malinowski escaped the confusions which have been associated with many behaviouristically inclined attempts at psychological interpretations of social behaviour. There is no indication in his writings that he was worried about the legitimacy of using verbal accounts of motives and sentiments or any suggestion that these should be treated as simple epiphenomena of some

---

[1] It may be noted, purely as a terminological matter, that Malinowski used the concept *institution* as referring to a concrete social system or, as he often said, a group. This is one of two alternatives both of which are deeply rooted in social science tradition, the other being to refer to an element of 'pattern' in the structure of social relationships. By Malinowski's conception obviously property and contract cannot be institutions. For British anthropology it is interesting to note that Radcliffe-Brown followed the other alternative (cf. for example, 1952, pp. 10–11), a usage he shared with Durkheim who may very well have been the source of it. I also have chosen to use the pattern rather than the group reference. Neither can be said to be canonically 'correct', but since there are considerable ranges over which they are irreducibly contradictory (e.g. property in much usage is certainly an institution but cannot in any way be made out to be a group) it is important to be clear which usage is meant.

underlying physiological process. However inadequately he analysed it, the independent significance of the cultural level of behaviour-structuring was deeply taken for granted by Malinowski. What now of the concept of function? In the first place it clearly fits into the scheme of culture as so far discussed. It is the primary basis of the differentiation of institutions within the same 'culture' from each other. Institutions differ in that they are 'organized about' different functions. But functions for what? The sense of the term Malinowski has in mind is clearly that current in the biological science referring to essential conditions of the continuing life and 'normality' of an organism, or an aggregate of organisms such as a species.

There are in Malinowski's writings a good many rather loose references to function where apparently are included individual human beings as organisms, groups of such human beings, institutions as such groups organized in a specific culture, and the culture itself. The two poles of Malinowski's analysis, however, between which the analysis is couched are clearly the individual biological organism, qualified mainly by the reproductive function on behalf of the species, and the culture, which is only equivocally and indefinitely related to any particular social system.

A key problem in this context is that of the classification of institutions. Malinowski attempted this on several occasions and in different ways. One such attempt which he spoke of as 'a fairly common sense statement' (1944, pp. 63–5), does not lean very strongly toward the biological pole, since only two out of seven main categories suggested have clear biological primacy, namely reproduction (a case of species, not individual primacy) and what is called 'physiological' referring above all to age and sex as points of reference for social differentiation. The other five categories, territorial, voluntary associations, occupational and professional, rank and status, and a final 'comprehensive integration' in which both political and cultural references are involved, are by no means obviously biological in reference. Indeed even the first two mentioned are biological only in the sense that relatedness through biological criteria constitutes a point of reference for ascriptive categorization of and assignment to social statuses.

This is a classification which any sociologist might take as a promising beginning for the analysis of social structure as such. Malinowski, however, showed surprisingly little interest in exploring such possibilities at all. In what was unquestionably meant to be his major theoretical work, after setting forth this classification he immediately went off on another tack and never returned to it. The tack in question was the development of a theory of needs, the main focal point of which is clearly a theory of the biological needs of the individual organism. He was quite clear about his own conviction that the primary reference of the concept of function was to such a theory of needs. Thus: 'It is clear, I think, that any theory of culture has to start from the organic needs of man, and if it succeeds in relating (to them) the more complex, indirect, but perhaps fully imperative needs of the type which we call spiritual or economic or social, it will supply us with a set of general laws such as we need in sound scientific theory' (1944, pp. 72–3).

Within the polarity defined by the human organism and the culture, then, Malinowski ascribed causal priority to the organism, and his basic theoretical attempt was to *derive* the main characteristics of the culture, and hence of social systems, from a theory of the causally precultural needs of the organism. This orientation is again made quite explicit in his many statements that, however important, however differentiated, culture is always *instrumental* to the satisfaction of organic needs in the sense in which he is using that term. Indeed what he did was to assimilate the concept of culture to that of environment in the specifically biological sense of that term. He referred to culture, thus, as a 'secondary milieu' in which the organism exists (p. 68).

Before attempting to follow the logic of Malinowski's theorizing farther let us make explicit a fundamental theoretical problem at this point. The primary focus of biological theory as it has influenced the behavioural sciences has been on the physiological as distinct from the behavioural interchanges between organism and environment. The typical object of primary environmental significance has not been another behaving organism but for example a source of food. Though with respect to reproduction and defence particularly, relations to other organisms are important to biology, the drawing of a sharp distinction between objects with which there is and is not a process of *interaction* on a behavioural level, has not been a prominent feature of biologically influenced theory in the social sciences. Indeed, where the focus has been on behaviour as such, as in the theory of learning in experimental psychology, the typical experimental situation has not included other organisms, but rather the maze is set up by the experimenter to operate entirely independently of any behaviour except that of the experimental animal.

But it is this very process of interaction between two or more behaving organisms which is the point of departure for a theory of social systems. Here the behaviour of one must acquire meaning as sign, cue or symbol for the other and vice versa. But in his assimilation of the culture to the concept of environment in a biological sense, Malinowski gives no intimation that he is giving special importance to this distinction; on the contrary it is clear that he conceived organic needs as altogether independent of any phenomena of interaction; it is only as instrumental means to their satisfaction that interactive features of the situation acquire significance. To be sure he speaks of symbolic behaviour from time to time, but apparently does not connect the problem with this context.

Thus we have seen that on two levels Malinowski missed an opportunity to take a path which would have led directly into a theory of social systems. First he did not follow up his 'fairly common sense' classification of institutions as elements of social structure, and secondly in relation to the idea that culture is an environment of behaviour, he did not bring out the significance of the phenomena of social interaction, but left them merged in the general biological concept of environment.

What he did was to attempt first to work out a theory of 'basic needs' which gave specific content to what he called 'human nature', i.e. 'the biological determinism which imposes on every civilization and on all individuals in it the carrying out of such bodily functions as breathing, sleep, rest, nutrition, excretion, and reproduction. We can define the concept of basic needs as the environmental and biological conditions which must be fulfilled for the survival of the individual and the group' (1944, p. 75).

His basic problem, then, was how to get from the system of biologically basic needs of the organism to the facts of culturally organized behaviour. As has already been noted he utilized one very general formula, namely that culture is always of instrumental significance in the satisfaction of biological needs. This formula represents in a sense the dividing line between the path Malinowski took and other paths of theoretical development, since in principle it categorically denied the independent causal significance of *learned* goals and values. There is a sense in which what Malinowski put into culture and institutions with his concept of the charter as the system of values for the pursuit of which human beings organize, he took away again with his conception of the causal priority of basic needs and the conception that culture must always be instrumental to the satisfaction of such needs. It is perhaps correct to say that on the clinical level Malinowski operated mainly with the conception of charter; here values were very real and were not treated simply as instrumentalities. But when he attempted to be a general theorist he tended to shift his ground to the detriment of the sociological quality of his thinking.

What, however, of his own explicit attempt to build the bridge? His first major step was to set up a classification of basic needs which could be directly related to a classification of 'cultural responses' which could then in turn be brought into relation to institutions. The familiar table (1944, p. 91, and p. 35 of this volume) includes among the seven basic needs reproduction, movement and growth; and as the corresponding cultural responses, kinship, activity, and training.

In the first place it would seem that the catalogue of basic needs is somewhat skewed from one which would be acceptable to biological theory. But this is not a very serious departure. The one item which is perhaps most dubious in his list is the need for movement which surely most biologists would refer to some other functional context, probably breaking it down into relevance to several such as safety, food-getting and the like.

But more serious is the arbitrariness involved in the way Malinowski attempts to relate this classification of needs to the classification of cultural responses. Let us take three examples. The relation of kinship to reproduction is obvious. But particularly in non-literate societies kinship units perform a wide range of functions which certainly include all seven of Malinowski's categories both of basic needs and of cultural responses. It is a very general fact of course that only in organized kinship relationships is human reproduction ordinarily legitimated but this fact does not justify treating kinship as a whole as primarily a cultural response to the biological need of reproduction.

Secondly let us note the category of 'training' as a cultural response. Most surely this cannot be said to be a response simply to the need of the organism to grow in the strict biological sense. The only basis for such a view would seem to be that biological maturation provides necessary conditions for the effectiveness of various sorts and stages of training. If culture is learned, there clearly must be some kind of ordered sequence in the learning process which is concomitant with and in part dependent on the process of growth of the organism.

Finally, third, perhaps the most tenuous connection of all is that between activities as a cultural response and the alleged basic need for movement. The basic difficulty here is the extreme generality of the categories, both of cultural response and of need. *All* social behaviour is in some sense activity. Presumably activity devoted to satisfaction of the other six needs would not be included in this category; hence it becomes a residual category of all activity which is not devoted to some other function than satisfying the need for movement. To be sure Malinowski suggests that particularly play and recreation should be placed in this category, presumably because they otherwise appear functionless. But this is an example of the familiar logic of the *ad hoc* hypothesis. There exists a category of empirical phenomena which are otherwise unexplained. Then what one does is to invent a 'need' or some other 'force' of which they can be treated as a manifestation.

Clearly Malinowski's classification of cultural responses, however, even granting that they stand in a satisfactory relation to a satisfactory classification of basic needs, does not get him very far toward bridging the gap between the concept of needs and even his own classification of institutions discussed above. He must have recourse to some further theoretical devices in order to get within shouting distance of his goal. The principal device he adopts is the insertion of a second category of needs between his basic needs and the institutional integrates of collective behaviour. These are what he calls 'derived needs' and are clearly the outcome of applying the concept of 'secondary drive' as utilized in Hullian learning theory to his problems.

Three main questions arise about this shift from emphasis on basic biological needs to that on derived needs and their relation to cultural imperatives. The first concerns the implications of the shift for Malinowski's thesis of the primacy of basic needs in functional theory. The second concerns the actual classification of derived needs at which he arrived and its implications, whereas the third concerns his analysis of the motivational mechanisms by which the connections are established. The three questions, particularly the first and third, are of course inter-dependent.

There seems to be no doubt that, in this part of his discussion, Malinowski talked about the relative independence of culture and institutions from biological needs in a way that stands in striking contrast to his many pronouncements about the functional primacy of basic needs. He thus speaks of culture as 'imposing a new type of specific determinism on human behaviour' (1944, p. 119). And again 'Man does not, by biological determinism, need to hunt with spears or bow and arrow; use poison darts; nor defend himself by stockades, by shelters, or by armour. But the moment that such devices have been adopted, in order to enhance human adaptability to the environment they also become necessary conditions of survival.' And yet again 'A permanent deterioration in material equipment, in social solidarity, in the training of the individual and the development of his abilities, would lead in the long run not merely to disorganization of culture, but also to starvation, large-scale disease, the deterioration of personal efficiency; hence also, obviously, to depopulation' (1944, pp. 121, 122).

On one level the bridge he attempts to build is through the concept of adaptation and hence of the instrumentality of culture. Once cultural instrumentalities have been adopted then man becomes dependent on them in such a way that biological survival itself, and of course the satisfaction of the basic needs, becomes dependent on them. In this connection the source of difficulty lies in such phrases as the one quoted, that man does not, by biological determinism, need to hunt with spears, etc. Then there is the problem, why, if biological determinism is para-mount, does he do so? In a broad way Malinowski's answer seems to be that he does so because he has found that he can *better* gratify his basic needs through cultural instrumentalities than without them. This raises certain questions in the theory of personality to which it will be necessary to return presently.

However this may be, there has, when Malinowski talks in this vein, been at least a relative abandonment of what may be called the 'passive' conception of the rôle of the cultural environment of action. Now, if man is even to survive he not only has this cultural environment available to take advantage of if he wishes, but he must do so in order to survive. Above all, perhaps, he must learn the content of his culture and he must conform to its norms and rules. To this extent at least the cultural level has acquired theoretically independent significance. The cultural element of the environment is *man-made*, and is perpetuated and sustained by human action. It is not something which is simply there, independent of human life, to which man must adapt because he is unable to change or control it.

From this type of consideration there emerges in Malinowski's work a classification of cultural imperatives and responses which is of the greatest theoretical interest to the sociologist. It is worth while to quote his tabular presentation in full (1944, p. 125):

Imperatives		*Responses*	
1	The cultural apparatus of implements and consumers' goods must be produced, used, maintained and replaced by new production.	1	Economics
2	Human behaviour, as regards its technical, customary, legal or moral prescription must be codified, regulated in action and sanction.	2	Social Control
3	The human material by which every institution is maintained must be renewed, formed, drilled and provided with full knowledge of tribal tradition.	3	Education
4	Authority within each institution must be defined, equipped with powers, and endowed with means of forceful execution of its orders.	4	Political organization

This, it can be said, is an authentic, if sketchy, classification of the functional imperatives of *social systems*. With respect to it, the formless encyclopedic character of Malinowski's more general discussions of culture evaporates and relatively clear relationships between 'material culture' at least in its economically relevant aspects, norms, values and social organization come to the fore.

This is the more notable to me personally because this classification corresponds very directly to one which I and various people associated with me have been using in our recent theoretical work. With some modifications, but retaining in essentials the four basic categories, and particularly the number four, it can be treated as the master-classification of functional imperatives of any social system, or indeed of any system of action.[1]

[1] I shall not attempt to elaborate this statement here. The classification in substantially the form now being used was first put forward by R. F. Bales (1950, Chap. II). It turned out that the 'pattern variable' scheme with which Shils and I had been working (Parsons and Shils, 1951; and Parsons, 1951) also involved this classification and could be derived from it. In its current form the fourfold scheme was first stated in Parsons, Bales and Shils (1953, chaps. III and V).

I should maintain, then, that Malinowski's late classification of the functional imperatives of culture, or as I should prefer to say of a social system, could well have constituted a basic starting point for a general theoretical analysis of social systems in their own right, not just as derivatives of basic biological needs. Unfortunately, however, this notable contribution stands as a virtually isolated fragment. Not only is it not developed or used in any technical theoretical sense, but Malinowski did not even attempt to relate it to the classification of institutions which he had presented earlier in the same volume.

Part of the explanation of this fact undoubtedly is to be found in the fact that this was one of the very last things Malinowski wrote; had he lived longer, it might have been developed. But at the same time, the further sequence of the *Scientific Theory* would seem to indicate that there was another aspect of the matter. For he immediately returns to his overpowering theoretical interest, namely how he can relate these derived needs to a theory of motivation of the behaviour of the individual. Theoretically at every crucial point he seems to have done this, to have abandoned the structural analysis of culture and of social systems in favour of a certain level of psychological interest. This brings us to the third of the three questions we raised in connection with the theory of derived needs, namely his analysis of the motivational mechanisms involved.

What he finally adopted, and is developed in the last part of the *Scientific Theory*, is, as I suggested, a modified version of Hullian learning theory. The essential point is that he adopted the concept of learned or acquired drive so that one could for example on this basis speak of a need to conform with rules or norms of the culture.

But even here it is notable how narrowly he circumscribes his analysis. First an acquired drive, which he refers to as 'drive (2)', is stated always to be instrumental in significance relative to a basic need which he refers to as 'drive (1)'. Secondly he roundly asserts that, presumably in every case the satisfaction of an acquired drive, of a derived need is also and in its meaning to the individual essentially a satisfaction of a particular and specific basic need in the original sense. As he says 'after the instrumental phase has been adequately accomplished, the immediate drive of nutritive or sexual appetite, of removal of pain or noxious bodily conditions leads directly to the physiological performance, whether this be positive or negative, the satisfaction of pleasure or the removal of pain' (1944, p. 138).

This is a very tenuous bridge indeed and almost undoes what Malinowski has been saying about the independent significance of culture and social organization. Furthermore even on the basis of learning psychology alone, Malinowski takes up only the one idea of instrumental learning and altogether ignores the possible significance of contiguity learning and classical conditioning. Even more serious, he seems to be guilty of a basic confusion, namely between the necessary conditions for a process of learning to take place, and the motivational structure of psychological process after the learning has occurred. There is no reason to doubt that the motivation of all secondary drives or derived needs goes back in the genetic history of the individual to the satisfaction of primary drives. But that in the mature individual the 'ultimate' motive for any specific act of learned behaviour must be the continuing satisfaction of a specific primary drive is certainly not an established psychological doctrine.

Above all, perhaps, the most serious source of the difficulty of Malinowski's position lies in his failure to consider the problems of the *organization* of human personality as a motivational system. He clearly leaves it as a bundle of biologically inherited basic needs, about each of which there then develops a cluster of learned instrumental patterns of behaviour. But the motivation of the instrumental patterns *remains*, in the last analysis, the basic need. Insofar as the personality can be conceived to operate as a system its fundamental organization must be referred to the cluster of discrete basic needs. There is no central organization of learned motivation.

Perhaps this aspect of the matter can be summed up by saying that Malinowski failed to establish a theoretically adequate link between the observed facts of cultural behaviour and the psychological sources of motivation to such behaviour. He reduced the connection to an instrumental one, leaving the structure of the motivational system essentially untouched as a system of given, i.e. biologically inherited, basic needs which are independent of, and prior to culture itself. Essentially Malinowski's social psychology turns out to be a modification of the instinct theory of McDougall.

Above all it is perhaps significant that Malinowski by-passed the opportunity to utilize the conception of internalization of culture patterns, which was very much in the air in the later years of his career. The difference between Malinowski's position and that of the 'culture and personality' school, however, which utilized this conception on one level (e.g. Kardiner or Margaret Mead) lies essentially in the relative weights that they gave to the organic and the cultural reference points in the scheme we have seen that Malinowski worked with. The culture and personality school took the fullest possible advantage of the conception of the plasticity of human nature, and tended to push it to the point where the personality was only a kind of mirror image of the culture, wholly formed by it. Malinowski on the other hand reduced the learned elements of personality functioning to instrumental status and essentially left the biologically given structure of 'instincts' untouched as the prime mover.

It seems to me that the dilemma between these two positions is a false dilemma. The only way to escape it, however, is to develop a more differentiated conceptual scheme than either Malinowski or the 'culture and personality' school have given us. The essence of the necessary differentiatedness is that the conception of a social system must be differentiated from the encyclopedic conception of culture which both groups on the whole share, leaving a more restricted conception of 'cultural tradition'. Secondly the personality as a behavioural system must be clearly differentiated from the organism as a physiological system.

If these theoretical differentiations are fully carried out it becomes possible to raise in a fully technical sense the questions of the structure of social systems and of personalities and their relation to each other. Malinowski was quite right that cultural man is subject to certain imperatives which are independent of the exigencies imposed by the physiological needs of the organism. Furthermore, it is legitimate to interpret these imperatives as above all those of the social systems in which he is involved.

All this is correct. But Malinowski grossly underestimated the theoretical import of these facts. The systems could not be made to fit together at all if their connection were restricted to the levels with which he deals. A much more radical step is necessary, to the doctrine that the *primary structure of human personality as a system* is not organized about the physiological needs of the organism, but about the social structure of the society and its various sub-systems. To a point the position taken by the personality and culture school is, seen in this light, correct. But it is not the 'culture' in the most general sense, but the circumstantially detailed rôle structure of the social system which is the focus of personality structure and its development. This starts, in virtually all societies, with the family, not as an agency for securing biological reproduction, but as an agency of the *socialization* of the child, and goes on by a series of successive stages of development which institute a process of differentiation of a simple structure and further organization and integration of the differentiated parts. Only by conceiving a process of personality development in an ordered system of social interaction situations can we conceive the development of complexes of motivation by which human beings could conceivably meet the exigencies imposed on them by the imperatives of their culture and society. Instrumental patterns for meeting physiological needs have their place in such a motivational system, but the departure from this simple paradigm which must be accounted for is far more profound than Malinowski realized.[1]

At the conclusion of this review of Malinowski's theoretical treatment of social systems, the verdict must be that on the level of general theory

[1] For an attempt to develop this point of view of the relation between social structure and personality development, see Parsons, Bales, et al. (1955). For a critical review of psychological theories in this context and others related to the motivation of social behaviour, see Parsons (1954).

his contribution left much to be desired, both in the most general respects and with respect to his field of special interest, the motivation of social behaviour. On the other hand his performance on what I have called the 'clinical' levels of theorizing about social behaviour is far more satisfactory.

At certain points suggestions of a general analysis of the social system and its structure did emerge in Malinowski's work, notably in his classification of institutions and in his account of the functional imperatives of cultural life. But he never disentangled the concept of the social system as such in any clear way from his encyclopedic concept of culture, which would have been a necessary prerequisite of further theoretical development. But above all he entirely failed to carry out any technical development from these starting points. It seems clear that his heart was not in it, that whenever he had established what he felt to be a useful reference point his theoretical interest immediately turned in a psychological direction.

In this connection it may again be noted that he failed to make significant contact with the eminent theorists of social systems whose work was available to him; there is so far as I am aware no reference either to Max Weber or to Pareto anywhere in his work, and his references to Durkheim are either on too particularized points to be of great interest to general theory, or were negatively critical with respect to certain general aspects such as the alleged 'group mind' aspect of his thought. He apparently entirely failed to appreciate the profound contributions Durkheim made to the analysis of social systems.[1]

Malinowski's special field of interest, the motivation of social behaviour, is one of the greatest importance to sociology and anthropology as well as to psychology. But here again in terms of general theory his work cannot be judged to have been highly successful. Essentially it was characterized by premature resort to psychology. His failure to carry through sustained structural analyses of social systems meant that he did not develop, or take over from others, an analysis of the structural setting which would have enabled him to state the problems of the nature of social motivation and its genesis in the individual more fruitfully than he did, or to get more deeply into the theory of personality in its relation to social systems.

Again in this context Malinowski seems to have been rather peculiarly insensitive to the sources available in the literature of the time which might have been of help to him. He was one of the early social scientists

---

[1] The purpose of this essay is not to make a comparison between Malinowski and Radcliffe-Brown, but the contrast in this respect is striking. Throughout his work Radcliffe-Brown has been extremely clear about the concept of social system—and Durkheim's use of it—and has consistently made it the main focus of his theoretical work. On a comparably general level this cannot be said of Malinowski.

to become interested in Freud's work. But having, to an important degree prematurely and without full understanding, decided that Freud's theory was culture-bound and could not explain Trobriand facts, he dropped it and never made serious use of it in his own theoretical structure. Moreover, there was a school of social psychology in the United States centring on the names of G. H. Mead and W. I. Thomas, which might have been very useful to him, but so far as one can judge from his writings, had no influence on him. What he did take up was one version of behaviouristic learning theory in perhaps its least directly fruitful form for these purposes.

In sum, I am afraid that my verdict must be that so far as the *general* theory of social systems is concerned, including as a vitally important branch, the motivation of social behaviour, there is with one exception no point at which Malinowski has more to teach us than one or several of his contemporaries or predecessors. The one exception to which I refer is the classification of the functional imperatives of 'culture' and the responses to which they relate. It is tragic that, having set this forth, he entirely failed to follow it up.

The harshness of this verdict [1] is mitigated above all by two circumstances. The first of these concerns the eminence of Malinowski's contributions to anthropology and more broadly to social science in other directions, as a field-worker, a teacher,[2] and a 'clinical' theorist. It is only as a general theorist of social systems that I think we must conclude that Malinowski was not definitely first-rate.

The second circumstance concerns the state of the subject in his time. By contrast with the older evolutionary and trait theories he unquestionably was, in his general theoretical orientations, on a fruitful track and exercised a healthy influence. This influence, I think it is clear, considerably increased sensitivity to the need for good general theory, and for recognition of examples of it when it was available.

[1] This verdict seems to be shared on the whole, though from a somewhat different point of view, by the only other attempt at a rather general appraisal of this aspect of Malinowski's work I have found, namely by Gluckman (1949).

[2] In this respect I have a heavy personal debt to Malinowski which I fully recognize and do not wish anything said in this essay to invalidate.

Malinowski's Contribution to Fieldwork Methods and the Writing of Ethnography

PHYLLIS KABERRY

I N his Preface to the *Argonauts of the Western Pacific*, Sir James Frazer wrote: 'It is characteristic of Dr. Malinowski's method that he takes full account of the complexity of human nature. He sees man, so to say, in the round and not in the flat. He remembers that man is a creature of emotion at least as much as of reason, and he is constantly at pains to discover the emotional as well as the rational basis of human action' (Malinowski, 1922*a*, p. ix).

Malinowski as 'the chronicler and spokesman of the Trobrianders' gave ethnography a dimension it had hitherto lacked: actuality of relationships and richness of content. Instead of a nondescript field where anonymous informants provided genealogies, recounted their folk-tales, stated the norms and apparently conformed to them, we become familiar with the Trobriands and its shaded villages, the changing aspect of its gardens through the seasons, its decorated yam houses, and canoes drawn up on the beach or moored in Kiriwina lagoon. We come to know the inhabitants, not as paid and perhaps bored informants, but as actors in a changing scene, as individuals who co-operate, quarrel, cheat, compromise, give generously, contradict one another (and also Malinowski on occasion), diverge from the rules, pay the penalty or sometimes avoid it. In short, we are always aware of the context of situation in which Malinowski made his generalizations; and with him we trace the intricacies of multiple interrelationships. 'We shall', he says, 'have to follow two lines of approach: on the one hand we must state with as much precision as possible the principles of social organization, the rules of tribal law and custom; the leading ideas, magical, tech-nological, and scientific, of the natives. On the other hand we shall try to remain in touch with a living people, to keep before our eyes a clear picture of the setting and scenery' (1935, Vol. I, p. 4). His attempt to

71

recreate incident and setting was not an introduction of a little local colour to enliven the narrative, but sprang from both his scientific and humanistic approach to social anthropology: his recognition of his duty as an anthropologist to document as fully as possible the empirical basis for the sociological principles he formulated; his desire to gain an insight into human motives and values. For him, the final goal of the ethnographer was 'to grasp the native's point of view, his relation to life, to realize *his* vision of *his* world. We have to study man, and we must study what concerns him most intimately, that is, the hold which life has on him. . . . Perhaps through realizing human nature in a shape very distant and foreign to us, we shall have some light shed on our own' (1922a, p. 25).

In his approach to social anthropology, Malinowski had much in common with Frazer to whom on more than one occasion he acknowledged his debt.[1] Both wrote with an awareness of the complexity of human nature and both wrote with imagination, subtlety and irony, though Malinowski had not Frazer's felicity and precision of style. Both delighted in and were fascinated by the ceremonial aspect of life; and for both the process of analysis of belief and rite was also a journey of exploration into the reaches of the human spirit. Both contextualized their facts; and both moved from facts to theory and from theory back to facts, though Frazer cast his net much wider. If there is much to criticize in Malinowski (and what anthropologist is not vulnerable), if our interest has shifted to problems with which he was not concerned, and if we have developed new frames of reference, nevertheless his ethnographical writings still provide us with a rich store of data for comparative purposes. More than this: he set a standard for intensive field-work and rigorous documentation of theory that few have achieved since; and his functional approach, in the sense of the study and analysis of institutional interdependencies, has become so much a part of the texture of our thinking that we are apt to forget its first full formulation and demonstration occurred only a generation ago in 1922.

If we are to evaluate in more detail and more critically his contribution to the writing of ethnography, we must place *Argonauts of the Western Pacific* in its context of situation; that is, examine it in relation to its predecessors.

Malinowski's Predecessors

Malinowski in his early writings expressed his debt to his predecessors in the field and in theory: to Haddon, Rivers, C. G. Seligman, and Baldwin Spencer on the one hand; and to Tylor, Frazer, Westermarck,

[1] In an address given in honour of Frazer in 1925, Malinowski described how as a young student he had been ordered to abandon physical and chemical research some twenty years before. But he carried away from Cracow the three volumes of *The Golden Bough*—the only solace of his troubles (1926c, p. 5).

Durkheim, Hubert, and Mauss on the other. A detailed survey of the development of field-work techniques has already been made by Audrey Richards in an earlier publication (1939). Here I am more particularly concerned with the work of those British anthropologists who directly influenced Malinowski.

Until the end of the nineteenth century, most anthropologists wrote from the armchair and relied for their raw data on material recorded by missionaries, explorers, travellers, government officials, and settlers. Among the missionaries, however, Codrington had himself published a study based on his observations from 1863 to 1887 in Melanesia and more especially in Norfolk Island, where Christian natives from the islands were brought together for instruction. He obtained from the latter systematic accounts of the religious beliefs, practices, and social regulations prevailing among the Melanesians. He was mainly concerned with existing institutions and he was persuaded that the first duty of the missionary was to try and understand the people among whom he worked (1891, pp. v and vii). In Africa, Junod published *Les Ba Ronga* (1898), and Callaway, *The Religious System of the Amazulu* (1868–70), the latter a reproduction of texts of informants with an annotated translation by the author.

The first relatively intensive field studies were made by Baldwin Spencer, in collaboration with Gillen, in 1894, among the aborigines of Central Australia (Spencer and Gillen, 1899); and by Haddon, who organized the Cambridge Expedition to Torres Straits from 1898–9 and enlisted the help of Rivers, Seligman, Ray, Wilkin, Myers, and Mc-Dougall.[1] Five weeks were spent on Mabuiag in the Western Islands, and four months on Mer in the Eastern Islands. Information was collected in pidgin-English or through interpreters, and the division of labour in the field was largely followed in the publication of the results (1901–35). For example, in Volume 5 (1904), Rivers was responsible for the chapters on genealogies, personal names, kinship, and the regulation of marriage, Seligman for birth and childhood customs and women's puberty ceremonies, and Haddon for trade, warfare, magic, religion, and the regulation of public life, while Haddon and Rivers did the chapter on totemism. What established the expedition as a landmark in British anthropology was the attempt made by a team of experts to collect data on all aspects of native life; the scrupulous specification of the conditions of field-work and the qualifications of informants; and, lastly, the development of the genealogical method by Rivers. After this

---

[1] In America, Cushing had lived among the Zuni from 1879–84; and in 1883–4, Boas had carried out research among the Eskimos, and later investigated the Indians of the North-West Coast. Boas emphasized the importance of learning the language and of studying cultures as wholes, but his work made little impact upon his British contemporaries in anthropology because he did not actually produce a detailed functional analysis.

expedition, Seligman made his survey of the Melanesians of British New Guinea in 1904 and, despite the brevity of his visit and his dependence on accounts of customs from selected informants, he laid the foundation for our ethnographic knowledge of that area. In 1907–8, together with his wife, he carried out research among the Veddas and this was followed by field-work in the Sudan.

Rivers, after his return to England, carried out research among the Todas for a short period between 1901–2. Despite the thinness of the material, *The Todas* (1906) is a major work in the history of British anthropology. It contains a precise statement of field-work conditions and, in the main text, descriptions of belief and custom are strictly separated from interpretation and theory. Rivers collected the genealogies of all the members of the community studied, together with their clan, moiety, and local affiliations, and he used the material to work out the regularity of types of marriages (pp. 11 and 462 ff.). He was obliged to depend on interpreters, but he obtained independent accounts from different people, compared them and cross-examined for discrepancies (pp. 8–10). In addition to formal statements about norms he also asked for concrete cases. His aim throughout was 'to apply rigorous methods to the investigation of sociology and religion' and to make his book 'a demonstration of anthropological method' (pp. v and 7).[1]

The next landmark in field-work, and especially in theory, was the expedition of A. R. Brown (Radcliffe-Brown) to the Andamans in 1906–8, though the results were not published until 1922. The book was dedicated to his teachers, Haddon and Rivers, and in the Preface to the 1933 edition he wrote: 'It was largely from this point of view [the historical] that I approached the study of the Andaman Islanders and attempted, by an investigation of physical characteristics, language, and culture, to make a hypothetical reconstruction of the history of the Andamans and of the Negritos in general' (1933, p. vii). During the course of his work he became convinced that speculative history could not give results of any importance for the understanding of human life and culture. He stressed the need for 'an intensive investigation of each culture as an adaptive and integrative mechanism and a comparison one with another of as many variant types as possible' (1933, p. ix). He devoted the first part of his monograph to a lucid if bare account of the social structure of the Andamanese, and the second part to an exposition of the meaning and function of ceremonies and myths. Here he formu-

---

[1] Later Rivers, in the Percy Sladen Trust Expedition to the Solomon Islands, carried out intensive field-work with Hocart in the Western group, and survey work elsewhere. But he stated that 'much of the material was collected during hasty visits to the islands, sometimes of only a few hours' duration', and that the book was intended to be a 'demonstration of ethnological, rather than ethnographical, method' (1914, Vol. 1, pp. vi and 1–2). For a critical reference to Rivers's description of Tikopia custom, see R. Firth (1936, p. xxiv).

lated his concept of function as 'the effects of an institution (custom or belief) in so far as they concern the society and its solidarity or cohesion' (1933, p. 234).

Radcliffe-Brown did not make any particular contribution to the development of field-work techniques; in his Australian research in 1911, and also subsequently, he systematically applied Rivers's genealogical method and laid an enduring foundation for the analysis and study of kinship and totemism. His 'Three Tribes of Western Australia' (1913) was his first essay in establishing a typology of Australian kinship systems and it was followed by a series of articles which culminated in his brilliant monograph, *The Social Organization of Australian Tribes* (1931). He always writes with balance, lucidity, and economy, but the precision with which he blue-prints the formal aspects of Australian kinship and local organization has also its negative side. Though again and again he asserts the basic importance of the family and the local group in Australian social structure, we are not given a description of them as functioning units in the tribes which he studied. Many of the questions posed by Malinowski in his *The Family among the Australian Aborigines* (1913a) about the actual working of the family as a social institution cannot be answered from Radcliffe-Brown's published field-work. And here we have an essential difference between these two anthropologists who for the last quarter of a century have exercised the dominant influence in British anthropology. Both denied the value of speculative reconstruction of history; both emphasized the need to study existing social institutions; both conceived of cultures as wholes; both developed a concept of function in terms of the social effects of any custom or institution. But here they diverged, and the difference in approach is nowhere more evident than in their ethnographic monographs. If, in Malinowski's, the people are always with us (and, some would say, too much with us), in Radcliffe-Brown's they are conspicuous by their absence; they are the invisible facts. One explanation lies not so much in Radcliffe-Brown's preoccupation with structure, but rather in the nature of the 'effects' which he thought most significant. They are also the most difficult to document from empirical data. 'The discovery of the integrative function of an institution, usage, or belief', he says, 'is to be made through the observation of its effects, and these are obviously in the first place effects on individuals, or their life, their thoughts, their emotions. Not all such effects are significant, or at least equally so. Nor is it the immediate effects with which we are finally concerned, but the more remote effects upon the social cohesion and continuity' (1933, p. x). Radcliffe-Brown became increasingly concerned with the more remote effects; Malinowski in his Trobriand monographs concentrated on the more immediate effects, the analysis of institutional interdependencies. He regarded the elucidation of such interrelations as the only valid basis for the next stage in abstraction—the evaluation of the function of an institution, or set of related institutions, in tribal life (1935, Vol. I, pp. 454–6).

If, then, we crystallize the situation in British anthropology as it was just prior to Malinowski's expedition to New Guinea in 1914, we may say that, largely owing to the influence of Haddon, a tradition of the first-hand study of primitive communities by anthropologists had been established, and that some rigorous techniques and standards for the collection of data had been developed. On the theoretical side, there was a preliminary formulation of the hypothesis of the interdependence of institutions in the writings of the French sociologists, and also to some extent in that of Rivers.[1] Malinowski's own emphasis on the adequate description of the facts and their mutual dependencies was not the mere consequence of his prolonged period of research in the Trobriands but had already been explicitly stated and demonstrated in his armchair study of the Australian aboriginal family (1913a), where he had attempted to analyse that institution in all its aspects. In the concluding chapter he put forward a formulation of the functional approach which bears many resemblances to that propounded by Radcliffe-Brown in *The Andaman Islanders*, published nine years later.

'If in any society there exist two institutions of very close resemblance, as in Australia, the individual family creating individual relationship and the various kinship organizations creating group relationship, the only way to understand their working is by describing minutely the social functions of each of them. This has been done for the individual family in the foregoing pages; it remains to be done for the kinship groups. Social institutions should in the first place be defined by their social functions; if the functions—religious, magical, legal, economic, etc.,— of the totemic class, the exogamous class, and other divisions be known and compared with the functions of the individual family, each of these institutions will appear as occupying a definite place in the social organization, and playing a determinate part in the life of the community. And such a knowledge would form a firm basis for further speculations' (Malinowski, 1913a, p. 303).[2]

---

[1] Rivers (1906, pp. 10–11) described the ceremonial and social life as an intricate web of closely related practices. He also pointed out (1914, Vol. 1, p. 1) that among primitive peoples 'these departments (of social life) are inextricably interwoven and interdependent so that it is hopeless to expect to obtain a complete account of any one department without covering the whole field'. Rivers, however, never gave a functional analysis of the cultures he studied, though he did concern himself with the correlations between kinship terminology and social behaviour.

[2] See also his earlier statement (1913a, p. 6) that 'the essential features of the individual family, as of all other social institutions, depend upon the general structure of a given society and upon the conditions of life therein'.

MALINOWSKI'S FIELD-WORK METHODS

Malinowski's Field-Work

Malinowski made three expeditions in all to New Guinea. The first, September 1914–March 1915, was suggested by Seligman and was spent mainly among the Mailu of Toulon Island, a West Papuo-Melanesian group. A brief visit was also paid to Woodlark Island. He returned to Australia and went to the Trobriands in June 1915 and remained there until May 1916. A second visit to the Trobriands lasted from October 1917 to October 1918. While on leave in Australia he sorted notes, digested and recast evidence, formulated problems and began to write up his material. He himself stressed the value of such intervals between bouts of field-work, and suggested that a break between expeditions of about a year each was preferable to two consecutive years in the field. After twelve or fourteen months in the field, the law of diminishing returns is apt to set in. Most anthropologists would confirm him in his opinion; but unfortunately few among the older generation have been able to plan their research along these lines, and for most of us even the prospect of a second visit to study social and cultural change lies on the remote and perhaps illusory horizon of the future. But among the younger anthropologists, especially those associated with research institutions at Ibadan or Makerere, or at the Rhodes-Livingstone Institute or the Australian National University, some have been able to adhere to a programme such as that suggested by Malinowski. We await their results with interest.

Malinowski first used pidgin-English in the Trobriands, but he was already familiar with the structure of Melanesian languages and had acquired some knowledge of Motu among the Mailu. After three months he was able to converse with informants in Trobriand, though he admitted that it was not until his second visit that he could 'follow easily conversations among the natives themselves' and could take notes rapidly in dialect (1935, Vol. I, p. 453). Although he made Omarakana in Kiriwina district his headquarters, he moved about from one part of the Trobriands to another and visited also the *kula* communities of the Amphletts, Woodlark, and Dobu (1922a, p. 32). Only six weeks in all were spent in the company of Europeans during his two years in the field.

His account of his 'tribulations' is one of the most human documents in ethnographical writing, and finds a response in even the most seasoned field-worker who has had to face the despondency of the first few weeks, when anything more than superficial contacts seems impossible once one has 'done technology', made maps of the village and, if lucky, collected a few genealogies without creating the suspicion among the natives that such data will be used for a new tax assessment. Malinowski pitched his tent among the native huts in the village and found that, in cutting himself off from the amenities of white settlement, he not only placed himself

77

in a strategic position to observe, but also quite naturally sought out the company of the natives for companionship as a relief from loneliness.

'There is all the difference between a sporadic plunging into the company of natives, and being really in contact with them. What does this latter mean? On the Ethnographer's side, it means that his life in the village, which at first is a strange, sometimes unpleasant, sometimes intensely interesting adventure, soon adopts quite a natural course very much in harmony with his surroundings. Soon after I had established myself in Omarakana, I began to take part, in a way, in the village life, to look forward to the important or festive events, to take personal interest in the gossip and the developments of the small village occurrences; to wake up every morning to a day, presenting itself to me more or less as it does to the native. . . . As I went on my morning walk through the village, I could see intimate details of family life; . . . I could see the arrangements for the day's work, people starting on their errands, or groups of men and women busy at some manufacturing tasks. Quarrels, jokes, family scenes, events usually trivial, sometimes dramatic, but always significant, formed the atmosphere of my daily life, as well as of theirs' (1922a p. 7).

But Malinowski was more than a passive, sometimes participant, observer. He actively sought his information by employing a range of techniques. However, the fruitful application of techniques was for him dependent in turn on a sound training in theory and some foreshadowing of problems. In the Trobriands, he used what he was later to call somewhat cumbrously the method of statistic documentation of concrete evidence. This involved the collection of statements of norms and concrete cases, genealogies, village censuses, maps, and especially the preparation of synoptic tables or charts to illustrate ownership of garden land, hunting and fishing privileges, the dovetailing of ritual and technical activities, the distribution of harvests, and the pattern of gift exchange in association with its sociological, ceremonial, and economic aspects (1922a, pp. 14–15). He regarded the construction of such tables not only as an instrument in the field to ensure the widest possible investigation of relevant facts, but as part of the writing of ethnography. They enable the reader to judge what is the result of direct and indirect observation; they constitute an empirical charter for generalization.

But Malinowski did not consider that the collection of the type of data described above was sufficient. It provided the bare outlines of tribal constitution and the anatomy of its culture. The ethnographer must also record the *imponderabilia of actual life*. And this cannot be achieved by the method of question and answer.

'Here belong such things as the routine of a man's working day; . . . the tone of conversational and social life around the village fires, the existence of strong friendships or hostilities, and of passing sympathies and dislikes between people; the subtle yet unmistakable manner in which personal vanities and ambitions are reflected in the behaviour of the individual and in the emotional reactions of those who surround him. . . . Indeed, if we remember that these imponderable yet all important facts of actual life are part of the real substance of the social fabric, that in them are spun the innumerable threads which keep together the family, the clan, the village community, the tribe—their significance becomes clear' (1922a, pp. 18-19).

Malinowski recognized that this involved not only the superficial registration of details but an effort to penetrate the mental attitude revealed in them; and this in turn raised the problem of the 'personal equation' of the observer. But he believed that it could in some measure be taken into account by keeping an ethnographic diary; and by systematically noting the normal and typical, and the slight and more pronounced deviations from them over a prolonged period of field-work.

Malinowski also insisted that the adequate investigation of a culture demanded not only the documentation of aspects of social structure, the details of behaviour and emotional interaction, but also the natives' commentaries on action, their beliefs and ideas. And here, it should be stressed, he was not concerned with the unique experiences and motives of individuals *qua* individuals, but as members of a community.

Such documents of native mentality, a *corpus inscriptionum*, entailed the recording in the native language of narratives, opinions, typical utterances, myths, folk-lore, magical formulae, and native explanations and interpretations of customs and beliefs (1922a, pp. 22-4).

Lastly, Malinowski considered it the duty of the anthropologist to render a careful and sincere account of his credentials and his mistakes in the field; and, in Appendix II to *Coral Gardens*, he recorded his 'Confessions of Ignorance and Failure'. In judging his methods he was his own most exacting critic. He admitted that a general source of inadequacies in all his material, whether photographic or linguistic or descriptive, consisted in the fact that, like every ethnographer, he was lured by the dramatic, exceptional, and sensational; and he castigated himself for not treating the 'drab, everyday, minor events with the same love and interest as sensational, large-scale happenings' (1935, Vol. I, pp. 241, 452-3, 462). But despite his strictures on his own work he did accumulate a mass of detail on the drab and the everyday routine; and despite his impatience with the purely technological enthusiasms of the museum ethnologist he conscientiously recorded the technical processes of housebuilding and canoe construction (1935, p. 460). And in this sphere of research he made his own contribution by emphasizing the need to study a material object within the context of situation: that is in terms of the purposes for which it is made, the uses to which it is put, the rules of ownership, and native attitudes towards it. Conversely, he regarded a knowledge of technology as an indispensable means of 'approach to economic and sociological activities and to what might be adequately called native science'. Finally, he collected a certain amount of quantitative data, though he admitted that there were gaps in his assessment of some of the material aspects of gardening. But he was of the opinion that the anthropologist should measure, weigh, and count everything that could be legitimately measured, weighed, and counted (1935, p. 459).

I have discussed Malinowski's methods in detail and have quoted freely from that manual of field-workers, *The Argonauts*, not only because of the importance of his contribution to research, but also because the principles he laid down for field-work are to some extent applied to the handling and presentation of material in his monographs and articles. More than this. In the course of narrative and exposition, we are again and again taken into the field situation and, with the ethnographer, examine and piece together the evidence and witness the gradual integration of data into a meaningful whole. There is no better example of this than his chapters on land tenure (1935, Vol. I, chaps. xi and xii).

Malinowski's Theoretical Framework

In his first publication of field data, from Mailu (1915a), Malinowski conformed closely to the methods adopted by the anthropologists of the late nineteenth and early twentieth centuries in describing the main social institutions of a particular people. He gave a short but competent account of the Geography, Social Divisions, Tribal Life, Economics, Magico-Religious Activities and Beliefs, Art and Knowledge of the Mailu.[1] It was a field report and its scope was largely dictated by the brevity of his visit among that people. But in the monographs which were concerned with specific aspects of Trobriand culture there was not only an increasing command of English, but a radical change in his handling of the results of research. The very richness of his material presented problems of exposition which few if any of his predecessors had been called upon to face. This, allied with his theoretical approach which defined the institution as the 'isolate' of culture and postulated the organic interdependence of institutions, accounted in some measure for the fact that by 1942 only certain aspects of Trobriand society had been analysed for publication. It is a matter for deep regret that the

---

[1] Similar categories were foreshadowed in the work of Tylor and his successors —Codrington, Haddon, Rivers, Seligman, and so on—though some of the data included occasionally strike a note of incongruity for the present-day reader. For example, in Volume I of the Cambridge Expedition to Torres Straits, we find 'Domestic Life (including disposal of the dead and mummification)' and 'Various Social Contacts (Head-hunting, *Sarup* and Trade)'. Contemporary anthropologists still employ with modifications many of the categories used by the earlier writers; but there is, firstly, an explicit recognition of the interconnection of institutions; and, secondly, a bringing together of facts relevant to social structure.

projected books on kinship and primitive warfare were never completed, but it should also be borne in mind that, owing to his functional method, we have a considerable amount of information on political and clan organization in the *Argonauts*, *Sexual Life of Savages*, and *Coral Gardens*. More important still, Malinowski's intensive knowledge of one culture, his enduring awareness of the complexity of social facts and of the 'amplitude of deviation' (1932a, p. 237), which may occur in even the most formalized social relationships, made him chary of carrying his generalizations to a point where, 'mounted on the airy stilts of abstraction', he overlooked 'the impertinent individualities of such poor concretions as mankind'.[1] In other words, in his ethnographic works he permitted neither himself nor his reader to lose sight of the facts and of the multiple and organic relations which obtain among them.

If we are to evaluate Malinowski's own contribution to the writing of ethnography, or indeed that of any other anthropologist, a number of factors must be taken into account: the period when the work was undertaken, the scope and intensity of research, and the theoretical orientation of the anthropologist in the field. We have already attempted to place Malinowski's field-work in historical perspective and have indicated some of his basic assumptions as formulated in *The Family among the Australian Aborigines*. There remain those factors which pertain to the actual processing of field notes; or what Malinowski himself described as the enormous distance between the 'brute material of information— as it is presented to the student in his observations, in native statements, in the kaleidoscope of tribal life—and the final authoritative presentation of results' (1922a, pp. 3–4).[2] And here we are concerned not only with the problems on which his articles and monographs were focused, but with the theoretical framework within which they were written.

It does not fall within the scope of this essay to examine his theory in detail but some discussion of his key concept of *function* is essential, since for him it had different meanings at different levels of organization. In this respect his practice offers some parallel to that of Radcliffe-Brown. At the first level of abstraction, the function of an institution or custom is its effects on other institutions or customs: 'Custom does not sit loosely in its context. It is organically connected with the rest of culture' (1926a). The functional method therefore entails the examination of institutional relationships; it is something more than 'pure ethnography' or the recording of uniformities of behaviour and belief; it is more than integrative description, for it is the eliciting of what

---

[1] Charles Lamb, 'Imperfect Sympathies' in *Essays of Elia*. Lamb's ridicule of abstraction carried to extravagant lengths also recalls Auden's satire on 'that Heaven of the Really General Case'.

[2] He also states that 'The real mental effort, the really painful and uphill work is not so much "to get facts" as to elicit the relevance of these facts and systematize them into an organic whole' (1935, Vol. I, p. 322).

Malinowski himself called the 'invisible facts', the principles of organization and their interconnection.

'The principles of social organization, of legal constitution, of economics and religion have to be constructed by the observer out of a multitude of manifestations of varying significance and relevance. It is these invisible realities, only to be discovered by inductive computation, by selection and construction, which are scientifically important in the study of culture' (1935, Vol. I, p. 317).[1]

At the second level of abstraction, the investigation of function involves an analysis of the effects of an institution on the maintenance of specific relationships and the achievement of specific ends as defined by the members of a particular community. At the third level, function may be interpreted as the part played by an institution in promoting social cohesion and the persistence of a given way of life or culture in a given environment. All three usages of the concept of function imply a teleological approach, and the differences in meaning are a correlate of differences in the scale of organization with which the anthropologist is concerned. But, as indicated in an earlier section, Malinowski in his ethnographic writings largely eschewed any formulation of the 'remoter effects' of a custom (or set of usages) on social cohesion; though in examining the rôle of polygyny and of marriage payments in relationship to chieftainship in the Trobriands he was of course dealing with the problem of political stability. Nevertheless he would not, I think, have seen in any one set of social relationships the key to the whole social system; or, to particularize, the key to its social structure, its values and its activities. At least he was not prepared to advance such generalized sociological propositions until he had analysed in turn the component institutions of Trobriand society.

And here it should be pointed out that while Malinowski stated that the first requirement of ethnography was an account of the 'tribal constitution', he did not consider, as did Radcliffe-Brown (1952, pp. 189–90), that society (and not culture) was the primary subject matter of social anthropology. Culture was a process *sui generis*, which must be studied by special methods. It was an organic unity, or a connected living whole with the three dimensions of social organization, material outfit, and belief (Malinowski, 1926a, *passim*). His concept of institution followed logically from his concept of culture. Whereas for Radcliffe-Brown an institution is a formalized mode of behaviour, for Malinowski an institution was multidimensional, having its personnel (social structure), its charter (or values), its norms, activities, and material equipment. It was a construct, but it was a model closely linked to empirical reality, that is to social situations in which pairs or groups of individuals in defined relationships carried out activities in pursuit of certain ends.

[1] Vide also 1922a, p. 397.

The task which Malinowski set himself in the writing of ethnography was therefore the analysis of a range of institutions and a demonstration of their organization into a cultural whole. What the next step would have been we shall never know. But in his theoretical writings he postulated that one of the main tasks of social anthropology was the comparative study of institutions; and it is clear that in his last years he was increasingly concerned with finding a framework of reference within which such complex units might be compared. But instead of abstracting one aspect of institution, such as structure or values, he re-formulated his concept of function as the way in which an institution satisfies biological or derived needs; and he suggested that institutions might be compared in terms of their functions. He himself never attempted a systematic survey of one type of institution from a selected range of societies. The difficulties would have been formidable, and one suspects that the generalizations would have been so vague as to be valueless. But if few anthropologists are prepared to grant the usefulness of a model based on biological needs for explanation at the sociological level, few would deny the value of his earlier model of the institution as a conceptual tool for field research and for the organization of data at certain stages of abstraction. Indeed, the validity of generalization in a purely structural analysis rests on comprehensive documentation at the institutional level.[1]

Malinowski's Ethnographic Works

Between 1916 and 1935 Malinowski wrote a series of monographs and articles which were concerned with the analysis of various aspects of Trobriand economy, social control, marriage and the family, ritual, belief, and mythology. But while each was focused on a particular institution or set of closely related institutions, the treatment or exposition was fugal in the sense that a number of themes were interwoven or counterposed. Where the subject matter permitted, he presented his data in the form of a narrative of events, developing in the process the implications of his generalizations for theory in the fields of economics, law, kinship, magic, and religion. *Argonauts of the Western Pacific* (1922a) is a typical example of his method and we shall examine it in some detail.

We are taken on a journey through the *kula* district: the landscape is re-created and, at each island, the physical characteristics of the natives and the main features of their social and economic organization are indicated. When we reach the Trobriands, it is with something of

---

[1] Among the classic accounts of social structure we would place that of Fortes (1945). But while his framework of reference is structure, his demonstration of the importance of the lineage system in Tallensi society is achieved by a functional analysis; that is, by a study of the lineage in its economic, residential, jural, moral, political, and ritual aspects.

Malinowski's own suspense and interest that we enter the community which is to be the centre of his field-work. A vivid picture of villages and gardens emerges and, in the course of some thirty pages, we are given an outline of Trobriand economy, kinship system, beliefs, ceremonies and, especially, rank and chieftainship since he regarded 'a firm grasp of the main, political institutions as essential to the understanding of the *kula*. All departments of tribal life, religion, magic, economics are interwoven, but the *social organization* of the tribe lies at the foundation of everything else' (p. 69). In subsequent volumes, *The Sexual Life of Savages* and *Coral Gardens*, the reader is not only referred back to the preliminary account of structure in the *Argonauts*, but further aspects are elucidated where relevant to the theme under discussion. If, for Malinowski, social organization (or what today we would call structure) was merely one aspect of culture, he nevertheless regarded an analysis of 'the sociology of enactment' as an essential part of ethnographic writing.

In the following chapter, the essentials of the *kula* system are given: the types of valuables involved and the norms governing their exchange, the basis of partnership, the importance of secondary economic transactions, and the background of ritual and ideology. The rest of the volume is devoted to a documentation of these generalizations by an account of the links in the chain of *kula* performance—from the building of a canoe, the departure of an expedition to Dobu, the ceremonial procedures which occur at each stage of the journey, to the return to Kitava and Kiriwina. While the sequence of events provides the main thread of the argument, the themes of the 'sociological mechanisms underlying the activities, and the system of ideas at work in regulating labour and magic' are developed (1922a, pp. 124–5). But in demonstrating the interlocking of structural, technological and ritual aspects Malinowski does not stop short at integrative description; he uses it as a basis for the enunciation and clarification of sociological concepts. Thus the lively account of a feast at the ceremonial launching of a new canoe is made the occasion for an analysis of the rules governing the organization of labour and the distribution of wealth, and for the formulation of the principle of reciprocity and its importance in kinship, political relations, and law (1922, p. 167 ff.).

Many similar examples of his method might be taken from his ethnographic works but a particularly good case occurs in *Coral Gardens* where, in discussing the distribution of the yam harvest among affines, he points out that an understanding of the economic aspect of *urigubu* involves a grasp of the laws of marriage and native ideas of procreation and kinship (1935, Vol. I, p. 199). In the process of brilliant analysis he elucidates the complex relations, with their potentialities for tension and conflict, between the genealogical unit of descent (or unit of filiation) on the one hand, and the patrilocal household (or family) on the other;

and he advances the hypothesis that the *urigubu* 'is the outcome and economic expression of a compromise or adjustment between the principles of the patrilocal household and matrilineal filiation' (1935, Vol. I, p. 208).[1]

In passing from one dimension to another, from the technological to the structural or the ideological, Malinowski has his own criteria of relevance and these are determined by the scientific rigour which he considers necessary for the documentation of his more abstract generalizations. If, in the eyes of some of his colleagues, he carries to excess his vivid presentation of detail and his wide contextualization of event, at least he is never guilty of concocting what Postan (1939, pp. 10–11), in another universe of discourse, has called 'a soufflé of whipped postulates'.[2] But Malinowski not only employs the technique of crucial incident to substantiate the formulation of a principle. As indicated in the earlier section on field-work methods, he includes in his text linguistic statements made by informants, quantitative material on harvests and economic transactions, plans of villages and garden lands, and charts which provide a synopsis of land tenure, exchanges, systems of ownership, calendars of events, and the interlocking of magic with technical activities.

Lastly, in his vivid eye-witness accounts of ceremonies, economic activities, domestic and village relations and quarrels he records the imponderabilia of actual life. Some anthropologists have regarded his technique in this respect as impressionistic and subjective. But, in her discussion of the peculiar difficulties which confront the anthropologist in the presentation of field material, Richards (1939, pp. 308–9) has pointed out that to omit such vivid eye-witness accounts as the anthropologist is able to give, often 'results in the loss of something which may be essential to an understanding of the group's social life. Writers who give abstract analyses of kinship terms without any description of the way the people behave do not necessarily obtain objectivity by this means, for they have merely given their own abstract generalizations, based on what they have observed.' If Malinowski's ethnographic writings in their rich discursiveness do not conform to the strict canons of

---

[1] See also p. 199, where he states that 'marriage puts the wife's matrilineal kinsmen under a permanent tributary obligation to the husband, to whom they have to pay yearly gifts of *urigubu* for as long as marriage lasts'.

[2] In his discussion of the degree to which abstraction can be carried in economic history, Postan raises many problems which are pertinent for social anthropology. 'Social study in its empirical ranges deals with entire social patterns; however abstracted and simplified, its facts are still too complex for a single and a simple prediction. And at the cost of yet another repetition we must insist that the penalty of being sufficiently concrete to be real is the impossibility of being sufficiently abstract to be exact. And laws which are not exact, predictions which are not certain, generalizations which are not general, are truer when shown in a concrete instance in one of their unique manifestations than they are when expressed in quasi-universal terms' (1939, pp. 32–3).

logical consistency, aesthetic proportion, and economy and precision of exposition, nevertheless he provides us with a wealth of information on native incentives, values and attitudes, on the tensions and conflicts which underlie the operation of structural principles, and on 'the amplitude of deviation' from the norm. In so doing he has drawn attention to a range of problems which increasingly are demanding the attention of anthropologists. I do not of course imply that Malinowski's influence has been the sole or even dominant influence in this respect; still less that he himself systematically developed and clarified his theory in relation to such problems. But I do stress his appreciation of the sociological importance of data on values, incentives, individual variation, and tension for a full analysis of a social system.

Malinowski's Effect on the Writing of Ethnography

There can be no question of Malinowski's radical influence on fieldwork methods. The anthropologists who are contributors to this volume, as well as many others, have profited by his precepts and example in carrying out their 'intensive sociological investigations' of particular societies. Richards in an earlier publication (1939) has already dealt with the development of field techniques up to this date and it is unnecessary to traverse the same ground.[1] Apart from an increasing emphasis on the collection of quantitative material in relation to marriage, kinship affiliation, residence patterns, family budgets, nutrition, labour and other aspects of economics, there have been two major changes since Malinowski carried out his field research in 1914–18: firstly, in the type of societies investigated, and secondly, in the theoretical orientation of anthropologists. Whereas Malinowski did his work in a small-scale community in which much of the traditional way of life was unchanged, many anthropologists—working in Asia, India, and Africa—have had to deal with large-scale political organizations and the complex economies of plural societies undergoing rapid change. More recently attention has been directed to the investigation of Western communities and immigrant populations. Apart from the difficulties of carrying out comprehensive research in such conditions, the anthropologist has been confronted with a new range of problems; and these, in conjunction with the preoccupation with the analysis of social structure, have led to the development of new techniques in the collection of data, a more rigorous sampling, the employment of assistants and, in some cases, the collaboration of a team of experts from the related disciplines of economics, psychology, and history.

[1] See also more recent surveys, by Evans-Pritchard (1951*a*, chap. iv); Firth (1951*a*, chap. i); Nadel (1951).

Malinowski's influence on the writing of ethnography is difficult to assess at this stage, though his immediate impact on his students is evident in the publications which appeared from 1929 to the mid-'thirties. Many of the contributors to this book, as well as many of his other students such as the late Camilla Wedgwood, the late Gunther Wagner, Margaret Read, Hilda Kuper and Monica Wilson, have produced studies of particular institutions which, while making a contribution to the elucidation of problems in the fields of kinship, economics, social control and ritual, have also utilized the functional approach for the organization of data at certain stages of exposition, and have followed his practice in the scrupulous documentation of generalizations.

But since the mid-'thirties, many of Malinowski's students have followed Radcliffe-Brown in his clear-cut conceptual distinction between society and culture, though not all are prepared to accept his formulation of the relation between them and their relative importance as a subject of study for social anthropology.[1] In fact, many would regard the two concepts as indispensable tools for the analysis of social life:

'The terms represent different facets or components in basic human situations. If, for instance, society is taken to be an organized set of individuals with a given way of life, culture is that way of life. If society is taken to be an aggregate of social relations, then culture is the content of those relations. Society emphasizes the human component, the aggregate of people and the relations between them. Culture emphasizes the component of accumulated resources, immaterial as well as material, which the people inherit, employ, transmute, add to, and transmit' (Raymond Firth, 1951a, p. 27).

Since 1937 Radcliffe-Brown's students and other adherents of his theory have produced a series of monographs and articles devoted to the study of the social structure of a range of societies: the Australian Murngin (Lloyd Warner), the Nuer (Evans-Pritchard), the Tallensi (Fortes), the Lozi (Gluckman), the Ngoni (Barnes), and the Tiv (Bohannan)—to mention but a few. In the utilization of ethnographic data, the underlying assumption in most of these structural analyses is that societies are in more or less stable equilibrium and that 'morals, law, etiquette, religion, government, and education are all parts of the complex mechanism by which a social structure exists and persists' (Radcliffe-Brown, 1952, p. 195). The terms society and social structure are often used interchangeably by Radcliffe-Brown and his students, and he himself has held that the application of scientific method in social anthropology involves 'the intensive study of single societies (i.e. of the structural systems observable in particular communities)' and 'the

[1] E.g. Nadel (1951); Firth (1951a); Fortes (1949b), p. 57; Wilson (1945), chap. 3; Evans-Pritchard (1951a); Leach (1954b).

systematic comparison of many societies (or structural systems of different types)' (Radcliffe-Brown, 1952, p. 194).

This somewhat Calvinistic doctrine of salvation by structure alone has had both its advantages and its dangers. It has led to the clarification and refinement of concepts for the handling of social relations and statuses, and has focused attention on a wide range of problems, including the nature and basis of social integration. The period between 1940, when Evans-Pritchard published *The Nuer*, and 1955 has been a fruitful one in British anthropology both in the field and in the development of theory; and, in this, the anthropologists who have used structure as a frame of reference have made a most substantial contribution. It falls outside the scope of this essay to examine the nature of their theoretical contributions further, but they have been discussed in detail by Fortes (1953) in his excellent and illuminating paper on 'The Structure of Unilineal Descent Groups'.

But the intensive preoccupation with structural analysis has also its dangers for field-work and for the presentation of field material. In the field, too rigid a concept of structure may lead to the neglect of other aspects of social life, to which in the last resort structure itself must be related. In the analysis of social systems or of sub-systems, the achievement of a high level of abstraction has frequently involved the sacrifice of circumstantial detail; and, with that, the ironing out of the ambiguities, inconsistencies, fluctuations and complexities of social process. Social facts are handled as though they were mechanical facts; that is, as though the relationship between them were of a one-to-one kind rather than multiple and organic. Compared with a number of monographs which dealt with problems in an institutional framework and which appeared between 1929 and 1940 (more especially those of Firth, Richards, Schapera, Hunter, and Hogbin), many structural studies carry only a light ballast of ethnographic content.[1] The people, in the sense of a group of personalities, are conspicuous by their absence. A few individuals may make a brief appearance in a preface, where an anthropologist acknowledges their assistance; but thereafter they become ciphers like their fellows in the community; they occupy statuses and carry out activities which maintain the social system.[2]

[1] Fortes's books on the Tallensi are an exception; but, in the work of Radcliffe-Brown and Evans-Pritchard, documentation is reduced to a minimum and rarely placed in a ramifying context.

[2] In the course pursued by some structuralists in making their analysis, one is reminded of Lytton Strachey's comment on Gibbon's method of writing history: 'He drove a straight, firm road through the vast unexplored forest of Roman history; his readers could follow with easy pleasure along the wonderful way; they might glance, as far as their eyes could reach, into the entangled recesses on either side of them; but they were not invited to stop, or wander, or camp out, or make friends with the natives; they must be content to look and to pass on' (*Portraits in Miniature*, London, 1931, pp. 161-2).

Illustrative case material is reduced to a minimum and, with that, any sense of the actuality of day-to-day relationships. Moreover it is frequently difficult to test the anthropologist's generalizations from his field data; at the best, one must await the publication of another mono-graph. More important still, we have no means of ascertaining how the abstract principles of structure find expression at the level of social organization, and how far they are in fact the determinants of choice and social activity. Anthropologists who have used a purely structural frame of reference and who have treated structures as closed systems are now faced with the problem of relating their models to empirical reality in all its complexity.

Anthropology, like any other social science or indeed like any of the humanistic disciplines, must abstract to a certain degree, but the question that faces us is the lengths to which abstraction can be carried. A structural model is of value in explaining certain aspects of culture in a particular society; but when we go on to compare, for example, kinship or political *structures*, how far are we in fact comparing kinship or political *systems*? In the past, there has been some tendency to regard structure as more real than other aspects of the social system; but it is a model of the anthropologist's own making, and in comparing structures he is comparing models.

In the last few years there has been a much more explicit recognition of the fact that structures are constructs; and there has been a greater willingness on the part of some anthropologists to admit that 'we cannot, for analytical purposes, deal exhaustively with our ethnographic observations in a single frame of reference' (Fortes, 1953, p. 21). Evans-Pritchard (1951a, pp. 60-62) has recently said that social anthropology has more in common with history than with the natural sciences, and has asserted that it 'studies societies as moral, or symbolic, systems and not as natural systems, that it is less interested in process than in design, and that it therefore seeks patterns and not laws, demonstrates consistency and not necessary relations between social activities, and interprets rather than explains'.

Leach, like Radcliffe-Brown, would still assert that as a social anthropologist he is concerned with social structure (1954b, p. 16, n. 28 *et passim*). But he has challenged the assumption that social systems are in stable equilibrium, and in his recent book he has devoted himself to the problem of establishing the nature of the relation between structural models and a changing empirical society. Firth has likewise been concerned with the investigation of social change and has found the concept of structure inadequate for the explanation of social adaptation and social continuity. 'A structural analysis alone cannot interpret social change.' He has elaborated his concept of social organization as 'the arrangement of action in sequences in conformity with selected social ends', and involving therefore the exercise of choice and the making of decisions in relation to social values (Firth, 1951a, pp. 35–6).

On the one hand, the study of societies undergoing change, and on the other, the study of values and their expression in the symbolism of ritual, ceremony, and belief, will undoubtedly constitute one of the main fields of research for British anthropology over the next decade or so.[1] But if the exploration of values and the wide field of symbolism is to result in something more than the translation of structure into other terms, it will demand intensive sociological investigations of communities, and it will give a new and richer ethnographic content to anthropological monographs. For clearly this type of study, by virtue of the non-empirical character of its subject matter, will entail a rigorous application of the technique of contextualization of evidence as a basis for its generalization; and, not least, a faithful recording of the imponderabilia of actual life.

Social anthropology straddles both the humanities and the social sciences and, like economic history, the degree of abstraction it may achieve in its formulation of principles must always be limited by the intransigent complexity of its lively subject matter. But this subject matter is so rich and various that it permits the exploration of many problems over the wide fields of human behaviour and endeavour.[2] One may ask that anthropologists in evaluating the work of their colleagues should make allowance not only for their own 'personal equation' but also for that of others. Malinowski, himself a scientist and humanist, thought that 'in the present state of Ethnography . . . each new contribution ought to justify its appearance in several points. It ought to show some advance in method; it ought to push research beyond its previous limits in depth, in width, or in both; finally, it ought to endeavour to present its results in a manner exact, but not dry' (1922a, p. xvii).

Any formula for the writing of ethnography spells sterility; and obviously the range and intensity of documentation will depend on the problem with which the anthropologist is concerned, and the scale of organization in reference to which it is handled. But documentation there must be; and a mean must be established between conscientious compilations of unillumined detail and masterpieces of ethnographic understatement. One may legitimately demand that the anthropologist should make his assumptions explicit and define his concepts; that he

---

[1] Radcliffe-Brown was of course a forerunner in the latter field and his example was followed by Evans-Pritchard in his classic monograph (1937) and by Firth (1940). More recently Nadel (1954) has made a study of Nupe religion (1954); Leach (1954b) has analysed the relation between structure, ritual, and myth; and there is a publication from Richards on girls' puberty ceremonies among the Bemba (1956).

[2] See also Redfield (1953b) for a discussion of social anthropology and the humanities.

should specify his problem and his criteria of relevance; that he should substantiate his propositions and indicate the range of variation; that he should avoid cumbrous repetition; and, lastly, that he should write with lucidity, economy, and balance. Lytton Strachey (1931, pp. 169-70) has defined the qualities that make a historian as 'a capacity for absorbing facts, a capacity for stating them, and a point of view'. They also make a good anthropologist.

Ethnographic Analysis and Language with Reference to Malinowski's Views

J. R. FIRTH

I N the field of linguistics, it has been said with some truth that the English have excelled in phonetics and in lexicography. They have always been interested in the spelling of their language, which has the longest literary tradition in Western Europe. The English were the first to make use of their native language in law, chronicle, and translation. The first grammar of Latin in a Western European language was written by the Anglo-Saxon Aelfric in the tenth century. I have elsewhere (1946) given some account of the English interest in spelling and pronunciation, culminating in an appreciation of our greatest philologist, Henry Sweet.

It is, therefore, a matter of some satisfaction to an Englishman, writing an appreciation of the linguistic work of Bronislaw Malinowski, to be able to quote him as follows (1923a, p. 495n.): 'I quote from H. Sweet (*Introduction to the History of Language*), because this author is one of the cleverest thinkers on language'. Malinowski notices Sweet's statement that Language and Logic 'often diverge from one another' and that they are constantly at loggerheads. In Section 4 of the same Supplement, he mentions his concern with the 'definition of single words and with the lexicographical task of bringing home to a European reader the vocabulary of a strange tongue. And the main result of our analysis was that it is impossible to translate words of a primitive language or of one widely different from our own, without giving a detailed account of the culture of its users and thus providing the common measure necessary for a translation' (Malinowski, 1923a, p. 470).

Malinowski faces the crucial problem of definition throughout his work. It should be remembered that all definitions of the 'meanings' of a word are arbitrary and that authoritative citations collected by the lexicographer or ethnographer are usually keyed to these selected uses of the word under description. Throughout Malinowski's ethnographic work, from his account of the natives of Mailu (1915a)[1] to his *Coral Gardens* (1935), it can be said that he makes every effort to give the native words the fullest cultural context of ethnographic description in English. There is one notable exception which he learnt to abandon in later years. In his account of the Mailu classificatory terms of kinship (1915a, pp. 532-4), he gives English terms first, even when the Mailu equivalents are often repeated for different entries.

In the nature of our history, British scholars have been faced with the necessity of offering some account of the exotic languages they have had to live with all over the world. Most of these accounts are, by modern standards, amateurish and inadequate but the pioneer work was there. Malinowski's contribution in English to the advancement of the study of such languages from the point of view of a professional anthropologist is a brilliant enhancement of the English tradition and we can be proud to include him as one of the makers of linguistics as we now understand it in this country.

Having dealt first with the definition of single words in his Supplement on 'The Problem of Meaning in Primitive Languages', we next find him looking at language in an ethnographic perspective, using the concept of context of situation in order to give an outline of a semantic theory useful in the work on primitive linguistics and throwing some light on human language in general. He goes on to describe language, in its primitive function, as a *mode of action*, rather than as a *counter-sign of thought*.

All this is truly in the tradition of British empiricism and of the philosophic radicals and utilitarians, whose influence was far reaching and is obvious in the works of the Vienna Circle. It finds echoes in Wittgenstein, who would probably have endorsed Malinowski's views on meaning. 'The meaning of words lies in their use' (Wittgenstein, 1953, p. 80). 'One cannot guess how a word functions. One has to look at its use, and learn from that' (Wittgenstein, 1953, p. 109). He likens the practice of various types of language in speech behaviour, to games with rules. 'A language is a set of games with rules or customs' (Wittgenstein, 1953, pp. 47, 81). The publication of Malinowski's essay on the problem of meaning as the first Supplement to a work largely inspired by C. K. Ogden is itself significant in this connection. Malinowski himself refers to his own *ethnographic empiricism* (1923a, p. 481).

Among the linguists mentioned in the Supplement, the leading German comparatists are missing but W. von Humboldt, Sweet, and Jespersen are there, and notably Wegener (1885), to whom Malinowski

---

[1] It is of some interest to note that a copy of this work was presented by the author to the Library of the School of Oriental and African Studies on Malinowski's return to England and is one of many indications of his appreciation of the work of his British colleagues in exotic languages.

owed his early notions of the Situation. Wegener was one of the first to propound what he called the *Situationstheorie*.

Malinowski explicitly informs us that he was not acquainted with the technicalities of Indo-European comparative linguistics. 'Of Brugmann-Delbrück's treatise, I tried to understand only the main outlines and the general theoretical parts' (1920*b*, p. 37, n. 1).

Of his outstanding ability as a practical linguist, we have abounding evidence. To begin with, it is perhaps enough to notice his mastery of English as a vehicle for his original thought. He tells us of what he calls his facility, in his introduction to his work on the Mailu (1915*a*, p. 501).

'I am afraid I must explicitly boast of my facility for acquiring a conversational command of foreign languages, since I understand that the time in which I learned to speak the Motu would have been normally too short a period for acquiring a foreign, and especially a native, tongue. I wish also to state that the ability to speak Motu and to follow a conversation was of no small advantage in my work. Over and over again, I was led on to the track of some extremely important item in native sociology or folklore by listening to the conversation of my boy *Igua* with his Mailu friends, who used to come from the village to see him.'

In associating him with Anglo-American rather than Continental traditions of linguistic scholarship, the further point might be made that he explicitly dissociated himself quite early from Durkheim's philosophical basis of sociology (1913*b*; 1916, p. 423, n. 1). He would have nothing to do with a collective soul and presumably had no interest in the French conception of *langue* as a function of the *collectivité*. It is well known that leading French scholars, notably Meillet, held Durkheimian views in their sociological approach to language. This was reflected in their contributions to *L'Année Sociologique* (Meillet, 1926). I know from personal association with Malinowski that those parts of de Saussure's general linguistic theory which led in that direction, he found not only unattractive but of little practical value in the study of meaning, which was his principal interest. In order to make way for his own approach, he declared that the postulate of a collectivity was barren and absolutely useless for an ethnographical observer. He wished to see his 'social ideas' embodied in institutions or traditional texts formulated on the basis of work with competent informants (1916, p. 424).[1]

As a social anthropologist and ethnographer, he was primarily interested in the analytical and functional study of culture, and throughout his work, he made the fullest use of language possible to him, in stating

---

[1] Malinowski's procedures and techniques with *informants* are fully described, and of high importance both in ethnographic and linguistic analysis. See especially: (1935) Vol. II, pp. 5, 23–6, 84, 95, 100–1, 119–21, 127, 129, 135, 156–7, 158, 175, and (1922*a*) pp. 396, 398, 400, 409, 429, 433, 453, 454, 455, 483, 490, 491.

J. R. FIRTH

and commenting on his facts. The linguist, however, must keep the language text in the focus of attention and his main work is the linguistic analysis of the language data collected in his *corpus inscriptionum*.

The London group of linguists associated with my own work have accepted the notion of the institutionalized word in the broadest sense and have always kept to the text as the point of departure. Throughout his ethnographic work, Malinowski had stressed the importance of the institution[1] viewed from the native point of view and interpreted by the scholar, and he makes copious use of native expressions almost as loan words in his descriptive writing. The importance of applying his idea of the institution to language and the liberal recording of textual material is fully recognized in present-day linguistics in England. The procedure is explicitly stated in his *Argonauts of the Western Pacific*. 'The best enthnographical writers—here again the Cambridge school with Haddon, Rivers, and Seligman rank first among English Ethnographers—have always tried to quote *verbatim* statements of crucial importance. They also adduce terms of native classification; sociological, psychological, and industrial *termini technici*, and have rendered the verbal contour of native thought as precisely as possible. One step further in this line can be made by the Ethnographer, who acquires a knowledge of the native language and can use it as an instrument of inquiry. In working in the Kiriwinian language, I found still some difficulty in writing down the statement directly in translation which at first I used to do in the act of taking notes. The translation often robbed the text of all its significant characteristics—rubbed off all its points—so that gradually I was led to note down certain important phrases just as they were spoken, in the native tongue. As my knowledge of the language progressed, I put down more and more in Kiriwinian, till at last I found myself writing exclusively in that language, rapidly taking notes, word for word, of each statement. No sooner had I arrived at this point, than I recognized that I was thus acquiring at the same time an abundant linguistic material, and a series of ethnographic documents which ought to be reproduced as I had fixed them besides being utilized in the writing up of my account' (1922a, pp. 23-4). In a footnote, Malinowski recognizes the encouragement given him by Dr. A. H. Gardiner, now Sir Alan Gardiner, in collecting and interpreting his *corpus inscriptionum Kiriwiniensium*. It is a considerable satisfaction to me to remember Malinowski's association with Sir Alan Gardiner at that time, to be followed by my own association with both these dis-

---

[1] Cf. Wittgenstein (1953), p. 108, para. 337. 'An intention is embedded in its situation, in human customs and institutions. If the technique of the game of chess did not exist, I could not *intend* to play a game of chess. In so far as I do intend the construction of a sentence in advance, that is made possible by the fact that I can speak the language in question.' See also above, p. 94, and footnotes, and p. 95.

tinguished scholars, since it provides a further illustration of Malinowski in his English setting and his part in the development of linguistics in this country. This is further borne out by his reference to 'Sir Richard Temple's most interesting attempts at a semantic theory adapted to the study of primitive languages. His outlines of a Universal Grammar and their application, although very condensed and carried out only in very broad outlines, seem to me of extreme importance: the problems are set forth in an excellent manner, and the solutions offered are undoubtedly correct in all essentials' (Malinowski, 1920b, p. 74, n. 1—with reference to Temple, 1899a).

The placing of Malinowski in the English tradition links him with the work of distinguished amateurs, so characteristic of scientific leadership in England in the nineteenth century.

He tells us that during his first stay in Kiriwina from 1915 to 1916, he had no linguistic preparation, but on his return to Melbourne he undertook a good deal of linguistic reading which enabled him to write on linguistics (1920b, pp. 73-4). He appears to have studied Sir Richard Temple's 'A Theory of Universal Grammar' carefully and especially Temple's detailed examination of Portman's *Notes on the Languages of the South Andaman Group of Tribes*. Temple reproduces Portman's texts of the Andaman fire legend with inter-linear word-for-word equivalents, followed by a rendering in running English with somewhat crude syntactical notes. Temple described this procedure as the analysis of the language in which the story is couched and, in a good deal of Malinowski's own linguistic work, little more than this is attempted. His reading of Temple reminded him of the difficulties of grammatical description in dealing with exotic languages. As he says, 'there is no universally acknowledged set of definitions and no consistent body of views about the various linguistic categories, everyone is compelled to use his own discretion and to coin his own terminology' (1920b, p. 74).

Sir Richard Temple devotes some time to the consideration of a new set of grammatical categories coupled with an original nomenclature in contrast with traditional terminology. This he summarized in 'The Skeleton of a Theory of Universal Grammar' (1899b). Sir George Grierson of the Linguistic Survey of India must have taken some interest in this matter since I have in my possession a letter addressed to him by Sir Richard Temple in November 1907, in which he says 'The question of terminology in my "Theory" resolves itself thus:—is it a smaller strain on the brain to put *new* definitions on to old words or have new words? I thought the latter was the best, but if the former is the best, it is all one to me. Of course, to a man immersed in a set terminology, a new one is a trouble—but for the learner at large, it may be best to discard what is old and give him something new for new notions. At any rate you avoid confusion in teaching by so doing.'

Malinowski expressly approves of the main essentials of Temple's approach. I certainly agree with some of the general principles myself. For example, Temple says 'Of course, grammarians will know that all this is syntax, and I will now explain why I consider that it is far more important to study function than form as essential to the correct apprehension of words, and how to my mind accidence arises properly out of syntax and not the other way round, as we have all been taught.

'It is obvious that any given word may fulfil one or more or all the functions of words, and that therefore words may be collected into as many classes as there are functions, any individual word being transferable from one class to another and belonging to as many classes as there are functions which it can fulfil. The functions a word fulfils in any particular sentence can be indicated by its position therein without or with variation of form, and, because of this, the form which a word can be made to assume is capable of indicating the class to which it belongs for the nonce. It is further obvious that words transferable from class to class belong primarily to a certain class and secondarily to the others, that a transfer involves the fulfilment of a new function, and that a word in its transferred condition becomes a new word' (1899a, pp. 4-5). Again, Temple is on the right track when he says, 'I found myself, in building up the theory, compelled, in order to work out the argument logically, to commence where the accepted Grammars ended, viz. at the sentence, defining the sentence as the expression of a complete meaning, and making *that* the unit of language' (1899a, p. 2). It is not surprising in the light of the development of linguistics since, that Malinowski found Temple's approach attractive. He did not however pay much attention to functional grammar or move in the grammatical directions suggested by Temple. He remained reasonably traditional, but grammatically unsystematic.

In developing a school of social anthropology in London, Malinowski gave all his emphasis to the need for linguistics, especially in connection with the establishment of sound ethnographic texts. It may safely be said that he was among a very few scholars who actively promoted descriptive linguistics both by the example of his own work and by what may be called propaganda. He realized the need for the development of linguistic theory different from the one prevailing, the main orientation[1] of which was the study of historical change and evolution. He even regarded his important article on Kiriwina as '... an example of a general proposition, namely, that there is an urgent need for an Ethno-

[1] See Malinowski, 1920b, p. 55. The establishment of texts in living languages by the descriptive linguist may prepare the way for studies of such subjects as the degree of obsoleteness of words and grammatical forms. 'It is extremely astonishing that, although this is the only way of gaining an insight into the historical changes of a native language, and although historic change and evolution have been the main orientation of linguistics, yet, to my knowledge, very little attention has been paid to the degree of obsoleteness of words and grammatical forms.'

linguistic theory,[1] a theory for the guidance of linguistic research to be done among natives and in connection with ethnographic study. It was stressed above, in the introductory paragraph, that as there can be no sound theory which is not based on an extensive study of facts, so there can be no successful observation of facts without the guidance of a sound theory. A theory which, moreover, aims, not at hypothetical constructions—"origins", "historical developments", " cultural transferences", and similar speculations—but a theory concerned with the intrinsic relation of facts. A theory which in linguistics would show us what is essential in language and what therefore must remain the same throughout the whole range of linguistic varieties; how linguistic forms are influenced by physiological, mental, social, and other cultural elements; what is the real nature of Meaning and Form, and how they correspond; a theory which, in fine, would give us a set of well-founded plastic definitions of grammatical concepts' (Malinowski, 1920b, p. 69). 'The field-worker relies entirely upon inspiration from theory' (1922a, p. 9).

Jespersen's book *Language*, published in 1922, opens with the sentence—'The distinctive feature of the science of language as conceived nowadays is its historical character'.[2] In 1931, Malinowski found it necessary to say that 'many linguists realize the importance of studying the language of living rather than dead specimens, and everyone would probably admit that the study of native languages is of paramount importance'. He brings in, as he says, 'even Delbrück' in support of the view that 'a finer analysis of given linguistic phenomena could be achieved on living languages only' (1920b, p. 71).

Sweet, in his Presidential Address to the Philological Society of Great Britain in 1887, pointed out the special English interest in the observation of the phenomena of living languages.[3] 'Our tendency is not so much toward the antiquarian philology and text-criticism in which German scholars have done so much, as towards the observation

---

[1] Eventually in Vol. II of *Coral Gardens and Their Magic* (1935), Malinowski stated what he there describes as an ethnographic theory of language.

[2] Cf. J. R. Firth, 1951a.

[3] Cf. J. R. Firth, 1951a, p. 72. 'In the session, 1950–1 the School of Oriental and African Studies was able "*to send out*" seven "*thoroughly and specially trained young men*" whose whole task was "*the observation of the phenomena of living languages*" and both they and at least a score of others are "*concentrating their energies mainly on what may be called 'living philology'*". In America there is a similar history to report since the foundation of the American Philosophical Society [1838], the American Oriental Society [1842], and the Smithsonian Institution [1846]. Today there is in the Linguistic Society of America which supports the annual Linguistic Institute; also the Linguistic Circle of New York, the *International Journal of American Linguistics*, and the Summer Institute of Linguistics for the training of missionaries for linguistic work in the mission fields of the world (see "Atlantic Linguistics", *Archivum Linguisticum*, Vol. 1, fasc. II, 1949).'

52159

of the phenomena of living languages . . . the real strength and originality of English work lies . . . in phonology and dialectology. Our aim ought clearly to be, while assimilating the methods and results of German work, to concentrate our energies mainly on what may be called "living philology". The vastness of our Empire, which brings us in contact with innumerable languages, alone forces us incessantly to grapple with the difficulties of spoken, often also unwritten, languages. We ought to be able to send out yearly hundreds of thoroughly and specially trained young men. . . .' As I have pointed out earlier, Malinowski in a sense joined this especially English trend and was unaware of the developments in the United States, as he says himself (1920*b*, p. 72, n. 1).[1]

While emphasizing by example and precept the importance of general linguisitics in theory and practice, Malinowski clearly appreciated the value and importance of comparative and historical studies and goes out of his way to notice them. Furthermore, he points out that 'so-called functionalism is not, and cannot be, opposed to the historical approach but is indeed its necessary complement. The functional method, if I understand it rightly, is interested primarily in the processes of culture as an explanation of its products. It introduces thus the time element, at first on a smaller scale, but none the less in the real historical sense. I myself have advocated the biographical approach in the study of kinship. In my work on language, I have attempted to show that the study of meaning should start with observations on infant speech and the growth of linguistic expression within the context of culture. In the study of law, I have tried to point out that the consideration of transactions in the long run, as the extensive and enduring balancing of interests, is the only way to understand primitive jurisprudence. The context of time as well as the context of culture essential to the functional approach are, on the one hand, historical concepts, and on the other, they lead to the formulation of general laws of process so necessary to any reconstructive work. Here again, therefore, I do not see that functionalism and historical reconstructions stand in antithesis. I agree with Professor Kroeber that "basically a functional approach is rather close to the historical approach" ' (Malinowski, 1939*a*, p. 43).

This view accords with my own approach which emphasizes the mutually complementary nature of historical and descriptive studies in linguistics though I am inclined to the opinion that the development of descriptive linguistics on a large scale is an essential preliminary for the reformulation of problems in comparative and historical work. This could only be the case if, as I have frequently emphasized, linguistics

[1] 'There has been much, and as it seems excellent, work recently done on the American native languages, but with that I am completely unacquainted'. Present-day American linguists return the compliment by remaining unacquainted with Malinowski's contribution to the subjects of their concern.

recognizes that its principle objective is the study of meaning in its own terms (J. R. Firth, 1950, pp. 8–14; 1951*a*, pp. 82–4; 1951*b*, p. 118). Malinowski's functionalism extended to language, as is clear from his Supplement to *Meaning of Meaning*. 'The lack of a clear and precise view of Linguistic function[1] and of the nature of Meaning, has been, I believe, the cause of the relative sterility of much otherwise excellent linguistic theorizing' (1923*a*, p. 471).

By no stretch of imagination could he be described as a 'structuralist', nor would I, myself, accept the appellation, if it be narrowly interpreted to require adherence to basic phonemic 'structures' or with 'alterations' in 'sub-structures' and 'super-structures'. The main reason being that 'the structure of all this linguistic material is inextricably mixed up with, and dependent upon, the course of the activity in which the utterances are embedded' (1923*a*, p. 473). He gets nearer the structural approach— which I distinguish from 'a structuralist approach'—in Section VI of the Supplement (1923*a*, p. 495) in which he faces the problem of the structure of language. 'Every human tongue has a definite structure of its own. . . . This body of structural rules with their exceptions and irregularities, the various classes into which the elements of the language can be ranged, is what we call "the grammatical structure" of a language.'

It is not easy to assess his contribution to linguistic analysis as understood today because his language material is closely wedded to his ethnographic work. Yet there are throughout his work, indications that he appreciated the bearing of function and structure in linguistics. In approaching his study of the classificatory particles in Kiriwina, he indicated his awareness of 'the general features of linguistic structure, rules of syntax, parts of speech, and word formation. Everybody agrees that in an ethnographic work these should be recorded, that all essential linguistic facts should be collected. But all collection of facts requires the guidance of definite theoretical principles' (1920*b*, p. 34).

Again, in his concluding paragraphs, he reiterates what seems almost like a wish unfulfilled—the need for a theory. 'We need a Theory, devised for the purpose of observation of linguistic fact. This theory would give a recast of grammatical definitions, based on an analysis of meaning. It would analyse the nature of syntax, parts of speech, and formation of words, and besides giving adequate and plastic definitions would open up vistas of problems and thus guide research' (1920*b*, p. 78). And here, I cannot refrain from repeating a favourite quotation from Goethe: 'Das Höchste wäre zu begreifen, das alles Faktische schon Theorie ist'.

It is clear that Malinowski contributed very little towards such a

[1] In the same Supplement, Malinowski uses the expressions 'speech function', p. 476, 'linguistic uses', p. 474 (cf. Wittgenstein, 'Meaning is use'—see above, p. 94).

theory for the statement of linguistic facts in terms of phonetics, phonology, the various branches of grammar or stylistics. This we shall appreciate by a close study of his linguistic work following the indications here given. His main interest, as he indicates in his Supplement, was in the problem of meaning, and such theory as he developed arose from his study of primitive societies. The key concept of the semantic theory he found most useful for his work on native languages was the notion of *context of situation*. He read widely in linguistics,[1] always looking for the kind of theory which could find a place and prove useful in his ethnographical work. He was always eager to discuss theoretical questions with linguists of his acquaintance, as I well know from personal experience. It is no accident that both he and Sir Alan Gardiner acknowledge their indebtedness to Dr. Philipp Wegener. In dedicating his book *The Theory of Speech and Language* to Wegener, Gardiner (1932) calls him 'a pioneer of linguistic theory'.

Malinowski and Gardiner[2] both make great use of the situation theory, and I, too, have developed its application in descriptive linguistics, though in a more abstract and general form as one of several levels in linguistic analysis, all of which should be congruent.[3] In Wegener's original work (1885), the concept of the situation is related to his distinctions between the logical and grammatical subject and predicate, and there is much which has to be abandoned. Nevertheless, a good deal survives which has, with modifications, been incorporated into subsequent work by later theorists.

Wegener's theory requires three types of situation: (i) die Situation der Anschauung; (ii) die Situation der Erinnerung; (iii) die Situation des Bewusstseins (1885, pp. 21–7).[4] He recognizes both speakers and

[1] Malinowski, 1935, Vol. II, Introduction, p. xi. 'Since I regard it as of the greatest importance always to stress the fact that only theoretical training enables us to see a sociological fact and to record and interpret it correctly, I should like to say that in no other branch of Anthropology has my reading been as extensive as in Linguistics.'

[2] See Gardiner, 1932. For *Situation*, see pp. 49, 51, 194. Gardiner's book was published in 1932, nine years after Malinowski's Supplement in which the phrase 'Context of Situation' is first used. For his reference to Wegener's *situationstheorie*, see pp. 60, 124, 127, and refer to the Index, where there are 16 entries. Gardiner points out that his own terminology is different from Wegener's—so is his whole theory.

[3] See J. R. Firth, 1935, pp. 60–1, 72; 1950, p. 8; 1951a, p. 83; 1951b, pp. 120–8.

[4] This philosophical use of the word *consciousness* in English really begins with Locke's *Essay Concerning Human Understanding*. His French amanuensis and translator, M. Coste, found great difficulty in rendering Locke's thought in this connection. Wegener's use of *Erinnerung* and *Bewusstsein* is also traceable to Locke. Under the entry *Personality* in Dr. Johnson's Dictionary, the following quotation from Locke is cited: 'This personality extends itself beyond present existence to what is past, only by consciousness, whereby it imputes to itself past actions just upon the same ground that it does the present.' See J. R. Firth, (1950).

hearers, objects and events as possible end-points in sets of relations set up to state the meaning of language. In other words, if language is studied in context of situation, mutual comprehension and co-operation is not by language only. Even using logico-grammatical terms, he would maintain that the predicate or the subject of a situational communication might be in the relevant objects and events of the situation. The situation is the basis, the environment for all the facts or data and we see the effective process of speaking and listening therein displayed. The presence of the persons and relevant objects, he regarded as providing essential environmental relations which may be thought of within the three sub-situations above mentioned. First, the objective situation as presented and observed; second, the immediately associated memorial elements or the factor of retentiveness; and, thirdly, the situation of the whole state of mind (with special reference to the consciousness of self or of personal identity in all participants) in which the content of the specific language finds its meaning completed.

In some respects, this analysis has links with my own point of view though I do not require his trinity of situations, nor do I wish to introduce a reference to retentiveness nor to consciousness of self or of personal identity. A serious confusion of the analysis of the context of situation with the other levels of analysis such as the grammatical level, has been one of the main weaknesses of early attempts to relate statements of meaning to other social and psychological factors. Nevertheless I place a high value on Wegener's realization that the context of situation provided a valid configuration of elements comprising persons, objects, non-verbal events as well as language between which significant relations obtained, thus constituting a set of functions as a whole.

This reshaping of the most interesting features of Wegener's theory, if related to other levels of linguistic analysis in terms of interior relations, would accord with the practice of a number of present-day linguists in this country. It should be borne in mind, however, that Malinowski and others who have used the situational approach, did not grasp the full theoretical implications of Wegener's hints, though he has been frequently quoted.[1]

[1] Let Wegener speak for himself in the following extract from his work, pp. 21-3. 'Die Situation ist der Boden, die Umgebung, auf der eine Thatsache, ein Ding u. s. f. in die Erscheinung tritt, doch auch das zeitlich Vorausliegende, aus dem heraus eine Thätigkeit entsprungen ist, nemlich die Thätigkeit, welche wir als Prädicat aussagen, und ebenso gehört zur Situation die Angabe der Person, an welche die Mitteilung gerichtet ist. Die Situation wird bei der sprachlichen Mitteilung nicht blos durch Worte bestimmt, viel gewöhnlicher und ausgedehnter durch die umgebenden Verhältnisse selbst, durch die unmittelbar vorhergegangenen Thatsachen und die Gegenwart der Person, mit der wir sprechen. Die durch die umgebenden Verhältnisse und die Gegenwort der angeredeten Person gegebene Situation kommt uns durch die Anschauung zum Bewusstsein, wir nennen sie daher die Situation der Anschauung. 'Stehe ich mit Jemandem vor einem Baume, so genügt vollständig das Wort

A general theory such as this must include similar approaches in other branches of linguistic analysis. Naturally, the sentence and syntactical analysis find a central place. Even the origins of all speech, considered biographically in the nurture of the young and in the history of the race, are to be found in sentences. 'Alle Sprachelemente sind ursprünglich Sätze' (Wegener, 1885, p. 181). It is not surprising that Wegener pays special attention to imperatives, interrogatives, demonstratives and pronouns. No wonder Malinowski found all this attractive in his search for concepts likely to assist him in developing a technique

---

Linde, um zu sagen: *dieser Baum ist eine Linde.* Der vor uns stehende Baum bildet, auch unbenannt, das Subject des Satzes. Oder sage ich bei dieser Situation: *das ist eine Linde,* so erhält doch das Pronomen erst durch die gegenwärtige Anschauung seinen Inhalt.—Stelle ich Jemanden in einer Gesellschaft vor, so wäre es gradezu unpassend zu sagen: *dies ist Herr Müller,* ich weise nur mit der Hand auf ihn hin, um ihn von den übrigen anwesenden Personen zu unterscheiden und sage: *Herr Müller.* Die lebendige Anschauung, präcisiert durch den Gestus, ist die Situation und das Subject. Es ist klar, dass ein gegenwärtiges Anschauungsbild nicht so einfach ist, dass alle Teile desselben das Subject sein könnten, noch auch das gesammte Anschauungsbild. Neben jener Linde im Parke steht vielleicht auch eine Eiche, und vieles Andere ist sichtbar, die angeredete Person ja auch. Der Gestus und die Richtung der Augen geben Anhaltepunkte für die Ausscheidung eines Teiles aus dieser complicierten Masse, doch auch ohne diese Illustration bleibt ein derartiges Prädicat beziehbar. Ja, der Gestus selbst ist ja eine Thätigkeit, die Hand, der Arm, ein Finger wird dabei gezeigt, warum bezieht der Hörende das Prädicat nicht anf diese Teile der Anschauung? Es muss ein Schluss von dem Hörenden aus der Natur des Prädicats sowohl wie aus dem Inhalte der Anschauung gewonnen werden, um die Beziehung richtig zu machen. Ich deute hier diese Frage nur an über welche die zweite Abhandlung einigen Aufschluss geben soll.

'Setzt Jemand ein Glas Wein vom Munde und sagt: *vortrefflich!,* so zweifle ich keinen Augenblick, dass er den eben genossenen Wein so nennt; selbst wenn ich nur das leere Glas sehe, so ergänze ich den Ausruf zu dem Satze: *der Wein ist vortrefflich.* Also die Situation wird auch bestimmt durch vollendete Handlungen, die noch im Vordergrunde unseres Bewusstseins stehen. Und das zu denkende Subject ist nicht blos die gesammte Handlung, wie hier das Weintrinken, sondern ein Moment dieser Handlung, der Wein,—also auch hier liegt ein Schluss des Verstehenden vor, von dem später die Rede sein wird. Diese Situation wird passend genannt werden Situation der Erinnerung. . . . Hört der Jäger von *Löffeln,* so ist er wenigstens ebenso geneigt an die Ohren des Hasen zu denken, als an die Suppenlöffel bei Tisch, selbst wenn er einen solchen bei Tisch in der Hand hält. So hat der Militär seine besonderen Gruppen der grössten Associationsfähigkeit, andere der Jurist, andere der Seemann, andere der Philologe, andere der Geistliche u. s. f. Daher die hübsche Anecdote, welche Steinthal erzählt, dass ein Menschenkenner sich anheischig macht, aus den Antworten, welche verschiedene ihm unbekannte Personen auf eine Rätselfrage geben, ihren Stand zu bestimmen. Diese verschiedenen Interessenkreise haben daher ihre eigenen Ausdrucksweisen, die bekannten termini technici, welche ihren Inhalt aus der Situation des Bewusstseins, d. h. aus den fest gewordenen Interessen ergänzen, so *die Löffel, der Lauf* des Hasen, *der Schweiss* des Wildes, die vielen juristischen Termini und die grosse Menge der Handwerkerausdrücke; *testudo* bei den Römern kann die Schildkröte, das militärische Schilddach, die Leier sein.'

for the elucidation of ethnographic texts. He had found similar notions in the work of Sir Richard Temple.

Ranging himself with the primitive man's pragmatic outlook and re-garding language as a mode of action rather than as a counter-sign of thought (1923a, pp. 459, 479), Malinowski selected for notice only such features of his languages as were essentially bound up with his contexts of situation in trading, fishing (1923a, p. 474), gardening and similar pursuits. There, he noticed direct indications of these activities, refer-ences to the surroundings, words of command, words correlated with action (1923a, p. 473), the expressions of feeling and passion bound up with behaviour, many of them stereotyped in form, such as spells, chants and narratives.

It is language material of this kind which he presents throughout his ethnographic work with little or no development of formal description as understood by linguists. The linguistic treatment of ethnographic texts, from *Argonauts of the Western Pacific* (1922a) to *Coral Gardens and Their Magic* (1935), is fundamentally the same though in *Coral Gardens* we are given a 'full treatment' of the 'language of agriculture'.[1]

In substantiation of the above criticism of his linguistic technique, it is sufficient to notice his chapter on 'Words in Magic' in the *Argonauts of the Western Pacific* (1922a, pp. 428–63).[2] In the course of this chapter, he makes repeated use of the expression 'linguistic analysis' (pp. 428, 433, 442, 459) with reference to his ethnographic texts, but it must be pointed out that the expression as used by linguists refers to highly abstract analyses of a given language—usually a restricted language—at the phonological level, at various grammatical levels and in the summary entries of dictionaries. Malinowski fully realized his short-comings in linguistic analysis, as we now understand it, and said so explicitly. 'The analysis to which I now proceed can be given only in an approximate manner, for in a full one, a long disquisition on grammar would have to be given first' (1922a, p. 433). He never managed

---

[1] Malinowski, 1935, Vol. I, Preface, p. xi. 'For the first time I am able here fully to document my ethnographic contribution from the linguistic point of view. This is not due to the absence from my field notes of the same, or of a reasonably comparable quantity of texts, commentaries, sayings and termino-logies to validate the statements which I have made in *Argonauts of the Western Pacific* or in *The Sexual Life of Savages*; in my booklet on *Myth* or in *Crime and Custom*. The reason is, that earlier in my career there would have been no chance of publishing as full a linguistic documentation as has become possible now, when the interest in the Trobrianders and in more detailed ethnographic accounts has on the whole increased. I trust that the theoretical parts of this book: the Introductions to the Linguistic Supplement and to the Magical Formulae (Parts IV and VI), will add to this interest and to the understanding that such full documentation is necessary; and that they will justify the methods here adopted.'

[2] 'These three texts will be quite sufficient to give an idea of the method of dealing with linguistic evidence, and of the documentary value of immediately recorded native opinions.'

to realize what may have been his secret ambition—a technique of analysis satisfying the demands of linguistic science.

The main features of his textual method can be summarized as follows: having placed the text functionally, from the sociological point of view, let us say, as a particular kind of spell tabulated in his systematic magic, linguistic statements of 'meaning' are to be made—first, by an interlinear word-for-word translation, sometimes described as a 'literal' or 'verbal' translation, 'each expression and formative affix being rendered by its English equivalent', secondly a free translation in what might be described as 'running English', thirdly by the collation of the interlinear and free translations, leading, fourthly, to the detailed commentary, or 'the contextual specification of meaning'.

The commentary relates the free translation to the verbal translation and deals with the 'equivalents' and adds phonetic and grammatical notes.

First then, he no doubt intended really to suggest *an* English equivalent for ethnographic purposes. When I was associated with Malinowski in his Linguistics Seminar in the early 1930's, he often referred to this word-for-word translation method, and even employed the expression 'fixed term equivalent'[1] for the English counters that he placed against the elements of native texts. He states as his fundamental principle that for each native word we adopt one English 'fixed meaning'. Unfortunately, in this connection, he reverts to notions characteristic of early work by such etymologists as Skeat, and makes an attempt to establish what he calls the 'primary meaning'[2] of a word, numbering derived meanings in the text. But, he found that it was not 'always feasible or convenient to use primary meaning as the fixed equivalent'.

In my opinion, the concept of primary and derived meanings must be abandoned, and even in Malinowski's work it served no useful purpose. I well remember discussing with him the primary meaning of the word 'ass' in familiar, colloquial English. To bring in the animal, we had to place the word in another 'language'. Such difficulties are met by applying the concept of meaning by collocation, which I have dealt with elsewhere (J. R. Firth, 1951b; see also T. F. Mitchell, 1952 and 1953). The word 'ass' in colloquial English is usually collocated with expressions of personal reference and address and the plural is not very common.

Moreover, 'fixed term equivalents' or counters are of doubtful value in the structure as I define it, that is to say, taken together in sentences

---

[1] This notion he adheres to in *Coral Gardens and Their Magic*, in which he formulates rules of interlinear translation. 'The fundamental principle here is that for each native word we adopt one English *fixed meaning*' (Vol. II, p. 28). My comment here is that such 'fixed meanings' are of value in stating systems but difficult to apply in interlinear translation. Such systems of differentiated words might be technically referred to as *distinctive meanings* in the relative sense of mutual exclusiveness.

[2] Cf. Malinowski, 1947, p. 86. 'Social science is still burdened with the superstition that words contain their meanings.'

and longer pieces.[1] The notion of a fixed term equivalent, arbitrarily chosen to cover systems of words, is another matter. Systems of units or terms, set up by the linguist, provide sets of interior relations by means of which their values are mutually determined. In order to have validity, such systems must be exhaustive and closed, so far as the particular state of the language, suitably restricted, is under description.

Malinowski's lists are rich in information and testify to the excellence of his field-work. But, as he says himself, not all of his lists are exhaustive and the reader is left to judge for himself (1935, Vol. II, p. 5). There is one example, however, of what a linguist would accept as a system, to be found in his treatment of the six[2] Trobriand words for 'garden'. That they can be regarded as a lexical system on the evidence supplied, is clear from his own statement that they 'are defined by placing them within a series of terms with mutually exclusive uses' (1935, Vol. II, p. 16).

We now turn from the verbal translation to what Malinowski calls a 'free translation' (1922a, p. 457). 'Comparing the free translation with the literal one, it is easy to see that certain additions have been made, sentences have been subordinated and co-ordinated by various English conjunctions which are either completely absent from the native text, or else represented by such very vague particles as *boge* (already), and *m'tage* (indeed)' (1922a, p. 458). Occasionally, the comparison of the interlinear version with the free translation is held to be sufficient. Indeed, a great deal of the method of statement depends upon this double-entry procedure in giving what is nowadays technically described as the 'translation meaning'.[3]

---

[1] My own theory of analysis requires that the terms 'structure' and 'system' be kept distinct in technical use. Structures are abstractions from utterances or parts of utterances recorded textually. Thus CVCVC and Noun-Verb-Noun might each constitute a structure specifically defined in a particular language, at the phonological and grammatical levels respectively. A *structure* is said to comprise *elements* or categories in mutual syntagmatic relation. At any given level of analysis closed systems of categories, units or terms are set up to give mutually determined values to the elements of structure. The terms of a *system*, or of a *sub-system* within it, *commute*, thus enabling account to be taken of the elements, constituents and features which are given order and place in structures. See my 'Synopsis of Linguistic Theory' in a volume on Linguistics to be published by the Philological Society of Great Britain, also R. H. Robins, 1953, p. 109.

[2] 1935, Vol. II, p. 15. 'For they really have no word corresponding to our general term "garden". Instead they have a series of words: *bagula, buyagu, tapopu, kaymata, kaymugwa, baleko*, each of which describes a certain type or kind, aspect or phase of "garden". But to "translate" any of these native terms by equating it to an English word would not merely be wrong, but impossible; or rather it would be impossible to find an English word exactly corresponding to any one of the native ones. Furthermore, to label the native term by even a combination of English words is at least misleading.'

[3] 1935, Vol. II, p. 38. 'In any case, comparing the interlineal version with the free translation, the text becomes quite clear.'

Throughout his work, he uses the double translation method of stating 'meaning'. He was in the habit of accumulating large numbers of texts and he even uses the method in dealing with native definitions provided by informants.[1]

The third and fourth features of his textual method, namely, the collation of the interlinear and free translations, must be considered together, since what is called 'the contextual specification of meaning' (1935, Vol. II, p. 37) is with reference to the text (and not the situation) and to the two translations requiring a full miscellaneous commentary.

In doing this, a great many words 'have to be reinterpreted when we pass from the interlineal word for word rendering to the free translation'. He claims that this transition is not arbitrary and that his commentaries on the texts illustrate definite principles. In the *Argonauts of the Western Pacific* (1922a, p. 457) he makes the astonishing claim that 'the verbal translation renders word for word the individual meaning of every particle and root, according to a definite grammatical and lexicographical scheme which has been adopted for this text in common with a few hundred more'.[2] In spite of the above statement, he confesses that he had not made any distinction in the verbal translation between the inclusive and exclusive first person, dual and plural. It is difficult to imagine the definite grammatical and lexicographical scheme, presumably expressed in the translation, and not easy to agree that the opening sentences of the formula given (1922a, p. 440) 'are so clear that the translation word for word explains itself without any closer commentary'. Malinowski's notion of 'translation' extends to his whole method of *'defining a term by ethnographic analysis*, that is, by placing it within its context of culture, by putting it within the set of kindred and cognate expressions, by contrasting it with its opposites, by grammatical analysis and above all by a number of well-chosen examples—such translation is feasible and is the only correct way of defining the linguistic and cultural character of a word'. He did, however, deal explicitly with 'the translation of untranslatable words' (1935, Vol. II, p. 11).

---

[1] 1922a, pp. 460-1. The 'two versions will give an inkling of how I was able to obtain from my native informants the definition of unknown and sometimes very involved expressions and how, in the act of doing it, I was given additional enlightenment on obscure details of belief and custom'. Further, on p. 463, he comments 'these three texts will be quite sufficient to give an idea of the method of dealing with linguistic evidence, and of the documentary value of immediately recorded native opinions'.

[2] Leading American ethnographic linguists are still using this somewhat primitive method of so-called 'equivalents', confusing at least three levels of analysis, and mixing up translation with grammatical and collocational statements. 'A point by point morphemic transformation of kwteletiiwena = *advise-animate-reciprocal-inanimate thing-plural* = *laws;* hence, saawanwa kwteletiiwena = *Shawnee Laws.*' See Voegelin, Yegerlehner, and Robinett, 1954, p. 32. Even Harris makes use of translation meanings, though not systematically. See Z. S. Harris, 1951, pp. 165-7, 182-4, 211, 213, 216-17, 223-4, 285-9, 339-44.

'The contextual specification of meaning' includes phonetic, grammatical, and lexical observations, many of which are of doubtful value and would not be technically recognized as useful in descriptive linguistics today. To say that the real difficulty of the Trobriand language is 'not in the complexity of the grammatical apparatus but rather in its extreme simplicity', may be an amusing paradox but it fails to satisfy the sophisticated reader, and we get very little further when we are told that 'its structure is on the whole what might be described as telegraphic; the relation of the words, as well as the relation of the sentences, has mainly to be derived from the context. In many cases the subject remains unmentioned, is represented merely by a verbal pronoun and has to be gathered from the situation' (1935, Vol. II, p. 36). Grammar is concerned with the interrelation of categories, not of the words as such, and cannot be derived from any context other than that of grammatical analysis. In referring to the subject of the situation, Malinowski goes back again to Wegener.[1]

Most linguists would regard his grammatical treatment of texts (1935, Vol. II, pp. 30-7) as unsatisfactory. To begin with, most of the grammar is notional, of the traditional pattern. We find for instance that 'this sound b changes the character of the verb'. He connects it with what he calls the 'future tense' but 'very roughly' and adds that it 'conveys the idea of potentiality, past, present or future; or at times it is simply emphatic'. The confusion of all levels of analysis is well exemplified in his summary sentence: 'As a fixed meaning distinguishing verbs thus modified by the potential b I have chosen the English auxiliary verb "might" ' (1935, Vol. II, p. 31). Levels are again confused and vagueness reigns supreme, in the following: 'This sound imparts a tinge of definiteness; at times it places the action into a regular past, accomplished state; at times it only gives emphasis. On the whole it is best to regard it as an implement of definiteness and accomplishment. The letter l I have rendered by the fixed meaning "did", lukugis, "thou didst see" ' (1935, Vol. II, p. 32). Traditional grammatical categories are obviously accepted as universals as is shown by his remarks (i) that the distinction between the transitive and intransitive verbs is not easy to make, and (ii) that the passive does not exist. He is much better on the classificatory particles, to which he gave special attention in an article previously quoted, and in his introductory note to Part V[2] of Coral Gardens, he specifically refers those grammatically interested to this article (1935, Vol. II, p. 78). He did not develop any precise forms of lexical entry, but attempted more or less systematic glossaries (1935, Vol. II, pp. 115, 150-5).[3]

---

[1] See above, p. 94, and pp. 102-4.

[2] Corpus Inscriptionum Agriculturae Quiriviniensis; or 'The Language of Gardens'.

[3] The following example is typical of the entries: 'kwanada: yam growing in odila; eaten in molu'.

He appears to be acutely conscious of his shortcomings in phonetics as a basis for what he calls his transliterations of the texts—they are certainly not phonetic transcriptions—and confesses that his phonetic distinctions probably do not go as far as they ought to, and he very often finds in his notes two or three transliterations of what he calls 'the same word'. He dismisses the difficulty by saying that perhaps phonetics carried too far is unprofitable. However, he appreciated the need to connect sound of the language in some way with what he regarded as meaning but had no technique of analysis at his command, nor language of statement. He had to be content with such observations as 'alliterative symmetry so dear to Kiriwinian magic'; 'a heavy thumping rhythm indicated by sharp and circumflex accents'; 'the manner of reciting these parts is more perfunctory, with fewer melodic modulations and phonetic peculiarities'; 'this phonetically very expressive word is used with very great sound effect'; 'this sentence, giving the vowels a full Italian value, such as they receive in the Melanesian pronunciation, does certainly have an impressive ring' (1922a, pp. 441, 444, 447, 450).

The abundance of the linguistic materials would justify revision in the field by a linguist since, as Malinowski says, 'belief in the efficiency of a formula, results in various peculiarities of the language in which it is couched, both as regards meaning and sound' (1922a, p. 451). It would be of considerable linguistic interest to know more of the 'effects of rhythm, alliteration and rhyme, often heightened and accentuated by actual vocal accent' (1922a, p. 452; 1929a, p. 304).

The use of synoptic tables in presenting at a glance the consecutive progress of work and magic as inseparables, is a useful example of the ethnographic method of analysis and justifies the expression 'systematic magic' with its formulae, rites and spells (1922a, pp. 414 ff.).

As I have already pointed out (p. 105, n. 1), Malinowski was fully aware that as his work became better known, it was easier for him to expand his linguistic documentation to great lengths. But he was also apparently conscious of the possible danger of his ethnographic apparatus becoming too obvious and wished to get beyond the field-worker's notebook (1935, Vol. II, p. 45).

A critical appreciation of his contribution to linguistics may be summarized under the following four heads:

I. General theory, especially his use of the concepts of context of situation and of types of speech function (1935, Vol. II, p. 53; 1923a, pp. 475-7).
II. The statement of the meaning of a word by definition with reference to culture context.
III. The statement of meaning by translation.
IV. The relations of (i) language and culture; and (ii) linguistics and anthropology.

ETHNOGRAPHIC ANALYSIS AND LANGUAGE

I. As we have seen, the situational approach in linguistic theory can be regarded as beginning with Wegener's work (1885), which has the merit of general theoretical abstraction with no trace of 'realism'. My own development of the situational approach has been of this kind.

In the work of Gardiner[1] and Malinowski, there are distinct traces of the realist approach which is in strange contradiction, in Malinowski's case, to his repeated insistence on the need for theory. He seems to imagine that there is such a thing as the 'existence' of the brute 'fact', independent of and prior to any statement of fact. 'To us', he says, 'the real linguistic fact is the full utterance within its context of situation.' There is belief in the 'concrete situation', the 'situation of action' in which the utterance is 'directly embedded' and he even used the phrase 'environmental reality' (Malinowski, 1935, Vol. II, p. 57). The word 'utterance' seems to have had an almost hypnotic suggestion of 'reality' which often misleads him into the dangerous confusion of a theoretical construct with items of experience. The factors or elements of a situation, including the text, are abstractions from experience and are not in any sense embedded in it, except perhaps in an applied scientific sense, in renewal of connection with it. In one place, however, he seems to have realized that if a sound film could be taken of a Trobriand gardening activity, so that the 'visual part of it would be self-explanatory', 'the accompanying sounds would remain completely incomprehensible' and would have to be explained by a long and laborious linguistic analysis (1935, Vol. II, pp. 10, 26).

It was perhaps in order to avoid giving 'a disproportionate amount of space and attention' (1935, Vol. II, p. 10) to language that he adopted the not altogether satisfactory methods we have just reviewed.

In my own work, I first turned to the context of situation in 1930[2] and, more recently, have held to the view that the context of situation and the notion of types of speech function are best used as schematic constructs to be applied to language events and that they are merely a group of related categories at a different level from grammatical categories but of the same abstract nature. The linguist sets up interior relations[3] of three main kinds:

(1) the interior relations of elements of structure, words and other bits and pieces of the text;
(2) the interior relations of systems set up to give values to elements of structure and the bits and pieces;
(3) the interior relations of contexts of situation.

[1] A. H. Gardiner, 1932, pp. 49–52, 127 and especially p. 193 for the expression 'the present situation of the utterance'.
[2] See J. R. Firth, 1930; 1950; 1937, Chapter X; 1951a, pp. 83, 84, 87.
[3] See above, pp. 106–7 and footnote 1, p. 107.

The interior relations of the context of situation may be summarized as follows (see J. R. Firth, 1950, p. 7):

    A. The Relevant Features of participants: persons, personalities.
        (i) The Verbal Action of the Participants.
        (ii) The Non-verbal Action of the Participants.
    B. The Relevant Objects.
    C. The Effect of the Verbal Action.

The situational approach, I believe, requires also the classification of types of speech function, in which Malinowski pioneered the way in his Supplement[1] and in *Coral Gardens and Their Magic*.[2]

A great deal of the linguistic work we have noticed, deals with studies of the magical word in the sociological sense; but language can be regarded as magic in the most general sense. Malinowski's treatment suggests many possibilities of research for all students of words in action. It was perhaps this magic which led him to regard speech in infancy and childhood as sources of magical meaning for all of us (1935, Vol. II, p. 62). The creative functions of language which he always emphasized are indeed miraculous.

These aspects of his general theory which were first sketched in the Supplement, are more clearly stated in *Coral Gardens*[3] and are his weightiest contributions in the sociological approach to the statement of meaning.

He pointed out the 'richest field of modern verbal magic'—advertisements—and his amusing parallel of Trobriand beauty magic and the advertisements of Helena Rubinstein and Elizabeth Arden, he commends to any young anthropologist interested in modern as well as primitive savagery. He concludes this interlude in a light vein with the remark: 'In my opinion, the study of modern linguistic uses side by side with those of the magic of simple peoples would bring high rewards'.[4]

    II. His attitude to words as such is curiously unsatisfactory when we remember his concern with institutions[5] and customs. There is no

---

[1] 1923a, see especially pp. 476–7.

[2] 1935, Vol. II, Part Four and Part Six, Division V.

[3] 1935, see especially Vol. II, Part IV, Division I, pp. 52–62, and Part VI, Division V, pp. 236–7. Cf. *The Sexual Life of Savages*, pp. 296–7, 299.

[4] 1935, Vol. II, p. 238. See also Harold Lasswell and Associates, 1949, in which quantitative methods are attempted in the study of key symbols, slogans and the *credenda* and *miranda* of politics.

[5] See 1916, p. 428. 'If you examine the "broad masses" of a community, the women and children included, you will find that, whenever they grasp your questions, their answers will not vary'. See also 1935, Vol. II, p. 172. 'These three texts are a good example of how time after time one receives the same answer from different informants belonging to different communities. Perhaps unfortunately, I did not usually take down statements which I found merely duplicated information already noted.'

doubt in literate societies such as our own, that words and other elements of language are institutionalized, and statements about them in dictionaries and even in common talk are treated with a respect felt to be due to some sort of authority. He says, for instance, that words do not exist in isolation and adds that they 'have no independent existence in the actual reality of speech' (1935, Vol. II, p. 23). The descriptive linguist does not work in the universe of discourse concerned with 'reality' or what is 'real', and is not concerned with the ontological question of whether his isolates can be said to 'have an existence' or 'to exist'. It is clear that one cannot deal with any form of language and its use without assuming institutions and customs. It has long been a commonplace of linguistics, as Malinowski himself says (1935, Vol. II, p. 22), that the sentence and not the word is its main concern but it is not the lowest unit of language, nor is it a 'self-contained or self-sufficient unit'. Let us again emphasize that 'facts' do not 'exist', they are *stated*, and it may indeed be a better guide to the handling of facts to regard them as 'myths' in which we believe, and which we have to live with.

I should agree that 'the figment of a dictionary is as dangerous theoretically as it is useful practically' and, further, that the form in which most dictionaries are cast, whether unilingual or bilingual, is approaching obsolescence, partly on account of the arbitrariness of the definitions and preoccupation with the historical value of the citations. In his method of definition (see above, p. 93), Malinowski makes some approach, though rather vaguely it is true, to the tendencies in modern linguistics to use contextual definitions and make statements of meaning at a series of levels. He does, however, pay great attention to systems of words having mutually exclusive uses in a given field of application— for example, the six words for 'garden' in Kiriwina. He fully appreciates what we might describe in technical linguistic terms as 'distinctive meaning' (see below, p. 114, n. 2). Throughout his work he is at great pains to describe in English, sociologically important distinctions in use (see 1929a, pp. 58, 388, 422).

Perhaps the most interesting full-length commentary on the use of a common word is to be found in his *Freedom and Civilization*, which is an analysis of the 'multiple meanings' of 'freedom in its universe of semantic chaos'. The whole work he himself describes as the semantics of freedom, and his treatment I find not only more sophisticated but more stimulating than similar general semantic studies which have appeared in the United States. Two remarks in this work are of central importance: first, 'all mental states which are postulated as occurrences within the private consciousness of man are thus outside the realm of science' (1947, p. 84); and secondly, 'we have completely to throw overboard any meek acquiescence in dictionary meanings, in the dictates of epigram, metaphor and linguistic vagary. We have often stressed that in science we must run counter to linguistic usage. This is even more important in social science than in the study of matter or organism' (1947, p. 80).

There are signs that in this work, his general theory had so developed as to make consideration of primary meaning and fixed equivalents obsolete. While recognizing as a social fact, that most people do take up attitudes towards words, he sounds the very necessary warning that the 'physicist does not inquire through universal suffrage or a Gallup Poll what the meanings of his concepts are' (1947, p. 81).[1] We know how obsessive is the desire to define the 'core of meaning' (1947, p. 68) of such a word as 'freedom'. His final decision is a 'complete rejection of this core of meaning'. At the same time, as we have already pointed out, he recognizes the influence of such beliefs on human behaviour. In science, however, as he rightly warns us, we are to beware of the tendency to reify and hypostatize such general words as representing valid general concepts (1947, p. 77). Such words are often conceived anthropomorphically. In the language of description in linguistics, we refer chiefly to structures, systems and relations. Our task is observation, analysis, synthesis, and renewal of connection. Words such as 'freedom' and 'law', he regards—in accordance with sound tradition in linguistics —as polysemic and the words themselves as summaries of homonyms and homophones.

III. Whatever shortcomings we may find in Malinowski's analysis of texts, we must concede his realization of the central importance of the statement of meaning by what may be termed 'systematic transla- tion'. He presents in his synoptic tables, the consecutive progress of work and linguistic magic as inseparables (see above, p. 110). His state- ments by double translation with commentary bring into the focus of attention the whole question of what may be called 'translation meaning'[2] in linguistics.

Comparative linguists have perhaps not fully realized the technical implications of the translation meanings by means of which they identify words, let us say, by employing in English such translation equivalents as 'horse', 'sheep', 'father', etc. Translation meanings as

---

[1] See also Voegelin, E., 1952, in which notice is taken of certain words of power as traditional language symbols evolved in the social process.

[2] This has also been dealt with, though less satisfactorily, by American lin- guists. See the Supplement to *International Journal of American Linguistics*, Vol. 19, No. 2, April 1953, 'Results of the Conference of Anthropologists and Linguists', pp. 58–9. Malinowski has covered in detail the three kinds of mean- ing for linguistics suggested by Professor A. A. Hill: (1) differential meaning (distinctive meaning); (2) translation meaning; (3) structural meaning. Such multiple, yet congruent, statements of meaning at different levels are character- istic of the approach of the London group of linguists. See also the examination of inferences from linguistic to nonlinguistic data by J. H. Greenberg (1954, pp. 13–14).

identification names require careful consideration in all descriptive work. Translation meanings consisting of pieces of phrases in analytical languages, set against words in other types of languages, are all too often carelessly conceived and often quite haphazard in application. But translation meanings, however systematic, do not in themselves constitute linguistic analysis.

It is perhaps useful in this connection, to apply the two words 'use' and 'mention' to our procedures. A distinction must always be maintained, even in unilingual descriptions, between the word, piece or sentence in *use* and a reference to these by using the same words as autonyms in *mention*. What Malinowski calls an equivalent, especially in such cases as the six Kiriwinian names for 'garden' (see above, p. 107), should be specifically noted as such, so that the translation meaning does not masquerade as analysis, but serves its identification function in linguistic description. It is in no sense to be regarded as a sociological equivalent.

This leads me to the triple distinction of (i) language under description; (ii) the language of description and (iii) the language of translation. The language of translation subdivides into word-translation meanings, and translation meanings offered as a means of identifying longer pieces, or as names for other native categories supplied by informants. What Malinowski calls free translation, though it may be regarded as contributing to the general statement of meaning, might be referred to simply as 'translation' to distinguish it from the more formal apparatus which we have referred to as systematic translation meanings. The rest of the language of description, being both technical and general, may incorporate translation meanings and translations as part of the description, alongside the necessary technical nomenclature and phraseology of the statement of the analysis proper.

IV. The subject of this essay 'Ethnographic Analysis and Language', which arises from the consideration of Malinowski's work between 1915 and his death in the United States of America in 1942, has been very much on the agenda of anthropologists and linguists among others, in recent years. In 1951, a Commission was set up by the International Council for Philosophy and Humanistic Studies of UNESCO, of which I am a member, to promote a number of linguistic investigations to serve as the basis for an examination of the relationships between language and the other aspects of culture, undertaken by linguists, cultural anthropologists, and philosophers (J. R. Firth, 1951a). May I repeat Malinowski's warning in this connection. 'But there is nothing more dangerous than to imagine that language is a process running parallel and exactly corresponding to mental process, and that the function of language is to reflect or to duplicate the mental reality of man in a secondary flow of verbal equivalents' (1935, Vol. II, p. 7).

In 1953, the results of a Conference of anthropologists and linguists was published as a Supplement to the *International Journal of American Linguistics*. This has been previously referred to. Although the Conference did not actually face the problems stated by Lévi-Strauss (1953*b*), his clear summary of the position should be noted. He distinguished the relations between (1) *a* language and *a* culture; (2) language and culture; (3) linguistics as a scientific discipline and anthropology. He also remarked on something I have often experienced myself, namely, the dangers which beset scholars of different disciplines when they meet to discuss what they consider to be common problems, often employing similar language. In recent conferences on communication theory, scientists and humanists have imagined that when they employ the same words, they mean the same things. A far more healthy state of affairs was indicated by my namesake, Raymond Firth, when he remarked in a humorous vein at a meeting in which we both took part, that the audience should not allow themselves to be confused by the identity of the patronymic but should remember that though we were colleagues working in similar fields, neither of us really knew, in any technical sense, what the other fellow was talking about. Lévi-Strauss expressed it as his belief that one of the main teachings of the Conference was that whenever they tried to express in the same language, linguistic problems and culture problems, the situation became tremendously complicated and they would always have to keep this in mind (1953*b*, p. 3).

If it be admitted that linguistics is a social science of some sort, it is certainly true that it is ahead of the others in theoretical formulation and technique of statement. The coming together of anthropologists and linguists in recent conferences may have the highly desirable effect of, first, convincing anthropologists that they need to look not only to their theories but also to their technical language of statement, including systematic nomenclature; and secondly, to demonstrate to the linguists that they are concerned with the statement of meaning in linguistic terms and that 'linguistics limited to the signal factor' was a 'necessary but fragmentary stage' (1953, p. 59). As Lotz remarks, linguists should not feel so pessimistic about statements of meaning in linguistics.

In a paper at the same Conference, Roman Jakobson, summing up his impressions of the Conference, declared 'One of the most symptomatic features of this Conference was that we lengthily and passionately discussed the questions of meaning', and concluded: 'Thus, meaning remains a No Man's land. This game of Give-away must end. For years and decades we have fought for the annexation of speech-sounds to linguistics, and thereby established phonemics. Now we face a second front—the task of incorporating linguistic meaning into the science of language' (1953, pp. 19, 21).

It is my personal opinion that linguistics is suffering from a surfeit of phonemics and that our energies must turn to the second front. As we have seen in our review of the work of Malinowski, approaches to the problem in Great Britain go back over three-quarters of a century. In my own work, associated with my colleagues in London, I have indicated a strictly formal study of meaning at all levels, in linguistic terms, without poaching either on the sciences of the mind or of society.

It is of considerable interest, therefore, to notice the published results of still another Conference in the United States on the interrelations of language and other aspects of culture. Even Hockett, who places semantics outside linguistics as he understands it, finds it possible to say that ethnography without linguistics is blind: linguistics without ethnography is sterile (1954, p. 225). From my own point of view, I should move a drastic amendment to the last phrase and say that linguistics without 'meaning' is sterile. I do, however, find myself in agreement with Hockett that 'it had better be the linguists who work on this systematic end of semantics' (1954, p. 250).

I should like to suggest once more that linguistics at all levels of analysis is concerned with meaningful human behaviour in society and that the structures and systems and other sets of abstractions set up enable congruent statements of meaning to be made in exclusively linguistic terms.

Let us now turn to Malinowski in this connection. His approach, as one might expect, was practical and concerned itself with teaching. 'A close co-operation between linguistic teaching and anthropological training seems to me of the greatest importance' (1929d, p. 29). Even earlier, he had pleaded 'for a more intensive interest in linguistics on the part of the student of man, and at the same time for a study of language more thoroughly correlated with investigations on other aspects of human culture' (1927c, p. 157). He encouraged the linguist in setting up his grammatical categories to look to other levels of linguistic analysis which would take note of the situation, including the personalities, institutions and customs. 'A grammar of a primitive language cannot be fully stated without reference to further analysis.' As he says, 'The various pronouns of possession[1] in Melanesia, some modifications of verb and noun, are deeply correlated with the practice to which the language is put within its various cultural contacts, and to separate the study of language from the study of culture means merely a waste of time and an amateurishness in most aspects of the work' (1929d, p. 29).

I think it is a fair criticism to say that Malinowski's technical linguistic contribution consists of sporadic comments, immersed and perhaps lost in what is properly called his ethnographic analysis. As he says

---

[1] In the Bauan dialect of Fijian, for example, the following expressions may serve as illustrations: (1) na nona *waqa*, 'his canoe'; (2) na mena *tī*, 'his tea'; (3) na *yava*-na, 'his foot'; (4) na mena *yaqona*, 'his kava'; (5) na kėna *uvi*, 'his yam'. The noun bases are underlined.

himself, 'I was able to incorporate a great deal of my linguistic information into the analysis of magical texts and into the ethnographic descriptions, so that not very much is left to purely linguistic commentary and etymological speculation' (1935, Vol. II, p. 170). There is a need to separate the two techniques of ethnographic and linguistic analysis and, at the same time, to correlate the results so that the trend towards a statement of meaning in linguistics shall be made clear at all levels. Linguistic analysis, I reserve for statements about language data in terms of phonetics, phonology, grammar, stylistics, lexicography, and textual analysis in a background of statements of collocation and of contexts of situation as I understand these terms.[1]

In conclusion, it may surely be taken as a tribute to Malinowski, that we have found it possible to discuss the wide subject of ethnographic analysis and language, still very much before us as the recent conferences show, largely in terms of his published work.

His outstanding contribution to linguistics was his approach in terms of his general theory of speech functions in contexts of situation, to the problem of meaning in exotic languages and even in our own.

[1] See my 'Synopsis of Linguistic Theory' in a volume on Linguistics to be published by the Philological Society of Great Britain.

The Epistemological Background to Malinowski's Empiricism

E. R. LEACH

MALINOWSKI'S contributions to the theory of social anthropology were of two sharply divergent kinds. In the first place he created a theory of ethnographic field-work. Although Malinowski's account of Trobriand culture is far from complete, his descriptions are so alive that we feel we know these people better than any other in the entire anthropological catalogue. The difference between the dry record of 'old style ethnography' and the vivid life of 'Malinowskian ethnography' is not merely an artistic device, it is a matter of theoretical insight. This theory has become a fundamental element in the general body of doctrine propounded by British social anthropologists. We do not now seek to imitate the rather Frazerian style of fine writing which Malinowski adopted but, most definitely, we do all emphasize that we are studying contemporary societies of living human beings rather than fossilized relics from the prehistoric past. Malinowski transformed ethnography from the museum study of items of custom into the sociological study of systems of action.

But besides altering the whole mode and purpose of ethnographic inquiry Malinowski made numerous theoretical pronouncements of a general, abstract, sociological kind, which were supposed to be valid for all cultural situations regardless of time or space. Here, I consider, he was a failure. For me, Malinowski talking about the Trobrianders is a stimulating genius; but Malinowski discoursing on Culture in general is often a platitudinous bore. The framework of concepts that is to be found in the posthumous *A Scientific Theory of Culture* (1944) or in the earlier article on 'Culture' (1931*a*) provides us with few tools which the anthropological field-worker can actually use in a practical situation. The 'Principle of Reciprocity', with its implied emphasis upon the priority of economic motives, may be descriptively preferable to Radcliffe-Brown's 'network of person to person relationships' but it doesn't get us very far. For most of us, 'functionalism' in its

Malinowskian form has become repugnant. Nor can I believe that this is merely a passing phase; the abstract theoretical writings of Malinowski are not merely dated, they are dead.

Paradoxically, I consider that Malinowski's anthropological greatness is to be found precisely in this circumstance. That Malinowski was an imaginative genius of a high order there can be no doubt; but he had a bias against abstract theory which kept his imagination firmly earthbound. The result was a unique and paradoxical phenomenon—a fanatical theoretical empiricist. After all, what was Malinowski's really fundamental contribution? Surely the intensive technique of field study? But of what does this consist? There was plenty of good ethnography long before Malinowski went to the Trobriands; Boas's work among the Kwakiutl, to take but one example, could hardly be described as anything but *intensive*. I should say that the special distinguishing characteristic of Malinowski's field technique lies in two things: firstly in the severely curtailed use of the professional informant, and secondly in the *theoretical* assumption that the total field of data under the observation of the field-worker must somehow fit together and make sense.

Malinowski, of course, used informants, but only to supplement what he knew already; his first line of evidence was always first-hand observation by the field-worker himself. Empiricism could hardly be carried further. Culture consists in what the field-worker himself observes; it is intelligible in terms of the field-worker's personal private intuitions. No data outside the immediate subjective-objective present need to be considered.

As a basis for abstract generalization such an attitude to sociological materials is surely disastrous, but as a device for convincing the field-worker that the minutiae of his present occupation are of supreme importance, it is magnificent. Malinowski trained his field-workers to observe the apparently unimportant in minute detail; the justification for so doing lay in a deeply rooted suspicion of every type of second-hand information. It is in the quality of the observation rather than in the interpretation that the merit of 'Malinowskianism' lies. The interpretations are mostly merely private intuitions, based in the minimal generalization that human beings, as members of a biological species, must satisfy their biological needs.

Holding then that an 'obsessional empiricism' was both the strongest and the weakest element in Malinowski's intellectual equipment, I am concerned in this essay to examine the source and nature of this empiricism. It was dogma in the Malinowskian teaching that facts are only intelligible in their social context; let us then consider some of the elements in Malinowski's own social context.

Malinowski entered the British academic field in 1910. At this period, the late nineteenth-century cultus of mechanistic materialism, linked with naïve doctrines of the inevitability of progressive evolution, still held the field, but was under serious attack. In the realm of pure science, Einstein's formulation of the theory of relativity had shaken the simple world of Newtonian mechanics to its foundations, while Whitehead and Russell had just broken through the boundaries of Aristotelian logic which had held fast for over 2000 years. In psychology, Freud was busily engaged in cutting away the foundations of the ordinary man's commonsense idea of the rational individual. In social studies, the evolutionist comparative method had achieved a kind of massive futility in the vast tomes of Frazer and Westermarck and the only real stimulus was coming from the writings of Durkheim and his school, where the empirical content was often extremely low. Diffusionism with its superficial emphasis on material facts seemed likely to become the dominant vogue in the near future.

Malinowski, with his training in the pure sciences, was certainly keenly sensitive to all these trends, but above all it is his studies under Wundt that seem relevant here. For on the one hand Wundt was an objective empiricist, the founder of the science of experimental psychology, while on the other he was an evolutionist of the old school, who, in his anthropological studies, threw especial emphasis on the study of language and upon the unitary personality of the tribe as a whole.[1] Malinowski, I suggest, approved of Wundt's empiricism but was repelled by the 'group-mind' implications of his historicist approach. He searched therefore for a body of theory which could somehow combine the 'materialist' basis of nineteenth-century Evolutionism with the attribution of free will to the individual soul.

It is my thesis that Malinowski found this body of theory in the Pragmatism of William James. It was precisely in the period around 1910, when Malinowski first came to England to study sociology under Westermarck and Hobhouse, that James's philosophy had its maximum vogue, and it is at this period that Malinowski is most likely to have been receptive to the ideas of the English-speaking world.

Certainly the word *pragmatic* was one which cropped up very frequently in Malinowski's discourse in later years, and certainly also there seems to be much in James's writing that finds a marked echo in the later Malinowski. The philosophic notion of Pragmatism has an interesting history. The term was invented by the American philosopher C. S. Peirce to cover his own rather dry and detached method of logical inference. Though Peirce achieved only a meagre reputation in his own day, his work is now recognized as one of the major influences leading to the development of mid-twentieth-century Logical Positivism. William James was a friend and colleague of Peirce but a man of very different temperament. Where Peirce was austere, retiring, philosophic, James was a public figure, a missionary propagandist with

[1] See Vierkandt (1935, p. 506).

a wide popular appeal. James's Pragmatism is a creed rather than a philosophy; it is a practical guide to correct behaviour. In propounding it, James may well have supposed that he was merely elaborating his friend Peirce's ideas, but in fact he misrepresents and distorts Peirce out of all recognition. Significantly Peirce repudiated all connection with James's doctrine; after 1906 Peirce called himself a *pragmaticist*, a coinage which he dryly referred to as 'ugly enough to be safe from kidnappers'.

Malinowski's Pragmatism is that of James rather than Peirce. Indeed James and Malinowski had a good deal in common. A recent extremely penetrating commentator (W. B. Gallie, 1952, p. 25) has summarized James's position thus:

'First, from the plausible thesis that certain biological interests under-lie, or provide some of the necessary conditions of, all our thinking, he (James) passed to the more exciting (and more ambiguous) thesis that the sole function of thought is to satisfy certain interests of the organism, and that truth consists in such thinking as satisfies these interests.' Substitute *behaviour* and *behaving* for *thought* and *thinking* in this quotation and we have in a nutshell the whole essence of Malinowski's functionalism.

The same author contrasts Peirce's more metaphysical approach in the following terms (W. B. Gallie, 1952, p. 29):

'For Peirce . . . ideas, ideals, movements of thought and feeling, traditional wisdoms, life-tendencies, and above all the life that is in-herent in symbols—these were to him every bit as real as the individuals who apply them or, rather, as the individual occasions, the actions and reactions, in which they are applied.'

The contrast here drawn between the Pragmatism of James and the Pragmatism of Peirce surely parallels closely the analogous contrast between the Functionalism of Malinowski and the Functionalism of Durkheim, Mauss and Radcliffe Brown? The heart of the matter is that James was deeply suspicious of any abstraction that could not im-mediately be referred to directly observable facts; so was Malinowski. This suspicion led Malinowski to his valuable emphasis on first hand observation as a field technique but it also led him to cast most of his theoretical ideas in a shape which makes sociological comparison nearly impossible.

It will be useful here if we distinguish three main types of epistemo-logical thinking. Down to the end of the nineteenth century most philosophies were based in Aristotelian logic, which assumes that all Truth is of one kind and that the validity of statements about God can be tested by the same criteria that might apply to statements about the sun. Today, largely as a result of the development of Logical Positivism, the technique of making scientific statements is becoming increasingly specialized. It has come to be recognized that the language of science deals with propositions quite different in kind from those of ordinary speech. Conversely, we see now that statements that concern metaphysics cannot be expressed in scientific language at all.

In terms of this contrast, James's Pragmatism occupies a kind of middle ground. On the one hand it recognizes that strict logic cannot lead directly to metaphysical judgements; yet metaphysical judgements are still supposed to have a psychological basis in reason. James maintained that we are entitled to believe whatever can be shown to be biologically satisfying even though the belief in question may be metaphysical and incapable of verification either by experiment or rational argument. He explicitly maintained that where proof is impossible it is 'reasonable' to hold beliefs that are arrived at by other than rational means (Gallie, 1952, pp. 25–6).

There is here a serious failure to distinguish clearly between several distinct meanings of the term *reasonable*. *Reasonable* may be held to mean *rational*—the outcome of logical analysis in the strictest sense, or *plausible*—a guess that is justifiable on the grounds of probability, or *sensible*—convenient in the given circumstances. *Reasonable propositions* of the first two kinds are meaningful in the language of science, because they are potentially verifiable; but *reasonable propositions* of the third kind might well include all sorts of metaphysical hypotheses which fall outside the field of scientific analysis altogether.

James is ambiguous, and a very similar ambiguity confuses much of Malinowski's theoretical argument.

We are all kidnappers of ideas. Any attempt to diagnose the epistemological context of Malinowski's functionalism runs into the difficulty that Malinowski borrowed the concept of social function from Durkheim (Malinowski, 1913a, p. 303),[1] but transmuted it in the process. Durkheim's use of the term is unambiguous, it equates with utility: 'the function of a social fact ought always to be sought in its relation to some social end (*fin*)' (Durkheim, 1938, p. 110).[2] But Malinowski changed 'social end' to 'biological end' and thereby loaded the argument with value judgements. Durkheim was simply concerned to investigate the relationship between social facts and their social consequences— he did not presuppose that the consequences were good, they were simply moral or a-moral according as to whether they fitted with the prevailing conditions of society. But for Malinowski social phenomena

---

[1] This first reference to social function follows directly on a discussion of Durkheim's work and is cast in strictly Durkheimian form.

[2] *Les règles de la méthode sociologique* (1895), p. 135. Earlier in *De la division du travail social* Durkheim introduced the notion of social function by drawing the analogy with organic function which 'expresses the relation existing between (a system of vital movements) and corresponding needs (*besoins*) of the organism'. Durkheim consistently makes social facts relate to social ends/needs on the analogy that biological facts relate to biological ends/needs. In contrast, Malinowski uses 'function' to relate social facts to biological ends/needs. Cf. *The Division of Labour in Society* (Free Press Edn.; 1947), p. 49.

exist in order to satisfy needs of the biological organism. Functions are thus both purposive and positive and to detect them requires intuitive judgement. Functionalism, in Malinowski's hands, became something very like a religious creed;[1] it is presented to us as reasonable (practically useful) rather than reasonable (logical or plausible). The 'truth' of Functionalism is itself simply a matter of functional utility.

The fervour that Functionalism aroused among a limited intellectual circle was not based in reasoned analysis. Malinowski had many of the qualities of a prophet, he was a 'charismatic' leader and such men always express their creed in slogans, which have a certain characteristic quality. These slogans assert in a clear-cut but crassly oversimplified form, a state of affairs which their followers would all like to be true. Malinowski's thesis that cultures are functionally integrated is no more true, empirically speaking, than Hitler's thesis that Germans are the master race, but both assertions *could* be true and both appeal to their respective adherents for somewhat similar reasons—they express a Utopian state of affairs.

Prophets are conscious of their powers. Malinowski had no doubts about his own greatness; he regarded himself as a missionary, a revolutionary innovator in the field of anthropological method and ideas. Like all such revolutionaries he tended to belittle the significance of his more conservative contemporaries and their immediate predecessors. His published comments on fellow anthropologists are seldom flattering[2] and in verbal discourse he was even more explicit; he claimed to be the creator of an entirely new academic discipline. A whole generation of his followers were brought up to believe that social anthropology began in the Trobriand islands in 1914.

Yet it is a matter of objective fact that the revolutions which innovators achieve seldom extend over a very wide field. The decisive steps, though all important, are usually quite small. In retrospect the original genius tends to look strikingly like his less imaginative conventional contemporaries. We can observe this over the whole range of science, art and philosophy. Newton, Masaccio, and Occam are cases in point. So too with Malinowski. We may grant that he was the originator of 'a new age' in social anthropology, yet we need to recognize that he was a scholar who reached maturity in the first decade of the twentieth century, and that consequently he took for granted most of the fads and prejudices of the men of that particular generation.

[1] 'The magnificent title of the Functional School of Anthropology has been bestowed by myself, in a way on myself, and to a large extent out of my own sense of irresponsibility' (1932a, p. xxix). Self mockery though this be, it nevertheless reflects Malinowski's belief in himself as the prophet of a new creed.
[2] Consider for example, from this point of view, the first 20 pages of *Crime and Custom in Savage Society* (1926b). The posthumous *A Scientific Theory of Culture* (1949), Chapter III, is, on the other hand, quite unexpectedly tolerant.

A significant example is his use of the term *savage*. Malinowski habitually refers to the Trobrianders as *savages*, implying thereby a whole catalogue of value judgements about the intrinsic superiority of European culture, which few of us today would unhesitatingly accept, but which were an unquestioned anthropological dogma at least as late as about 1925. True enough, Malinowski ridiculed the missionary view that the Trobriander was 'lawless, inhuman and savage' (1922a, p. 10 n.), but when he himself spoke of the Trobrianders as savages he did not do so only in mockery. Tacitly, for all his anti-historicism, Malinowski used the word *savagery* as Morgan has done, to denote a 'stage' in cultural evolution: 'When we move in our survey from the lowest primitives to a somewhat higher level, we are met by a complexity of forces and facts. We enter the world of real savagery . . .' (Malinowski, 1947, p. 280; cf. also 1944, pp. 16–17). There was, admittedly, an important middle phase in his career when Malinowski formally recanted from evolutionary presuppositions. Writing in 1932 (pp. xxii–xxiii) he draws the reader's attention to the fact that the evolutionary premises present in his work down to 1927 were dropped when he came to write *The Sexual Life of Savages* in 1929. Even so, a paper dated 1930 makes a simple equation between 'savage societies' and 'early societies' and half seriously compares 'my present-day Stone Age savages of the South Seas' with our European ancestors of 'forty thousand years back or thereabouts' (1930a, pp. 113, 123), a viewpoint borrowed straight from Tylor and Lubbock.[1]

Now whether or not evolutionary doctrine is true, it is certainly quite irrelevant for the understanding of present-day human societies, and Malinowski was perfectly well aware of this, but somehow the categories of his thinking were still partially trapped in the cage of nineteenth-century orthodoxy. Along with his insistence that the fieldworker must recognize the tribe under observation as consisting of living human beings, he still used the verbal conventions of the evolutionists which set a great gulf between the savage primitives of ethnography and the civilized European intellectual who was observing them.

The notion that the culture of primitive peoples represents in some sense a *survival* from the past was of course a basic premise of the Tylorian anthropology which Malinowski considered it his duty to overthrow. The fact that the same premise was incorporated as a dogma into the very roots of 'functionalism' had important and logically fatal consequences.

Thus: 'This (functional) method has been worked out with the purpose of describing and analysing one culture, and a culture at that, which *through age-long historical development* has reached a state of well

[1] The use of 'evolutionist' phraseology in this essay is particularly revealing, since the essay itself is largely concerned with the demolition of evolutionist presuppositions.

balanced equilibrium' (Malinowski, 1938a, p. xxxvi—my italics). It was Malinowski's proud boast that he had taught anthropologists the futility of the pursuit of conjectural history, yet all the time, the primary assumption of the functionalist creed—the dogma that there is an intrinsic integration between the institutional mechanisms of any one cultural whole—called for a major historical conjecture, namely that equilibrium had been achieved through 'age-long historical development.'

Oddly enough this is an hypothesis that is particularly inappropriate to the Trobriand situation. Chieftainship is quite abnormal in Melanesia and this circumstance suggests strongly that the political structure observed by Malinowski in 1914 may have been of recent origin and perhaps a quite transient phenomenon.

This is one of the cases where Malinowski's ethnography is strikingly superior to his theory. In *Coral Gardens* (1935, Vol. I, p. 365 f.) he actually describes in some detail the process by which the Tabalu chiefly clan was, at the time of his visit, actively expanding its political influence, a condition of affairs hardly consistent with 'a state of well balanced equilibrium'.

The very notion of the 'cultural whole', which is, at all stages, central to Malinowski's thesis, is a concept taken over uncritically from earlier writers (e.g. Wundt) whose 'tribes' were clear-cut, easily distinguishable entities, with completely stereotyped characteristics. Malinowski professed to ridicule the resultant picture of bodies of men conforming to meticulously detailed customs in a rigid and mechanical manner. He sought to replace the notion of custom as an accidental product of history by the notion of custom as a rationally designed tool. Yet when he indulged in cultural comparisons outside the immediate context of Trobriand functionalism, he made statements just like those of his predecessors. What, for example, could be more untrue than the following?

'Were we to take the map of any continent, Australia, Africa, Asia or America we would be able to divide it neatly into ethnographic tribal boundaries. Within each such ethnographic area we would find people of "the same" tribe. On the other side of the boundary another tribe would be found, distinguishable from the first by a different language, different technologies and material objects, different customs and forms of grouping' (Malinowski, 1947, pp. 252-3). There is almost no part of the world in which recent first-hand accounts have not tended to contradict this assertion in every particular.[1]

The simple fact is that inter-cultural comparison was not a field which Malinowski ever bothered to think about or investigate at all carefully.

---

[1] For example, see recent accounts of Arnhem Land by R. M. and C. H. Berndt, of New Guinea by Hogbin, of North Burma by Leach, of West Africa by Nadel, of Bechuanaland by Schapera.

When he expressed an opinion on such a topic he merely repeated the stock dogmas of an earlier generation.

This paradox is a geniune one which might be documented by numerous quotations. On the one hand it was Malinowski's outstanding contribution that he 'brought ethnography to life'. In the pages of *Argonauts* and its successors, the 'savage' ceases to be a marionette 'bound in the chains of immemorial tradition' (1926*b*, p. 10). He is a live human being operating a bizarre system of social organization through the exercise of rational choices about alternative means to alternative ends. Yet somewhere at the back of Malinowski's mind there still seems to have persisted the earlier convention that savages are mechanical dolls surviving from the Stone Age. It was in *Argonauts*, of all places, that he wrote (1922*a*, p. 62): 'It must not be forgotten that there is hardly ever much room for doubt or deliberation, as natives communally, as well as individually, never act except on traditional and conventional lines.'

Let me then sum up this part of my argument. Briefly it is that Malinowski, like William James, was a rebel against the mechanistic implications of late nineteenth-century thought and that his 'functionalism', like James's 'pragmatism', was an aspect of this revolt.[1] Yet at the same time Malinowski was intellectually a 'child of his time', rationalist and materialist in his outlook, and he was himself much influenced by, and even a victim of, those very epistomological windmills against which he charged so valiantly.

The particular aspect of this thesis which I now propose to discuss concerns Malinowski's views of rationality and the effect of those views upon his theories of magic, technology, and kinship.

It may fairly be said of Malinowski, as it has been said of James, that 'he was an individualist, interested in the experiences, perplexities, and satisfactions of individual souls, and anything claiming to be more-than-individual he distrusted from the depth of his soul' (Gallie, 1952, p. 29). Malinowski's biggest guns are always directed against notions that might be held to imply that, in the last analysis, the individual is not a personality on his own possessing the capacity for free choice based in reason. Morgan is repeatedly lacerated for postulating group marriage (Malinowski, 1932*a*, p. xxxii); Durkheim's sin is that he emphasizes religious euphoria, with its implication of a group mind (1925*a*, p. 55); Freud gets it in the neck for postulating a collective unconscious (1927*a*, pp. 156 f.); Hartland is attacked for suggesting that primitive man is a legal automaton (1926*b*, pp. 10, 55 ff.), and so on.

It was dogma for Malinowski that all human beings are reasonable (sensibly practical) individuals. To understand the significance of this belief we need to remember that at the beginning of Malinowski's anthropological career the 'savage' was commonly regarded as a sub-rational

[1] Cf. Gallie (1952), pp. 23–4.

human being. Marett's criticism of Tylor was then in vogue and the *mana* concept was bearing fruit in Durkheim's *représentations collectives* and Lévy-Bruhl's 'pre-logical mentality', abstractions utterly repugnant to Malinowski's way of thinking.

It is against this background that we need to consider Malinowski's attempt to impose 'rationality' upon his savages—for that is what it amounts to. He maintains persistently that primitive man makes a fundamental category distinction between fact and fiction, using criteria that might have been acceptable to John Stuart Mill.

In all Malinowski's writings concerning the relation between magic and science this argument is latent. He himself found the conceptual distinction between the rational and the metaphysical self-evident; he insisted that it must be self-evident to the Trobriander also:

'Thus there is a clear-cut division: there is first the well known set of conditions, the natural course of growth, as well as the ordinary pests and dangers to be warded off by fencing and weeding. On the other hand there is the domain of the unaccountable and adverse influences, as well as the great unearned increment of fortunate coincidence' (1925*a*, p. 31).

Malinowski accused Tylor of treating primitive man as 'a ratiocinating philosopher' (1944, p. 27) yet this simple dichotomy between the objective-rational and the subjective-metaphysical is strictly in the Tylor-Frazer tradition.

Actually Malinowski went one better than Tylor, for he postulated that the Trobriander was more rational than himself. Although he maintained that, for the Trobriander, there is a clear-cut division between the domain of knowledge and work and the domain of magic, he later confessed that 'I was not able to judge for myself where rational procedure ended and which were the supererogatory activities, whether magical or aesthetic' (1935, Vol. I, p. 460; cf. Vol. II, p. 113).

In Malinowski's analysis magical procedures are distinguished from non-magical procedures according to the kind of reasonableness involved. All behaviour is regarded as a means to an end (functionally orientated) but whereas non-magic is reasonable because it is based in scientific fact, magic is reasonable because it is based in psychological need:

'Experience and logic teach man that within definite limits knowledge is supreme; but beyond them nothing can be done by rationally founded practical exertions. Yet he rebels against inaction because *although he realizes his impotence* he is yet driven to action by intense desire and strong emotions' (1931*a*, p. 635—my italics).

Notice the insistence that the actor himself distinguishes between the strictly rational and the psychologically sensible.

It is in accord with Malinowski's dogma that reasonableness is natural to mankind that witchcraft beliefs—being neither sensible nor rational

—were never effectively incorporated into the Functionalist schema. Such beliefs had been reported in the Massim area by Seligman (1910, Chap. XLVII). Malinowski at first expressed complete scepticism (1915*a*, p. 648n.), then he moved to a position of partial agreement (1916, p. 356, n. 2), and finally accepted Seligman's views in their entirety (1922*a*, pp. 237 ff.). Yet he seems never to have adjusted his other ideas to this empirical discovery. Trobriand witches (*mulukuausi*) do not fit into the rationalist schema. In *Coral Gardens*, where magical beliefs and practices are dealt with at length and treated as functionally positive practical working tools, the existence of witchcraft beliefs is completely ignored, the word *witchcraft* being used merely as a synonym for sorcery, in the sense of negative magic.

Malinowski maintained, no doubt rightly, that Trobrianders are at least as rational as twentieth-century Europeans. He stressed that 'civilized' as well as 'savage' life is packed with magical practices (1931*a*, p. 636). Where he seems to err is in maintaining that the ordinary man distinguishes consistently between the magical and non-magical.

Here we need to remember that in Malinowski's youth non-rationality had been deemed to be one of the characteristic marks of the savage; it was likewise deemed to be characteristic of civilized man that he could distinguish clearly between the logical and the non-logical. Frazer's description of magic as 'bastard science' epitomizes this view. In seeking to break down the dichotomy between savagery and civilization Malinowski argued that primitives were just as capable as Europeans of making such distinctions. 'Since the superstitious or prelogical character of primitive man has been so much emphasized, it is necessary to draw clearly the dividing line between primitive science and magic' (1931*a*, p. 636). He would have had a much better case if he had insisted that Europeans are ordinarily just as incapable as Trobrianders of distinguishing the two categories. In seeking to prove that Trobriand savages are not really savages after all, he endeavours to impose upon them a precision of mental classification such as is ordinarily demanded only of professional logicians.

A striking example of this is the doctrine of homonyms which became very prominent in Malinowski's writing during the *Coral Gardens* period.[1] According to this thesis, it is incorrect to suppose that 'native terminologies represent native mental categories'. This very surprising proposition is developed by saying that when the Trobrianders use the word *taytu* to mean (*a*) a plant, (*b*) the food derived from it, (*c*) the crops, (*d*) the year in which the crops ripen, they do not 'lump these meanings together in one confused category'. On the contrary 'there

---

[1] 1935, Vol. II, see index reference to *homonyms*, but especially pp. 65–73. Cf. 1930*a*, p. 159. The germ of the homonym argument is present in *Sexual Life of Savages* (1929), but is not obvious in the 'Problem of Meaning' article of 1923.

is no confusion in the use of these terms; the series is really a series of homonyms, each of them invariably well indexed in actual usage by the context of speech' (1935, Vol. II, pp. 69, 73, 124).

Malinowski alleges that 'arm-chair anthropologists' have inferred that primitive peoples have a 'pre-logical mentality' because they make verbal categorizations unfamiliar to modern Europeans (1935, Vol. II, 69n.). His way of repudiating this allegation is to assert that these verbal categories do not really exist at all; they are merely accidental homonyms which the arm-chair anthropologists mistakenly assume to constitute a single word.

The same doctrine can be applied to kinship terminologies: 'to correlate kinship terms with kinship facts is based on the mistaken assumption that when there is one term for two people these two people must somehow be lumped together or telescoped or united in the mind of the native, or even that they must be one and the same person' (1935, Vol. II, p. 65 n. 2). This is the equivalent of saying that because the English subsume under a single word *tree* a number of different botanical species, it is a 'mistaken assumption' to suppose that Englishmen find anything common as between one tree and another, and that those who hold a contrary opinion are seeking to maintain that all members of the class *tree* are one and the same.

It is certainly a curious argument. Perhaps because they lend themselves so easily to a kind of abstract algebra, kinship terminologies, as such, were repugnant to Malinowski. It is significant that the volume on formal kinship structure, promised in *The Sexual Life of Savages* (1932a, p. 434), was never written. Classificatory systems somehow 'stood for' Morgan and Rivers and everything out of date and antiquated in anthropological theory. They were a type example of non-rational behaviour—judged by European standards—and Malinowski seems to have felt impelled to do away with them root and branch, even though the Trobrianders inconveniently possessed such a system of terminology themselves. The facts were inconvenient but he could deny the implications. Without a vestige of proof, he asserts categorically the unlikely proposition that for the Trobrianders 'the word *tabu* in the sense of "grandmother", in the sense of "maternal [*sic*] aunt", and in the sense of "taboo" are accidental homonyms' (1935, Vol. II, p. 28),[1] meaning thereby that the three meanings here listed are in no way associated.

Now this assertion that the several meanings of *tabu* represent separate words rather than variant meanings of the same word is something which Malinowski projected on to the data in the light of his homonym theory. It is indeed a rational but not a reasonable (sensible) argument! The separate words were not obvious to Malinowski the field-worker, nor even to Malinowski the author of *The Sexual Life of*

[1] The word *maternal* is here a mistake for *paternal*.

Savages. Thus: 'The primary meaning of this word (*tabu*) is "father's sister". It also embraces "father's sister's daughter" or "paternal cross cousin" or, by extension, "all the women of the father's clan"; and in its widest sense, "all the women not of the same clan" ' (1932*a*, p. 423).

The whole doctrine of homonyms, with the added arguments about 'metaphorical extensions' to the 'primary meanings' of terms, seems to me very much on a par with the artificial rational-metaphysical dichotomy upon which I have commented above. Here again Malinowski seems to be trying to force Trobriand categories of thought into the watertight logical containers fashionable among rationalist European thinkers around the beginning of the century. He would surely have disapproved most strongly of certain important trends in contemporary anthropological thinking.

Consider for example the following remarks by Godfrey Lienhardt (1954, p. 97):

'If I report without further comment that some primitive men speak of pelicans as their half brothers, I do little more than offer the reader a form of words which, as it stands in English, suggests the atmosphere of fairy tale and nonsense. . . . In order to make this understood in English it would be necessary to give a full account of views about the relations of the human and non-human quite different from those we entertain, but not therefore, necessarily, less reasonable.' This reaches to the very heart of the matter. Lienhardt finds it quite possible to suppose that his primitive peoples are reasonable (sensible) men although they order their world by principles of logic different from those current in contemporary Europe. Malinowski on the other hand insisted that, belief or dogma apart (1916, p. 418n.), all intelligent behaviour must be based in nineteenth-century logic. The doctrine of homonyms is brought in as a *deus ex machina* to explain away the fact that Trobrianders do not, on the face of it, use nineteenth-century logic. In a similar way Malinowski would doubtless have got rid of Lienhardt's example by saying that, among the tribes in question, the word for pelican and the word for half-brother are accidental homonyms!

Malinowski's contributions to the sociology of language are very relevant here. A linguist of outstanding brilliance, he emphasized that the effect of the spoken word is entirely dependent upon the context in which it is uttered. 'The meaning of words consists in what they achieve by concerted action, the indirect handling of the environment through the direct action on other organisms' (1931*a*, p. 622). 'Language in its primitive function and original form has an essentially pragmatic character' (1923*a*, p. 480). 'It is a type of behaviour strictly comparable to the handling of a tool' (1931*a*, p. 622); it operates as an instrument of communication, as a tool does, 'by direct action'. The symbolic significance of language, its use as a vehicle of thought, is consistently minimized—'to regard it as a means for the embodiment or expression of thought is to take a one-sided view of one of its most derivate and specialized functions' (1923*a*, p. 481).

On the other hand, despite the important insistence that 'language is an integral part of culture . . . . body of vocal customs' (1931*a*, p. 622) Malinowski isolated spoken language as a thing in itself and gave it special importance—'the spell is the most important element in magic' (1925*a*, p. 68). For Malinowski, the 'meaning' of every type of custom was to be seen in its 'pragmatic effect', but there was a tendency to maintain that every type of custom had a special type of effect (function) peculiar to itself. Mere communication—symbolic statement —was not one of the effects which Malinowski considered to be of any importance.

We arrive here at a very important source of confusion. Malinowski's notion of pragmatic function differs radically not only from the 'organic function' concept of Durkheim and Radcliffe-Brown (Radcliffe-Brown, 1935, p. 3), but also from the 'symbolic function' concept employed by mathematicians and logicians (Stebbing, 1945, pp. 128 ff.). In logic, if we have a symbolic equivalence such that X stands for Y, then the form of the symbolization—that is to say the description of Y in terms of X—is referred to as a function. For example, if we write $y = \log x$ then y is a function of x, and if x has the particular value 3 then the expression log x stands for, or is a description of, the number 0·4771. The expression 'log' ('the logarithm of') is here 'the function'. Since, in principle, anything can symbolize anything else the number of forms in which any particular proposition or statement can be expressed is limitless. In any particular case the problem of determining 'the function' is that of ascertaining the symbolic rules and conventions that link the thing described with the form of its description. When Malinowski propounded his extremely valuable thesis that the function of myth is to provide a charter for proper social relationships (1926*c*) he seems to have been using function in this *logical* sense, but in most other contexts he uses the term as very nearly the equivalent of *purpose*. In Malinowskian theory, the function of a custom is the direct effect it produces. In practice, because of the impossibility of establishing causal relationships, Malinowski's 'functions' were determined intuitively, with a very general tendency to allocate one specific function to one specific aspect of culture.

This part of the Malinowskian scheme seems seriously defective.

If culture be regarded as a set of tools (institutions), designed for specific purposes, or causing specific effects, one must face up to the epistemological problems involved in distinguishing the 'designer' and in separating out 'purpose' from 'cause' and from 'consequence', and this Malinowski most signally fails to do.

Moreover even if we take a pragmatist position and say that Malinowski's system is justifiable on grounds of utility, though defective in strict logic, we must still recognize the narrowness of his exposition.

Let us concede that speech can have direct empirically observable effects, does that lessen the importance of communication of a less 'pragmatic' kind? Malinowski's savage has no time for philosophy. For him, culturally defined behaviour is concerned only with *doing* things, not with saying or thinking. But surely all Culture (both verbal and non-verbal) is also concerned with 'making statements' about the social order? In many ritual contexts non-verbal symbolic communication seems to be an end in itself quite independent of the practical-technical outcome (the 'pragmatic function'). Persistently right through his work Malinowski manages to minimize the significance of this aspect of social behaviour.

His treatment of the *kula* provides an example. Malinowski's description represents the *kula* as primarily an economic institution, though the economic principles involved differ from those axiomatically assumed by professional European economists. The picture presented is that of a vigorously competitive market in which the 'currency' consists of 'social debts' of all descriptions. Yet, as Mauss points out, Malinowski's account 'tells us very little about the sanction behind these transactions' (Mauss, 1954, p. 24). In Malinowski's own terms, the *kula*, as described, is pragmatically useless; why then is it maintained? Malinowski's reaction to this criticism was to complain that it is no part of an ethnographer's task to inject private theoretical interpretations into his material, though he proposed to reveal his views in a further work—which never materialized.[1] In retrospect, one feels that Malinowski was here handicapped by his conviction that all behaviour must have a practical end—using the term practical in a narrow mechanistic sense. Mauss's interpretation though not 'pragmatic' provides a most important supplement to Malinowski. Mauss, in essence, sees 'potlatch' behaviour of the *kula* type as 'symbolizing' the ambivalent friendship-hostility aspects of the relationship ties which constitute the component elements in the social structure. It is an abstract interpretation which implies that Trobrianders, in carrying out their *kula* rituals, are also, in a symbolic way, 'saying things' to one another which they certainly could not put into words.

Of course there is a large measure of agreement between Malinowski and Mauss; both are talking about the same material, and the material is that provided by Malinowski. But the underlying difference of basic viewpoint is very fundamental—Mauss sees gift giving as symbolic behaviour, a way of making statements; Malinowski sees it exclusively in operational terms, a way of achieving desired results. Today we can learn from both masters, but that should not blind us to their differences.

[1] See Malinowski, 1935, Vol. I, pp. 455–6. Malinowski seems to have oscillated between thinking that the ultimate practical reason for the *kula* was economic and the potentially much more structural idea that it 'is to a large extent a surrogate and substitute for head-hunting and war'.

So far as I know Malinowski's only published comment on *Essai sur le don* is a footnote (at p. 41 of *Crime and Custom*). He here accepts Mauss's criticism of the concept of 'Pure Gift' but claims that he revised his views independently.

This brings me back to a point I made much earlier, Malinowski's deep suspicion of 'abstract theory' as such. I would emphasize again that this prejudice proved both an advantage and a handicap. The advantages are clear. Consider for example the opening paragraphs of Chapter XI of *Coral Gardens* which carries the title "The Method of Field-Work and the Invisible Facts of Native Law and Economics'. Here Malinowski lays down rather precisely the relationship, as he saw it, between theory and observation, and the limits to which abstract theorizing might legitimately proceed:

'The main achievement of field-work consists, not in a passive registering of facts, but in the constructive drafting of what might be called the charters of native institutions.... While making his observations the field-worker must constantly construct: he must place isolated data in relation to one another and study the manner in which they integrate ... "Facts" do not exist in sociological any more than in physical reality; that is they do not dwell in the spatial and temporal continuum open to the untutored eye. The principles of social organization, of legal constitution, of economics and religion have to be constructed by the observer out of a multitude of manifestations of varying significance and relevance. It is these invisible realities, only to be discovered by inductive computation, by selection and construction, which are scientifically important in the study of culture' (1935, Vol. I, p. 317). Malinowski, then, approved of the use of sociological theory in the interpretation of first-hand fieldwork observations; what he objected to was 'arm-chair theorizing' about behaviour recorded in hearsay statements. On the face of it this is a sensible and scientific attitude, and yet it has implications which are entirely paradoxical. Logically speaking, Malinowski would need to maintain that, for the Trobrianders themselves, 'Trobriand culture as a whole' does not exist. It is not something that can be reported on by Trobrianders, it is something that has to be discovered and constructed by the ethnographer. It is entirely consistent with this position that the most intelligible account of the total social structure of Trobriand society which Malinowski gives us occupies the *last* 50 pages of the *last* book he published on the subject (1935, Vol. I, pp. 328–81).

In an earlier work he specifically mocked at the account of Trobriand social structure that one might expect to obtain from a professional Trobriand informant,[1] though when he himself attempted to write a concise description of 'The Constitution of Trobriand Society' (1935,

[1] 1932a, pp. 416–24, gives the formal description of the structure; pp. 425–9 are devoted to ridiculing the validity of this native description.

Vol. I, pp. 33–40) the result resembles most strikingly that given by his imaginary despised 'informant'.

Now it is certainly true that in recognizing quite specifically that there is a marked divergence between 'ideal' and 'actual' behaviour, Malinowski made explicit a fact of the greatest sociological importance: 'the hasty field-worker who relies completely upon the question-and-answer method, obtains at best that lifeless body of laws, regulations, morals and conventionalities which *ought* to be obeyed, but in reality are often only evaded. For in actual life rules are never entirely conformed to, and it remains, as the most difficult but indispensable part of the ethnographer's work, to ascertain the extent and mechanism of the deviations' (1932a, pp. 428–9). Moreover he was perfectly justified in asserting that most of his predecessors had relied heavily on hearsay statements so that existing ethnographic accounts of tribal custom consisted everywhere of abbreviated descriptions of idealized behaviour. But he went much too far in the other direction. He appears to have regarded the ideal construct of the native informant as simply an amusing fiction, which could at best serve to provide a few clues about the significance of observed behaviour. Truth was 'pragmatic', objectively observable; it lay in what men did, not in what they said they did. Yet surely in Malinowski's own analysis of myth a counter argument is already apparent? If myths are to be regarded as charters for social institutions, surely the intelligent informant's descriptions of his own society are also 'a kind of myth', a charter for human action, none the less important because the rules are not precisely obeyed?

In the case I have cited, Malinowski uses the fact that Trobrianders frequently have love affairs with their clan sisters (*kakaveyola*) but only very seldom with their lineage sisters (*veyola*), as evidence for the uselessness of general statements about clan exogamy. But in recent years facts strikingly similar to those recorded by Malinowski have been reported from other societies, and have been shown to be meaningful precisely because they provide differentiating criteria in terms of which the different segments of the formal social structure become apparent (Evans-Pritchard, 1951b, chap. 2; cf. also M. Fortes, 1949a, pp. 101, 115). The same is certainly true in the Trobriand case also. In this instance, as in a number of others, Malinowski's pupils have progressed further than Malinowski himself largely because of their willingness to recognize that symbolic functions are at least as relevant as pragmatic ones.

In writing this essay, the impression I have been trying to convey is that Malinowski was a highly original thinker who was nevertheless held in bondage by the intellectual conventions of his youth. But did he point the way to escape from the dilemmas with which he was faced?

It would be absurd to suggest that Malinowski's thinking was 'permanently stuck at 1910'. Although his last books, written in illness, give the impression of regression to a position formally repudiated in 1932,[1] there is otherwise a very noticeable 'development' throughout Malinowski's work. If we take *Mailu* (1915*a*), *Argonauts* (1922*a*) and *Coral Gardens* (1935) as three points on a time scale, the increase in sophistication is very marked indeed, and is an indication of the extent to which Malinowski's famous seminars were a vehicle for learning as well as for teaching.

But we need to see this development as part of an intellectual problem: Malinowski's persistent struggle to break out of the strait-jacket of nineteenth-century historicist theory without getting hopelessly bogged in empirical detail. Despite his advocacy of empiricism Malinowski was really searching all the time for concepts of the middle range of gener-ality,—not so abstract as to amount to mere verbal speculation, not so concrete as to defy generalized comparison. Culture is too abstract; the individual too concrete.

Now if we compare the stated content of 'functionalism' at different stages of Malinowski's career we find an interesting and significant shift of emphasis. The original stress on *Culture* as a unitary integrated whole seems gradually to lessen, as also the emphasis on the simple family as the basic unit of social structure, while in their place we find a new 'concrete isolate of organized behaviour'—the *Institution* (1944, p. 52; cf. 1931*a*, p. 626). Here, I would suggest, Malinowski was pointing the road for his successors.

Sociologists have used the concept of 'Institution' in a variety of senses.[2] Malinowski's version tends to confuse the individual with his institutionalized rôle. As a result his institutions emerge as collections of individuals (personnel) who possess a common vested interest (1944, pp. 52 ff. and pp. 62–3), a conception closely analogous to Weber's 'corporate group' (*Verband*) (M. Weber, 1947, pp. 124 ff.). A recent American study makes this parallel very clear (Gerth and Mills, 1954, p. 13 *et passim*; Vidich, 1954).

Since Malinowski's death British social anthropologists have in-creasingly tended to think of their special field as the study of the behaviour of small groups operating within a defined structural-cultural matrix.

It is in line with this that the concept of the *corporation* with its associated hereditable estate—its 'bundle of rights' over things and people—is tending to become central to our analysis. We have reached this position by borrowing ideas from the lawyers and the theoretical

[1] Both *Freedom and Civilization* and *A Scientific Theory of Culture* are strangely 'evolutionist' in tone when compared with his explicit repudiation of 'speculations about origins' in the 1932 Edition of *Sexual Life of Savages*, pp. xxii–xxiii.

[2] Cf. S. F. Nadel (1951), p. 108.

sociologists—Maine, Durkheim, Weber, Talcott Parsons in particular, but the resulting development seems to parallel that of Malinowski in same respects. Malinowski's *Institution*, as he left it, is not a precise isolate, but it does provide a kind of bridge between the crude intuitive functionalism of the 1930's and the increasingly sophisticated structural analysis of today. It is in concepts of this type that we find a meeting point between the arguments of those who stress the importance of the ideal order conceived as a system of jural relationships and those who see social behaviour as the outcome of competitive individual self-interest. To that extent we may now be coming back to where Malinowski left off.

One thing at any rate we should remember. All the authors of this book were 'grounded in Malinowski', just as I have suggested that Malinowski himself was grounded in William James. If I am correct in thinking that Malinowski was partly frustrated by the persistence of youthful intellectual prejudices, the same certainly applies to ourselves. Malinowski, I have insisted, was 'in bondage' to his predecessors; he resented their existence because he was so much indebted to them. Some of us perhaps feel the same about Bronislaw Malinowski.

Malinowski's Theories of Law

I. SCHAPERA

(i)

MALINOWSKI'S conception of 'law' changed several times during the course of his career. Before going into the field, he restricted the term to social norms 'which enjoy an organized, more or less regulated and active social sanction' (1913a, p. 11). His basic premise was that 'All social organization implies a series of norms, which extend over the whole social life and regulate more or less strictly all the social relations' (p. 10). Different kinds of norms are enforced by different kinds of 'social' or 'collective' sanction, and norms may accordingly be classified according to their sanctions. For Australia, about which he was writing, he distinguishes three main classes of norms: religious rules, punishment of whose breach ('sin') is 'supernaturally entailed by its very committal'; customary rules, whose breach ('improper conduct') is punished by ridicule and social contempt; and legal norms, whose breach ('crime') is 'punished by the decision of the community, acting as a whole, or by its central organs, or certain groups of it' (pp. 14 f.). 'A given norm or rule is Legal', he emphasizes, 'if it is enforced by a direct, organized, and definite social action' (p. 15). 'Without the norm the social action would be mere violence. Without the social enforcement, the norm would be a moral or customary rule; so enforced, it may properly be called a law' (p. 14).

'To make this definition plausible', he adds, 'we may remark that it makes the Australian legal institutions correspond to what we call law and legal in higher societies' (p. 11). In his monograph on Mailu (1915a), the first major study based on his own field-work, he is more cautious. He says that it would be an obvious mistake, in describing native conditions, to use such terms as law, legal, criminal and civil law, etc., in the strict sense in which they are defined in jurisprudence. On the other hand, 'To use them loosely and without troubling as to their meaning would be essentially unscientific, because, in the case of the field ethnologist, it would show that he has not been considering very carefully where to look for his facts and how to group them' (p. 576).

Accordingly, he now introduces a distinction of his own, 'following as closely as possible the conditions of native social life', between civil and criminal law. 'Civil law', he says in one context, 'comprises all the rules governing social life' (p. 578). Elsewhere he is more specific and narrow. 'Under civil law in a native society we can understand the set of rules regulating all the normal relations between persons, as kinship, marriage, economic co-operation and distribution, trading, etc.; and between persons and things, property inheritance, etc.' (p. 578). These are 'fundamental rules which must be observed'. Their infraction 'is a lurking temptation, and there are always individuals who succumb. As a preventative, or reaction, to this there exist some measures of restriction and redress; broadly speaking, some restraining forces' (p. 577). From this follows the distinction between civil law, 'a set of rules regulating the social mechanism in its stationary, normal course', and criminal law, 'the safety arrangements, putting things aright whenever there is any hitch in their normal course' (p. 578). The Mailu have 'no central authority which would spontaneously and automatically' deal with offenders, but there are various ways of reacting to murder, adultery, theft, and 'evil magic', which he discusses under the heading 'Rudimentary Measures, corresponding to Criminal Law' (pp. 578–80). Then follows a much longer section (pp. 580–8) on '*Taboo (Góra)*', of which he says (p. 587): '*Góra*, in its broadest and most abstract meaning, means taboo, rule, prohibition; it is distinctly the conception covering what we would call law in our society.' It is 'enforced by a supernatural sanction—by the fear of the evil results, automatically following the offence' (p. 583).

In his writings on the Trobriand islanders, where for the first time he discusses law in extensive detail, Malinowski returns to the concept of 'fundamental' rules of conduct. Although at the very beginning of *Crime and Custom* (1926*b*) he refers loosely to 'primitive law' as 'the various forces which make for order, uniformity and cohesion in a savage tribe' (p. 2), he later emphasises that law is 'clearly distinguishable, and distinguished by the natives, from the other types of norm, whether morals or manners, rules of art or commands of religion' (p. 74). 'There must be in all societies', he says, 'a class of rules too practical to be backed up by religious sanctions, too burdensome to be left to mere goodwill, too personally vital to individuals to be enforced by any abstract agency. This is the domain of legal rules' (pp. 67 f.). 'The rules of law', he says in another context, 'stand out from the rest in that they are felt and regarded as the obligations of one person and the rightful claims of another' (p. 55).

This definition of law differs from those given in his earlier works, notably the book on the Australian family. But he does not use it consistently. For example, the 'body of binding obligations, regarded as a right by one party and acknowledged as a duty by the other', he sometimes distinguishes as ' "civil law", the positive law governing all the phases of tribal life' (p. 58). Elsewhere he defines civil law more comprehensively as 'a class of binding rules which control most aspects of tribal life, which regulate personal relations between kinsmen, clansmen and tribesmen, settle economic relations, the exercise of power and of magic, the status of husband and wife and of their respective families'. On the other hand, 'the fundamental rules safeguarding life, property and personality form the class which might be described as "criminal law" '; in this class he also includes the rules safeguarding 'such institutions as chieftainship, exogamy, rank and marriage' (p. 66).

If he is here trying to distinguish between civil and criminal law in terms of subject matter the attempt is hardly successful, since both categories obviously have certain 'rules' in common. However, as he himself makes very clear, civil and criminal law (in his use of the terms) differ primarily in mode of enforcement. Criminal law has as its sanction 'tribal punishment, due to a reaction in anger and indignation of the whole community' (p. 65). But there is no formal administration of justice 'according to a code and by fixed methods' (p. 99). Instead, 'the principles according to which crime is punished are very vague, [and] the methods of carrying out retribution are fitful, governed by chance and personal passion rather than by any system of fixed institutions'. The most important methods are 'such institutions and usages' as 'sorcery and suicide, the power of the chief, magic, the supernatural consequences of taboo and personal acts of vindictiveness'. These, 'far from being legal in their main function, only very partially and imperfectly subserve the end of maintaining and enforcing the biddings of tradition' (p. 98). Nevertheless, he devotes a whole chapter to 'Sorcery and Suicide as Legal Influences', and only later, and as 'a brief digression', does he inform us that of 'the two standard criminal acts, theft and murder', the former is punished by shame and ridicule, and the latter by either vengeance ('vendetta') or the payment of blood-money (pp. 117–19).

Civil law, in contrast to criminal, is 'the law obeyed and not the law broken' (p. 73). This is the same distinction as previously made in the monograph on Mailu; but much more detail is now given about the manner in which the rules of civil law are sustained. They have 'no religious sanction. . . no fear, superstitious or rational, enforces them, no tribal punishment visits their breach, nor even the stigma of public opinion or moral blame' (pp. 66 f.). Instead, they are 'kept in force by a specific mechanism of reciprocity and publicity'. Their observance rests upon a sense of duty and recognition of the need for co-operation. The dominant factor is enlighted self-interest. By carrying out his obligations to others, the Trobriander satisfies his 'ambition, vanity, pride, [and] desire of self-enhancement by display', and also testifies to his 'attachment, friendship, devotion and loyalty to the kin' (p. 58).

Conspicuous fulfilment brings him social esteem, whereas failure to do as he should not only entails loss of the reciprocal services to which he is entitled and upon which he depends, but also (despite the statement quoted above) adverse criticism and sometimes even ostracism.[1]

In his 'Introduction' to Hogbin's *Law and Order in Polynesia* (1934*a*), Malinowski again stresses the importance of 'reciprocity, systematic incidence, publicity and ambition' as 'the main factors in the binding machinery of primitive law'. Here too he discusses more fully the rôle of 'positive inducements' (i.e. rewards of various kinds) in securing observance of the social norms; and he goes so far as to say that 'this is probably the most important aspect' of the functional theory of primitive law. 'It is very closely related with the fact that most laws are the expression of some sound biological reality, of some important and functionally founded trend of culture' (p. lxvi).

But he is no longer so insistent upon establishing and maintaining a verbal distinction between 'law' and other rules of conduct, and sometimes uses the terms 'law' and 'custom' interchangeably (e.g. pp. xxviii, xxx, xli). Instead, he now emphasizes a new distinction, between 'valid, sanctioned customs' and those that are 'neutral or indifferent'. The latter, to which only casual reference is made in *Crime and Custom* (1926*b*, pp. 52, 65), 'are never sanctioned in the sense that their breach provokes dissatisfaction in any one, hence reaction, communal or individual, hence organised punishment. Such rules are not broken since no one wants to break them, hence their breach does not exist and cannot be punished' (1934*a*, p. xxvi). But the former, mostly rules relating to sex, property, and safety, 'invariably imply the sharp sting of temptation' and 'are sanctioned by technical arrangements, supernatural threats, moral opprobrium and last not least, by law. They have to be legally sanctioned, that is provided with some mechanism of enforcement or validity, not merely in the form of punishment for transgression, but also through strong positive inducements to compliance' (p. xxvii). Just what he means by 'law' in this context is not clear, but it is at least evident that 'valid, sanctioned custom' includes more than merely the rules kept in force by 'reciprocity and publicity' or whose breach leads to 'tribal punishment'.

In his introduction to Hogbin's book Malinowski also refers briefly to his conception of law as one of the 'derived or instrumental needs' which in all societies 'have to be satisfied as urgently as biological requirements if man is to survive' (p. xxxii). His general theory of 'cultural determinism' (the term is his own) was originally expounded in an article on 'Culture' (1931*a*). Here in addition to law he lists economic organization and education among what he calls the 'instrumental imperatives' (pp. 633 f.). The significance of this for our present purpose is that now, in contrast with his treatment of the subject in *Crime and*

---

[1] See below, p. 146.

Custom, he explicitly includes education among the mechanisms of social control.[1] Except for an unimportant passing reference, he again ignores it in his Introduction to Hogbin's book. But in the posthumously-published *Scientific Theory of Culture* (written in 1941) he stresses that training during childhood and youth 'not merely compels general respect and obedience to tribal tradition but also reveals to the individual the consequences and penalties of deviation or breach' (1944, p. 129).

In almost the last publication to appear during his lifetime (1942*a*) Malinowski restated his views on law, in a manner superficially different from everything before, but nevertheless repeating some earlier ideas. Asserting that in the study of law confusion has been created 'by the multiple meanings given to the main term', he seeks to introduce clarity by speaking of 'Law (1)', 'Law (2)', etc. He recognizes four different meanings, which (he says) can be readily kept apart by 'contextual or adjectival distinction'.

Law (1) is 'the law of cultural determinism'. Here the term 'law' is used in the same sense as in the phrase 'law of science', but with specific reference to 'the natural laws of physical and biological process' that affect human behaviour and determine the basic pattern of culture. Such laws, 'the laws of the science of culture', can be formulated only by the scientific observer, and although 'implicitly followed' are neither 'known nor stated' by the native.

Law (2) is 'the law or rule of native conduct'. It embraces rules of 'knowledge, technology, co-operation, common life, and convention', all of which are 'standardized in behaviour or verbally formulated'; they are 'automatically sanctioned by the coercion of efficiency or by the convenience of conventionality', and since there are 'no temptations to break or to stretch' them, since they are not subject to tensions and conflicts, they 'remain outside any socially organized enforcement'.

Law (3), 'the law of order and maintenance', is also described as 'the law which is positively primed and baited', i.e. to which rewards for conformity are attached. It 'applies to rules of conduct which refer to relations between individuals and groups, delimit divergent interests, and curtail disruptive physiological and sociological tendencies'. It embraces most rules of property, contract, status, and authority, as well as those protecting life and limb and defining sexual rights.

Law (4), 'the mechanisms of law when breach occurs', is defined as 'the specific mechanism which is brought into existence when a conflict of claims arises or a rule of social conduct is broken'. It is also described as 'retributive and restitutive social action', and as 'the more or less

---

[1] In his essay on 'Magic, Science and Religion' he had emphasized the rôle of initiation ceremonies as 'an extremely efficient means of transmitting tribal lore, of insuring continuity in tradition and of maintaining tribal cohesion' (1925*a*, p. 40; 1948, p. 23).

organized coercive reactions of a community which are set in motion when a rule is broken definitely and conspicuously' (1942a, pp. 124–5).

'Law (1)' need not detain us here, since, as Malinowski himself indicates, it is of no interest to jurisprudence. 'Law (2)' obviously corresponds to what he previously termed 'neutral or indifferent custom'. The distinction between 'Law (3)' and 'Law (4)', respectively representing the two processes of 'maintenance or order' and 'restitution or re-establishment', is one to which he attaches great importance and which, he insists, 'has to be emphatically stated'. 'When we speak of a law-abiding community, we mean Law (3). When we say that "law" has been brought into action, we mean Law (4). Law (4) comes into being when Law (3) ceases to work. As long as Law (3) reigns, there is no room for Law (4)' (p. 1244). In effect, we have here again the distinction made in the Mailu monograph between 'civil law' and 'criminal law'.

In the posthumously-published *Freedom and Civilization* (1947), the four uses of the term 'law' are reduced to only two: Law (1), 'a rule of intrinsic determinism of a process' or 'a phase of natural determinism', and Law (2), 'a promulgated command of authority sanctioned by force' or 'a human precept' (1947, pp. 173, 178). Law (1), as now described, refers both to 'the law of nature' and to certain 'rules of technique . . . which cannot be evaded' if a technical process is to be carried out successfully. Law (2) seems to be essentially the same as the 'valid, sanctioned customs' mentioned in the Introduction to Hogbin's book. 'By law in the sense of a socially established rule we mean a command or rule of conduct sanctioned by organized constraints. Here belongs obviously modern law in the lawyers' sense. All the rules of morals, manner, etiquette, ceremonial, and custom, as these are taught to children at all stages of civilization, also belong to this class' (p. 175). In brief, the distinction between 'law' and other rules of conduct is abandoned, and the term is now used to cover all kinds of sanctioned norm. But, in the accompanying discussion (pp. 178–80), primary emphasis is laid on coercive sanctions; 'reciprocity and publicity' fade into obscurity, 'rewards' are mentioned only incidentally, and the new catchwords are 'authority', 'punishment', and 'exercise of force'. This also appears in a later passage: 'The principle of authority comes into being from the beginnings of mankind. In disciplining the individual, authority is an indispensable factor of the process of training at any level of culture. In the enforcement of criminal law it is at all stages and in all societies a *conditio sine qua non*' (p. 234).

(ii)

In discussing Malinowski's views about law, other writers generally concentrate upon what he said in *Crime and Custom* and in his Introduction to Hogbin's book. Since these are in fact the two works in which he developed his ideas on the subject most fully, and to which is largely due such influence as he exercised on its study, they need further comment.

One cannot help starting with some adverse criticism. In order to emphasize his own views more sharply, Malinowski uses the technique of contrasting them with what others have written on the same topic. This is a valid and even commendable mode of procedure. But it can hardly be maintained that he always tries to deal justly with the work of his predecessors. Occasionally he distorts what they say, as when Radcliffe-Brown's statement that 'some simple societies have no law, although all have customs which are supported by sanctions', is represented as implying that 'law [is] sanctioned and custom not' (1934a, pp. xxiii f.). Similarly, he accuses Hobhouse of neglecting to explain why customs are 'felt as binding', and links him with writers who assert that 'all custom is obeyed automatically and rigidly by sheer inertia' (1926b, pp. 12, 56, 63 f.). Yet Hobhouse explicitly states that primitive peoples obey custom because they hold that 'its breach will bring misfortune upon the wrong-doer, or some one connected with him, or on the community', and that 'the man whether civilised or uncivilised who conforms to custom is not acting like an automaton. He is perfectly well aware of what he is doing at the moment. He knows that it is expected of him, and he himself would expect it of another placed in similar circumstances' (Hobhouse, 1915, pp. 61n., 419, 624; 1924, p. 45).

Malinowski says also that 'Law in modern Anthropology is still almost exclusively studied in its singular and sensational manipulations, in cases of blood-curdling crime, followed by tribal vendetta, in accounts of criminal sorcery with retaliation, of incest, adultery, breach of taboo or murder' (1926b, p. 73). Yet Hartland's *Primitive Law* (1924), which he singles out for special disapproval, contains chapters on constitutional law, personal rights and liabilities, property (together with ownership, inheritance, barter, and money), international relations, and legislation. Similar topics feature conspicuously in such well-known regional studies as Barton's *Ifugao Law* (1919), Dundas's articles on Bantu law in East Africa (*J.R.A.I.* 1915, 1921), and Gutmann's *Das Recht der Dschagga* (1926), as well as in such older works as Post's *Afrikanische Jurisprudenz* (1887) and Steinmetz's *Rechtsverhältnisse von Eingeborenen Völkern* (1903). Admittedly they are sometimes treated there in a highly formalized manner, occasionally even as a mere catalogue of rules; but the fact that they are dealt with at all, and in detail, shows how little justification Malinowski had for saying: 'It is generally held that with the description of crime and punishment the subject of jurisprudence is exhausted as far as a savage community is concerned' (1926b, p. 56).

That is not the only rash generalization in which he indulges. Ignoring virtually all the work done from the time of MacLean (1858) down to Rattray (1929) he affirms, mistakenly, that according to the conventional view law in centralized African chiefdoms 'was mainly concerned with the interests of the sovereign, or of a small privileged class, or of one or two interested individuals. Otherwise the rules of conduct within the clan, the family, the village community, seemed to have no special enforcement from outside' (1934a, p. xxi). Again, ignoring the work of even such standard authorities as Ehrlich, Pound, and Vinogradoff, he says that jurisprudence 'emphatically, circumstantially and ponderously' isolates 'the field of law from that of other rules of conduct. . . . If anthropology can influence jurisprudence to the extent of making it recognise the positive side of law and also acknowledge that law is only part and parcel of a wider system of norms, this will be of some benefit to all social science' (pp. lxvi f.). In reply one need merely quote Vinogradoff (1913): 'Laws take their place among the *rules of conduct* which ensure social order and intercourse. . . . Laws are, of course, not the only rules of conduct which govern men's actions. People conform also to fashions, to manners and customs, to conventional standards, to precepts of morality' (1949 ed., pp. 13, 16).[1]

Malinowski's exposition of his own views contains various instances of inconsistency and contradiction. We have already seen that even within a single work, such as *The Natives of Mailu* or *Crime and Custom*, he uses the term 'law' in several different senses. He accuses his predecessors of maintaining that 'all custom is obeyed automatically and rigidly by sheer inertia' (1926b, p. 63), yet himself writes (p. 104) that for a Trobriander 'anything but immediate compliance with a ritual request is unthinkable' (the 'ritual request', in this context, ordering a man to depart from a village where he is a 'resident outsider'). He says (pp. 66 f.) that not 'even the stigma of public opinion or moral blame' attaches to breach of what he calls civil law, yet elsewhere remarks that 'failure to comply places a man in an intolerable position, while slackness in fulfilment covers him with opprobrium' (p. 41), and that 'The ceremonial manner in which most transactions are carried out . . . entails public control and criticism' (p. 55).

Nor does his general description of crime and punishment among the Trobrianders (1926b, pp. 71–119) bear out his earlier assertion that criminal law is sanctioned by 'tribal punishment, due to a reaction in anger and indignation of the whole community' (p. 65); indeed, as already mentioned, he himself states elsewhere that the principal methods of punishing crime are 'sorcery and suicide, the power of the chief, magic, the supernatural consequences of taboo and personal acts of vindictiveness' (p. 98). He also makes statements such as the following: 'A dual organization may appear clearly in the division of a tribe into

[1] The first two chapters of this little book discuss the relationship of law to other rules of conduct.

two "moieties" or be almost completely obliterated—but I venture to foretell that wherever careful inquiry be made, symmetry of structure will be found in every savage society, as the indispensable basis of reciprocal obligations' (p. 25). If this is intended to mean more than that in every society persons are often connected with others by reciprocal rights and duties, it is ethnographically incorrect; if it means nothing more, the use of the phrases 'dual organization' and 'symmetry of structure' is extremely rash.

One could readily find other instances where Malinowski has criticized his predecessors without paying due attention to what they wrote, or has himself made careless statements that could be turned to his disadvantage by quotation out of context. But these defects, and they are defects in his manner of presentation rather than in the substance of his views, do not detract from his outstanding contributions to the study of social control in primitive societies.

Among those contributions was his insistence that in such societies rules of conduct are not all of the same character, but differ both in kind and in the degree to which they are made obligatory. Already in his Australian book (1913a) he had distinguished between rules of custom, religion, and law. In *Crime and Custom*, similarly, he says that not all social rules are 'legal', and that 'besides the rules of law, there are several other types of norm and traditional commandment', such as morals, manners, rules of craftsmanship and ceremonial, and religious precepts (1926b, pp. 52–4). He also maintains, as he did in 1913, that the only way in which rules of conduct can be classified is by reference to the motives and sanctions enforcing them, and that the sanctions characteristic of law are 'entirely different' from those pertaining to other rules (pp. 50, 54).

There is of course nothing original in this approach. At the time when he wrote it was already a commonplace in the general literature on social control, and Vinogradoff, for example, had used it in discussing 'social rules' (*op. cit.*). But if not new it certainly needed emphasis in regard to primitive society. Hartland, for example, claimed that 'primitive law is in truth the totality of the customs of the tribe', every portion of it being 'equally binding', and that although some customs have 'definite sanctions', and others 'none', the savage 'does not distinguish between them' (1924, pp. 5, 8, 138). Similarly, MacIver said in 1921 that in primitive society the whole body of social usages is 'unwritten law': custom is law and law is custom, custom and morality are one. In 1937 he still maintained that primitive peoples make no formal distinction between legal, religious, and economic codes and 'the code of the customary law'; but in deference to Malinowski's views he was now willing to concede that 'There are, of course, varying degrees of importance attached to the several prescriptions of any code, and this holds of the code of custom' (1921, pp. 159, 165; 1937, p. 332). And

Timasheff, although also not accepting Malinowski's definition of law, says that the merit of his work 'is to have shown that there are many layers in the nonlegal regulation of life in primitive society' (1939, p. 277n.)

Malinowski further added much to our knowledge of the reasons why primitive peoples observe their social norms. Tylor (1881, pp. 407 ff.) and Hobhouse (1915, p. 28; 1924, p. 46), among others, had previously stressed the rôle of habit and public opinion in securing conformity, and one suspects that it was largely such factors that Rivers and Hartland, for example, had in mind when referring to the dominant sway of custom. Malinowski himself recognized their validity when he wrote: 'The force of habit, the awe of traditional command and a sentimental attachment to it, the desire to satisfy public opinion—all combine to make custom be obeyed for its own sake' (1926b, p. 52). And again: 'The Melanesian of the region here treated has unquestionably the greatest respect for his tribal custom and tradition as such. . . . All the rules of his tribe, trivial or important, pleasant or irksome, moral or utilitarian, are regarded by him with reverence and felt to be obligatory' (pp. 64 f.). Isolated from their context, such passages read very much like some of those that led him to denounce what he called 'the dogma of the automatic submission to custom' (p. 14).

'But', he continues, 'love of tradition, conformism and the sway of custom account but to a very partial extent for obedience to rules' (1926b, p. 52, cf. p. 65); and he asks if it is not contrary to human nature for people, whether civilized or savage, to accept any constraint as a matter of course and without being compelled by some irresistible force or motive (p. 10). This problem was also visualized by some of the writers whom he criticizes. But, confronted with the lack of central authority and organized judicial institutions in many primitive societies, they sought the answer in supernatural control and intervention. Hobhouse, for example, held that 'in the lowest grades of ethical thought the sanction of conduct is found in taboos and other magical terrors or in the fear of vindictive and resentful spirits' (1915, p. 624).[1] So, too, MacIver wrote that the customary observances of primitive peoples 'are guarded by rigorous sanctions, and the dreadful powers of a misknown universe jealously attend their violation. If the community punishes the offender against custom, it is often to avert the less discriminate interposition of these formidable guardians of the social way. The acts which are forbidden are even more numerous than those which are enjoined, and taboo is the invariable concomitant of custom' (1926, p. 37).

[1] Cf. pp. 61n., 419 ff. Tylor, on the other hand, said that among primitive peoples 'religion . . . has not the strong moral influence it exerts among higher nations; indeed their behaviour to their fellows is little affected by divine command or fear of divine punishment' (1881, p. 407).

To views such as these Malinowski rightly replies that 'primitive law does not consist exclusively or even chiefly of negative sanctions' (1926b, p. 56), nor is it merely through fear of punishment, whether human or supernatural, that people observe the social norms (pp. 15, 56). On the contrary, life in a primitive community involves every individual in specific obligations to others, who in turn are similarly duty-bound to him. Those obligations he fulfils partly because of early training, and partly because of public opinion and self-interest: it pays him in various ways to do as he should, and if he does not he suffers loss of material benefit and of social esteem.

In emphasizing that there are always such positive inducements to carry out one's duties, and that they are more effective than the threat of punishment by force, Malinowski has unquestionably shown more adequately than any of his predecessors what are the reasons underlying the observance of 'law and order' in primitive society. Roscoe Pound, indeed, refers to his conception of 'binding obligations' as a 'fruitful and significant' contribution to the theory of social control (1936, p. xxxiv). But not everybody has been converted to this view. Simpson and Stone, for example, write categorically: 'Despite the recent challenge of Malinowski the orthodox explanation of the effectiveness of social control in a kin-organized society still seems the most satisfactory. The pressure of a body of custom sanctified by a belief in its supernatural origin points to social opinion and the fear of the gods as the two major weapons in the armory of rudimentary social control' (1948, p. 3). And Kelsen, who seems unaware of Malinowski's work, also continues to maintain that 'fear of the revenge of the spirits' is chiefly responsible for the preservation of 'social order' in primitive society (1945, p. 18).

Malinowski tried also to dispel the old idea that violations of social norms are much less frequent in primitive societies than in civilized. He quotes statements by Hartland and Lowie contending that the savage 'never seeks to break forth' from the fetters of custom but submits to them with unquestioning obedience (1926b, pp. 10, 13). To these he might have added what Marett says: 'One reason why it is hard to find any law in primitive society is because, in a general way of speaking, no one dreams of breaking the social rules' (1912, pp. 182 f.). As Malinowski mentions, the writers holding such views have to concede that the savage does in fact sometimes break the law—which is why they are able to dilate upon self-help, vendetta, and other forms of punitive sanction. But what they did not observe, and what he himself illustrates convincingly, is that even 'under the normal conditions', when the law 'is followed and not defied', observance of social norms 'is at best partial, conditional, and subject to evasions' (1926b, p. 15). If the native can do so without loss of prestige or prospective loss of gain, and if it offers him some immediate personal advantage, he will often try to evade his obligations, 'exactly as a civilized business man would do' (p. 30). In this connection, incidentally, Malinowski shows also that even supernatural sanctions, such as those attaching to breach of taboo, can be averted by special forms of magical antidote (pp. 80 ff.) —which in itself indicates that fear of those sanctions is not always effective.

This brings us to another of his main contributions: his insistence that the field-worker should not merely ascertain what the rules of custom are, but should also study by direct observation 'the ways and means' by which they are carried out and how 'they function in actual life' (1926b, p. 125). The use of case-histories to supplement and illustrate formal statement of rules had already been recommended by Hobhouse (1912, p. 176), and was a distinctive and valuable feature of Barton's work on Ifugao law. But where Malinowski advanced on his predecessors was in stressing that legal rules should be studied 'in their effective influence on human behaviour' (1934a, p. xliii) and as part of the general process of social control; and he showed how such an approach would lead to the investigation of problems that are usually neglected, such as the psychological and social inducements to conformity, the 'elasticity' of rules, and the reasons why they vary so much in the sanctions supporting them (pp. lxi ff.). As outlined in one of his latest works, his general conception of social control (1944, pp. 128 f.) provides an admirable guide to research in the field: 'In every community there are to be found means and ways by which the members become cognizant of their prerogatives and duties; there are impelling reasons and mechanisms which keep each individual to the by-and-large performance of his duty, and thus also to the adequate satisfaction of his privilege; and finally, in case of deviation or breach, there are some means for the re-establishment of order and the satisfaction of unfulfilled claims.'

(iii)

Malinowski's influence upon the study of primitive law can most readily be seen from even a casual survey of the relevant literature immediately preceding and following his main writings on the subject— by contrasting, for example, the fourth edition of *Notes and Queries on Anthropology* (1912) with the fifth (1929), Hartland's *Primitive Law* (1924) with Diamond's book of the same title (1935), Lowie's 'Anthropology and Law' (1927) with Cairns's 'Law and Anthropology' (1931), and Lowie's chapter on 'Justice' in his *Primitive Society* (1920) with that on 'Law' in his *Social Organization* (1948). Instead of concentrating mainly on formal description of norms, sanctions, and procedure in cases of breach, the more recent publications also discuss such topics as the nature and functions of law, psychological and other grounds of obedience, the relationship of law to other social institutions and its place in the scheme of culture generally, and the distinction between primitive and civilized systems of law.

It cannot be claimed that Malinowski alone is responsible for the more dynamic approach to problems of law and other aspects of social control that is nowadays characteristic of anthropology. But it seems true to say that he initiated and stimulated the trend reflected in such books as Llewellyn and Hoebel's *The Cheyenne Way* (1941) and Gluckman's *The Judicial Process among the Barotse* (1955), both exemplifying a far greater preoccupation with theoretical issues than is to be found, for example, in such earlier classics as Barton's (1919) or Gutmann's (1926). His work has also influenced the writings of such non-anthropologists as Cairns, Diamond, Hankins, MacIver, Paton, Robson, Seagle, and Timasheff, all of whom use him as a basic source; and, as already mentioned, they give him credit for demolishing the old idea that primitive man is the slave of custom, and for showing that rules of conduct in primitive society are by no means all of the same character.

But with a few exceptions, notably Robson (1935, pp. 12 ff., 303 f.), jurists and sociologists are unwilling to accept his general conception of law.[1] The reason is not far to seek. In the advanced societies with which they are primarily concerned, law is clearly distinguished from all other rules of conduct; and although it has been defined in many different ways, stress is usually placed upon enforcement by some recognized authority or specific mechanism (such as courts of law).[2] As Malinowski himself mentions (1934a, p. xxi), some African and Indonesian societies also have specialized legal institutions of a similar kind. But, on the other hand, there are likewise very many primitive societies that are devoid of 'codes, courts, and constabulary' (to quote an alliterative phrase that he often used). We must accordingly adopt one of three points of view: (*a*) such societies do not have law; (*b*) law among them is something different from law in advanced societies; or (*c*) the definition of law commonly used in regard to advanced societies is inadequate and should be extended.

Defining political organization as 'the use of direct force by individuals in authority over the other members of the group', Malinowski is prepared to believe that among certain primitive peoples it does not exist (1944, pp. 61, 130). But that he will not do in regard to law. Criticizing Radcliffe-Brown he says: 'If we have to deny the existence of law to many, perhaps most primitive communities; if we have to give up our concept of civil and criminal law and substitute specific terms such as "public and private delicts"; if we assume that primitive law

---

[1] Reference may be made in this context to Seagle's criticism (1937).

[2] That (or some variant thereof) is the basic criterion recognized by such writers as Diamond, Hankins, MacIver, Paton, Seagle, and Timasheff, and responsible for their rejection of Malinowski. I am of course aware that it is not universally accepted in modern jurisprudence.

functions by an entirely different social mechanism from our own—we obviously assert a complete breach of continuity between the working of primitive institutions from the legal point of view and the working of our law' (1934a, pp. xxviii f.).

He thus rejects the first two of the three alternatives mentioned above. His own basic definition of law, in *Crime and Custom*, is as follows: 'The rules of law stand out from the rest in that they are felt and regarded as the obligations of one person and the rightful claims of another' (p. 55). If applied to advanced societies, this definition, as Timasheff observes (1939, pp. 277 f.), would cover not only 'law' as known in those societies, 'but also large parts of nonlegal social regulation endowed with comparatively strong sanctions' (such as 'rules of politeness' and the now obsolete duelling code). And it would still leave us with the necessity of showing why some of the rules to which it refers are enforced by special institutions whereas others are not. Nevertheless, if for the moment we ignore that problem, the definition does delimit a field of human conduct that can be distinguished everywhere from, say, rules of craftsmanship or religious observance. It is also consistent with, though more precise than, some of the broader definitions of law, such as that given in the *Shorter Oxford English Dictionary* ('the body of rules, whether formally enacted or customary, which a state or community recognizes as binding on its members or subjects'), or implied in the following quotation from Allen (1951, p. 63): 'In many societies of which we have evidence, before any clearly articulated system of law-making and law-dispensing has developed, the conduct of men in society is governed by customary rules. To call these *legal* rules is something of an anachronism, for in very many cases they are equally rules of religion and morality, which, at this early stage, have not become distinguished from law; but they are "legal" in the sense which is nowadays attached to that term, inasmuch as they are binding and obligatory rules of conduct (not merely of faith and conviction), and that the breach of them is a breach of positive *duty*.'

But we cannot as readily accept Malinowski's equation of 'civil' and 'criminal' law respectively with 'the law obeyed' and 'the law broken' (1926b, p. 73)—an equation originally made in the Mailu monograph and reflected again in 'Law (3)' and 'Law (4)' of the Yale article (1942a). In drawing this distinction, which is certainly not what is meant by civil and criminal law in modern systems, he violated his own plea that we should not differentiate between 'primitive legal institutions' and 'our law'. Nor does he adhere to it consistently. He tells us that legal rules, unlike all others, 'are kept in force by a specific mechanism of reciprocity and publicity' (1926b, pp. 58, 55); but he says also that when 'binding obligations' are not fulfilled the penalty is social disesteem and loss of return services, whereas the sanction for crimes is 'tribal punishment'. In other words, 'civil law' now becomes not only 'the law obeyed' but also 'the law broken' and penalized by the sanction of reciprocity, and 'criminal law' is restricted to 'the law broken' and penalized by sanctions of various other kinds, such as sorcery, self-help, vendetta, and taboo. What Malinowski was trying to do is clear enough: he wanted to show that people fulfil obligations because thereby they benefit socially and materially; he wanted to show also that breach of duty sometimes entails loss of benefits and sometimes more direct punishment. But he introduced needless confusion by the peculiar sense in which he used the term 'civil law', and by his failure to specify precisely which rules are sanctioned by reciprocity and which by physical or mystical penalties.

That he was not wholly satisfied with his treatment of law in *Crime and Custom* is suggested by the later developments of this theory. In his Introduction to the book by Hogbin he implicitly abandons the attempt to isolate law from all other rules of conduct. Instead, he now speaks merely of 'neutral custom', which no one wishes to break, and 'valid, sanctioned custom', where temptation is always present. The same distinction is reflected in 'Law (2)' and 'Law (3)' of the Yale article (1942a). Once again it is not original; it was, for example, made more neatly and precisely in 1921 by Ginsberg, who spoke of usage, 'those actions habitual to members of a community, which do not possess normative character or lack the sanction of moral constraint', and custom, which is 'not merely a prevailing habit of action or behaviour, but implies a judgment upon action or behaviour . . . Custom, in other words is *sanctioned* usage' (pp. 106 ff.). In *Freedom and Civilization* Malinowski goes further, and explicitly classes together law and 'all the rules of morals, manner, etiquette, ceremonial, and custom' (1947, p. 175). He thus departs from the principle, originally advocated in his Australian book, that 'norms and regulations' can and must be distinguished 'according to the kind of sanctions they enjoy', and in effect associates himself with those whom in *Crime and Custom* he castigated for speaking of the 'amorphous mass of tribal usage or "cake of custom" ' (1926b, p. 66).

Modern anthropologists have also tended to differ from Malinowski in their conception of law.[1] Some of those working in societies with constituted judicial institutions restrict the term either to 'any rule of conduct likely to be enforced by the courts' or to 'the whole reservoir of rules . . . on which the judges draw for their decisions'.[2] Wider definitions have been suggested by others, to include societies lacking courts or similar specialized agencies of enforcement. Radcliffe-Brown (1952, pp. 208, 212), adopting Pound's definition ('social control through

[1] Reference may be made in this context to the chapter on 'The Trobriand Islanders: Primitive Law as seen by Bronislaw Malinowski' in E. A. Hoebel (1954), pp. 177-210.
[2] I. Schapera (1938), p. 38; M. Gluckman (1955), p. 164.

the systematic application of the force of politically organized society'), speaks of sanctions as legal 'when they are imposed by a constituted authority, political, military or ecclesiastic', and adds that 'The obligations imposed on individuals in societies where there are no legal sanctions will be regarded as matters of custom or convention, but not of law.' Nadel does not insist upon sanctions 'ordered or executed by an authoritative body', but says that we can speak of law where 'social constraint' implies the use of force 'with the authority of public consent', and that 'where force is absent from the sanction, we have custom' (1947, p. 500). Hoebel, again, says that 'A social norm is legal if its neglect or infraction is regularly met, in threat or fact, by the application of physical force by an individual or group possessing the socially recognized privilege of so acting' (1954, p. 28).

Although differing in detail the definitions just quoted all agree, in contrast with Malinowski, that the essential characteristic of 'law' is socially approved use of force. The same conception is stressed in definitions given in some recent general textbooks of anthropology.[1] The implication is that Malinowski's definition, in *Crime and Custom*, is not on the whole acceptable to his colleagues. He himself, as already mentioned, adopted 'social enforcement' as the distinctive criterion of law when discussing the Australian aborigines, and reverted to it in *Freedom and Civilization*. One cannot help thinking that had he adhered to it when writing about the Trobriand islanders he would have avoided some of the confusion into which he fell. He might then have regarded self-help, vendetta, payment of 'blood-money', the chief's penal powers, and the punitive applications of sorcery, as specifically legal sanctions, taboo as a ritual sanction, etc.; and reciprocity would have been classed, like public opinion, among the various sanctions enforcing what in the Australian book he called 'customary rules' (which, indeed, is the rôle assigned to it by such writers as Diamond and MacIver). But in his anxiety to emphasize 'positive inducements' to conformity he failed to do justice to the significant fact that even among the Trobrianders there is 'socially approved use of force', and hence he did not sufficiently distinguish from all others the rules to which this particular sanction applies.

Malinowski may have been mistaken (though, if so, he erred in good company) in using the term 'law' for all types of binding obligation, regardless of their sanction; he may have given us an unbalanced and inadequate account of the Trobriand reaction to crime; and he certainly cannot be upheld in the distinction that he makes between civil and criminal law. But anthropologists, even if they disagree with his views on such matters, have learned much from his general approach to the study of law and from his contention that the basic problem is social

[1] Cf. Lowie (1948), p. 156; M. J. Herskovits (1948), p. 345; M. Titiev (1954), p. 390.

control generally. As Hoebel says, 'Malinowski's positive contribution to the theory of law has been in his vigorous insistence on law as an aspect of society and culture at large and on the occurrence of gaps between the ideal and the actual norm of law. He broke the crust of legal formalism in anthropology and gave a new impetus to the anthropology of law. For this service social science is in his debt' (1954, p. 208).

Malinowski and the Study of Kinship[1]

MEYER FORTES

IT is impossible for anyone who was a pupil of Malinowski to write about his work quite impersonally. One has to be able to visualize the histrionic, not to say the exhibitionistic, streak in him to understand the tone of some of his later books. It arose from his view of himself as the leader of a revolutionary movement in anthropology; and such was his magnetism, his wit and his virtuosity that he made us, his pupils, fall in eagerly with that view. This happened in spite of his sometimes offensive prejudices and his impatience of criticism; for he was basically right. But it warped his work. He could not shake off the compulsion to present his theories and his ethnographic discoveries in the form of an assault on the *ancien régime*. It drove him to wrap up some of his most original ideas and observations in laboured paradoxes and prolix repetition. *Coral Gardens* (1935) illustrates this. I mention it in particular because the typescript was discussed, page by page, in the seminar of 1932–3 of which I was a member. As the Preface implies, Malinowski regarded it as the *Summa Ethnographica* of the Trobrianders and, almost by corollary, as the best example of functionalism in action. Malinowski did indeed strain himself and his seminar to make it such an example; and that is perhaps why it shows up so well the blind spots due to his preoccupation with his war against obsolete theories and imputed opposition.

Not surprisingly, this came into almost everything Malinowski wrote on kinship; for kinship is a subject that bristles with temptations for the anthropologist who feels strongly about slipshod thinking and well-rooted fallacies. Even today Morgan's preposterous scheme of the evolution of the family through the stages of promiscuity, group marriage, matriarchy and patriarchy, is still accepted as a sociological law, and not only in the U.S.S.R. Though no reputable anthropologist in

[1] I am indebted to Professor Raymond Firth and to Mrs. B. Z. Seligman for helpful suggestions in the course of writing this paper; and to the Behavioral Sciences Division of the Ford Foundation for a grant which provided research assistance for its preparation.

this country or America now accepts it, non-anthropological scholars do. One recent example is that of a distinguished classical scholar's reconstruction of pre-Aegean Greek social organization on the basis of Morgan's and Engels's theories (Thomson, 1949). Another example is the following statement by one of the most eminent biologists and sinologists of this century, Joseph Needham, writing about Chinese social organization in Shang times: 'Matriarchal traces, noted by many authorities, seem to give place during this period to a rigidly patriarchal society' (1954, p. 85).

For Malinowski and his contemporaries who agreed with him, these temptations were much stronger than for us, their heirs. They were brought up on the Matriarchal Controversy; and the pseudo-historical and pseudo-psychological theories of classificatory kinship, incest, totemic descent and so forth which have now been relegated to the limbo of historical curiosities as a result of their exposure by Malinowski and Radcliffe-Brown, had powerful support as late as the nineteen-thirties. One of the worst offenders was Sir James Frazer.

Malinowski's training in sociology and anthropology was completed under Westermarck's direction and this set the pattern of his interests in the field of kinship for the rest of his life. It also involved him in the controversies of the turn of the century when scholars were still vehemently debating whether the family or the clan came first in man's cultural evolution, and whether 'group marriage' could be demonstrated from Australian sex customs. Malinowski accepted the theory put forward with such massive documentation by Westermarck that the individual family is a universal feature of human life and is also prior to the clan in the historical sense. His first book, *The Family Among the Australian Aborigines* (1913a), was a notable, contribution on Wester-marck's side. He often recurred to the absurdity of the 'group marriage' theory as an instance of how misleading it can be to ignore the total institutional setting of marriage and sex. But he might well have thrown aside these and related controversies in his Trobriand studies if it had not been for W. H. R. Rivers and what he stood for in British anthro-pology.

As the founder of field research on primitive kinship, Rivers still deserves our homage. He was at the height of his fame and influence during the very years when Malinowski was carrying out his field-work in the Trobriand islands and was publishing his first results. It is a sign, both of Rivers's standing, and of the state of British anthropology up to the time of the publication of *The Argonauts of the Western Pacific* (1922a), that Rivers was awarded the Gold Medal of the Royal Society in 1915, mainly for *The History of Melanesian Society* (1914). This monument of bizarre logic and misunderstood ethnology showed, however, that Rivers was incapable of thinking sociologically about kinship even though he advocated what seemed to be a sociological theory of the subject. In his early contributions to the *Reports of the Torres Straits Expedition* (1904), in his remarkable field report on *The Todas* (1906), and in his lectures on *Kinship and Social Organization* (1913) which Malinowski attended before he went to the Pacific, Rivers purported to be seeking for the 'social conditions' that, in his view, 'determine' 'kinship systems', that is, systems of relationship terminology. In fact, the 'social conditions' he invoked, in the first place, were speculative rules of marriage supposed to have prevailed in the past; and his shrewd field observations of kinship custom were often twisted to fit his conjectures. The basic assumption was one that went back to Morgan, who considered kinship terminologies to be fossil relics of earlier stages of social organization; and not even Radcliffe-Brown's cogent persuasions (1952, p. 51) moved Rivers from his position. Taking relationship terminologies as his primary data he sought in them evidence of determination of kinship relationships by obsolete marriage rules. The much discussed classificatory nomenclature he was ready to explain as relics of an earlier stage of sexual communism. He had critics but they differed from him only in what they read into the terminologies.

What Rivers stood for accounts for much of Malinowski's over-emphasis on the 'biographical method' and especially for the scorn he poured on 'kinship algebra'. He probably felt the more strongly in these matters just because Rivers was regarded as an authority on Melanesian social organization. And it went deeper than a disagreement over a point of theory. Kinship terminologies were usually quoted by him as instances of what he contemptuously called linguistic 'collectioneering'. His pragmatic theory of language with its exaggeration of the instrumental meaning of words, and his 'conditioning' model of language learning, were in part a reaction against the prevailing obsession with kinship terminology.[1]

Malinowski was much given to paradox in order to bring out the point of an argument. In his later analysis of the relation between language and culture (1935, Vol. II) he writes almost as if he sees an antithesis between 'language' as a mere tissue of words, and 'culture' as the tangible 'reality' of social life. This is, however, only a special instance of an ingrained mode of thought in Malinowski's work. He claimed that functionalism was a '. . . theory which, begun in field-work, leads back to field-work again' (1932a, p. xxix) and by field-work he meant observation of '. . . what exists . . . how it works, and what it means to the natives' (ibid., xxxi), in contrast to the hypotheses built on hearsay and on statements from informants.

This general approach was the basis of *Crime and Custom* (1926b) where it is most forcefully expounded by reference to a problem of

---

[1] See, for example, Malinowski, 1935, Vol. II, pp. 65 ff., where he goes out of his way to ridicule 'the assumption that language simply mirrors reality' and specifically cites Rivers.

kinship, the Trobriand law of exogamy. What Malinowski tried to drive home—and this is a recurrent theme in the book—is the discrepancy between 'the ideal of native law' and the 'application of morality and ideals to *real life*' (1926*b*, pp. 79, 120—my italics). Analogously, as he repeatedly claimed, the 'ill-omened kinship nomenclatures' (1932*a*, p. xx) only made sense when seen in the contexts of speech, act and feeling, that is, the context of 'reality'.

This dichotomy between the 'ideal' and the 'real', between native 'theory' and 'practice', has, overtly or implicitly, played a large part in the work of Malinowski's followers and successors. It has stimulated ethnographic discoveries of very great importance, but has also given rise to some theoretical misunderstandings. For Malinowski himself it went back a long way in his thinking. It is foreshadowed in *The Family among the Australian Aborigines* (1913*a*) both in the kind of questions asked about the 'actual' conduct of husbands and wives or parents and children, to one another, and in the method of getting at the facts by confronting ethnologists' interpretations with statements about the actual habits and practices of Australian aborigines made by travellers and other observers. Here, for example, is the list of questions he wants answered in order to discuss the relations of parents and children: 'Is there between parents and children any kind of affection? What is the general character of the treatment of children by parents? Are rudiments of education given by father or mother to offspring? . . .' etc. Verbal statements by missionaries or even by native informants cannot answer such questions. Only direct observation in the field can do so.

My point is not that Malinowski insisted on field observation as the only reliable source of ethnographic data. Haddon, Seligman and others had proclaimed this before Malinowski went to the Trobriand islands and, indeed, it was because of this belief that Seligman found the ways and means for Malinowski's field-work. What is significant is the emphasis on *practice* (the activity; the behaviour; the concrete mutual services; the exhibited self-interest, ambition, and vanity; the facts of mother love and paternal affection; in short the actions and feelings and thoughts of individuals in social situations, as directly observed by the ethnographer and as admitted by the actors) as the 'reality' of social life, as against '*ideal*', or '*theory*', the merely verbal formulation.

Malinowski was, of course, not alone in this way of thinking. The precursors of modern billiard-ball sociology[1] held similar views, only in more extreme forms. But his vigorous and brilliant propagation of

---

[1] By this I mean the kind of sociology that seeks to derive social systems and institutions deductively from the 'interactions' of individuals who are visualized as devoid of biography and therefore of social experience with its implication of custom-bound behaviour. Given the 'particles' all that is needed is to posit a biologically endowed learning process motivated by inborn drives and arising in the 'interaction' context in order to derive the social system.

the idea had a direct influence on anthropologists and that is what concerns us here. In Malinowski's case it arose in part from the conditions of his field-work in the Trobriands; but it gained inspiration also from his interest in and study of the new psychologies of the nineteen-twenties. First Shand's theory of the sentiments, then psycho-analysis, and finally behaviourism[1] were the dominant influences. This is easy to understand. For what these theories stressed in common was the supremacy of the emotional and instinctive dispositions and tendencies in the human make-up and the unreliability, if not impossibility, of knowing them through introspection and reasoning.

Psycho-analysis (to which he was introduced by Seligman) was the critical influence on Malinowski's thought after his return from the Trobriands. Now the most obvious lesson of psycho-analysis is that there is a large hiatus between the declared (conscious) motives and affections of men and their deep-lying (unconscious) 'real' wishes and feelings. Furthermore, it shows that antagonistic feelings can co-exist in the same person though he may not be conscious of this. Malinowski's stock dramatization of the conflict between 'the main principle of law, Mother-right, and one of the strongest sentiments, paternal love', is the translation into ethnographic description of the Freudian concept of ambivalence. The 'reality of actual life' in which the father is attached to his son rather than to his nephew, is opposed to the 'legal' status of being not his son's kinsman—almost as if 'legal' here was identical with the conscious fictions with which repressed motives are covered up, according to psycho-analysis.

Malinowski no doubt wrote in this way partly for effect. Yet his insistence on the test of 'reality' was a salutary rule in his pupils' field-work. It demanded a thorough mastery of the native language; and this needed time and patience. The excellence of British ethnographic field-work since Malinowski set the standard and laid down the methods is due chiefly to his insistence on 'concrete' data. And yet it is by trying to satisfy this demand that the sociological untenability of Malinowski's dichotomy has been made apparent.

In almost every publication on the Trobriand Islanders from *Baloma* to *Coral Gardens*, Malinowski gave notice of a forthcoming book on kinship, several times significantly announced with the title of THE PSYCHOLOGY OF KINSHIP (e.g. 1932a, p. 434). Why was this book never completed?

It may be because Malinowski had said all he had to say about kinship in other publications and had nothing new to add. None of the major Trobriand works covers every aspect of kinship, in the way, say, that Firth's *We, The Tikopia* (1936) does. But kinship figures in every one

[1] Cf. the remark (Malinowski, 1935, Vol. II, p. 236): 'In one way the whole substance of my theory of culture . . . consists in reducing Durkheimian theory to terms of Behaviouristic psychology.'

of them, and not merely incidentally. It forms the true, though much concealed, framework of all except *The Argonauts* (1922a). This alone would provide a substantial first-hand documentation on Malinowski's theories of kinship. But in addition we have the series of articles on the family and kinship[1] in which his ideas are explicitly and occasionally aggressively presented; and it is clear from them that his theoretical views on kinship remained basically the same from 1922 till the end. But I do not believe that Malinowski would have been restrained from bringing out his book on kinship by the thought that he had nothing new to add. He was, in fact, rather given to repetition, the same hypotheses and even the same handful of dramatic cases being used over and over again.

I suggest that Malinowski could not write this book because his theoretical premises ran counter to those on which any analytical study of a kinship system or kinship in general must be based. In other words, the obstacle was Malinowski's concept of kinship as 'the facts of sexuality, marriage, family and clanship' inter-related in 'one integral institution—the Procreative Institution of Mankind'.[2] The prerequisites for an analytic study of kinship, that is, one which treats of kinship in its own right, have been familiar for thirty years. Indeed they go back to Rivers and Morgan. They require the isolation of kinship as 'genealogical relationship recognised for social purposes' to quote the simple formula used by Radcliffe-Brown (1929, p. 50). This means seeing kinship as part of the total social organization or social structure which holds a society together. It means defining social organization as a system of social relations, arising out of the modes of ordering and arranging the members of a society in all their activities and therefore common to—cutting across—the 'procreative', 'nutritional', 'recreational', 'educational', etc., etc., institutions to which Malinowski gave the name of functional aspects. These premises are the very opposite of those on which Malinowski's need-centred concept of a Procreative Institution parallel to a Nutritional Institution or an Educational Institution rest.

The theoretical divergence, epitomized in the conceptual distinction we now make between the social structure and the total body of traditional custom and usage to which the label of culture is usually attached, was once brought home to me by Malinowski himself. He was discussing with me my field-work plans and we got on to the subject of totemism.

---

[1] Notably, the articles on 'Kinship' and 'Marriage' in the *Encyclopaedia Britannica*, 14th edn., 1929; 'Kinship', *Man*, 1930, no. 17; 'Parenthood the Basis of Social Structure' in Calverton and Schmalhausen, *The New Generation*, 1930. Kinship is also considered in the Introduction to H. I. Hogbin's *Law and Order in Polynesia*, 1934, and in the lively Foreword to M. F. Ashley-Montagu's *Coming into Being Among the Australian Aborigines*, 1937.

[2] I am quoting from the article 'Parenthood the Basis of Social Structure' but the same words were repeatedly used by Malinowski.

Comparing his own views with those of Radcliffe-Brown, he said, 'The difference is that I am a functionalist, and Radcliffe-Brown is a structuralist.' Better evidence of his attitude is the tart, if somewhat oblique, rebuff in his Preface to Raymond Firth's *We, The Tikopia*, to the criticism of the 'biographical method' implied in Firth's approach to kinship. Firth's main point (pp. 117–21), demonstrated by his meticulous examination of Tikopia social life department by department, is that there is a common 'institutional map', a 'kinship structure' that can be extracted and seen as the common 'articulating' framework for all the different 'contextual situations' of residence, farming, fishing, marriage, ritual, etc. The 'biographical approach', he says, is concerned with a special problem that *presupposes* a kinship system. Hence the 'biographical' explanation of the 'extension' of kinship terminologies outside the individual family is not tenable; for kinship terms are not merely metaphors indicative of extensions of sentiment but correspond to 'codified obligations' and to modes of 'social regulation' as seen, for instance, in the 'representative status' of members of units that are 'fundamental to the particular social structure' (p. 268).

This is an analytical theory of kinship. 'Kinship behaviour and not kinship sentiment is the study of the anthropologist', says Firth (p. 576), thus explicitly rejecting a psychological starting-point. In parenthesis, he also rejects the interpretation of social institutions, 'in terms of basic human needs'. No doubt that is why Malinowski makes a point of restating his main convictions in the Preface.

I have referred to Firth's book because it was the first to confront Malinowski with field data fully measuring up to his own standards and aimed at testing his kinship theories. It helped, also, to make clear to those of Malinowski's pupils who were just embarking on research in the field the meaning of social organization as the analytically distinct framework of all customary action and belief, in contrast to Malinowski's concept of social organization as merely the 'personnel' of an institution tied to a 'material apparatus' used in fulfilling basic needs in accordance with a 'charter' and 'rules'.[1]

In pointing out the blind spots in Malinowski's view of kinship institutions, I want to make it clear that there were good reasons for them in the beginning. As Radcliffe-Brown had said (1929, p. 53), there was then a 'really important conflict . . . between conjectural history on the one side and the functional study of society on the other'. Functional ethnography, in this context, had to emphasize the descriptive reality of primitive social life, as for instance in the observable concatenation of sexual motives and customs with courtship, marriage, family arrangements, local grouping, work, magic and chiefship to

[1] An excellent summary and evaluation of Malinowski's concept of the Institution is given in R. Piddington's *Introduction to Social Anthropology*, Vol. I, chap. VI, sect. 6.

which Malinowski devoted his superb gifts of exposition. Malinowski's interest in psychological theories fitted naturally into his descriptive aims and corresponded to his intuitive understanding of individual motive and attitude. Functional theory as developed by him is an impressive attempt to provide what he would have called a 'charter' and a systematic procedure for the kind of field research and ethnographic reporting of which he was the unrivalled master.

No better technique has yet been devised for monographic studies, and we, Malinowski's pupils, have done no more than follow the patterns he established. But Malinowski's conceptual scheme does not give to social organization a generalized character and a systematic coherence of a different order from that of custom, habit and motive. The facts of social relationship and social grouping are, in this scheme, merely facts of custom and motive broadly on a par with, for instance, magical beliefs, and springing in the last resort from such universal human instincts as those of parenthood or such common human sentiments as vanity and ambition. So we have nowhere a connected analysis of Trobriand local organization, kinship, and political structure as an analytically separable framework of social life, though the facts, or at least the bulk of them, are given piecemeal where they are needed as the indispensable bones and joints on which to hang the flesh and blood of his descriptions. This justifies my guess as to what stopped him from finishing the promised book on kinship.

In sum, what is inadequately stressed by Malinowski is that kinship relations have to be seen as a system, within the framework of the total social structure. Their fundamentally juridical nature then emerges, as Rivers appreciated. This is specially relevant to the Trobriands where rank and residence rules directly affect conduct in kinship. Questions of right and duty are, however, secondary to emotion and sentiment in Malinowski's analysis of these data. This follows from his psychological approach; it is consistent with the opposition he made between 'ideals' and 'laws' on the one hand and the 'reality' of action and motive on the other. 'The unity of the clan', he says (1926b, p. 119), after a vivid summary of the expression of this unity in rules of vendetta and mourning, exogamy and food distribution, 'is a legal fiction in that it demands . . . an absolute subordination of all other interests and ties to the claims of clan solidarity, while, in fact, this solidarity is almost constantly sinned against and practically non-existent in the daily run of ordinary life'. It is not only a question of individual loves, hates and self-interest undermining 'the law' but of a mysterious force called 'customary usage' which 'seconds' the free and affectionate generosity of father to son and thus 'defies' and 'circumvents' the 'rigid matrilineal law' of avuncular obligation to the sister's son (cf. 1935, Vol. I, p. 205). The same kind of inference is drawn in connection with every facet of kinship that appears in the Trobriand works. And the important thing is that it is the alleged defiance of solidarity, the purported circumvention of the law that is held up as being more 'real', certainly more authentically due to kinship, than the formal rules. If this were not a matter of theoretical principle with Malinowski one would almost be inclined to accuse him of *suggestio falsi* in these statements for, as we shall see, it is easy to show from his own field material that his emphasis is distorted. What he is doing is to turn the facts inside out, so to speak. This is most obvious in his handling of the odious subject of kinship nomenclatures, to which I will return later.

If it is easy to criticize Malinowski in retrospect, it is just because he towers so high. The faults and failings, which we have learnt to avoid by studying him, loom far larger than in lesser men. To criticize his treatment of kinship is not to deny the brilliance and originality of some of his discoveries in this field, or to disparage the inspiration his work gave to others. Indeed, I would maintain that Malinowski's most productive hypotheses are concerned with problems of kinship and social organization in the jural sense, and not, as he claimed, with questions of motive and of the meaning of custom in the psychological sense. This may seem inconsistent with my criticism of him but it is not really so. We must remember that his training in sociology was on the literature of Australian family and kinship organization and that the Trobriand discoveries which most startled the anthropological world were his revelations of matrilineal family relations in action. Even without his initial interest he would have found that it was impossible to present his descriptive data in an orderly way without considerable attention to the kinship framework. Among these productive ideas I would include: the analysis of the sociological consequences of native notions of procreation; the concept of the Initial Situation; the Principle of Legitimacy; the theory of the incest taboo; and the concept of the 'splitting' of the paternal rôles between mother's brother and father. These are due, in large part, to the stimulus of psycho-analysis as Evans-Pritchard pointed out in an appreciative article (1929). But it is very interesting to see that Malinowski's response to psycho-analysis had roots going back to his Australian book. Almost all the kinship problems to which he repeatedly returned in his Trobriand books, and his theoretical articles, too, are foreshadowed there. He himself drew attention to this in one of his most pungent and concentrated early statements of his kinship theory (1930*b*).

Kinship, for Malinowski, all through his career, was not merely focused in the 'individual family'; it was nothing but the individual family, considered either from within, or as the source of the 'extensions' that in his theory account wholly for extra-familial genealogically ordered relationships. This point of view was firmly established in the Australian book. In a review, which described the book as 'by far the best example in English of scientific method dealing with descriptions of the customs and institutions of a savage people', Radcliffe-Brown (1914) drew attention to the consequences of subordinating everything to the family. 'The Australian notions relating to kinship', he said, 'cannot be studied without reference to what the author calls "group relationships" . . . the relationship systems, classes, and clans. . . .' This difference of orientation at that date was, it seems, prophetic, if we think of the later contrast between Malinowski's notion of the Procreative Institution and Radcliffe-Brown's concept of a Kinship System. As we know, at the very time that Malinowski was working on his vindication of the individual Australian family as the 'basis of their social structure', Radcliffe Brown (1913) was in the field investigating those aspects of Australian kinship institutions that Malinowski considered to be of secondary importance.

Malinowski's book demolished the theories of primitive promiscuity, group marriage, and clan priority. But far more important was his contention that all the economic, social, legal, and ritual customs and practices of the Australians converge on the nodal point of the family organization; and, partly because it began as a move in opposition to group marriage, etc., the emphasis is on the 'actual working' of the family in terms of the individual relationships of its members.

Instead of discoursing on marriage classes and clans, he deals at length with the economic, sexual, and affectional relationships of spouses, insisting particularly on the 'individual appropriation' of the wife by the husband. He soon comes up against the controversy that was destined to be one of his main theoretical preoccupations thereafter. This is the problem arising out of Spencer and Gillen's researches, of whether or not the Australians have a knowledge of the physiological function of the male in procreation. After minutely studying the evidence he concludes that they do not, over most of Australia, and he argues that this is as might be expected from their general ignorance of natural science. This leads him to expound what later became the important distinction between physiological paternity and social father-hood. The reader gets a foretaste of the later Malinowski at his best in the analysis of the sociological significance of incarnation beliefs. These are shown to imply a pre-existing kinship relation of every child with its parents, and to fit in with ignorance of the physiology of repro-duction. 'Consanguinity (as a sociological concept)', he says, 'is there-fore not the physiological bond of common blood; it is the social acknowledgement and interpretation of it' (1913a, p. 182). When, following on this, Malinowski tries to ascertain just what the 'emotional character of the parental kinship relationship' (1913a, p. 199) is and what are the actual procedures and tasks of feeding, caring for and bringing up a family, we have the ground laid for the Principle of Legiti-macy, the Initial Situation and the working out of the theory of incest.

It is worth observing how the same interests run through *The Natives of Mailu* (1915*a*). Malinowski made a special point of investigating the sexual customs, the beliefs about conception, and the individual family relationships of the natives. He finds that the Mailu are ignorant of the nature of physiological paternity. His primary interest is in the 'reality' of action, behaviour, sentiment, and conduct. This is nicely shown in the discussion of legal institutions (1915*a*, chap. III, sect. 5, pp. 576 ff.). The nucleus of *Crime and Custom* (1926*b*), with its insistence on the division between 'ideal' and 'real', is here. The ethnographer's task is defined at length. 'Actual, concrete facts' are what he must get; and Malinowski complains that he was unable to get 'authentic stories about murder, adultery, theft' and other crimes in the old days. He asserts that 'in every community there exist fundamental rules which must be observed. The infraction of these rules is a lurking temptation and there are always individuals who succumb. . . . To discover the rules, the possibilities of infringement, the restraining forces . . .' is his aim. And after some discussion he expresses his conclusion that 'the conception of criminal law or of civil law, or of the distinction between the two' has no 'counterpart in native ideas'.

I am giving prominence to the continuity between Malinowski's theoretical training, his first experience of field-work and his mature ideas and theories because it seems to me that this helps to explain why he, more than any other anthropologist of his time, responded so eagerly and creatively to the influence of psycho-analysis. This may seem an exaggeration if we think of the impact of psycho-analysis on the leading anthropologists of the nineteen-twenties—for example, on Rivers and both the Seligmans, in this country, and on Sapir and Benedict in America. Even Radcliffe-Brown, later so rigorous in his sociological thinking, must have been influenced by Freud, for his theory of joking relationships obviously owed something to Freud's theory of wit. But for Malinowski psycho-analysis was the light by which he was able to make a new synthesis of his ideas and experiences.

It is important to understand clearly what Malinowski's innovations were. For, of course, ethnological field-workers and scholars usually included accounts of sexual customs and practices, beliefs about the nature of conception, and customary modes of conduct between parents and children and between other kinsfolk, in describing primitive kinship institutions. The nineteenth-century classics are full of such discussions. Was not the controversy about primitive promiscuity and group marriage chiefly concerned with the question of the connection between sex and parenthood? More pertinently, the pioneers of scientific field-work had paid considerable attention to these matters. Thus Rivers provoked Malinowski's scorn by his confused speculations about the origins of such customs as the Banks islanders' avoidance of affinal kin in earlier conditions of 'sexual communism' (e.g. Rivers, 1914, Vol. II, pp. 136 ff.). But these speculations, related to Rivers's preoccupation with the problem of the mother's brother, were associated with shrewd observations similar to those on which Malinowski later built his analysis of the position of the father in the Trobriands. Rivers noted, for example, that a person was not considered to be his father's kin in the Banks islands because he belonged to the opposite moiety.

Malinowski's break with this kind of ethnology lay, therefore, not in his choice of topics but in his handling of them, especially after his field experience in the Trobriands. This was first shown in 'Baloma' (1916), where his 'contextual' or 'institutional' method led him to make a particular point of what he called the 'social dimension'. Individuals and groups in fact vary greatly in their observance of custom and in their knowledge of the beliefs and practices which we conventionally attribute to a tribe as if they were uniformly present among all its members. Hence, he argued, the actual language and gestures used, the feelings, motives and ambitions of actors and informants, the whole psychological setting, are important data for ethnography. Custom and belief thus appear as the motives of action, both in the positive sense of furnishing aims and incentives, as in the *kula* or gardening, and in the negative sense of provoking instinctive rebellion, as in the evasion of incest taboos. To seek for psychological explanations of the springs of conduct came naturally to Malinowski and was consistent with his rejection of both historical theories and collectivist sociologies of a Durkheimian type. In common with most scholars in the social sciences at that time, Malinowski was an admirer of McDougall and Shand. Psycho-analysis could be regarded as taking their theories a step further and this made it the more acceptable to him.

Thus, psycho-analysis fitted Malinowski's general approach. It also fitted his conception of human nature. We see this from the following statement of what it was in psycho-analysis that appealed to him: 'The open treatment of sex and of various shameful meannesses and vanities in man—the very thing for which psycho-analysis is most hated and reviled . . . should endear psycho-analysis above all to the student of man.' 'Man is an animal', he continues, 'and, as such, at times unclean, and the honest anthropologist has to face this fact' (1927a, p. viii).

This unflattering view of man was in the spirit of the nineteen-twenties; but it was not just a case of drifting with the tide. Malinowski played a lively part in creating this climate of thought, more particularly with his writings on sex and the family. Did not the Trobrianders become a byword among novelists and sex-reformers, as well as the model primitive society (I am tempted to say, the Twentieth-Century Noble Savage) for textbook reference among the most diverse of scholars and scientists? What better testimony could there be to the authenticity of Malinowski's understanding of man? To him, as to Freud, the seamy side of human conduct and belief was a matter of observation not of fashionable ideology. To sum up, Malinowski's debt to psycho-analysis is obvious in much of his work (e.g. on magic) but nowhere so markedly as in his descriptions of Trobriand family structure and in the theory of kinship that grew out of them. Indeed I would maintain that it was the notion of the Œdipus Complex that gave Malinowski the inspiration for the main features of his kinship theory.

Two features of Freudian theory specially impressed Malinowski. The first was the picture of the ambivalent emotional relationship of father and son arising out of the clash between the son's instinctive sexual urges and the culturally enforced power and authority of the father. Duly transposed into 'matriarchal' terms this gave coherence and meaning to the ostensibly contradictory facts of Trobriand family relationships. Here was a mechanism which accounted neatly for the coexistence, one might almost say the necessary coexistence, in a system of mutually opposing forces, of the distinctive elements of the matrilineal family. Father love and avuncular authority, the sexual bonds of spouses and the sexual barriers between brother and sister, the obligatory friendship and common interests of uncle and nephew alongside of their mutual enmity ('in real life to a certain degree and quite openly in myth'—1927a, p. 121), the ignorance of paternity, the incest rule and the urge to break it, all fall into a unitary and consistent scheme on the revised Freudian hypothesis. It accorded well with Malinowski's way of thinking about 'real' emotions and sentiments as being in perpetual struggle against 'ideal' laws and morals.

The hypothesis had another merit. It was economical and realistic. Given the irreducible biological facts of sex and of child nurture, everything else followed from the necessary constitution of the individual family. No extraneous data or assumptions were needed. And the conflict between sexual wishes on the one hand, and the demands of law and morals on the other, which was deemed to give rise to the Œdipal ambivalence, could, it seemed, be confirmed by direct observation in the field.

This brings up the second aspect of psycho-analytic theory which specially impressed Malinowski. The Œdipus mechanism seemed to be rigorously accounted for by a kind of causal process. It was the result of a genetic sequence beginning with inborn infantile sexuality and running through all the stages of child development in an interplay of innate impulse and the 'moulding' influence of cultural training. The whole process was, Malinowski thought, verifiable by field observation (i.e. 'real') and had the support of general psychological theory.

This genetic conceptualization became and remained the first principle of Malinowski's kinship theory even when, later on, he turned against psycho-analysis. The concept of the Initial Situation and the notion of kinship extension arise directly from this principle. He spoke of it as 'doing, somewhat tardily, for social anthropology what psychology has been doing for the study of the mental development of the individual', as the study of the 'moulding of innate dispositions' (1930a). He summed up the method of approach in such formulas as 'It is, therefore, the process of the extension of kinship from its extremely simple beginnings in plain parenthood [sc. the Initial Situation] to its manifold ramifications and complexities . . . which . . . forms the *real* subject-matter of the study of kinship' (1930b—my italics).

As I have said, a psychological framework was essential to Malinowski's functionalism. Everything he wrote was riddled with psychological explanation partly because his functionalism meant seeing custom as motive, partly because its instrumental and utilitarian form led back to physiological needs, and the simplest way in which these can be visualized as emerging in action is as the driving forces behind instincts, sentiments and emotions. A graphic instance is Malinowski's theory of magic, where, it will be remembered, he uses the notion (originated by Freud and adopted, in a watered-down physiological form, by Rivers) of 'spontaneous ritual and verbiage of overflowing passion or desire' related to 'natural responses' of fear and hope and 'illusions of subjective experience' (1925a, pp. 75–6).

But necessary as psychological theories are for it, a *genetical process* need not, strictly speaking, be posited in order to introduce concepts of motive and feeling into ethnographical description. Every ethnographer uses such concepts. Malinowski himself does not give a genetical derivation for the psychological concepts he uses in describing breaches of the incest taboo or the conduct and feelings of the Trobriand husband to his wife and father to his children. For these, like most ethnographic descriptions, are set in the generalized present.

The truth is that the concept of genetic development was less a psychological hypothesis than a methodological one for Malinowski. It was the functionalist answer to 'imaginary speculations' about kinship, in fact a sounder theory of origins and of temporal sequence because ostensibly verifiable by observation. It could be seen happening in the reality of social life. The origins of the clan, said Malinowski, scoffing at these speculations, 'happen . . . under our very eyes . . . I have myself witnessed (them) . . .' (1930b). And what he puts forward is his hypothesis of the 'biological development of kinship', which leads to the conclusion that 'the clan develops as a derived sociological form of grouping by empirical processes . . . along the life history of the individual'.

Malinowski disliked the systematic statement of theory. He even made a virtue of using technical terms loosely and was criticized by Radcliffe-Brown (1929) for confusing the concept of descent with that of bilateral kinship. As he had a flair for coining valuable new terms this was exasperating. But inconvenient as this may be to his readers, avoidance of system and precision suited his habits of thought. For his insight worked in leaps, like stepping stones in the flood of his divagations. Thus the 'life history' principle was ideal for his mode of thought. It was naturalistic enough to fall in with the 'institutional' form of presenting his descriptions and arguments, and yet flexible enough to give him plenty of room to spread about without losing the semblance of an objective order. Most of all, it enabled persons to be shown as active agents in the process of developing sentiments, dispositions, habits and ideas. Thus the extrapolation from the 'initial situation' in the parental family to descent concepts, clans, and tribal structure is effected by successive genetical steps. The logical flaws and the empirical selectiveness that are obvious when these facts are looked at in terms of their contemporary relations in a total social structure, are easily concealed in such a piecemeal presentation.

I want to underline this methodological value of the genetic concept for Malinowski. For, in spite of his protestations, he never himself made any true 'life history' studies. What he wrote under that rubric are highly generalized and abstract statements of sequences of customary activities and patterns of relationship in a model matrilineal family and clan system. Even in his ethnographic work, as for instance *The Sexual Life of Savages*, where he follows a rough order of chronological succession in describing the vicissitudes of the sexual instincts and proclivities of the Trobrianders, there are no individual 'life histories'. The 'biographical' method gives only a convenient framework on which to hang the descriptive facts of kinship, as Firth and others after him have found.

But it would be a mistake to think that what Malinowski got from psycho-analysis was only a model for a procedure of description. He also, as I have noted, got the clues towards some of his most cherished and valuable theoretical ideas on the nature of family relationships. For this he had to reinterpret Freudian theory to accommodate his ethnographic insight. The main problem was the empirical status of the unconscious emotional formations and conflicts, overtly visible only in disguised or symbolic forms, upon which the hypothesis of the Œdipus Complex relies, and how they could be compared with the observed facts of customary and publicly accepted behaviour which are the ethnographer's data. Freud himself, incidentally, was well aware of the problem. In *Totem und Tabu* he frequently comments on the danger of identifying the symptoms and mental states of neuroses with primitive customs. He emphasizes that it is analogies and coincidences not identity that he is investigating.[1]

---

[1] It is obvious, from the internal evidence of *Sex and Repression* alone, that Malinowski made a careful and thorough study of *Totem und Tabu*. What I am referring to is the numerous qualifications and cautious asides in Freud's book. Thus he contrasts the 'private' reality-shunning world of neurosis with the institutions 'achieved by the collective efforts' of society and has many remarks such as '. . . but taboo is not a neurosis, it is, on the contrary a social formation'. We must not forget, by the way, that *Totem und Tabu* was first published in 1913, when a non-specialist wishing to make use of anthropological findings could hardly have chosen a better authority than Frazer.

Malinowski at first followed Freudian terminology and claimed that his observations supported Freudian theory (e.g. 1927*a*, pp. 82, 92, etc.). He spoke of the 'repressed passions' breaking through, of 'the repressed sexual attitude of incestuous temptation . . . towards the sister', and of the 'ambivalent attitude' of sister's son to mother's brother (p. 80). But the controversy with Ernest Jones, and criticism of the hypothesis of a primordial parricide, led him to formulate his notion of the 'nuclear family complex' as 'a functional formation dependent upon the structure and upon the culture of a society' and 'determined' by 'the manner in which sexual restrictions are moulded . . . and authority apportioned' (p. 143). This was Freud rephrased but with the stress on the primacy of culture over instinct in the formation of the nuclear complex. Instead of a parallelism between the customary attitudes and behaviour of Trobrianders and the partly unconscious emotional formations revealed by psycho-analysis, Malinowski was led to assert that custom is in fact the equivalent of unconscious emotional forces and to reject the need for the concept of unconscious motive (pp. 173 ff.). The 'nuclear family complex' became 'a configuration of sentiments typical in a patriarchal or a matriarchal society' (p. 178) and by definition directly accessible to ethnographic observation. This was a significant discovery and has been tacitly, if not openly, accepted by ethnographers since then.

Malinowski was thus confronted with the task of showing how culture regulates the elements of family organization, 'apportions' authority, and 'moulds' family sentiments. He found part of the answer in the hypothesis of the 'rule of legitimacy' which, he said, reinforces the instinctive parental feelings of the human male and gives cultural definition and legitimacy to motherhood as well as to fatherhood. It is connected with the 'two main perils of humanity: the tendency to incest and the revolt against authority'. It was in establishing his thesis about the nuclear complex that Malinowski arrived at his remarkable reinterpretation of the Freudian theory of the incest taboo. The stroke of sociological inspiration was to relate the incest taboo to the function of the family as the agency through which the knowledge and sentiments essential for maintaining culture are transmitted from generation to generation. This educational task requires emotions of 'reverence, dependence, respect as well as strong attachment' to the mother and 'thorough submission to the leadership' of the father. So if, as psycho-analysis holds, incest is a universal temptation it must be forbidden because it is incompatible with the existence of the family as the medium through which culture is transmitted. If incest were permitted 'the fundamental pattern of all social bonds, the normal relation of the child to the mother and father would be destroyed' (1927*a*, p. 252).

To this general hypothesis he added a supplementary analysis of the differences between 'patriarchal' and 'matriarchal' family and descent

systems from the point of view of incest prohibitions. 'Unilateral kinship' as he calls it (p. 268) is casually disposed of as 'the only possible
way of dealing with problems of transmission of possessions, dignities,
and social privileges'. Father-right is thus characterized in rephrased
Freudian terms: 'In the patrilineal society the father has to incorporate
in himself the two aspects . . . of tender friend and rigid guardian of
law. This creates both a disharmony . . . within the family . . . disturbing
co-operation and . . . jealousies and rivalries at its very heart' (p. 270).
Matriliny, on the other hand, is represented as being better adjusted
to the psychological facts. As it is the mother's brother, not she herself,
who wields 'coercive powers' this does not introduce jealousies between
her and her son. The sentiment between mother and child is not disturbed by the transmission of legal and economic powers. The mother's
brother 'who represents stern authority, social ideals, and ambitions
is very suitably kept at a distance outside the family circle'. We note
here that the emotional attitudes attributed to father, mother and uncle
are of a highly general kind and are presumed to be quite overt.

One of the paradoxes in Malinowski's work is that his theoretical
writings are mostly couched in terms of the highest generality, in strong
contrast with the rich and concrete detail of his ethnographical books.
This is conspicuous in everything he wrote on the theory of kinship.
The specific facts of custom, with their variability from culture to
culture, disappear behind abstract terms. Closely looked at these terms
—even quite conventional terms like marriage, paternity, maternity,
etc.—prove to be concerned with the limiting principles and factors of
kinship rather than with the realities of custom, belief and sentiment.
Where they do not deal with physiological and psychological principles
that form necessary prerequisites for the functions of social and cultural
reproduction in human society, they deal with structural prerequisites.
Such, for instance, is the notion of the universal need for a husband-
father, in the first place as protector of the mother and child, but also
in order to confer legitimacy on the procreative rôle of the mother. And
what is more, all these principles and hypotheses are deductively
reached.

One of Malinowski's chief debts to Freud was that psycho-analysis
joined to his Trobriand field data provided the premises for his most
fertile deductive hypothesis. The theory of incest is an outstanding
instance. I do not think this is a purely tautologous generalization. For
it does specify definite rules of sexual behaviour that must be obeyed
for the social and cultural tasks that can only be performed in the
relation of parenthood to be fulfilled. It is the relation of parenthood,
be it noted, that is central to Malinowski's hypothesis, not the composition of the individual family, though he states it in language that
implies an arrangement of co-resident parents and children. This is
important; for the generalization is susceptible of being refuted by

direct observation of the relations of parenthood, irrespective of residential arrangements or even of the duration of marriage.

If Malinowski's contribution to kinship theory on the conceptual side was, in effect, a series of loosely connected, largely deductive hypotheses about family structure, what was it on the ethnographic side? This is important because Malinowski was at his best in the descriptive exploration of an idea through the medium of his own field observations, and his influence was chiefly exerted through his ethnographic writings.

As far as the study of kinship systems is concerned, I think his influence has been greatest through the models he has provided for field research and for the descriptive presentation of kinship custom and behaviour. The genetic framework or, more appropriately, the life-cycle sequence is well suited for this and the insistence on observing and recording what takes place in the living situation is fundamental. More specific models are provided by almost all of his books and it would be easy to give a list of ethnographic publications that have been inspired by them. No ethnographer with a 'functionalist' training writing about kinship today will overlook the rivalry and conflict aspect of the relations between the legal possessor of parental authority and the filial generation, or the significance of reciprocity rules in kinship, or the educational (sc. 'socialization') function of the family and its connection with incest prohibitions.

One of the best examples of such a model is the essay on *The Father in Primitive Psychology* (1927b). Though much of the ground it covers is the same as in *Sex and Repression* (1927a) and in later works, this essay brings into particularly clear relief both Malinowski's ethnographic method and his most influential contribution to kinship theory. This was the now classical picture, to which I have already several times referred, of matrilineal paternity divided between the father, with his personal bonds of affection and solicitude for his child, based on his exclusive sexual rights over the mother and his part in the task of child-rearing, and the mother's brother with his bonds of right and duty with his sister's son, rooted in the incest barrier, in legal authority and in descent, and accompanied by suppressed hostility.

Malinowski found the clue for this analysis in the Freudian concept of ambivalence in the Œdipal relationship of father and son but he had the insight to apply it to the structural arrangements of the 'matrilineal family', and his method showed him that the emotional pattern was supported by the physiological ideas, the ritual beliefs, the conventional loyalties and hostilities, the residence patterns and the legal rules of the society. As a demonstration of the significance of functional consistencies in social organization it is noteworthy, and has inspired many confirmatory studies, like those of Richards (1934, 1950a), Fortes (1950) and Nadel (1950). But this was not Malinowski's own judgement of his analysis. For him the issue was one of a dramatic conflict between passion and law which was undermining the family at its core. He saw it in terms of '. . . beliefs, ideas and customary rules which smuggle extreme patrilineal principles into the stronghold of mother right' (1927*b*, p. 85).

This was not just rhetoric or an example of Malinowski's ingrained contempt for precise analytical concepts. He held, as a point of theory, that what he was describing *was* 'patrilineal principles' in conflict with 'matriliny'. He adhered to this conception throughout his work. Even in *Coral Gardens* (1935) where there are indications of appreciation of the analytical autonomy of social organization in its jural aspect, this point of view still prevails. Its significance for later research is that it treats the analytically heterogeneous topics of sex and sentiment in the setting of dyadic personal relationships, on the one hand, and the legal and political order of the total society, on the other, as if they were all on one level. This may be justifiable in the context of the parental family taken as a more or less closed system where jural and political status are subsidiary to the inter-individual relationship— though even in this context they are not negligible, as Malinowski himself showed. It breaks down when the family is considered in the external context of local, jural and political relations.

The proof lies in Malinowski's failure to understand the nature of classificatory kinship terminologies; for to give Rivers his due, however wrong his explanations were his empirical insight was sound. These terminologies are not just metaphors and homonyms as Malinowski proclaimed. They are indicators of social relations and of modes of grouping and arranging persons which are present in the social structure of any people at the same time as family relations and which serve to bind the family into the total jural and political order. The notion put forward quite early (e.g. 1927*a*, p. 221) and adhered to all his life that 'in all primitive societies, without exception, the local community, the clan or the tribe, is organized by a gradual extension of family ties' needs only to be stated for its absurdity to be seen. It led to entanglements such as the contradictory assertions that the 'clan always grows out of the family, forming round one of the two parents . . .' and three lines later, 'family and clan differ thus profoundly in origins, in the functions which they fulfil . . . etc.' (1930*b*). It led to the series of logical in-consistencies that culminated in the curious hypothesis of 'strata' of kinship nomenclature in which the same sounds had different meanings because 'the individual, the extended, the local and the classificatory are differentiated by phonetic distinctions . . . circumlocutions . . . con-textual indices' (loc. cit.), these being 'real' as opposed to the 'spurious' nature of the terminologies in the verbal sense.

We can see that Malinowski's error was to confuse the frame of reference of the individual life history—or rather of the conventional life history of the standard individual—with that of the total social structure. It is excellently documented in his only effort to explain Trobriand kinship terminology. In *The Sexual Life of Savages* (1929*a*, pp. 434–5) there is a table of Trobriand kinship terms, and this is followed by some discussion of the terms. His approach is well illustrated in the explanation of the term for sibling of opposite sex. It is linked to the incest taboo. The term is given its meaning by the emotional conditioning of the child due to the reprimands and horror of 'its elders' whenever it makes 'playful advances to the other small being'. On the same principle, Malinowski soon arrives at this extraordinary fallacy: 'The anomalous extension of the word for father (*tama*) to the father's sister's son is important, for it demonstrates the influence which language has upon customs and ideas . . .' and so on. The whole paragraph deserves study as an example of a beautiful methodological and logical howler due to preconceived ideas; and this was no slip of the pen for the rest of the discussion on Trobriand kinship terminology follows this line.[1] What Malinowski refused to accept was the fact that kinship terms designate jural relationships and groupings. The Trobriand kinship system, we would say today, has an obvious 'Choctaw' type terminology, well exemplifying principles formulated by Radcliffe-Brown at this time and published in 1931. The usages tortuously made to look anomalous by Malinowski are perfectly normal for such systems and enable one to infer certain jural consequences, such as the probability of property rights being vested in a matrilineal descent group.

But if we know this now, could Malinowski have anticipated these results of recent theoretical research? We must, I think, answer that he could have avoided the blunder, if he had made more of an effort to understand the findings and interpretations of other students of kinship. He might, indeed, have done this if he had adhered to a rule of method reiterated in *The Family Among the Australian Aborigines*, that it is specially important to bear in mind the connection of family organization 'with the general structure of society' (1913*a*, p. 300). What he in fact did was to revive, in a new-fangled form, Kroeber's early view[2] of kinship terminologies as primarily linguistic and psychological facts, not 'determined' by 'social conditions'. He knew very well, from the investigations of Seligman (1910) and Rivers (1914), that the alleged idiosyncrasies of terminology he was discussing have a wide distribution in Melanesia; and he might have asked himself whether it was not as ludicrous to invoke linguistic anomalies to explain such general features of social organization as to refer them to antecedent marriage rules. He might have given serious consideration to some of Rivers's ideas—not to mention earlier writers such as Kohler, and

---

[1] I have commented on the methodological problems arising out of this fallacy elsewhere (Fortes, 1953*a*; 1955).

[2] See Radcliffe-Brown's reflections on this controversy (1941).

contemporary scholars like Radcliffe-Brown and Lowie. Thus he might have followed up Rivers's contention (1913, p. 72) which Lowie adopted (1920, chap. VI)—but stripped of its pseudo-history—that certain types of kinship nomenclature are correlated with exogamous clan systems, for he himself remarked that one of the 'proofs' of Trobriand 'clan solidarity' '. . . is the classificatory use of kinship terms' (1929a, p. 425).

Malinowski's unwillingness to see the meaning of kinship terminologies in the setting of the total social structure did not, it should be added, pass without criticism at the time. A good instance is Mrs. Seligman's paper on incest and descent (1929). While accepting Malinowski's hypothesis of the relationship between incest prohibitions and family organization and agreeing with him about the central importance of the family in the transmission of culture, she insists on the 'equal importance' of a 'larger group' in which a 'system of descent' is the essential element. Though not quite clear in her remarks about classificatory kinship terminologies, she sees that 'the acceptance of the classificatory system of relationships carries with it the status of those relationships, not its emotional equation'. Again, Malinowski never succeeded in persuading his pupils to follow him wholeheartedly in this matter. Thus, without directly debating the point, Raymond Firth makes it quite clear, in his elaborate analysis of Tikopia kinship language (1936, chap. VII), that he does not accept Malinowski's ideas on this subject. His argument is eclectic but he underlines the fact that kinship terminologies serve as indices of jural groupings and classifications, such as the attribution of 'representative status'.

There is one particularly telling example of how Malinowski confused issues by lumping together indices of the jural order of society and usages showing up individual motive and sentiment. We know how obsessed he was with the dichotomy between 'ideals of tribal morality' and 'the real behaviour'. He maintains (1929a, p. 426) that 'the smoothness and uniformity, which the mere verbal statements suggest as the only shape of human conduct, disappear with a better knowledge of cultural reality'. The thesis was repeatedly illustrated by reference to breaches of the law of incest and exogamy. Now one of Malinowski's most firmly held hypotheses was that the law of exogamy is simply an extension to the clan of the prohibition of sexual intercourse between brother and sister or parent and child which is incest in the strictest sense. This idea gained wide currency as an established generalization. For though Malinowski did not originate the idea[1] he, more than

---

[1] It is inherent in Westermarck's conception of the origins of the incest taboo. The persistence of the theory is well documented in Leslie A. White (1948) and B. Z. Seligman (1950). See also Parsons (1954). A different view, in agreement with the criticism I shall be making, is put forward by Radcliffe-Brown, e.g. (1949) and (1950).

anyone else, gave it the appearance of cogency by showing it in action. It was indispensable for his views about the nature of 'cultural reality' and the basically linguistic and psychological meaning of kinship terminology. But his own comments and descriptions afford ample evidence that the Trobrianders, like many other peoples in whose social structure unilineal descent groups enter into the regulation of marriage, do make a jural distinction between the two rules; and not only that, it is also quite clear that they have severe and effective means of enforcing the 'ideal' rules. It is simply not true—or at any rate, not proven by the one or two cases quoted—that 'the breach of exogamy within the clan, intrigues with . . . kindred-in-clan . . . though officially forbidden, ruled to be improper, and surrounded by supernatural sanctions, is *yet everywhere committed*' (my italics). But the point I particularly want to bring out is best put in the remark that follows immediately on the paragraph from which I have just quoted (1929*a*, p. 431). '*Marriages*—as distinct from intrigues—*within the clan* are definitely regarded as a serious breach of the rule' (Malinowski's italics); and, a bit further on, '. . . the rule of exogamy, far from being uniform and wholesale in its application, works differently with regard to marriage and to sexual intercourse . . .' Finally comes the information that incest with the own sister or the mother's sister's daughter is 'a real crime . . . a dreadful crime' which may lead to suicide.

It is obvious that the Trobrianders do distinguish, in thought and in their institutional arrangements, between exogamy, the rule prohibiting marriage 'within the clan', and the incest prohibition which applies to sexual relations between close kin. Moreover, exogamy is evidently enforced without exception, as we should expect with a jural obligation that can only be entered into with the consent of the woman's kin and is validated by prestations on both sides (cf. the description of the procedure, Malinowski, 1929*a*, chap. IV, sect. 2 and 3). Again, the range of close kin subject to the incest taboo is equally clear. It includes the members of the same sub-clan (*dala*) or, as we should probably now call it, local lineage,[1] not only the closest circle of maternal kin; and within this range the breach of the incest taboo is evidently so outrageous and rare that it evokes the extreme sanction of suicide. The 'everywhere' in the earlier quotation seems to come down to occasional intrigues, but definitely not marriage, between members of different local 'sub-clans' of the same clan. By the test of regularity and incidence of observance, the 'cultural reality' of incest and exogamy rules is just what the 'ideal' states it to be.

This example well illustrates some of the weaknesses of Malinowski's theory and method in the study of kinship. He would have avoided the error if he had started with a different frame of analysis. Thus, a crucial problem is the exact local and genealogical make-up of, and relationships

[1] Or 'local descent group' in Leach's terminology (1951).

between, the sub-clan and the clan. Taking all the sources (and especially 1935, Vol. I, chap. XII) together we can construct some kind of picture of the sub-clan as the corporate, permanent, localized, land, rank, and magic-owning group made up of ranked 'lineages' connected by assumed common descent; and of the clan as one of four widely scattered, named divisions based on a totemic myth of remote common matrilineal ancestry. But we can only guess what the implications of this significant fact are for marriage rules and relationships. We can note, for instance, that the cases actually quoted of so-called breach of exogamy seem to occur between members of *different* sub-clans of the same clan (e.g. 1935, Vol. I, p. 385). In the context of a strict analysis of clan and sub-clan structure, the law of exogamy would have been seen in its true quality as a jural institution. This would have been equally clear if Malinowski had examined his data from the point of view of the marriage contract and the rights and duties arising out of it for the spouses as married partners and as parents. And there is yet another alternative. If (remembering his Durkheim) he had bethought himself of the chronic *anomie* into which Trobriand society would fall if the laws of incest and exogamy were commonly flouted, he would have seen the issue differently. He would have realised that such a state of affairs would make nonsense of the Principle of Legitimacy to which he rightly gave so much importance in the context of marriage and parenthood.

I have dwelt on this example partly because it concerns a subject which was prominent in Malinowski's interests all his life and partly for a personal reason. During my first year of field-work among the Tallensi I tried to confirm Malinowski's hypothesis in the field. It was thus that I learnt to distinguish between the jural and the personal, or psychological, components of kinship institutions.[1] Moreover, it is an example which explains why there is and always will be inspiration to be found in the careful scrutiny of everything Malinowski wrote. This is because the quality and amount of his ethnographic observations, coupled with his exacting, almost pernickety thoroughness in setting them down, give us a wealth of data for checking his theories by direct comparison with the facts. *Coral Gardens and Their Magic* is the acid test of this. On the surface, kinship and social organization appear as incidental topics only. But patient study reveals that here, more than in any of the other Trobriand books, they serve as the hidden 'articulating principles' of the whole book.

The reader has, of course, to work this out for himself since the relevant data are scattered piecemeal through the narrative of gardening activities. In doing so he will find that the data are there to check and sometimes to modify and even to refute Malinowski's generalized statements. He will be helped also by digressions on particular topics of

[1] I tried to bring this out in my article (1937).

social organization where Malinowski's insight breaks through and he gives a structural analysis very close in form and even in idiom to the practice of today. It may be that he was responding to a tendency that was already 'in the air' in 1932. A good instance is the description of 'the structure of the sub-clan' in the chapter on Land Tenure. To judge by his own remarks (1935, Vol. I, p. 481) Malinowski was specially satisfied with this description. It is carried out in quite rigorous sociological and jural terms, the red herring of 'real' *versus* 'ideal' in conduct being, for this task, left aside. Thus we are told that 'magic, strictly speaking, should always be handled by the *eldest member of the senior lineage* in every sub-clan' and that 'sometimes . . . it is not given to younger brother or maternal nephew, but to a person who has *no legal place in the lineage* . . . the headman's own son', who, however, usually 'becomes naturalized by the act of cross-cousin marriage, which gives him almost *full legal right* to reside in his father's community' (1935, Vol. I, p. 349—my italics). We learn that 'the *right of citizenship* . . . the absolute and unquestionable right of residence' from which the right to cultivate soil derives, is gained only by membership of a sub-clan which, if we patiently pursue the theme, we find has not only a 'local character' but also a 'spiritual unity and continuity' expressed in beliefs about the after-life and in the ownership of magic (1935, Vol. I, pp. 344 ff.—my italics).

There is much more in this vein in the book. I have quoted these short extracts just to show the affinity of this mode of handling the data with present-day structural theory, even in some items of terminology.[1] Not that the mode of thought followed in previous books is discarded. The narrative relies heavily on the attribution of motive and imputation of sentiment. But descriptions and discussions of what Malinowski called the 'juridical' aspects of social structure are more prominent and abundant here than in the previous works, perhaps because of the subject matter, and the governing principles can be extracted. As this is not an essay on Trobriand social structure but on Malinowski's ideas, I will consider only one or two examples. They show both the brilliance of Malinowski's insight in ethnographic particulars and his failure to follow up his analysis in a systematic way.

An excellent instance is the *urigubu* gift of agricultural produce annually handed over by men to the husbands of their sisters. It appears in every description Malinowski gave of Trobriand family organization. It is a major topic in *Coral Gardens*, where it comes up in one context after another and is given a comprehensive chapter to itself.

---

[1] Malinowski's cavalier attitude to terminological precision is particularly unfortunate in this book for his terms are sometimes brilliantly apposite. For instance, his concept of *filiation*, used in several of his works, and frequently in *Coral Gardens*, is rich in possibilities but his definitions of it are not uniform. This applies also to the terms *lineage, clan*, etc.

It was the descriptive features of this picturesque custom that loomed foremost, from the first (e.g. 1922*a*), in Malinowski's imagination and he therefore turned the limelight on to the apparent paradoxes in it. In *Coral Gardens* it is presented from the outset as being 'perverse' and 'so difficult to grasp' that even 'long-time white residents . . . married to native women . . . who . . . benefit under the Trobriand harvesting system . . .' cannot understand it. The problem thrust into the forefront is 'what motive can make one man offer the best part of his harvest to another?' And it is made to look more portentous by long disquisitions on the 'terminological looseness', the numerous 'exceptions', the paradox (to the ignorant European often dragged in as a lay figure by Malinowski for rhetorical emphasis) of a man's giving away his choicest crops, the 'puzzle' as to whether they are given to the sister's husband or herself or her family, the ceremonial transport of the gift, the economic waste implied, the conflict between a man's 'interests and his heart' which are fixed in his own household of wife and children, and his 'pride and moral duties' which are 'in the household of his sister'. (These references are from 1935, Vol. I, chap. VI, but they can be paralleled from the other Trobriand books.)

In *Coral Gardens* this familiar build-up is followed by something new. This is an analysis, in fairly strict structural terms, of the overlap between the 'unit of filiation' made up of brother, sister and sister's children, and the 'paternal household'. Marriage is defined as a 'publicly acknowledged relation, approved and accepted by the girl's family, and binding them to definite economic prestation'. This includes not only the reciprocal services of husband and wife and of father and child, but the *urigubu*; and we now get a structural and juridical analysis of this gift which makes all the preceding dramatization of it look irrelevant. 'The *urigubu*', Malinowski sums up, 'is the endowment by its real head of the unit of filiation . . . the expression of the real constitution of Trobriand kinship grouping. . . .' Hence the conclusion emerges that 'if the *urigubu* is regarded as a gift from an outsider . . . it appears absurd . . . but . . . as the endowment of his own kindred group by its head, it becomes natural, almost obvious'.

But there is still the essential juridical point to come. For this we have to wait till Malinowski reverts to the harvest gift in the chapter on land tenure. There he emphasizes that though a woman is bound to go and live with her husband she 'legally remains a member of her own subclan'. This means that the *urigubu* can be regarded as the 'annual return from the joint patrimony . . . due to the woman from her brother', a consequence of the fact that 'she and her children are real owners of the soil' on which it is raised. If this principle is grasped all the complicated details and purported exceptions fall into place. The incidence of rights and obligations determined by the bonds of kinship and affinity is seen to be regular almost to the point of rigidity. By this analysis it is, for instance, quite reasonable for a woman's son to assume the *urigubu* obligation if she has no brother. The caption 'Hunger, Love and Vanity as Driving Forces in the Trobriand Harvest Gift' (1935, Vol. I, chap. VI, sect. 2) is seen to refer to psychological elements that are only secondary to the jural compulsion. Of course Malinowski himself did not perceive or admit this, but his analysis leaves the issue in no doubt.

Equally instructive is a reconsideration of Malinowski's favourite topic of the gifts given by fathers to their sons. It illustrates very well how, being engrossed in the descriptive detail, he failed to follow up the analysis in its theoretically more important juridical aspects. What he constantly emphasizes is that these gifts of magic, material property, and legal and political privileges are freely and affectionately made; and the implication is always that they are outright gifts. The subject is discussed *passim* in *Coral Gardens*. The following statement (1935, Vol. I, p. 205) is typical:

'The father, in actual fact, always tries to give as much as he can to his own sons at the expense of those of his sister, who are his legal heirs. His natural inclinations are seconded by customary usage which almost defies and certainly circumvents the rigid matrilineal law, by giving the father a number of opportunities to favour his sons and to curtail the rights of his matrilineal nephews.'

The narrative goes on to contrast the gift to a son with the nephew's obligation to 'buy' the magic from his uncle. The interpretation follows earlier lines. Thus the gifts are described (p. 360) as 'a dynamic adjustment between the patriarchal and the matriarchal principle'; but certain qualifications are now made more explicit. We learn more about the way in which rank tips the balance in favour of the son as against the nephew. It is in the interest of a chief to make gifts to his son and he can do so, whereas a commoner lacks the means and authority to do so.

But an important point emerges. The benefit of gifts is associated with the rules of marriage and residence. A son gains by them as long as he remains in his father's village. But this cannot outlast a generation since sons move to their matrilineal villages in adulthood. Even if the son marries his father's sister's daughter, as chiefs desire, and stays on in his father's village in uxorilocal marriage, his offspring automatically become full-titled citizens and the introduced lineage is eliminated (p. 364). If he marries an alien his children go off to their maternal kin, and the outcome is the same. In the first case the son is an 'intermediate heir' (p. 205) between his father and his son, who will, of course, inherit from the father's sister's son. But the point here is that the first recipient of the gift, by an act of fatherly gift-giving to *his* son in the second generation, restores the inheritance from which he has had an illegal 'cut' to where it rightly belongs by descent. This is the ideal case, for in the second one the gifts are in the end a dead loss to both the father's and the son's lineages.

The concept of an 'intermediate heir' is of great interest. It is presumably metaphorical since the essence of Malinowski's whole analysis is the antinomy between the nephew's *legal rights* to inherit and the son's *exclusion* from these rights. However the implication is clear. It is that what every man (especially chiefs) tries to do is to reconcile his love for his son with his legal duty to his heir. The solution, *via* an arranged cross-cousin marriage, is for the magic and property held back from the lineage for the son, to be returned to it through the heir of the next generation. This, incidentally, is a rationalization of cross-cousin marriage that is common among tribes with matrilineal descent systems. The crux, here, however, is the implication that the gifts given outright to a son return to the true heirs-by-descent through the same medium of paternal gift-giving in the context of the chances of marriage. The very action by which the laws of inheritance are 'circumvented' turns round on itself and redresses the balance in the next generation. It is just the kind of paradox Malinowski loved, though it would, of course, only work, if he is right, in the relatively unusual case of cross-cousin marriage. What eventually happens to the son's 'introduced' lineage is irrelevant and the statement that it is 'automatically eliminated' by his marriage is, in fact, quite beside the point. For it is only a man's *daughters* who can, by uxorilocal marriage in their father's village, if that were possible, there perpetuate the lineage to which his *sons* belong.

This is not the place to follow out the further ramifications of Malinowski's argument. What I want to seize on is that his picture represents a father's gifts as outright alienation contrary to the laws of inheritance but inevitably bound to revert to the true owners after a generation as a result of further gift giving, the motive force behind this movement being the personal relationships of fathers, sons, uncles and nephews. He is so determined on this that when he records how magical leadership was passed on at Omarakana for three successive generations from father to son, it is almost as an afterthought that he mentions the last holder's status as a legitimate heir to these powers in virtue of his father's cross-cousin marriage. But what is also striking is that paternal gifts, whether of magic or of land or of privilege, benefit the recipient mainly, if not only, while he is a resident in his father's village. Localized or not, these benefits are bound to terminate with the son not for personal reasons, but because the combination of the rules of descent, marriage, and residence makes it impossible for them to be transmitted to the son's heirs and, in so far as they are localized, useless to hand on to his sons unless they are village citizens by descent.

This suggests an alternative to Malinowski's interpretation of the data and one that is, in my opinion, more consistent with the total social structure of the Trobriands. On this view we should regard the gifts as being in reality a sharing with his sons, by the father, of his possessions and rights on the same principle as a child is permitted and indeed entitled to share any food offered to his father, whatever its source. This sharing, or lending, is for the time being only, and holds only during the father's lifetime. It arises quite normally out of the father's duty to rear his children to adulthood; and it is not a 'circumvention' of the laws of inheritance. On the contrary, it is an aspect of the rightful employment by a father, in his capacity of legal holder for his lifetime, of any properties or privileges that accrue to him as a member of his lineage and as his uncle's heir. While he is the holder he is entitled to use his inheritance as he pleases, provided that his heir is not deprived when he in turn comes to inherit. To allow his children to use and enjoy his inheritance during his lifetime—perhaps only during their minority —is both his pleasure and his duty as a father. When he dies the rights of the lineage, in the person of his heir, are immediately reasserted. The whole estate, including the portions of which the sons have had temporary benefit, reverts to the lineage by rights of inheritance. This explains why the so-called gifts do not outlast a generation and fits in well with Trobriand rules of descent, inheritance, marriage and residence.

I should be willing to argue that some such interpretation must be right on first principles; for constant, even frequent, evasion of the rules governing the control over property and legal privilege and the transmission of rights between successive generations would not be tolerated in any society. But confirmation for it is found in Malinowski's own data, though in an unexpected quarter. In *The Sexual Life of Savages* (1929*a*, p. 178), a contrast is drawn between the nephew's payment of *pokala* tribute to his uncle in order to establish his claim to his inheritance, and the 'gratis' gifts to the son, received 'without the sanction of tribal law'. And then comes this sentence: 'Of course he [i.e. the son] has to return them, at least in part, after his father's death; but the use and enjoyment he has had of the material benefits remain his, while the magic he cannot return.'

It is a remark that raises many questions. What part of the gifts must the son return? How is this enforced, as it obviously is, by tribal law? If much magic is given away to sons how is the right to it that we know (cf. p. 180 above) to be vested in the descent group maintained at all? Does a son's knowledge of the magic automatically confer on him the right to utilize it freely or can he only practise it with the consent of his father's heir? Or perhaps some kinds of magic are a form of 'liquid' resources that do not accrue to a heritable estate. These questions receive no direct answer in the Trobriand *corpus*, for they are significant only in relation to the kinship system viewed as a total system of primarily jural relationships. This Malinowski never did. Indeed he barely touches on kinship relations outside those of parents. The relationships of grand-parents and grand-children, for example, who appear, from the terminology, to be closely identified, are only incidentally mentioned.

My conclusion is that it is, in fact, impossible for a Trobriand father to endow his sons with gifts at the expense of his matrilineal kin. Indirect evidence and the sentence just quoted support this hypothesis. The interpretation I have proposed would explain why tribal usage appears to accept with tolerance a father's partiality to his children. It would explain the *pokala* as a formal, jural institution by which the rights of the heir are affirmed, almost as a reminder to a man that he has not got the freedom to give away what belongs to the lineage. It is consistent with Malinowski's own statements about cross-cousin marriage, and about the relations of affines. A chief's son first enjoys local benefits by sharing them with his father, and continues to enjoy them for another generation in virtue of his privileged relationship with his father's heir (his cross-cousin wife's brother) and perhaps as a sort of trustee for his son, the next heir. It shows Malinowski's drama of father-love pitted against the 'ideals' of the law in the more acceptable perspective of conduct for which provision is made in the law itself. The evidence I have quoted shows that Malinowski was aware of this aspect of the problem. His failure to follow it up, especially in *Coral Gardens* which is so largely concerned with questions of the ownership and inheritance of property and of other legal rights, is attributable, I believe, to his theoretical bias. But it is characteristic of his ethnographic insight and objectivity that the facts are recorded in such a way as to make it possible for us to find in them the answers to our questions.

I have, in this essay, taken the liberty of criticizing some of Malinowski's ideas and hypotheses. The criticisms I have made seem to me to be well founded when we examine Malinowski's work from the point of view of the structural theory which is yielding such valuable results in the present stage of kinship research. I have suggested that Malinowski's conceptual frame was not adapted to the study of kinship systems in their own right, as a part of the total social structure. But that it is important and extremely profitable to re-examine Malinowski's contribution to our knowledge of kinship institutions is beyond question. It is worth criticizing his ideas just because they are still vital and relevant. By contrast, the theories of Rivers and of those who agreed with him are merely of historic interest.

Malinowski's virtuosity as an ethnographer partly explains his continuing significance. But there are other reasons as well. For one thing, there are the rules of procedure in field research which we owe to his example. His insistence that our primary data must come from living societies is pertinent *par excellence* to kinship studies. We now regard it as indispensable for such studies to be based on the observation of conduct and action, thought and feeling, among people rather than on the interrogation of selected informants. This applies particularly to the data used in the ethnographic monograph, which has become the standard medium of contributing to kinship theory by means of intensive field-work. Such monographs now regularly follow the 'life-history' pattern laid down by Malinowski. In addition to Firth's book (1936) there are studies like Schapera's *Married Life in an African Tribe* (1939), my own *The Web of Kinship among the Tallensi* (1949a), and Evans-Pritchard's *Kinship and Marriage among the Nuer* (1951b), which show the influence of Malinowski's ethnographic techniques.

More important are a number of postulates about the nature and sources of kinship custom and conduct which we owe chiefly to Malinowski. No study of kinship, whether it is purely ethnographical or analytical or comparative, can now ignore the part played by sexual institutions and values. Murdock (1949) shows this by devoting a detailed chapter of his comprehensive comparative survey of kinship and social structure to the 'regulation of sex'. Even if we think of sexual tendencies and habits as belonging to the biological factors which set limits to kinship forms, rather than as directly constitutive of them, we can no longer overlook them. And when anthropologists describe the sexual elements in social organization they do so in terms of Malinowski's general approach, and often of his re-interpretation of psycho-analytical hypotheses. Thus Evans-Pritchard, writing of Nuer marriage (1951b, p. 49), says: 'Sexual activities are from their earliest manifestations given the stamp of cultural values. They are from the first associated with marriage, which is the final goal of the sex life of men and women.' There follow in succession descriptions of children's sexual play, the flirtations of adolescents, the love affairs leading to courtship and, finally, marriage. In this connection, too, it is now usual to describe the beliefs held about the nature of procreation and to show their relationship to family and kinship organization (cf. Schapera (1939) and Fortes (1949a)).

Here we must give particular recognition to the problem of incest and exogamy, which is a central topic in kinship studies. In my opinion there is no evidence of any advance on the theory first sketched out with such penetrating insight in *Sex and Repression* (1927a). Take Lévi-Strauss's disquisition on the subject in his erudite and complex study of cross-cousin marriage (1949). The title of his first chapter, 'Nature et Culture', reminds us of the heading in Part IV of *Sex and Repression* ('The Transition from Nature to Culture'); and the conclusion that it is the incest prohibition that marks the transition (p. 13) accords with Malinowski's. His theory of incest-cum-marriage-regulation—for, like Malinowski, he confounds the two—is not, in my judgement, tenable. 'The prohibition of incest', he sums up (p. 596), 'is less a rule that forbids marrying the mother, sister or daughter than a rule which obliges the giving of the mother, sister or daughter to another. It is the rule of the gift *par excellence*.' Taken literally, this conflicts directly with native statements reported by the majority of ethnographers and with our own notions. The incest taboo is universally thought of and stated as the prohibition of sexual relations between specified kin. This argument, and the case made by Lévi-Strauss against Malinowski's theory, in my view have no ethnographic basis. The common opinion in anthropology and sociology (which, as I have indicated, I do not myself share) is better shown in Murdock's statement that '. . . incest taboos and exogamous restrictions of whatsoever sort seem clearly to be extensions of the sex taboos between parent and child and between brother and sister' (1949, p. 284). This is pure Malinowski.

More to the point, perhaps, is the testimony of Parsons in a recent article (1954, p. 102). He writes: 'The universality of some order of incest taboo is of course directly connected with the fact that the nuclear family is also universal to all known human societies. The minimal criteria of the nuclear family are, I suggest, first that there should be a solidary relationship between mother and child lasting over a period of years and transcending physical care in its significance. Secondly, in her motherhood of this child the woman should have a special relationship to a man *outside her descent group* who is sociologically the "father" of the child, and that this relationship is the focus of the "legitimacy" of the child, of his referential status in the larger kinship system'. Leaving aside the phrase italicized by Parsons, to which no satisfactory anthropological meaning can be attached, this is a reasonable summary of Malinowski's notion of the family almost in words he might have used.

The extent to which Malinowski's hypotheses have been incorporated in current social science is best seen in the postulate that the nuclear family is the source and mainspring of all kinship custom and behaviour. 'The point of departure for the analysis of kinship is the nuclear family,' says Murdock (1949, p. 92), citing Malinowski in support. He goes on to state that the 'developing child's . . . behaviour in these primary intra-family relationships tends to be extended or "generalised" ', citing Evans-Pritchard in support. I have indicated why I do not accept Malinowski's hypotheses about the nuclear family but most anthropologists would agree with Murdock's restatement of it rather than with my criticisms. I suspect, however, that they would regard the specific notion of the Initial Situation as expressing a truism rather than a law of social organization.

The Principle of Legitimacy implied in Parsons's remarks is another thing. Ethnographic evidence seems to support it. The same idea, without the implications of the assumption that it is related to the necessity for the mother and child to have a male protector, underlies Radcliffe-Brown's distinction between the genitor, or physical father, and the pater, or jural father. There is no doubt that the recognition of this principle has led to important discoveries about kinship.[1]

It was the stroke of inspiration in interpreting the position of the father in the Trobriand family that confirmed this principle for

[1] Every article in *African Systems of Kinship and Marriage* (A. R. Radcliffe-Brown and D. Forde (eds.), 1950) contains evidence of this.

Malinowski, though he foreshadowed it in the Australian book. It is undeniable that his isolation of the 'split' in the father's rôles, and his description of how the critical features of the opposed rôles, are distributed in the matrilineal family, gave anthropology a new perception of family organization. Some anthropologists now interpret the expression of this split in custom and belief as deriving from the structural arrangements rather than from emotional conflict. It might properly be argued that the two points of view are complementary not antithetical. In any case, the root of the matter is Malinowski's analysis.

In the current emphasis special attention is fixed on the systems of rights and duties represented in kinship systems; and in analysing these, a place of cardinal importance is given to rules of reciprocity. Malinowski's elucidation of the part played by reciprocity in social life is one of his most notable contributions to modern theory. The distinction between freely given gifts and services and those rendered as legally binding obligations is essential to modern theory. As is well known, Malinowski's analysis of gift giving among the Trobrianders was enthusiastically hailed by Marcel Mauss in the famous *Essai sur le Don* (1925). He singled out the analysis of the husband's gifts to his wife in return for her sexual services as a 'très grande découverte'. Lévi-Strauss has built his theory of the exchange basis of cross-cousin marriage on Mauss's concept of the gift and it is not unreasonable to connect his theory, albeit indirectly, with Malinowski's 'great discovery'. Criticism of this discovery does not diminish its importance in stimulating the development of theory.

But perhaps, when all is said and done, Malinowski's most valuable legacy to us is the fabric itself, as he might have said. I have had to pull it apart for discussion, but the fabric into which all the separate strands of thought and observation and intuition were woven by him is unique. It is from the intimate study of Malinowski's work that we have learnt to see the inter-relatedness and coherence of all those numerous components of social life to which he gave the name of culture; and the effect on ethnographic craftsmanship and theoretical insight is conspicuous in the study of kinship and social organization. It is bound up with his revelation of the seamy side of culture as an inevitable and socially meaningful concomitant of the life of a society, reflecting its vital purposes and giving strength to it. What Malinowski revealed was that the deepest layers of conduct, feeling and social relationship are manifested in custom and are therefore accessible to scientific inquiry without overstepping the bounds of ethnographic method. I do not think we have fully assimilated this discovery. Perhaps the book on *The Psychology of Kinship* is still waiting to be written by somebody who will do so.

Malinowski on Magic and Religion

S. F. NADEL

THE advance of any science is punctuated as much by the disappearance of old problems as by the emergence of new ones. This is little better than a truism if we have in mind problems disappearing and discussions or controversies ceasing because the issues in question have been resolved. But often it is not a question of solution; rather it is a question of changes of viewpoint and interest. The old problems are abandoned because they no longer seem important; the controversies cease because all that can be said has been said; and if certain questions still remain unanswered they are yet shelved in spite of it, or perhaps because of it—because one realizes that they are unanswerable and should be replaced by other, more profitable, ones.

This is undoubtedly true of the development of social anthropology in the last fifty or sixty years. And the study of religion had more than its fair share of these fluctuations. Think of the controversies, now silent, about the origin of totemism, the distinction of magic and science, the 'meaning' (or 'nature', or 'function') of taboo or sacrifice, and many other, similar topics. These were brave attempts, aiming at final explanations and universally valid principles, even though they contained much that was speculative, much that was over-simplified, and a great deal of purely verbal argumentation. Today, we have grown much more modest, but also more conscious of the need for precision and solid empirical evidence. And many of the questions which inspired the earlier scholars are simply no longer asked. Perhaps we shall return to them one day. Meanwhile the position has been fairly summed up by Evans-Pritchard (1951a, p. 91) when he says, 'Whereas the nineteenth-century anthropologist sought to answer such questions as "what is the sociological significance of religion?" no anthropologist or, at any rate, no sensible anthropologist, would ask such a question today. Rather, he seeks to determine, for instance, the part played by the ancestor cult in a social system . . . among certain African peoples.' Malinowski was one of the last to ask these brave, 'big' questions, and in this sense stood at the close of an era. Equally, he signalled the beginning of a new one; for while his theoretical writings raised many of the problems which we are now ready to put on one side, it was his pioneer work in the field which showed anthropologists the more fruitful, restricted tasks of careful empirical research and concern with the particular rather than the universal.

There is, on the other hand, a firm linkage between broad generalizations aiming at universally valid statements and the empirical studies of particular problems. At some stage, someone must ask, and attempt to answer, those 'big' questions if empirical work is to proceed systematically and fruitfully. No one has seen this more clearly than Malinowski, the teacher no less than the writer. But methodologically, the relationship between the two is highly complicated; and here Malinowski did not always see the full extent of this complication. It would even be true to say that it never really occurred to him that the transition from the particular to the universal constituted a problem. Throughout his work he aimed at combining the two viewpoints, as he would claim, harmoniously, as we might be tempted to say, a little naïvely.

Putting it somewhat crudely, Malinowski's thought moved on two levels only—on the level of the particular society, the Trobriands, where he did his fundamental and exemplary field research; and on the level of primitive man and society at large, and indeed of Man and Society at large. In his more general writings Malinowski did refer also to other primitive societies; but he did so in main only for the sake of supporting evidence, of secondary importance. He never thought strictly in comparative terms. His generalizations jump straight from the Trobrianders to Humanity, as undoubtedly he saw the Trobrianders as a particularly instructive species of Humanity.

I shall hardly be the only contributor to this volume who finds occasion to make this comment. But Malinowski's discussion of magic and religion exemplifies the point at issue most strikingly. There, many of his statements are simply misleading unless they are seen in this light. More important, in treating of magic and religion he not merely betrays his over-readiness to generalize but goes out to prove its legitimacy.

Concerning religion, Malinowski would claim that we cannot but view it from the all-embracing perspective of human fate and destiny: 'We must always keep in sight the relation of faith to human life, to the desires, difficulties and hopes of human beings' (1936b, p. 2). And as regards magic, the broad generalizations seem doubly justified, by the very nature of the subject matter. For we are assured that 'primitive magic—as every field anthropologist knows to his cost—is extremely monotonous, strictly limited in its means of action, circumscribed in its beliefs, stunted in its fundamental assumptions'. It follows that when you study one rite or spell, one particular type of magic effort, you know them all—not only the magic system in the one society but ('adding a variant here and there') in every part of the world where magic is practised and believed in (1948, p. 51).

Is primitive magic indeed so uniform and 'monotonous'? Anthropologists who have worked in other fields will hardly subscribe to this statement. Let us be clear, however, that this is not a question of the 'basic' features of magic, the sort of features we should include in any initial definition, and which *must* be uniform in all cases to which the name magic is legitimately applied. Malinowski does on occasion provide such minimum definitions, for example, when he describes magic as an attempt to govern the forces of nature directly, by means of a 'special lore' (1922a, p. 73). But in pronouncing upon the uniformity of magic he has more in mind than some such minimum definition. He draws a picture of magic rich in descriptive detail and including a whole array of features: they all, according to him, are uniform and 'monotonously' repetitive.

Take these two—the emotionally charged atmosphere of magic acts, and the firm link between magic and mythology. In a picturesque passage Malinowski invites us to imagine ourselves watching a sorcerer in Melanesia. If we did not know who he was we might think him a 'lunatic' or a person 'acting under the spell of uncontrollable anger'. Magic acts, Malinowski holds, are inseparable from the expression of violent emotions; and though this may be true more especially of 'black magic' or love magic, that is, of occult acts explicitly concerned with the realization of passionate desires, ultimately all magic acts, whatever their apparent 'rationale', are *prima facie* expressions of emotions' (1948, p. 53). The very meaning of magic is sought in this 'affinity' with 'emotional outbursts, . . . with strong unrealizable desire' (1931a, p. 637).

Magic is similarly inseparable from mythology. The belief in magic power rests on the inherited myths, which are full of descriptions of magic feats. Equally, magic also creates and constantly replenishes its own 'running mythology of magic miracles', which relates all the presumed magic successes that can be remembered (or presented as would-be memories), and hence validates in advance any future magic effort (1931a, p. 640). If myths thus testify to the efficacy of magic, any contemporary act which seems to bear out such beliefs, in turn testifies to the 'authenticity of myth'. Thus magic is a 'link between mythical tradition and the present day', while myths provide the 'foundation for a system of magic'. Whichever way one looks at the circle, it justifies the assertion that, whenever magic appears in institutionalized form, an appropriate mythology will also be present (1922a, p. 303). But the nexus between the two is even closer. For the myth is said to 'crystallize into the magic formulae', as the magic spell in turn is always an occasion for 'mythological allusions' (1948, p. 55; 1931a, p. 638).

S. F. NADEL

As suggested a moment ago, the ethnography of other areas provides a great many examples which fail to bear out these categorical statements. There is the prosaic, matter-of-fact magic which shows none of the drama and passion Malinowski imputes to it, and which, incidentally, occurs in his own description of Trobriand garden magic (1922a, p. 424). Nor are we unfamiliar with magic spells entirely devoid of mythological allusions, and of whole systems of magic lacking any mythological superstructure (or 'foundation').

Enough has been said about Malinowski's over-readiness to generalize. Let us, then, regard his generalizations merely as hypotheses, stimulating even if inadequately supported, and concern ourselves with the underlying theoretical assumptions. For these are not necessarily affected by whatever corrections we are tempted to make in the ethnographic evidence. Thus behind the emphasis on the link between magic and mythology lies the tenet that magic is essentially traditionalistic. Often placed in the hands of the powers that be, it is 'invariably a conservative force', protecting 'vested interests' and the 'established order' (1931a, p. 640). Furthermore, the very power of magic depends on skills and techniques understood to be traditional, even unchangeable and timeless—'never invented and never tampered with'. Though in reality magic techniques change and adapt themselves all the time, in the belief of the people, they have been preserved intact since the beginning of things. To practise such inherited skills thus means to reaffirm and buttress the 'established order'. And few will gainsay the assertion that primitive magic does indeed add to the social forces maintaining the continuity of society.

Behind the emphasis on the affective character of magic acts lies another basic tenet, that magic manifests the inevitable human effort to achieve the fulfilment, however illusory, of 'strong, unrealizable' desires. This thesis, fundamental as it is to Malinowski's whole approach, deserves fuller treatment.

Primitive man, as Malinowski would paint his picture, is placed in a world where his technical skills and his capacity for rational thought assure him only of a limited measure of self-reliance and mastery over conditions. Within that range, he can confidently employ the knowledge gained from ordinary experiences. Beyond it, that knowledge avails him nothing. It is here that magic has its part to play, as a 'complement' to rational knowledge and skills (1944, p. 173); as an extension of human efforts beyond their natural competence; in a word, as a power reaching beyond the normal.

This 'beyond' has several somewhat different meanings. In a first sense it includes the chanciness of life—the risks, dangers, and incalculable accidents which even a highly efficient technology cannot quite eliminate. The chanciness is not equally great in all spheres of life; and

192

where we have relatively simple activities, involving few or no risks, we should, logically, find them unaccompanied by magic. This thesis is clinched by Malinowski's classical and oft-quoted illustration from the Trobriands, where the safe fishing in the lagoon has no magic associated with it, while fishing and sailing on the high seas involve all the paraphernalia of fully-fledged magic (1931a, p. 636).

A second meaning of the phrase 'beyond the normal' indicates the area of truly miraculous and, by 'normal' standards, impossible achievements. Myths describe an age of miracles in this sense, when canoes could fly through the air and aging men could rejuvenate themselves. Magic is still enacting 'limited miracles', that is, feats transcending ordinary capabilities and expectations. They need not be 'spectacular events': any repetitive magic rite that is believed in, any event 'where supernatural forces enter as cause or effect', is such a miracle (1936b, pp. 47-9). Thus, for people who know nothing about the processes of natural recovery after illness or the empirical treatment of disease, the regaining of health becomes the miraculous business of magic; and it is once more through the miracle of magic that an ugly man, normally repulsed by women, will hope to become attractive to them.

Thirdly, and finally, the effects of magic may go 'beyond the normal' both in the material and moral sense. This is the realm of black magic, sorcery, and witchcraft, when one can kill at a distance, miraculously as well as with evil intent.

Not all the instances of magic acts described by Malinowski fall convincingly within these three categories. The principle of chanciness, for example, would suggest that so simple, well-grounded a technology, facing so few risks, as gardening on a tropical island, should be in little need of magic support. Yet the opposite is true. To be sure, droughts and failures of the crops are always possible: but as surely these relatively remote risks are not comparable with the dangers of long sea voyages in dug-out canoes, to far-away, alien islands. There is, however, another point. In the Trobriands (as in many other primitive groups) the production of food and surplus enters deeply into social relationships, providing a means whereby personal bonds are maintained and prestige is won and kept. Here, then, we can understand that emotional involvement and even passions will enhance the gravity of risks and chance. But the risks are in a sense artificial ones. This is no longer a question of the tragic shortcomings of human inventiveness in the face of nature. Rather, magic serves to protect a particular people from failures which are failures only because their own social system has decreed them to be such and, in a sense, invented them. Differently put, magic is a tool used in the realization of the fortuitously given social values, not only a weapon in man's eternal fight against fate.

Much the same is true of another, minor type of magic recorded by Malinowski which, in the terms of his theory, would appear simply as unwarranted and even frivolous. I am thinking of the Trobriand magic used to achieve 'excellence in dancing' or, for that matter, to protect the excellent dancer from the envy (and black magic) of his rivals (1932a, p. 301). It is clearly the society itself which decrees that this excellence is desirable and enviable: so that the society invents both the desire and the tragedy of its frustration, and then, in addition, has to invent also the supernatural device to save the people from a risk of their own making.

Malinowski's interpretation of magic, it seems to me, is weakest when it has to account for magic evilly used. If the essence of magic lies in the promise that primitive man can indeed master the risks and dangers of his environment, why should he have added to them, by conceiving also of black magic and evil sorcery? Malinowski offers two answers. One is that black magic comes from 'the natural human reactions to frustrated hate and impotent anger', being merely a variant of similarly impassioned love magic (1931a, p. 639). The other, that the belief in magic must protect itself against being weakened through the absence of success. This is achieved in two ways. The rules governing magic may be so strict, complicated, and delicate that they are easily, and even unwittingly, infringed—which helps to explain away any failure one may have to admit. And again, every magic has its counter-magic, including the destructive magic prompted by evil desires—so that, if the efficacy of a magical device cannot be vindicated, its in-efficiency is at least accounted for. In other words, the need for a magic one can believe in creates the belief in a magic one must fear. But behind all this there is a more general psychological principle: 'Such is human nature', that any man's desire is satisfied not only by his own achievements but as much by the thwarting of others: which is a final source of the belief in black magic (1948, pp. 65–6).

These explanations are all incidental rather than systematic, failing to treat the evil use of magic as a problem in its own right. Also, borrowing heavily from common-sense psychology, Malinowski ignores the fact that the belief in black magic poses sociological and ethical questions as much as psychological ones. For if a society acknowledges the presence of occult destructive powers in its midst, that is, of agencies threatening its very norms and stability yet available to its members, this must indicate that the structure of the society itself invites or even requires the presence of these agencies. Sociologically, this is a problem of social cleavages and perhaps balances, setting norm against anti-norm; psychologically, of mechanisms creative of the respective fears, accusations, and incentives. In either case the social concession to occult aggression needs to be treated specifically, and within a systematic framework, not so to speak *en passant*. Evans-Pritchard, Kluckhohn and others have seen the problem much more clearly. And Malinowski's failure to do so is borne out by his treatment of the related subject of witchcraft. On this he has little to say save that, in the Trobriands, the various witchcraft beliefs are not 'consistent pieces of knowledge'. Witchcraft, since it appears confused in the minds of the people, can be dismissed as another example of emotional responses—of how 'the native feels and fears his belief rather than formulates it clearly to himself' (1922a, pp. 238-9).

Withal, naturally, the powers 'beyond the normal' promised by magic are only an illusion, if one reinforced by spurious successes and by the general human reluctance to abandon cherished and comforting beliefs. But though magic is akin to 'wish-fulfilment' and 'day-dreaming' it is not of the stuff that dreams are made of. It shows in activity; it encourages and permits action where a dispassionate assessment of conditions might leave no scope for rational effort. Malinowski puts the question bluntly—'What does man do naturally', if there is no sustaining belief in magic, when facing situations involving uncertainty and chance? The answer is, he cannot but realize his impotence. But human nature, like the physical universe of the ancients, abhors a vacuum. Man's organism and mentality 'drive him to some sort of activity' (1948, pp. 59-60). Magic is this activity: it relieves the tensions and the 'unstable equilibrium' created by anxieties and the feeling of impotence, placing man once more into 'harmony with life' (1948, p. 61; 1931a, p. 639). Even when it is merely a question of waiting for the favourable season, the Central Australian, for instance, 'instead of merely waiting in idle and demoralizing anxiety, marks time in carrying out his totemic ceremonies' (i.e. some relevant ritual) (1936b, p. 43). Nor is the ritual or magic action merely a vicarious one: rather, it carries with it the hope and promise of success, and hence the stimulus to essay in real life, and essay confidently, any action made feasible by the magic faith. In short, magic 'ritualizes optimism' (1948, p. 70).

This is a pragmatic and explicitly utilitarian theory of magic. The whole truth of magic, for those who practise it, is a 'pragmatic truth'; and the student of magic must admit that 'it is useful' in that it 'raises the efficiency' of the believer (1931a, p. 639). Indeed, without magic, primitive man 'would not have mastered the practical difficulties' of life nor 'advanced to the higher stages of culture' (1948, p. 70). So that magic is a necessary step in human survival and evolution.

Note that in this final formulation the 'negative' side of magic—the fears and threats created by its evil use—no longer find any mention. But note also that Malinowski's pragmatic interpretation of magic does not stop at this speculative level. It applies equally to the strictly empirical data of primitive work and economic enterprise. And here Malinowski's approach to magic has undoubtedly opened up a new vista. For he was the first to show how magic rites can be used as signals inaugurating work and leading it through successive stages, and how the concentration of magic powers in the hands of a leader serves to

S. F. NADEL

organize labour and control co-operative efforts (e.g. 1935, Vol. I, pp. 457–8). Perhaps Malinowski over-rationalized the rôle (or 'function') of magic; at least, he found difficulty in handling forms of magic not unambiguously 'useful'. A magician can easily be turned into a sort of supernaturally qualified 'foreman'. But in other respects, considering the many ritual rules, taboos and the like which often surround economic activities, magic, as it makes work run more smoothly, so it also seems to impose extra work, in the form of 'apparently unnecessary, hampering taboos and regulations'. One can only assume that 'in the long run' these too are 'economically invaluable', through regulating and systematizing work (1922a, p. 60). Clearly, whether applied to the psychology of Primitive Man or, more prosaically, to aspects of primitive economy, Malinowski's view of magic (as his whole 'functional' approach) is typified by what I have elsewhere called the *presumption of adequacy* (Nadel, 1951, p. 376).

For Malinowski, the core of the magic procedure is the formula or spell, rendered faithfully, without deviation. It is no accident, therefore, that he should have explored the linguistic concomitants of magic with such thoroughness (1935, Vol. II). He overrated, I think, the part played by *intelligible* language: obscure, incomprehensible spells and invocations are as often vehicles for the magic intent. However this may be, Malinowski more than anyone else has taught us the importance of language in the whole study of supernatural beliefs and practices. One point, in particular, deserves mention.

In any study of primitive magic there is the problem of distinguishing between magical procedures proper and others which represent merely empirical knowledge misapplied. To some extent, this is the old question of the relationship of magic and primitive science. But let me leave this wider issue for the moment and consider only the strictly practical question, how to judge a doubtful situation. That such doubtful situations exist is certain. Think of some matter-of-fact procedure that looks like magic *to us*, implying effects which are irrational and empirically unsound or even impossible, such as poisons believed to work at a distance or healing practices based on the principle of 'like causes like'. Might not such a procedure represent, for the people, only a profane, technical, would-be empirical effort (however objectively crude or misconceived)? Whatever other facts we should consider, the crucial evidence must clearly be the people's own conceptions, and hence the words they use. Though Malinowski does not explicitly refer to this linguistic criterion, he made use of it—which is still a lesson worth learning. Thus he mentions that in the Trobriands there is a special term, *megwa*, indicating all non-ordinary, non-normal effects, that is, all effects due not to virtues residing in man or in objects, but to the virtues residing in the magical spell (1922a, p. 424).

Though the main force of magic rite resides in the spell, the latter rarely stands by itself. Usually it is accompanied by a rite more or less complex or 'autonomous'. In the simplest case it is a rite of 'impregnation', whereby the ritual gestures convey the spell to the object which is to be 'magicked'; more commonly, the rite involves the use of a further object, operating as a 'medium' through absorbing the force of the spell and transferring it to the final object (1922a, pp. 404–7). Yet whence this power ascribed to gestures and 'media' or, for that matter, to the words themselves?

Malinowski's answer might be guessed: the power derives from the basic character of magic as an expression of desires and of overwhelming emotions. More precisely, primitive man believes in the efficacy of gestures, objects and words to bring some desired goal within his reach, if they in some manner reflect his desire or give it visible shape. Thus certain substances or paraphernalia, as they happen to bear on the purpose of the magic act, so they become 'emotionally associated' with it and offer themselves as promising tools or media (1948, p. 53). 'Sympathetic magic', in which objects and gestures resembling the desired end are used to achieve it, is nothing but the figurative anticipation of the longed-for events: it goes with the 'imagery and symbolism' that 'haunt the magician' (1931a, p. 638). And as for the faith in the magic of words, this seems irreducible: we can say no more than that 'the native is deeply convinced of the mysterious intrinsic power' of these forms of expressive speech (1922a, p. 451).

This is a highly subjective interpretation. It may explain why the individuals using magic to further their own ends, and perhaps the magician acting for them, become convinced, at that moment, of the efficacy of their acts. But it must fail to explain the general magic knowledge (Malinowski's 'lore') existing in the society and providing a body of rules and prescriptions in which everyone trusts. For this knowledge must surely be such that it convinces also the dispassionate person, and convinces him at all times. It must have an objective appeal. It must contain something in the nature of a *theory*, persuasive because of the principles and arguments on which it rests, and akin, however remotely, to scientific theories.

Here, then, we touch upon the old controversy as to whether or not magic represents the primitive equivalent of science. Malinowski's stand in this respect is unambiguous. Magic and science, he argues, are alike in that both have specific aims, develop specific techniques, and are strictly practically oriented. Yet though magic might be called a 'pseudo-science' (or, better still, an extension beyond the natural limits of science) it can in no way be equated with it. Even on the most primitive level the two exist side by side, as distinct entities, controlling 'different phases of human behaviour' and differing 'in substance, form, and function' (1944, p. 197). They involve diverse social settings and diverse bodies of tradition—one profane, the other sacred, being 'hedged round by observances, mysteries, taboos' (1948, p. 67). Magic is unambiguously 'supernatural', occult, apart from being dominated by emotion: where magic promises miracles to the primitive, his science circumscribes the realm of rational efforts and of skills based on experience.

No anthropologist will quarrel with the gist of this. But the whole argument is rendered misleading by the all-too-ambitious term 'science'. For the thing magic is separated from or contrasted with is not really science, that is, a logically coherent body of empirical knowledge, but merely technology and the disconnected items of practical knowledge sufficient to sustain it. When Malinowski says—'We know now that primitive humanity was aware of the scientific laws of natural process' (1944, p. 196), this is simply untrue. What primitive peoples are aware of are scattered facts about natural processes, which can be turned to practical use: they have nowhere reached the notion of 'scientific laws' or any other conception meriting the name of science. At least, they have not done so in the 'phase' of profane behaviour.

If magic were truly compared with science, this would mean discussing theories about the world, principles discovered in phenomena, and the deductions made from them. Now it is perfectly conceivable that the earliest speculations about the universe and the first crude conceptions of 'principles' occurred in the realm of magic, not in that of practical technology. Frazer had this in mind when he regarded sympathetic magic with its axiom of 'like causes like', and magic based on the notion of contiguity, as being in the nature of such principles, and hence as demonstrating the analogy of magic and science. Mauss (1950, p. 69) similarly saw in the magical affinities imputed to objects and substances the beginning of scientific classification. Both scholars should, perhaps, more correctly have spoken of 'metaphysics' rather than 'science'. In any event, when Malinowski, and others after him, set out to prove that the primitive, in his profane actions, is never guided (or misguided) by these spurious laws and classifications, the proof missed its target; for they did not really disprove the assumption that magic conceptions may be the primitive analogue, not of applied science, nor perhaps of experimental science but of its theoretical and speculative side, however crude and 'metaphysical'.

But Malinowski would attack this assumption also. He explicitly denies that magic has anything to do with speculations about the universe or the desire to understand it. Undoubtedly, there exist primitive beliefs of the latter kind, such as the belief in *mana*, in some kind of undifferentiated 'force' or 'universal power'. But this 'early generalization of a crude metaphysical concept' is utterly distinct from magic; magic cannot be derived from it since it arises 'spontaneously', from particular situations, ideas, and emotional tensions. It is not in nature but only in man, and in man's relation to nature. Above all, magic arises from action, and *is* action—the 'power of creating desired ends': it has no reflective or metaphysical side (1948, pp. 56-9; 1931*a*, p. 638).

If this is pragmatism carried to the extreme it is no more than the logical sequel of Malinowski's psychological-utilitarian theory of magic. And to argue against it, say, by adducing evidence to show that elsewhere magic *is* linked with efforts to understand the universe or 'symbolize' its nature—as Lévi-Strauss might put it (1950, p. xlix)—would be arguing about definitions. For if you start out with the thesis that magic is the 'expression of overwhelming emotions', then any feature failing to conform to it would make the thing in question, not magic, but something else—a 'crude metaphysics' or perhaps religion. I said 'perhaps', because Malinowski equally rejects the assumption that religion might be 'born out of speculation and reflection' (1931*a*, p. 641). For him, Tylor's view of primitive man 'as a ratiocinating philosopher' is nothing better than a myth (1944, p. 27).

We turn, then, to that other boundary problem, concerning the relationship between magic and religion. Here too, Malinowski aims at a clear-cut distinction. Magic and religion are alike in that both arise from emotional stress, from felt crises of life, and from the realization that man's control of the universe, by reason and empirical skills, is tragically limited. They are alike also, in that both have their mythology, their miracles, and the taboos and observances separating the sacred from the profane. But though both represent an escape from the 'impasse' of human impotence, they differ radically in the nature of the escape they afford.

Magic is characterized by limited techniques and a practical orientation; religion is a 'body of self-contained acts', complex and rich in content, and expressing itself in rituals and beliefs which have 'value' (not utility). Magic rests in the simple trust in efficacious spells and rites; religion commands the 'whole supernatural world of faith', with a pantheon of gods, spirits, benevolent powers. While the mythology of magic only 'boasts' of 'primeval achievements', religious mythology turns into cosmogony, and opens vistas of a future life. Magic is in the hands of specialists—technicians as it were; religion is 'an affair of all', the specialization (of priests or visionaries) representing 'not a profession but a personal gift'. Finally, while magic can be good as well as evil and is concerned as much with the 'doing of things' (positive magic) as with the 'undoing of things' done by others (counter-magic), religion is essentially moral and has to do with 'irremediable happenings' (1948, pp. 67-9).

From this point-by-point comparison (which is Malinowski's) one might gain the impression that he was unable to see religion save against the foil of magic. Certain other passages even suggest that, for

Malinowski, religion was little more than a bigger and better kind of magic. Thus he says of religion that it involves wider issues of personal and social integration than those 'catered for by magic'; and if magic deals with the 'impasse' of human impotence in the face of the practical problems of living, religion deals with 'the whole range of anxieties, forebodings and problems concerning human destinies and man's place in the universe' (1931a, p. 641). But more often, Malinowski reads a much more subtle meaning into the relationship of magic and religion. He views them as two opposed yet complementary crystallizations or forms of transcendental belief. If one is the foil of the other, this is merely because primitive human existence seems to require them both, human evolution having caused both to emerge and to coexist over long periods of time. The point-by-point comparison merely indicates that, for Malinowski, the 'boundary problem' of separating the two was both genuine and relevant.

I have said just now that Malinowski viewed magic and religion as 'opposed yet complementary' forms of transcendental belief. Let me explain this more fully. Magic and religion are opposed in that the magic act is not only utilitarian but instrumental: it has an explicit purpose known to everyone, being simply a means for bringing about a particular end as a subsequent event or state of affairs (1948, p. 20; 1935, Vol. I, p. 455). Religious acts have no purpose in this sense; or at least, the rite and its purpose 'are one', the end being 'realized in the very consummation of the act' (1948, pp. 21, 23). In pure acts of worship (with which Malinowski does not deal) or in 'feasts of rejoicing' (such as a birth ceremonial) this is self-evidently so. But it is true also, in a somewhat different sense, of religious ceremonials more explicitly linked with particular ends or aims. The ceremonial sanctifying marriage is so linked with an 'end'. Yet it is plainly not meant to cause the end in question—the union of man and wife—as a 'subsequent event': it establishes that union by its performance; it creates and demonstrates 'the supernaturally sanctioned bond' which is marriage. Initiation rites similarly imply an aimed-at state of affairs. But they are not procedures meant to effect this change—the transformation from adolescence to manhood: they *are* this transformation, demonstrating and heralding it.

Now what religious rites do thus establish, demonstrate or herald are lasting attitudes, stable relationships, the awareness of rights and obligations, in brief, a piece of the social order. And in this sense magic and religion are also complementary. For magic engineers (or promises to do so) immediate, tangible benefits; religion, remote and abstract ones. Indeed the latter are not benefits in the same sense of the word. They do not meet the felt needs of individuals, whatever they may be— success in economic venture, love or war, or the defeat of rivals; they only meet impersonal needs or necessities such as we, anthropologists or sociologists, discover in societies or impute to them. So understood, religion sanctifies and hence sustains social usages; it sacralizes the assumption of relationships. Broadly speaking, it lends its sanction to the structure and values of the society, and in this sense is 'indispensable to the integration of the community', which means, to its whole orderly existence (1936b, p. 59).

Malinowski does not use the word 'benefits'; he refers to these abstract and remote effects of religious practice as its 'function' or 'raison d'être', which it is the task of the sociologist to establish (1948, p. 21). Yet since any such explanation is in terms of usefulness (for anything 'indispensable' is surely useful), it seems legitimate to speak of benefits and to juxtapose, as I have done, individually and socially beneficial consequences. Nor does Malinowski, in a different context, hesitate to describe the disappearance of religion from modern society as a process fraught with danger and tragedy—the danger that goes with social instability, and the tragedy of moral aimlessness. Which means, once more, acknowledging the benefits of religion. But of this wider significance of religion I shall have to say more a little later.

For religion to have all these effects, there must be suitable occasions when it can be brought into play. There are, of course, the periodical ceremonials, feasts, and religious gatherings of general import which every religion 'demands' (1948, p. 36). More important, there are the crises of human life, which are most readily elaborated by religion. They may be no more than occasions in the strict sense of the word, when religion steps in and displays its remote, impersonal efficacy. In initiation rites, for example, when the tribe's traditional lore and moral values are impressed upon the adolescents, the human crisis as such is only as it were the raw material. The psychological and biological effects of puberty are transformed into social ones: what counts is the learning of new habits and viewpoints, the physiological transition being turned into a moral and 'spiritual metamorphosis', which far transcends the original biological event (1948, pp. 22-3). Similarly the social import of the marriage ceremonial is 'superadded to the primarily biological fact'.

But the crises of human life, being crises, also exercise their own, direct pressure on ritual and belief so that, from mere 'occasions', they become demands—for psychological comfort and assurances. The perennial crises concerning food, inescapable in primitive societies on the subsistence level, are of this kind. Thus in the sacralization of food (in sacrifice and communion) the crucial theme is the dependence upon providence and faith in divine benevolence. The more remote, impersonal efficacy of religion is not absent: the sacrificial act, too, demonstrates socially relevant viewpoints or values in that it involves the idea of 'giving' and 'exchanging'—the same kind of giving and exchanging which pervades and sustains ordinary social intercourse. But behind it all is the hope or promise of abundance, that is, the effect of a personal access of confidence.

The paradigm of this psychological significance of religion is the sacralization of death. We might add that, for Malinowski, the ritual of death is more than a paradigm: it indicates the very source from which religion must have sprung. Death, he holds, is the paramount crisis in the lives of individuals and the community. But in the primitive attitude to death the feelings of horror or fear are not paramount. Rather, they are mingled with love for the dead, the continued love for those one held personally dear. Which twofold attitude is evidenced in the manner of disposing of the dead, in the longing to preserve them, and in the shrinking-away from the visible transformation wrought by death. There is the desire both to maintain the tie with the departed, and to break it. In this psychological crisis the new notion is born of a future life and the survival of the spirit (1948, p. 32). If all this seems to refer only to the emotional conflicts of the individual and to the rôle of religion in quieting or resolving them, social factors yet enter. For this love-fear of the dead expresses attachments and sentiments which both arise from social living-together and are sanctioned by the social order. If there is, in every human being, a 'deep need to deny personal destruction', from which spring ancestor worship, domestic cults, and every form of mortuary ritual, it indicates also the rebellion against the destruction of loyalties and relationships born of social life (1931a, p. 641). Men who exist in 'life-long co-operation and mutual assistance' cannot easily face the dissolution of. these bonds when life ceases. Ultimately, then, it is social existence, the involvement in social relationships, which creates the sacralization of death and the concept of immortality.

We note that here the social relevance of religion, its capacity to sustain a society, is reduced to an incidental aspect of that other capacity of religion, to give comfort to individuals facing some deep crisis. The personal crisis of death simply cannot help being a social one as well since the sentiments assailed by death are sentiments that only arise with social relationships. And in sustaining the fear-stricken or grief-stricken human being, religion cannot help sustaining a society periodically including such human beings. To be sure, Malinowski would have denied that he failed to give due recognition to the social concomitants of mortuary rites and beliefs about death. He saw the two effects as merging in a double purpose: as religion prevents man giving way to fear and horror, which would disintegrate the group and destroy the culture, so it re-establishes solidarity and morale and saves the continuity of social existence (1948, p. 35). And as religion offers the vista of immortality to men, so it teaches them 'to act in common with past and future generations' (1931a, p. 641).

In retrospect it seems only a short step from this obliquely sociological interpretation to one fully so, that is, to the interpretation of mortuary rites as social mechanisms, dealing not only with the emotional disturbances of individuals, but with the readjustment of groups depleted by death. Malinowski did not quite take this step. Nor perhaps did he fully think out the implications of the 'sociological function' of religion, even though he formulated it in broad terms. But this broad formulation meant, in his time, a momentous step forward. When scholars still thought of religion as springing entirely from speculations about man's place in the universe or from some emotional craving causing man to people his world with supernatural beings, even the bare announcement that religion owed its origin, in part, to social factors, meant giving a new direction to anthropological study.

I used the words 'origin' and 'in part' advisedly. Malinowski still thought in evolutionary terms, of the emergence of religion and of the sources from which it sprang. Equally, social factors never meant to him more than one such source, the other being the experiences and needs of man as a psycho-physiological organism. If Malinowski did not side with those who found the answer to all such questions in the creativeness of some undefined 'individual mind', neither did he agree with the 'collectivists' such as Durkheim and his school, who spoke of 'collective representations' and saw in religion merely the precipitate of group existence. Malinowski would argue that, whatever religion may achieve, for instance, in upholding the moral values of the group, it cannot but work 'through individual mental attitudes'. Religion, therefore, is not entirely social but arises 'to a great extent from purely individual sources' (1948, p. 41). Malinowski did not quite succeed in striking a balance. Partly, this was no doubt due to the conceptual framework he inherited, which still preserved the misleading antithesis of individual and society, and crudely separated the 'individual mind' from anything 'social'. But partly, he did not really want to strike a balance. For him, the decisive weight lay with the psychological, and in this sense individual, sources of religion. The 'social share in religious enactment' is only a necessary, not a sufficient condition for the emergence of religion: the latter cannot be finally understood save through the 'analysis of the individual mind' (1948, p. 50).

In Malinowski's later writings the social (and social-ethical) aspects of religion receive much greater emphasis. Even so they remain secondary and almost incidental aspects. The crucial feature of any religion is still man's emotional dependence on the supernatural powers, though this in turn entails dependence on one's fellow men: 'You cannot worship in common without a common bond of mutual trust and assistance, that is, of charity and love.' Social relationships and the cohesion of the group are still little more than by-products: it simply happens that worshippers will also 'have natural duties towards each other', conceive of mutual responsibilities, and acquire common sentiments. Similarly, every organized belief, as it needs to 'have been felt by many thinkers instructed by scholarship and common sense', so it makes religion a common possession of society and part of its order. Taboos, finally, vigils, and other forms of religious discipline become social-moral disciplines as well, since they imply 'a sacrifice of man's personal comfort for the common weal' (1936b, pp. 3, 6–7).

Malinowski's reluctance to admit the autonomy of the 'social sources' of religion involved him in some awkward questions. One is, why religious rites are collective and primitive religions an affair of the community. The answer is given, once more, in terms of secondary effects and incidental utility. Thus, when experiencing the death of someone loved, the bereaved individual by himself would be unable to withstand sorrow and fear. Here the group steps in, other people, un-affected by the calamity and 'not torn by the metaphysical dilemma', bringing him consolation and strength. In initiation, the public character of the rite ensures 'homogeneity and uniformity in the teaching of morals'. And more generally, the collectivity gives powerful public testimony to the positive, optimistic aspects of religious belief. The collective character of religious rituals, then, is only 'a matter of technique': the vital ends or ideas served by the technique 'exist in the individual' (1948, pp. 44–5).

Another question is whether there is such a thing as a 'religious instinct'? Malinowski argues both against the assumption of an 'intrinsic' human propensity for religion and against the assumption that religion is merely 'superimposed' by culture and society. In truth, religion is something in between—a 'derived need', though one with deep foundations. It is derived from the social organization in which man acts and lives, and through which alone he can assure his biological survival. And since it is in this social existence that many of man's mental conflicts arise, religion, in showing a way to resolve them, also sustains the survival of man (or man-in-society).

Magic, it should be noted, has deeper foundations still; for it 'corresponds to a real physiological need' (1931a, p. 639). Thus, if magic 'ritualizes optimism' for man as an organism, religion may be said to inject it into the society in which he exists.

At the same time Malinowski's view of religion is itself an optimistic one, and consciously so. To 'understand' religion, he says, is to bring to light its 'culturally valuable core' (1936, p. 3). In itself, this may be a defensible thesis. But it is treacherous when handled naïvely, as Malinowski did handle it. He is simply silent on all the features of religion not easily reconciled with his optimistic interpretation—the concepts of sin and temptation, the belief in powers of darkness, or the fatalism that goes with beliefs in predestination. Nor does Malinowski ever consider the tragedies so often wrought in human history by fanatical and rival creeds. The fact that primitive religion sustains the structure, values and the uniform code of morality of any given society seems enough to place it among the unambiguous benefits given to humanity. As this fact explains the 'orthodoxy of primitive religions' so it 'excuses their intolerance' (1948, p. 49). But surely when judging the value of religion the *status quo* of single societies cannot be our universe of discourse. And in the wider perspective of human society at large and of the whole history of human civilization, the justification of orthodoxy and the 'excuse' of intolerance are poor supports of Malinowski's theology of optimism.

With the naïvety of this theology goes a streak of casuistry. Malinowski, as I have said, could not conceive of religion disappearing from human society without leaving behind collapse and tragedy. He expressed this view thus forcibly only once. He did so in those dark hours when Europe seemed destined to be overwhelmed by the forces of a new barbarism. It is with this in mind that we must read his passage about humanity, devoid of religion, becoming the playball of other, cruder and more dangerous faiths, in egotism, intolerance, and collective brutality. He goes on to ask—'Is religion going to surrender its equipment of faith, ritual and ethics to cross-breeds between superstition and science, between economics and credulity, between politics and national megalomania?' The question bears witness to Malinowski's sincere humanism; but the answer is more than a little disturbing. 'The rationalist and agnostic', he says, 'must admit that even if he himself cannot accept the truths [of religion], he must at least recognize them as indispensable pragmatic figments without which civilization cannot exist' (1936b, p. 62). If this is still humanism, even pragmatic humanism, it seems dangerously close to the cynicism of Plato's 'noble lie'.

One suspects that to the pragmatist Malinowski the subject matter of religion was less congenial than that of magic. There is some simple evidence for this. In the comprehensive article on Culture which Malinowski wrote for the *Encyclopaedia of the Social Sciences*, three double columns are devoted to Religion and thirteen to Magic. An accident? I think not. Malinowski's account of magic is rigorously coherent and internally consistent; if you wish to quarrel with it you must quarrel with a systematic theory. Against this, the treatment of religion is loose and disjointed: there seem to be too many things incapable of conceptual integration. In a sense, Malinowski admits as much when he comments on the multiplicity of aspects and purposes that may appear combined in any religion, and on the absence of any simple technique. Religion has unity rather 'in the function which it fulfils and in the value of its belief and ritual' (1948, p. 68). Now my point is not that Malinowski failed to perceive or define such an ultimate unity: he did perceive and define it. My point is that, to him, the many-sidedness of religion meant an obstacle to understanding. He could not conceptually handle religion, as it were, as a multi-dimensional entity: there had to be some simple unity of function, in which, inevitably, many sides of religion were obscured or lost. There is Malinowski's denial of any intrinsic link between religion and reflective or speculative thought. The crucial moral implications of religion, as evidenced in religious sanctions and notions of divine retribution, are touched upon only in passing. Anything in religion which is not optimistic or optimism-promoting, is disregarded. Finally, there is that uneasy balance between the two 'competences' of religion, psychological and social, individual and collective.

By the same token, mythology was undoubtedly the topic most congenial to Malinowski. Here everything is clear-cut, consistent, and indeed forceful. If his treatment of religion and magic opened up certain new vistas, his interpretation of myth was altogether revolutionary. Today, we use many of his formulations as a matter of course; his signal phrase, 'mythical charter', has become an indispensable part of the modern anthropological vocabulary—which is probably the strongest testimony to the importance of Malinowski's contribution.

The 'revolution' lay, stated simply, in the denial of the explanatory or symbolic function of myth. Its function is direct and pragmatic. Myth is a statement relevant for the establishment of the existing social order; a justification by sacred precedent: a warrant or 'charter' (1931a, p. 640).

There are, to be sure, incidental aspects of myth which serve quite different purposes. Myths may occupy the place of poetry and epics: the mythology of the Trobriand *kula*, for example, also supplies 'one of the heroic elements in tribal life' (1922a, p. 297). Myth enriches people's perception of their environment: it fills the landscape with dramatic happenings and with meaning (p. 330). And myth also attempts to provide a total story of the world, from its creation to the phase one knows as the present, with its living customs and institutions (p. 305). One might ask if this is not in part 'explanation' and hence an intellectual effort born of the desire to understand, to complete and transcend the fragmentary knowledge human beings ordinarily possess? Malinowski would argue that there is still a deep gulf between the 'sacred tradition' of myth and any attempt at 'scientific explanation': the former 'does not explain things; it tells how they were created' (1936b, p. 42). And even if there is an explanatory element in sacred tradition, it is only 'secondary'; it would still be subordinated to that other notion, of explaining that which exists today, exists by right— by the right that flows from the anchorage in primeval happenings.

Myth is thus intimately bound up with tradition and continuing custom. And this means two things. One is that myth buttresses the adherence to traditional ways of life by tracing them 'back to a higher, better, more supernatural reality of initial events' (1926c, p. 125). The other is that myth must itself foreshadow such a continuous and unchanging state. Myth, Malinowski holds, is not a history composed of 'epochs' or suggestive of evolutionary stages and successive changes. Rather, it reveals a conception of the past which is only 'one vast storehouse of events'. It has no demarcated periods and no defined duration. It does not 'unroll itself' stage by stage; nor yet is the past of myth anything like an extension of the 'historical' past, being more distant and more dimly perceived. For the primitive the past is an undifferentiated, continuous area of time, describable only by such phrases as 'long ago' or 'very long ago'. And where the mythical past ends, there is at once the present, an ever-shifting and extended present so to speak, that is, the period documented by the memory of living people, one's own or one's father's (1922a, pp. 300–1).

Malinowski is throughout thinking of truly 'primitive' peoples, having no techniques, however crude, of measuring past time and of historiography, and lacking all historical perspective in our sense. Much of what he says is therefore inapplicable to the more complex societies since studied by anthropologists. But certain points remain valid. For even in the would-be history of these societies the succession of events is often ambiguous, suggestive of that generous 'storehouse' rather than of any consistent conception of epochs and sequences. Nor will the people always be able (or inclined) to say—'thus far we have history, and beyond it, myth'. Above all, the events of history, spurious or 'real', may only have the same reality as events we should call mythical, namely, the reality of precedents legitimizing the present.

Let me return for a moment to Malinowski's discussion of the conception of the past as revealed in primitive myth. Though he set himself only this narrow problem, implicitly he touched upon a much wider one, the very notion of time of primitive peoples. Here we may recall the more recent attempts, by philosophers and anthropologists, to show that the conception of time is shaped or determined by the character of the society in which people live. Most sharply put—time, for the primitive, is simply 'a conceptualization of the social structure' (Evans-Pritchard, 1951, p. 46): In spite of the different phraseology, there is a close link between Malinowski's thesis and this modern view. I suggest, in fact, that Malinowski has foreshadowed it, even though the nexus between the conception of time and the conditions of society, as he saw it, concerned only the unchanging, tradition-bound character of the latter. Let me quote a passage from Halbwachs: 'That time can remain in some fashion static during an extended period, this results from the fact that it serves as a common framework for the thoughts of a group, which itself, during this period, does not change its nature, preserves more or less the same structure, and turns its attention to the same objects' (1940/48, p. 128). I would not suggest that Malinowski could have written this. This kind of analytical approach was foreign to his way of thinking. If he had attempted to formulate his thoughts on the matter he would probably have argued the other way around— that a society bound to unchanging custom creates a conception of time similarly unchanging, as its support or 'charter'. But whether viewed analytically or pragmatically, it is the same nexus, and one first perceived by Malinowski.

There seems no better way of summing up Malinowski's contribution to the study of religious belief than by saying that he first perceived new ways of looking at these phenomena and a new logic in them, which his successors have inherited, developed, and no doubt also corrected. The 'logic', for Malinowski, was the logic of rationality. Magic, religion, mythology—they all had to make sense. If this 'sense' was often over-simplified and too closely akin to common sense, his search for it was a guide without which we, his successors, could probably not have charted our way.

Malinowski would have claimed that this 'sense' was a scientific one. And there was only one science he considered relevant to social inquiry— biology, more precisely, the biology at the beginning of this century, still strongly evolutionary and teleological, and dominated by the concept of survival. Nor would Malinowski have considered affinity with common sense a weakness. He could still hold that 'fundamental scientific truths in physics and biology, as in the science of man, are never sophisticated' (1936b, p. 7). The conception of a science which, by lay standards, is abstruse and opposed to common sense, was yet alien to the climate of thought of his day.

Even so, we should give due recognition to Malinowski's faith in the 'scientific study' (as he saw it) of human culture, including the 'imponderables' of religion and the 'irrationality' of magic or myth. But has a faith thus qualified still any valid meaning, as a message or example, for the new generation of anthropologists? I believe so. And I believe that there is also another message or example to be found in Malinowski's work.

In that fusion of rationalism, a biological viewpoint, and, equally, a 'theology of optimism' lay Malinowski's strength as well as weakness. It undoubtedly limited his awareness of the problems thrown up by primitive religion and magic, in ways we have discussed. But from the same threefold source sprang also Malinowski's clear perspective, upon man and human destiny. We still cannot do without this perspective, even though our greater consciousness of the complexity of facts and the vulnerability of our methods might make it appear less fruitful than it did to Malinowski. To disregard it, would mean utterly to emaciate the ideas of religion and magic.

The Place of Malinowski in the History of Economic Anthropology[1]

RAYMOND FIRTH

THERE is a paradox in Malinowski's contribution to economic anthropology. At an early stage of his work he wrote, 'There is no other aspect of primitive life where our knowledge is more scanty and our understanding more superficial than in Economics' (1922a, p. 84). If this view (which he stated on a number of occasions) is less true now, most of the credit for leading the way to a better appreciation of the subject is due to Malinowski himself. Yet his knowledge of formal economics was always very limited; his approach to economic analysis began largely on a descriptive, common-sense level and for the most part continued to be unsophisticated. To what then can we attribute the value of his own work and the stimulus which he gave to the work of others in this field?

I think it is due to three things: to the novelty of his first-hand field investigations with their specific consciousness of economic implications; to the verve and sincerity of his concrete exposition; and to his insight in being concerned as much with the relations between the economic and other aspects of the social system as with economic phenomena in themselves. This concern with the social content of economic phenomena was due probably to the fact that Malinowski's theoretical knowledge of economics and its emergence in economic anthropology was derived rather from those who may be termed broadly sociologists than from economists as such—with whom he never seems to have had very much to do. In his critique of L. H. Dudley Buxton's book on primitive labour (1925b) he expressed his disappointment at the neglect of work by Hahn, Schurtz, Cunow, Lewinski, Bücher, Thurnwald, Max Weber, and Koppers. It was from such authorities—though not much, it would seem, from Weber—that he largely derived his own framework of

[1] I am indebted to Mr. M. G. Swift for helpful comment on an earlier draft of this chapter.

concepts. But while Karl Bücher in particular had a very considerable effect upon his presentation, from the older writers Malinowski drew inspiration largely by reaction. From Bücher's examination of the effect of rhythm on work, I think that Malinowski gained more perhaps than he himself realized of inspiration for his own analysis of incentive and indeed for the parallel relation of magic to labour. But he was highly critical of Bücher's evolutionary scheme and in particular of his postulate of a pre-economic stage in history being represented in the life of modern primitive peoples.

From this and analogous negative propositions Malinowski proceeded to the establishment of a number of positive analyses. Through such correction of fallacies, he demonstrated, for example, the following points:

1. The assumption of primitive man as being purely rational, utilitarian and logical in his economic affairs was a grave error; social convention, social restriction and the principles of the social structure dictate much 'savage' economic behaviour (see e.g. 1922a, p. 516).

2. Among Australian aborigines, the Mailu, the Trobrianders, there was economic organization—hence no pre-economic stage was likely among any modern primitive peoples. (In his earliest work—1912a— he had not formulated his position clearly on this point.)

3. So far from being indolent, individually self-seeking and irresponsible in his economic affairs, the 'savage' was capable of long and arduous work.

4. Contrary to common view, 'savages' had highly organized and systematic forms of labour.

5. Trade and exchange among primitive communities were by no means necessarily rudimentary, but could be regular, elaborate and complex, both in operations and as regards their stimuli.

6. Concepts of primitive ownership were not to be defined either by group attributions of 'communism' or by individual exclusive possession, but in terms of multiple rights of groups and individuals.

Such generalizations, so obvious to us now, were of great importance more than thirty years ago at a time when the framework of evolutionary concepts was still dominant in anthropology, with a rigidity which inhibited perceptive analysis of behaviour. Even in his earliest work Malinowski insisted on the need for discussion of economic phenomena in an empirical framework. 'In order to prove that we find in the Intichiuma Ceremonies any form of division of labour, a detailed analysis of fact would be necessary, with a precise indication of the details displaying this aspect' (1912a, p. 82n.). As with his affirmations about the existence of law in primitive societies, the precise character of these general economic propositions was less important than the stimulus which they gave to discussion and field research.

Yet the theoretical phrasing of his economic propositions was often open to question. Indeed it is not quite clear throughout his work how Malinowski really understood the concept of 'economic'—or how far his refusal to phrase this concept in professional idiom rested upon a lack of understanding of its full implications. In his earliest essay, while arguing for a recognition of co-ordination of labour in the *intichiuma* ceremonies, he appeared to vacillate about admitting such labour to the category of 'economic'. He found an analogy between co-operation in these ceremonies with 'economic co-operation' as 'no more than a superficial resemblance' (1912*a*, p. 82n.). In his preoccupation still with the evolutionary schemes of Bücher, he was concerned to identify *economic* and *economic labour* with the type of work performed in civilized industrial enterprises. The difference lay not in the amount of work done but in its character. To be termed economic it must be systematic, periodically repeated, rationally planned, etc. Malinowski even states that 'primitive labour is quite unfit for economic purposes' (1912*a*, p. 106). This is an echo of Bücher. The essence of his view is that the special kinds of stimuli given by the increase rituals which convert the ordinary non-economic work of the Aranda and other tribes into labour are by the qualities of collectivity, regularity, and organization, the parallel (so to speak) of a proper economic type. The importance of these ceremonies is that under certain conditions they 'educate society in the exercise of forms of labour capable of economic utilization'. In this way they have had an 'educational' influence in the economic field (p. 102). In other words, Malinowski here was not dealing with the problems of control of resources in any general or theoretical sense; he was foreshadowing his later theory of the rôle of magic as a stimulus to production. Further proof of this lack of realization of economic issues is the fact that he did not deal in his essay with an important problem, that of assembly cost. In such a sparse environment the ability of these natives to hold ceremonies involving large numbers of people for several weeks must imply a very considerable degree of planning and organization of food supplies. Malinowski does not deal with this basic problem at all.

As his work progressed and in particular as the realities of field experience brought home to him the nature of economic problems, Malinowski's conception of economics broadened and conformed more closely to modern usage. But even in almost his last essay his consideration of the subject oscillates between the highly conventional (indeed old-fashioned) and the very unorthodox. He defines economics in conventional terms as the 'study of production, exchange, distribution and consumption of wealth' (1944, p. 126). He even limits his notion of wealth unduly by specifying it as 'material goods specifically appropriated' (p. 128). He makes no mention of *services* in this connection. On the other hand, he expresses the view that the classic economic theory has to be partly tested and partly re-framed in more elastic terms in the definition of the main factors of production and the organization of enterprise on 'levels' where these terms cannot be borrowed from our own culture (p. 127). He states that in his opinion the general structure of the classical theory is applicable with such modifications. But his concept of economic value is expressed as 'that specific culturally determined drive towards exclusive appropriation of certain claims to use, to consume, and to enjoy material possession to the exclusion of others' (p. 128). While this should not be taken as his final crystallization of the meaning of the term, it does express an idiosyncratic view, far away from any economic conception of value as established by the relations between supply and effective demand.

The defects in his approach to economic problems were due partly to his lack of knowledge of economic literature, and partly to his failure to scrutinize economic concepts with the same care which he gave to many other ideas. But they were also due partly to his perception, however indirect and unformulated, that the economic study of a real world required a partnership with principles and techniques from other social disciplines. Moreover, he regarded himself primarily as practising 'economic sociology' (1922a, p. 167n.), rather than 'ethnological economics' (1912a, p. 82). It is above all in the richness of his institutional analysis that Malinowski's contribution to economic anthropology lies. While nowhere did he finally present his Trobriand material in the framework of a complete economic system of the community, he did give for the first time both in this and in his earlier work the concept of a major primitive economic institution as a 'going concern' and relate it intimately to the social structure which gave it meaning and which it reinforced. There is no other detailed field contribution comparable to that of Malinowski in those early years.

Malinowski's contributions to economic anthropology extended over practically the whole of his working life. In reviewing them briefly one must start with his study of labour co-operation in his essay for the Westermarck *Festskrift* (1912a). Here the primary value of the treatment is three-fold. Perhaps its major importance lies in the specific selection of *economics* as a theme in conjunction with ritual, but it helped in the analysis of anthropological concepts of labour and it also pointed to the rôle of totemism as providing economic incentive. In a sense the essay was contra-Frazer, though it appeared as just a gloss on his proposition. Frazer had concluded that while the chief economic function of totemism lay in an elementary division of labour, this economic function was not of great importance. Malinowski, on the other hand, argued that there was little or no real division of labour in the totemic field but that there were very important economic (or we might translate him as saying quasi-economic) functions in the way in which the *intichiuma* ceremonies promoted economic ends, in particular arduous collective labour of an organized kind. The essence of the argument is the statement that

'magical and religious ideas must be taken under consideration as . . .
coercive mental forces to account for the training of man in economic
activity' (p. 107).

If this essay, despite its title, did not add much to the *economic* analysis
of the activities of primitive peoples, his next publication on the
Australian aborigines (1913a) dealt with several topics which were the
leitmotiv of all his later economic treatment. He examined the nature of
property rights, including those to land, and the division of labour,
especially on a sex basis; he examined the economics of the individual
family, thus relating overtly social structure and economic organization.
He asked such relevant questions as, 'How far in Australia was the
individual family an economic unit?' 'In what way is the individuality
of the single family determined by the economic facts?' He replied that
it was just the division of labour within the household which established
the unity of the social group from the economic point of view.

In his more detailed analysis he showed that the sexual aspect of
marriage should not be exaggerated, and he also brought out the fact
that the rôle of women among the aborigines involved the hardest work
and the work most essential to the maintenance of the family as an
economic unit. Drawing undoubtedly upon Durkheim for theoretical
inspiration he marked his appreciation of the way in which the sexual
division of functions defines individual family and marriage in Australia.
But he made a point of correction against Durkheim's view that in the
most primitive societies the division of labour and conjugal solidarity
are both quite rudimentary (p. 289n.).

On the other hand he stressed how the exact division of labour
between the sexes in aboriginal society depends also upon sociological
factors. In part here he was misled by his material. He saw the work
done by the aboriginal women as repulsive in that it 'differs most
essentially from sport' (p. 287—an echo of Bücher again). He regarded
it as carried on only from strong compulsion by the men and backed
this up by reference to the terrorism of women by the initiated males.
As Kaberry in particular has shown (1939, pp. 142-5, 159-60, 186) this
interpretation is not confirmed by modern observation. Methodologically there is a hint of Hobhouse in Malinowski's survey of the economic
facts of family life, with a block of quotations and his mention of 'thirty-
five statements' on the division of labour. But this essay shows his
interest at that time in comparative studies from the literature and his
ability to handle such material critically and sympathetically (see also
1921, p. 12). It shows also his perception of the importance of ritual
values in aboriginal land ownership and the critical rôle of the local
group therein (1913a, p. 153).

Though Malinowski's interest in economic anthropology was clearly
not due to his field-work, this undoubtedly widened his perceptions and
stimulated his interest. In particular it allowed him to correct by

observation the more naïve formulations which he was almost forced to make from the literature. An unexpectedly early practical contribution to the subject after he had visited the field is the very brief evidence on Papuan labour conditions and behaviour given by him at Melbourne on October 27th, 1916, to a committee reporting on British and Australian trade in the South Pacific (1918a).

His field report on the Mailu (1915a), though a straightforward ethnographic account, has some interesting economic material. He examines the Mailu 'agrarian laws' with some pertinent caution on the use of legal conceptions of ownership. The correct course, he said, was to investigate all the rights enjoyed exclusively by individuals or social groups with regard to a particular portion of land. Such rights are not to be found concentrated in one and the same 'legal person', whether a social body or an individual man (1915a, p. 592). He gave data also on the use and ownership of canoes with details of the price for hire, composition of crews, routes, cargo and the handling of trading expeditions. After a characteristic 'knowing how interesting and important are the problems of labour in modern sociology' (p. 630), he apologized for his inability to study this subject in the short time available to him, but he did give some consideration to incentives for labour and its organization, in gardening, hunting and fishing. All this was brief and concrete besides being somewhat unsystematic. But in it are phrases pointing towards his later analytical treatment, e.g. that the main psychological element in the ownership of hunting territory, nets or canoes, 'seems to be rather the craving for social prominence than desire for a greater share of material goods'; that the right to give away things, to grant access to privileges, was undoubtedly highly valued by the natives (pp. 635, 636).

The rich harvest of economic data from the Trobriands took some time to appear. Malinowski's article on fishing (1918b) has only a few notes on the economics of ownership and distribution of the catch. But by 1920 he had begun to analyse his material and crystallize his views. In the summer term of that year he gave a course of lectures at the London School of Economics on the subject of 'The Primitive Economics of the Trobriand Islanders' (1921), and he published a preliminary account of the kula as 'a special system of trade', about the same time (1920a).

The general article is an epitome of most of his later work on the subject. In it appear not only the positive propositions about the existence of distinct forms of economic organization, of hard and effective native labour and of complex principles of distribution, but also analysis of the principles of land tenure, of the integration of productive effort by the exercise of authority and leadership, of the rôle of magic in economic life, of the relation between chieftainship and control of wealth, of the nature and value of tokens of wealth and of the character of primitive exchange. There is some explicit conception of an economic system, of a public and a private economy and of a network of reciprocal obligations and dues enmeshing the whole community. There is also the dual approach which characterizes so much of Malinowski's later work—the social framework of economic effort and the economic basis of social action. Both these he saw illustrated in what he termed the 'Tribal Economy'. There is also, implied rather than stated, the *relational* concept which underlay his later functional propositions. The final sentence of this article may be taken as the keynote of this whole treatment: 'To study the interplay and correlation of the economic with other aspects of the social life is the ethnographer's duty, for to overlook the relation between two or several aspects of native life is as much an error of omission as to overlook any one aspect' (1921, p. 16).

From this point Malinowski's treatment developed in two directions. One was a detailed analysis of the economic data from his Trobriand record in particular relation to the social data. This appeared primarily in his analysis of the *kula* and of Trobriand agriculture (1922a; 1935). The other was a more general examination of the rôle of economic organization in social and cultural life—a theme which he developed as part of his general analysis of culture (1931a; 1937b; 1938b; 1944).

What have been the achievements and defects of Malinowski's contribution, and to what has it led?

In the first place, Malinowski saw economic behaviour as part of the whole system of social behaviour. He perceived that in the mode of utilization of the resources of the community lay a vital set of data for scientific study, interesting in themselves, but still more so in relation to the social activities from which they could be only conceptually separated. He did not himself make this full conceptual separation, and in that sense remained always an anthropologist, not an economist. But he was interested in the mode of allocation of resources not only as a sector of the social system, but as basically significant for the development of the system. He did not phrase his analysis explicitly in such terms. This was primarily because he was not impressed by what he thought were slick formulations which appeared to nullify the operation of individual incentives and actions. But it was partly a matter of terminology. As in his analysis of the Australian material he had seen the individuality and persistence of the elementary family determined in considerable measure by economic facts, so in his Trobriand analysis he did see, for example, the *urigubu* system of distribution as a basic principle in maintaining the matrilineal structure. Moreover, he demonstrated how the Trobriander was spurred on to the expenditure of a great amount of time and energy in work, the product of which went to other people, because of his status interests and ambitions, his response to legal and moral rules and to the expected norms of a structural framework. In all this Malinowski provided what is easily the most penetrating analysis of incentives of production yet made for a non-European society. Few people are likely ever to make great practical use of his specific analysis. But modern economists over the last two decades have become more and more impressed by the importance of understanding 'economic incentives'. It is to the work of Malinowski above all that anthropologists owe their own development of this interest and the possibilities of making a significant contribution in this field.

One of the most important aspects of Malinowski's studies was his development of the notion of the economic rôle of magic. His study of the Mailu led him to observe how magical rights connected with hunting, agriculture, etc., were clearly regarded as of economic value (1915a, p. 636) and this theme he documented in considerable detail from his Trobriand data. Applied more generally, this proposition is clearly empirically valid and very useful, and it has never been challenged. More debatable are his views on magic as a factor in production, especially as a technological aid or substitute.

In his first general analysis of Trobriand economics (1921) Malinowski outlined succinctly the rôle of the garden magician. Directly, this functionary gave a stimulus to production by his supervision of certain activities such as fencing, which were of general importance to the gardens. Indirectly he contributed to production in four ways. He supplied initiative in beginning the garden work; he regulated the pace of the work by inaugurating its successive stages; he set standards of quality by his control of certain key plots for magical purposes; and, finally, by his imposition of taboos he gave specific sanctions to work performance. It will be admitted that all these are functions of a positive productive character. They were further demonstrated in Malinowski's analysis of the *kula*. Here his notion of magic as a *system* came out very definitely (1922a, p. 59), and he showed its relation to the systematization of economic activities.

That part of his theory which has been subjected to most criticism is his insistence that magic also tends to promote *confidence* in those who use it or believe in it. This, of course, is a speculative hypothesis, difficult to furnish with supporting evidence of which Malinowski, in fact, supplied very little. Since the proposition can be easily reversed, as Fortune pointed out, the association of magic in some fields can be as much that of anxiety as of stoutness of heart.

Another criticism of the same general order, made in various forms (Viljoen, 1936, p. 32; R. Firth, 1939, pp. 185-6; Childe, 1950, p. 5), is that Malinowski failed to discuss adequately the negative effects of some forms of magic in inhibiting technical progress. Even granting the confidence theory, the use of magic, by the false security it gives, may tend to reduce the search for alternatives of a more realistic technical kind. Yet the 'confidence theory' of magic is at least as plausible a theory as its opposite, which equally lacks systematic proof, and it has provided a starting point for empirical investigation. In any case, it is to Malinowski above all that we owe the entry into anthropological discussion of the theme of magic as an economic entity, a factor or service in production, and a good or object of *economic* value.

It was Malinowski's acute awareness of social context, and of the importance of factors such as ritual obligations and performance, which led him to his strictures on the concept of primitive Economic Man. Herskovits (1952, pp. 57-8) states that the first explicit manifestation of the reaction against the reluctance to study primitive economics took the form of a vigorous attack on the doctrine of Economic Man. But no such attack was made by Malinowski in his early work in economic anthropology. It came only with his analyses in *The Argonauts of the Western Pacific* and then occupies only four pages of this five-hundred-page work (1922a, pp. 60-2, 96). Malinowski contrasted 'this fanciful dummy creature, who has been very tenacious of existence in popular and semi-popular literature, and whose shadow haunts even the mind of competent anthropologists' with the Trobriander whom he knew.

He criticized severely the notion of a primitive man 'prompted in all his actions by a rationalistic conception of self interest' (1922a, p. 60). He argued that even *one* well-established instance should show how preposterous was this assumption. Were his strictures justified? In a sense, no. To reputable economists, even at that date, Economic Man was the personification of a hypothetical construct—in modern terminology he would surely be called a model. In references to Economic Man, argument proceeds by logical inference from a few simple assumptions about human nature. Starting from such postulates, certain conclusions are reached about the structure and functioning of economic operations. Hence up to a point it was unnecessary to deny that men in primitive communities had such characteristics. But the economic construct did lead to certain misconceptions. In particular, there was apt to be a confusion between the simplicity in the motivation or *quality* of operations of Economic Man, and the simplicity in the range or *kinds* of economic operations of contemporary primitive man. When economists used primitive man as an example, as they sometimes did, they could argue that like Robinson Crusoe their creation was fiction. But there still remained the idea that, like Crusoe again, fiction had a basis in fact. Even now it is sometimes necessary for economists to explain that in assuming rationality all they mean is that they tend to find people behaving in ways which would be identical with those eventuating if people did conform to principles of rational action. What Malinowski helped to do for those working in this border field was to clarify the distinction between the economist's lay figure for purposes of his analysis, and the ethnographic reality in specific primitive cultures.

Some of Malinowski's most important contributions to economic anthropology have lain in his analyses of aspects of value and of exchange.

Malinowski's examination of the *kula* as a type of primitive exchange system is, of course, a brilliant piece of work—all the more so for the time when it was written. (I remember my own surprise and delight in Auckland in 1923 when I was fumbling with some ideas about developing a study of primitive economics, at finding this unique, vivid and stimulating analysis, based on actual research from the field.)

In this analysis Malinowski elucidated various categories of theoretical interest. He distinguished between the technological category of objects as overgrown for practical use, the ceremonial category of objects as instrumental in ritual, and the economic category of objects as having value in exchange. In distinguishing between the different forms of gift and exchange in the Trobriand socio-economic field, he drew attention to relevant criteria of general significance: e.g. regularity of the transfer, degree of customary sanction, immediacy of return, equivalence of return, extent of haggling. Further, he was one of the first to show clearly the existence in primitive economic systems of what others have later referred to as different circuits or spheres of exchange, in which the goods or services in each cannot be expressed in terms of one another (e.g. R. Firth, 1939, pp. 338–44; P. Bohannan, 1955). Moreover, he drew to the surface, as it were, and introduced overtly into anthropological literature, the concept of reciprocity. Misleading if regarded as an axiomatic principle, it is invaluable as an instrument for inquiry into the nature of transactions, if only because it tends to draw attention to the possible wider implications of any single transfer of goods or services. It focuses attention on the place of an item in a *system* of transactions. Again, he showed how the constant give-and-take, not only between specific partners in an overt exchange, but also between kinsfolk and community members over a wide field, tends to give coherence and meaning to social life. 'If we drew up a scheme of sociological relations, each type of them would be defined by a special class of economic duties' (1922*a*, p. 191). Fundamental to all his treatment, though not always equally stressed, is his recognition of 'the deep tendency to create social ties through an exchange of gifts' (1922*a*, p. 175). As Goodfellow has pointed out (1939, p. 55), Malinowski demonstrated with great force that a group or society does not hang together from any mystical impulse of unity, it continues to exist because in general each person feels that in return for what he gives to other people, he receives a corresponding service. Moreover, throughout his analysis is the demonstration of how such gift-exchanges symbolize and maintain status relations. Hence it is easy to see how Labouret (1953, p. 15), using

Malinowski's material freely, concludes that exchange thus becomes a most remarkable and solid basis of a social structure, and finds that Malinowski's exposition can be applied without difficulty to other societies.

Various critical points can be made on Malinowski's treatment. His theoretical conception of economic value was not clear, nor was it always felicitously expressed. He was anxious to dispel the impression that economic values in the Trobriands were simply a matter of rational calculation. But he left aside any consideration of the concept of value in relation to that of price and thereby deprived himself of at least one opportunity for theoretical discussion, and possibly of an avenue into a clearer perception of supply and demand relations (cf. R. Firth, 1939, pp. 332-40). Malinowski concentrated primarily on factors of demand—though not so terming them—and their social content or determinants. He considered mainly the value of food and the value of manufactured articles. The value of food, he said, in the Trobriands depends primarily on its display and ceremonial preparation, on its 'cult' qualities, on the enhancement of prestige through its possession, on the dedication of surpluses to rot—all involved in a socialized 'sentiment' related indirectly to the pleasures of eating it. 'This value again makes accumulated food a symbol, and a vehicle of power' (1922a, pp. 168-72). One can see what he means here, but it is difficult to disentangle the elements neatly. Moreover, while Malinowski discussed in great detail Trobriand food production, he did not relate the *problems of supply* effectively to the determination of food values. Food, he argued, was not a scarce good there—'all the necessities of life are within easy reach of the Trobriand Islander' (1922a, p. 173). Now it is clear that food in the Trobriands is usually plentiful and that the demand for it is extremely elastic, as is evidenced by the way in which surpluses to direct consumption give social satisfaction when they are seen to decay. In other words food values do not necessarily fall radically when destructible surpluses accumulate; these are absorbed by the liberal demand schedule of the economy. But this demand cannot be indefinitely expansible in comparison with that for other objects. Food growing is hard work—that Malinowski demonstrates. Yet the question of marginal increments—the relative advantage of extra work in the gardens on the one hand, or of additions to *urigubu* or related food transfers on the other, in comparison with the gains from other kinds of activity—is never raised. The market for *kula* valuables is also extremely elastic. Yet Malinowski does not discuss any processes of calculation whereby work on food production is matched against work of other kinds which might yield *kula* valuables. Again, there have been periodic famines in the Trobriands (1935, pp. 160-4), yet the relevance of this potential scarcity factor for food values is never brought home.

Similarly, Malinowski argues that the value of manufactured articles depends on the satisfaction given by the rarity of their materials and the elaboration of their workmanship. Here he does seem to leave the demand field. The explanation of their value 'must take into account, not so much the user of these objects, as the workman who produces them' (1922a, p. 172). But he is invoking demand factors in another form. While these people are keen and industrious workers 'they do not work under the spur of necessity, or to gain their living' (p. 172), but on the impulse of their fancy, for their enjoyment, often believing their talent to be the result of magic. Hence, led away by their interest in fine work, they over-develop and over-elaborate some craft objects, spending on them 'excess of labour', a 'disproportionate amount of labour'. Hence such objects are 'a kind of economic monstrosity', too big, too over-charged with ornament to be used, and yet highly valued just because of that (p. 173). Here is the same ignoring of the expenditure of time and energy in labour on these items as being relevant to their value. There is also some inconsistency in the concept of 'use' or 'utility' which is restricted by implication to capacity to fulfil immediate, practical ends. The *kula* valuables 'are not "utilities" in any sense of the word' (1920a, p. 98). Elaborate craft objects are 'too good to be used, but only so much the more desirable for possession' (p. 172); 'great quantities are produced, beyond any possible utility they could possess, out of mere love of accumulation for its own sake' (p. 173). This is not the terminology of economics, it is almost the language of the housewife. If the labour were really 'excess', if the goods were really 'produced beyond utility' and not used, according to economic analysis this should be speedily followed by changes in the values of the work and the goods, and diversion of energy to other things. Of course from an economist's approach these things *have* utility; their use lies precisely in the storing and display of them, or—as in the case of 'surplus' food—in its deliberate dedication to decay. Hence their value is maintained. Yet despite such imprecision of statement Malinowski makes his point: the components of economic value for primitive economic systems, as for our own, have a social content which cannot be postulated *a priori*, but which demands empirical examination, which is complex and which includes factors of status and power relationships as much as those of immediate practical use. The point that *exchange* in such economic systems is first and foremost a *social action*, has since emerged in various guises in nearly all analyses in economic anthropology; and its growing clarity is due to Malinowski's initiative.

Where perhaps Malinowski fails most in his analysis of exchange is in the lack of any precise indication of how relative values of *kula* objects are determined. For objects of the same type, armshells on the one hand or shell necklaces on the other, considerations of size, colour, and transaction-history are clearly relevant. But these two types of objects travel in opposite directions in the *kula*, so that an object of one category must be matched against one of another. By what criteria is this done? Malinowski speaks of a necklace as 'equivalent' to an arm-shell (1922a, pp. 98, 355, 356). He speaks also of a native giving up to £20 for a fine object, in olden days its value being 'an equivalent of that sum' in yams, pigs, etc. (1920a, p. 98). But he does not make it clear how such equivalence is precisely arrived at (comparable for example with data given by Armstrong—1928, chap. V). Moreover, he gives no quantitative data, particularly desirable where there is so much variation in the individual objects, to enable us to see the relation between objects of the same category. There are 'no definite correspondences or indices of correlation between the various kinds of valuables' (1922a, p. 359). Yet the idea of equivalence in the *kula* transaction is very strong and definite (p. 356) and one would have expected a more systematic analysis of this concept—especially since some data are given on barter relationships (p. 363). A point which is probably of great significance in explaining how such variable objects are matched, is the use of the different kinds of 'solicitary' gifts (pp. 354-6), the number and kind of which seem to vary considerably according to the *kula* valuable desired. A judicious arrangement of these could fill in gaps perceived between, say, an armshell and a necklace of the same general equivalence, but differing in precise evaluation. Moreover, the possibilities of com-petition in offering such solicitary gifts, and of coyness in accepting and acting upon them, offer a most important opportunity for what in essentials are the pricing operations of the market. They amount in effect to a *sub rosa* haggling of a polite kind, and illustrate the operation of supply and demand relations. Here is a basic point not really seen by Malinowski, though he has illustrated its workings.

Other instances of Malinowski's occasional theoretical absent-mindedness are his affirmation that in the Trobriands 'payments are never deferred' (1921, p. 13; cf. 1922a, pp. 187, 362), and his distinction between 'organized' and 'communal' labour (1922a, p. 159; cf. R. Firth, 1929, p. 221n., for critique). Neither point is tenable in the form in which he put it. So also with his discussion of 'pure' gifts. He defined a 'pure' gift as an act in which an individual gives an object or renders a service without expecting or getting any return (p. 177). He said that this type of transaction is rare in Trobriand life. But he did regard presents between husband and wife and father and child as coming in this category. As Mauss pointed out (1954, p. 71), Malinowski himself stated that the Trobriands described these gifts as *mapula* pay-ment for matrimonial relations; they are not 'pure' or 'free' without expectation or return. Malinowski later (1926a, pp. 40-1) agreed with this. But his original distinction has some validity. His conception of 'pure' or 'free' should have been rephrased, but it differentiates a category of Trobriand transfers of goods and services of a special kind. They are not characterized by expectation of *immediate* return, there is no *specific* equivalent to which they correspond, and they are empirically characterized as things which the donor *wants* to give. In this sense they are 'free' transfers. Moreover, the citation of such gifts as *mapula* implies a kind of assimiliation to the general idea in the Trobriands that there *should be* no service without return. As Malinowski hints, these gifts were rationalized by the natives in a manner that agrees with this rule— in other words, explanation is socially determined and reflects a predominant structural principle; they underplay the sentiment of personal affection because it runs counter to their overt and basic matrilineal rule.

Mauss complains that Malinowski did not reveal properly the sanctions for reciprocity in the *kula*—a point on which Warnotte follows him (1927, p. 15). Is the sanction only mystical and moral? Mauss asks (1954, p. 24). But it is clear from Malinowski's general treatment that one basic sanction is obviously loss of reputation to one who does not play his part, and another is loss of future benefits of partnership. Moreover, Mauss himself has misread the *kula* data in several places. He states that it seems to be reserved for chiefs (1954, p. 20), whereas Malinowski clearly states that commoners also participated (1920*a*, p. 98; 1922*a*, p. 91). Mauss states that *kula* valuables are worn by women, and only rarely by men; Trobriand women serve as a means of displaying wealth (1954, pp. 21, 94). But this rests upon Mauss's interpretation of a photograph and ignores Malinowski's specific statements, in close connection with it, that 'a chief will not put on his ornaments himself unless he intends to dance, but any of his relatives, his children and his friends, and even vassals can have the use of them for the asking' and 'if you go to a feast or a dance where there are a number of men wearing such ornaments . . .' (1922*a*, pp. 87–8). With these differences in mind, it is perhaps not surprising that Mauss has tried to read into the *kula* exchange his own mystical notion— that reciprocity in exchange is based upon the persistent attempts of the spirit of a gift to return to its original possessor as part of his personality. But this notion is itself based upon Mauss's misconception, and to some extent, mistranslation of Maori evidence, as I myself have pointed out (R. Firth, 1929, pp. 412–15). All this of course does not depreciate the value of the comparative treatment which Mauss gave to Malinowski's data.[1]

Other criticisms have been put forward, in reference to the 'meaning' of the *kula*. Malinowski's chapter with this heading (pp. 509–18) is certainly thin from the sociological point of view. Evans-Pritchard (1951, p. 95) has argued that Malinowski failed to see clearly 'what is perhaps the most significant feature of the Kula; the bringing

---

[1] It is interesting to note that the well-known term *prestation*, used by Mauss, by Lenoir, and later by Malinowski (1935, p. 204) and Radcliffe-Brown (1950, p. 47), was originally used by W. Robertson Smith (1889, pp. 403, 413).

together, through the acceptance of common ritual values, of politically autonomous communities'. In a formal sense this is true. But in his earliest publication on the subject, Malinowski did point out that the *kula* expeditions 'link together the various island groups' and that the *kula* 'presents a type of inter-tribal relationship of unprecedented magnitude' (1920a, p. 105). Later, he referred to the different Trobriand districts engaged in the *kula* as different political units, stated that a firm grasp of the main, political, institutions was essential to an understanding of the *kula* (1922a, pp. 69–70), and described the *kula* as 'an international affair' (p. 33); 'inter-tribal' (p. 81); 'welding together a considerable number of tribes' (p. 83); 'the foundation of a big inter-tribal institution' (p. 86); 'a type of inter-tribal relationship on an enormous scale' (p. 85). He pointed out that *kula* partnership provides friendly allies in the far-away, dangerous, foreign districts (p. 92). He also suggested that a study of the *kula* may shed some light upon 'the influence of economic aims and ambitions upon the evolution of intertribal intercourse, and of primitive international law' (p. 515). Moreover, it is clear from Malinowski's account that the different politically autonomous communities are not just 'brought together'. An important part of the procedure lies in the reciprocal visiting; and the exchanges take place, not as community transactions, but as many individual transactions taking place simultaneously. It is the symmetry and reciprocity of the inter-tribal relationship, and the individualism of it in permanent partnership relations, that are also so significant.

An indication of the stimulus of Malinowski's work has been the way in which not only Mauss and Labouret, but also Lenoir and Warnotte have tried to put the *kula* in a wider perspective. Warnotte (1927, p. 72) has suggested that, in common with the potlatch, it depends upon certain economic, political and demographic characteristics: small groups with relatively large space in which to operate, relative social equality—or at least instability in the system of social subordination—and freedom from military domination. Moreover, social control in such groups is relatively easy, through the wide-flung personal knowledge of one another by the participants. This points up the fact that a system of the *kula* kind, with its long-term credit, depends essentially upon personal knowledge of one another by the partners. It also suggests a reinforcement to Malinowski's view—that possibly one important function of the *kula* is the provision of symbols which help to maintain Trobriand chieftainship in a Melanesian area where on the whole social stratification is weak and the tradition of chieftainship is sparse.

From this comparative point of view, it is perhaps worth noting the contrast which Malinowski draws between the use of *kula* objects in three areas of the *kula* ring—in respect of mortuary rites. In Kitava and allied communities, death imposes a taboo on receiving visitors who come on the *kula*, and hence *kula* objects are dammed up in the village of the corpse, since at the same time they are collected by the mourners. Later, after a year or so, they are released in a flood at a post-mortem feast (1922*a*, p. 489). The Dobuans, who do not have that custom of distribution, adorn themselves with *kula* valuables at the final mortuary feast, and the subsequent release of valuables is therefore less sudden (p. 492). In the Trobriands, there is no mortuary distribution of *kula* valuables nor any ornamental use of them by mourners. Here, it is the corpse who is covered with them; they are on loan from kin, and are later withdrawn (pp. 512–13). At the mortuary feast it is food that is distributed. If further information were available, it would be interesting to relate this differential use of valuables to the differential rank structure of these respective communities, the chiefs in the Trobriands presumably retaining greater control than elsewhere through the lack of mortuary display and distributions there.

Malinowski himself stresses the importance of the *kula* as providing an opportunity for parallel trade of an ordinary economic kind (1920*a*, p. 105; 1922*a*, pp. 361–4; 1935, p. 456). This is a view which Fortune (1932, p. 208) has confirmed, and which Labouret (1953, p. 24) has accepted. Labouret has further added the significant point that the monopolistic trading the *kula* confers on its participants overseas helps to explain the importance with which it is invested. This is largely a matter of inference from Malinowski's observation. But more a matter of hypothesis is Malinowski's own suggestion that the *kula* may have been a 'surrogate' or substitute for head-hunting and war (1935, p. 456). This is perhaps reminiscent of Lenoir's more evolutionary view of the development of the potlatch from a state of war into a mechanism for the establishment of a political 'hierarchy', and his consequential distinction between *uvalaku* and *kula*. However farfetched be this hypothesis, it is clear from Malinowski's material, as Lenoir has brought out, how much latent hostility is ritualized in the *kula*, and how the acts of exchange provide a release of tension similar to peace-making (Lenoir, 1924, pp. 387, 394–5, 403). Moreover, if it be conceded that the various Massim communities could not ignore one another's existence, the *kula* overseas clearly offered certain advantages over war. It was less dangerous in its risks, more certain in its rewards. But what the *kula*, sociologically, does seem to offer above all is a means through the use and exchange of symbolic objects, of expressing, maintaining and building up status relations on a scale not possible in any single Massim community. If it be said to provide a charter for social symbiosis between these various communities, this is presumably expressing in a generalized way what both Malinowski and Evans-Pritchard have indicated.

One of the more controversial economic issues on which Malinowski expressed a decided opinion, was the use of the terms 'currency' and 'money' for the valuables exchanged in the *kula* and allied operations.

His uncompromising rejection of these terms by reference to the classical definition of the functions of money has not found favour in general with subsequent writers, including Mauss, Herskovits, and Einzig. This issue is now largely a verbal one since, to a considerable extent because of Malinowski's challenge, anthropologists have a much clearer understanding of the range of functions which these various types of object actually serve. Whether these shell strings and analogous valuables are to be called money or not is a matter of convenience of exposition. What is quite clear is that they are not money in the same sense as the objects so termed in Western economic systems. Their circulation does tend to promote a flow of other goods and services. They do tend to provide, though in an inprecise way, some standard of reference for the exchange value of other goods and services. They are also in most cases an important store of wealth. But it must be remembered that for the most part they do not serve in any direct sense as a medium facilitating the exchange of other objects or services, one for another. Nor are they used as the means whereby these objects and services are expressed in other terms. They might conveniently be referred to as having only 'quasi-monetary' functions.

I have already indicated some of the defects of Malinowski's other work in economic anthropology, due in particular to his inadequate appreciation of the range and meaning of economic theory. A few further points may be added, in reference to his later Trobriand work.

In his general theoretical approach he tended to ignore the concept of scarcity in resources. He does not really discuss problems of relative scarcity of land, although it seems clear that the Trobriand kinship interest in land connotes scarcity in some directions. He ignores also the relatively low level of capital available and the implications of this for planning of enterprises, though he does contribute an important point, novel in his day, of the way in which food resources can be converted into basic capital. His treatment of yam resources as 'the foundation of native expansion, wealth and power' (1933, p. 156), though brief, is very significant. But he left largely to one side the problems of accumulation and disbursement of capital stocks, apart from indicating their general importance in relation to the structure of Trobriand authority. In his stress on the social regulation of saving and spending, he tended to leave out of account consideration of the manner in which the magnitudes involved conditioned the economic processes. It would be unfair to say that Malinowski had no notion of quantity as a dimension in his economic analyses. He does, in fact, give in many different contexts quantitative data—numbers of canoes, estimates of proportion of the total area of the island under cultivation each year, of the proportion of crops distributed to different destinations, of rates of payment and exchange, etc. But there is very little linkage of the various quantitative items. So we cannot get any clear conception of

RAYMOND FIRTH

the volume of Trobriand production for instance, or of the income and outlay of any individual or group.

Related to this is the serious under-estimate, as far as the published material is concerned, of the impact of the Western economy upon the Trobriand tribal economy. There is mention of pearling, and of its relation to the *kula*. There is also mention of the export of 'surplus' crops to feed the labourers of European employers, and some discussion of the relative earnings from European employment and from native agriculture. There is also (1935, pp. 479–81) a reference to the decay of custom under European influence. But there is no examination of the total effect which the possibility of production of a surplus for export has had upon the tribal economy, nor of the way in which alternative avenues for the use of labour had radically affected, even before 1920, the Trobriand disposal of productive effort (cf. Austen, 1945*b*).

Yet such objections are more than balanced by other positive contributions in Malinowski's economic analyses: by his elucidation of the primitive credit system; by his elaborate description of the socialized modes of distribution represented by the *urigubu* yam transfers; by his meticulous dissection of the system of rights involved in the tenure of land; by his demonstration of the close relation between political authority and economic control. Implicitly and often explicitly, in these and other ways not only did he analyse Trobriand economy, he also showed how the system of economic arrangements tended to maintain the structure of Trobriand society.

How does Malinowski's general contribution to economic anthropology stand by comparison with modern work? In a sense of mastery of any considerable proportion of the body of economic theory, Malinowski did not contribute greatly to specifically economic studies. But his contribution on the economic borderlands was very great. He found the formal propositions of economic theory of his day arid and unrevealing. He himself had a different conceptual universe, preferring postulates about economic operations which to him represented the richness of interpretation of actual human behaviour. Now modern economics, where not content with the deductive problems of purely formal analysis, involving assumptions about closed economic systems, is seeking to gain an understanding of the phenomena of the real world. Increasingly, economists are becoming interested in the material provided by historians, sociologists, psychologists, and anthropologists to furnish them with those assumptions of content which are necessary in any explanation of concrete economic behaviour. As yet the rapprochement is tentative and uneven. But for this approach Malinowski helped to lay most significant foundations. He gave immense stimulus to parallel analyses in other primitive economic systems with a low technological content, and he opened up some of the basic problems— problems of organization of economic effort, of material incentives compared with those of social status and prestige, of the relation of political and ritual leadership to entrepreneurship in economic affairs, of the economic implications of the use of social symbols, of the subtle compounding of rights in ownership, of the complexity of primitive market operations and the character of collective economic action in its social context.

In brief, with sensitivity and insight, he described many of the major economic functions of primitive society and, in so doing, established for himself a lasting place at the foundation of economic anthropology.

Malinowski and the Study of Social Change

LUCY MAIR

The Beginning of Interest in the Subject

A T the time when Malinowski did his work in the Trobriands, the dramatic changes that the emissaries of 'Western' culture have brought about in the organization of most small-scale societies were not regarded as belonging properly to the field of anthropological study. The anthropologist was held to be concerned with the 'untouched primitive', and where untouched primitive societies could not be found it was considered legitimate to think away those intrusive external elements, the trader, administrator, and missionary. He himself wrote of his approach to his subject at this time: 'Anthropology, to me at least, was a romantic escape from our overstandardized culture.' In the Trobriands the impact of the modern world, though no doubt it had produced observable effects, had not so distorted the traditional institutions that these could not be profitably studied as an example of social organization. 'I was still able with but little effort to re-live and reconstruct a type of human life moulded by the implements of a stone age' (1930c, p. 406).

After anthropologists extended their interest to societies which are rapidly changing under the influence of colonial rule or of the spread of commerce and industry, this attitude began to be treated as a weakness to be repudiated or else admitted only in a rather shamefaced way; and to outsiders it was held to justify the stereotype of the unpractical academic, idealizing a vanishing order and withholding his sympathy from constructive policies. It returned to respectability, however, when attention was directed to the comparative study of social structures, which necessarily draws investigation to societies where a recognizable structure can be observed.

The theoretical discussion of the early part of this century tacitly assumed that the societies concerned were static, though they were

229

always envisaged as representing the end point of a process. Both the diffusionist and evolutionary hypotheses were in fact theories of social change, though the concentration of many studies of diffusion on material objects and techniques has tended to obscure this point. Malinowski's original criticism of these theories, as is well known, was not concerned with their adequacy for the analysis of change; indeed his insistence on the interpretation of institutions in terms of their contemporary significance would logically have precluded an attack from this angle.

Though anthropologists had earlier stressed the 'practical' value of an understanding of native custom, largely from the point of view of avoiding unnecessary disturbance, the first academic course of lectures in which the modern phenomena of change in small-scale societies formed the central theme was that given by Radcliffe-Brown at Cape Town in 1924 on the effect of western economic influences on the social organization of the Bantu. The study, in the South African field, of societies which had been so much affected by the European impact that it was impossible to disregard this was due as much to the difficulty of finding any others as to any theoretical preoccupation. The major influence in directing attention to these phenomena, however, was an ethical one—the concern of missionaries and of some administrators for the condition of the peoples among whom they were working. In the Pacific Islands they were distressed by a decline in population which seemed to be general and to threaten many peoples with extinction. Discussions of this question led to the promulgation by Rivers (1922, pp. 84–113) of the theory that whole societies might lose the will to live if they were deprived of the institutions on which their interests were focused, and its development by Pitt-Rivers (1927). As an explanation of depopulation this theory became unnecessary when the demographic trend was reversed; it is worth recalling because in his discussion of the head-hunting expeditions of some tribes as their principal incentive to economic activity of all kinds, Rivers touched on that interdependence of institutions which Malinowski demonstrated so much more fully in his account of the Trobriand *kula* published in the same year.

In regard to Africa the missionary activity of the period bore more fruit, in a number of representations in the political field and in the creation of the International Institute of African Languages and Cultures, an organization for research with the express aim of concentrating interest on the changing African in the hope that the results would be a guide to action. Among its founders J. H. Oldham (1929) was concerned with the meaning in practice of the concept of trusteeship; Edwin Smith (1926) with a more tolerant attitude towards African customs, and respect for African values such as had been wantonly outraged by incidents like the claim made by a British Governor for the surrender of the Golden Stool of Ashanti; Lord

Lugard (1928) with a fuller understanding of the political institutions and legal rights on which his system of administration through traditional rulers depended. The study of culture change (as it was always called at that time) was, then, closely bound up with the practical application of anthropological knowledge, and in the thinking and writing of Malinowski they were never separated. His visit to Africa in 1934 reinforced his conviction that the anthropologist had an important contribution to make to the formulation of policy, and also led to a shift in the emphasis of his writing from warnings of the disintegrating effect of enforced changes to criticisms of colour-bar policies and pleas for the extension to the African of every aspect of European culture. It must be admitted that his absorption in this theme inhibited his interest in the formulation of theories of social change as a general process.

The first Fellows of the African Institute had a year's training with Malinowski before beginning work, and in the interval between their first and second field trips they returned to London and took part in the discussions of his seminar. The preliminary training was given in terms of his general theory, and his pupils had to work out their own method for the application of this to studies in which special attention was to be given to the effects of external influences. His own first published writing on the subject took the form of a critical introduction to a collection of essays by them on *Methods of Study of Culture Contact in Africa* (1938a). After this, he wrote additional articles and delivered lectures on the subject to various learned societies, and in the years immediately before his death he conducted seminars on culture change at Yale University. He had planned to write a book on 'culture contact and change', and after his death such writings of his, published and unpublished, as might have formed the substance of such a book were collected and edited by P. M. Kaberry in the volume *The Dynamics of Culture Change* (1945).

'Cultural' or 'Social' Change?

During the greater part of Malinowski's lifetime the use of the terms 'culture contact' and 'culture change' did not imply a different approach to the phenomena studied from that connoted by the description 'social change'. The division of anthropologists into students of 'society' and of 'culture' was made explicit in Radcliffe-Brown's presidential address to the Royal Anthropological Institute in 1940, when he said that the difference in definition of the subject 'leads to two different kinds of study, between which it is hardly possible to obtain agreement in the formulation of problems' (1952, p. 189). Later in the same lecture he made a criticism of Malinowski's theory of culture change which would be generally regarded as valid. He did not, however, explicitly assign

Malinowski's whole body of theory to the category of those which had no common ground with his own, and in fact Malinowski's approach to anthropological problems was nearer to his, as their common debt to the French sociologists would lead one to expect, than to that of the American writers who are avowedly interested in culture as opposed to social structure. The first anthropologists to use the term 'Social Change' in the title of a book were G. and M. Wilson (1945); but their treatment of the subject could fairly be described as predominantly cultural.

Malinowski's own experience, as a Pole under Austrian rule, of the situation of ethnic minorities in Europe, was never far from his mind when he was considering the problems of the imposition of change by external authority. In Europe this consisted essentially in the suppression of overt modes of behaviour such as appear in enumerations of cultural traits—distinctive rituals and public celebrations, the use of a language other than that of the ruling group. He was acutely aware of the subjective attitude of the member of a minority group denied the right to perpetuate his own cultural tradition. As a student of social phenomena, however, he never thought of cultural traits as separable from the persons in whose behaviour they are manifest; the main responsibility for the reification of culture does not lie with him.

His 'functional' theory of culture has been severely criticized, and few, if any, anthropologists now accept it in its entirety. Nevertheless, it deserves, like all theories, to be considered in the light of the ideas that were current at the time when it was evolved. In so far as it is sound, one line of criticism runs, it consists of truisms which have never been in dispute. One of his own favourite phrases is apposite here: 'It is sometimes valuable to state the obvious.' At a time when the leading exponent in Britain of the study of social organization could invite his readers to 'suppose a people whose old men monopolized the young women, among whom there arose the custom of handing superfluous wives to the sons of the sister' (Rivers, 1914, Vol. II, p. 61), the interpretation of social institutions, at whatever level of development, as systems in which universally necessary ends are attained by the co-operation of organized groups was not only a salutary corrective but, as far as anthropological teaching in Britain was concerned, an innovation. Its weakness is that it does not account for all social phenomena, not that it does not account for any.

During most of the period when Malinowski was teaching in London it was taken for granted that an anthropologist in the field studied 'the culture' of 'a society'. Only later did the words 'culture' and 'society' come to stand for quite different approaches to social phenomena. Malinowski insisted that the field-worker must study the 'whole culture', but if he had been driven to admit the necessity for some elimination, he would have given priority to what he called 'institutions'.

In America, however, the view has been widely held that the 'wholeness' of culture is a matter of 'pattern'. Not only is behaviour 'patterned' in a sense in which the word means little more than 'standardized', but different aspects of culture are linked by a sort of implicit logic, so that each culture, taken as a whole, has a distinctive character—what Bateson (1936) called its ethos. The pattern can be seen in art forms, in ceremonies, and in the type of personality that is admired. The earliest form of this theory, in which a hypostatized 'culture' was held to 'impose its pattern' on the individuals through whom it was expressed, and to 'select' or 'reject' traits according as they were or were not compatible with the pattern, has been refined by studies directed to show how a given cultural environment tends to encourage the development of a particular type of personality. Of this approach to the subject it can fairly be said that in the formulation of problems it has nothing in common with the study of society, which, as Radcliffe-Brown has remarked, is essentially that of socially regulated interpersonal relationships.

Malinowski was concerned primarily with social relationships, as is clear from his insistence on the *institution*, which he defined sometimes as a system of activities and sometimes as a group of persons, as the isolable unit for purposes of comparison. His study of cultural change was therefore one of institutional change and not of the diffusion of traits. 'The units of transformation', he wrote, 'are not traits or trait complexes but organised systems or institutions' (1945, p. 119). This principle has been followed by all his British successors, whether they seek to combine in a single monograph an account of the totality of the changes occurring in a given society or, as is becoming more and more common, take separate institutions and follow out their development.

He himself, however, failed to make the complete break with the culture-trait and culture-pattern theory that is implicit in his own statement. Partly because much of his writing and teaching on this subject was done during his years in America, he linked his own views with an attack on this theory, and thus found himself tied to its language.

His theory of the integration of institutions led him to emphasize the subsidiary adaptations that are involved in most modifications of long-established custom. He quoted with approval Fortes's metaphor (1938, p. 62) that the process of cultural change (culture contact) is not 'a mechanical pitchforking of elements of culture, like bundles of hay'. Yet, while on the one hand he deprecated the 'invoicing back' of cultural items to their parent sources, even in such a clear case as the performance of a traditional Pondo ritual of blessing over a plough, on the other he used the metaphors of giving and taking in a manner not very different from that of the American anthropologists who so curiously write of the 'borrowing' of cultural traits. He differed significantly from them in his insistence on the 'new cultural reality', something more than a combination of pre-existing traits, or even a 'transformation' of the 'borrowed' trait, which results from the contact of two cultures.

Yet this concept is itself unnecessary once it is taken as sufficient to focus attention on any given institution and trace its development in response to whatever forces can be observed to affect it. Malinowski referred frequently to the cultural determinism of the two societies in contact, and affirmed that the 'institutions which are the result of contact and change . . . obey a specific determinism of their own' (1945, p. 12). He did not develop this concept. In writing of the 'specific determinism' of the new institutions, he may have had in mind that influence upon the form of related institutions which was not only implicit in his 'functional' theory but has also been summed up by Firth (1951*a*, p. 89) in the refreshingly common-sense statement that 'the same people tend to be involved in all of them'. By the 'cultural determinism' of the two societies in interaction he must have implied something like what is usually called today the 'value system' or scheme of goals or preferences current in each. The word 'determinism', implying as it does in this context something like the contact between the invincible force and the immovable object, is not the happiest possible. A significant development of the study of social change since his day has been the refinement of the analysis of social organization so that the fields in which the structural system allows for some play to individual choice are distinguished from those in which it is rigid (see e.g. Firth, 1951*a*, chap. III). When this distinction is made the process of social change can be traced in terms of response to new situations, or even to dissatisfaction with socially standardized situations, without postulating any confrontation of cultures or parallel institutions. It also enables us to interpret the failure of peasant societies to respond to plans for the raising of their material standards, the technical advantages of which seem to their promoters to be self-evident.

The Scope of Malinowski's Theory

Malinowski's theory of cultural change was not in fact a general one, but was concerned with the impact of industrialization on peasant societies. His illustrations were drawn from Africa, and largely from the research carried out there by his pupils. But he remarked that 'culture change in Africa does not differ profoundly from that which is at present transforming the rural and backward countries of Europe from peasant communities . . . into a new type closely akin to the proletariat found in the industrial districts of the United States, England or France' (1945, p. 2). This view would be generally accepted, and indeed field methods developed from his, and guided by a body of theory based originally on work done among 'primitive' peoples, have been applied within the last decade to village communities in France,

Spain, Turkey, and the New World, and even to selected localities in large cities.

The scope of his generalizations was further limited by the fact that his African material came from societies subject to political domination by European governments or immigrant communities of European stock. Again in part because of his own experience as one of a subject people in a European empire, he was deeply sympathetic to African discontents, and in generalizing on the process which he observed he was concerned not with laws of change as such but with the conditions of satisfactory adaptation to the new situation, or, as he called it himself, 'successful' cultural change (1945, p. 56). His principle of the 'common factor', to be found wherever there is 'a long-run identity of interests between Europeans and Africans' and hence a 'basis for collaboration', establishes an ideal, not an empirically based proposition. Nor does it apply to the increasing number of cases where there is little or no conflict of interests and yet plans for technological advance miscarry.

Methods of Inquiry

His prescription for the analysis of the process was a tabular scheme which, he held, ensured that all relevant facts would be noted and the connection between them brought out. In this 'three-column approach' the contributions of the two cultures in contact—conceived always as those of an imperial Power and its colonial subjects—were listed under separate headings, while between them stood the 'new cultural reality' resulting from their interaction. Not only did he regard institutions as the significant cultural realities, but he saw the process of cultural change as an *interaction* of institutions, and held that 'organized systems of *European* activities' must be co-ordinated directly with corresponding phenomena of change (1945, p. 32—italics mine).

In the scheme as eventually worked out, and published in his posthumous volume, the column devoted to the European contribution was not in fact filled with data on the nature of institutions. It is probable that, had he lived, he would not have published this volume without considerable revision, or possibly at all in the form in which we now have it, and certain inconsistencies might have been eliminated. He might then have made explicit what is implied in the heading 'White Influences, Interests and Intentions'—that in this particular situation we are concerned with deliberate attempts to alter customary ways of behaviour and with the response to them, and not even with what he himself termed 'selective giving' on the part of the dominant group. Indeed it is of some interest to note how often his entries under this head refer to prohibitions; as it is to observe that his illustrations deal with policies and their effects and not at all with institutions in

LUCY MAIR

juxtaposition. Moreover, the column headed 'Surviving Forms of Tradition' included the same activities that other writers might have 'invoiced back' to their native source.

Radcliffe-Brown has criticized the interpretation of the situation in terms of the interaction of cultures when, as he remarks, the process is in fact 'the interaction of individuals and groups within an established social structure which is itself in process of change' (1952, p. 202). He does not make it clear, however, that it is precisely this interaction of individuals and groups which produces the change. Both Schapera and Fortes have made the point that the observable phenomenon is the interaction of individuals. As Fortes put it, 'Individuals and communities react under contact; and not customs' (1938, p. 62). Schapera insisted on 'the tremendous importance of personalities, as opposed to institutions, in the process of cultural change' (1938b, p. 34). This goes rather beyond the purely methodological point that only individual reactions can be observed, and introduces the question how far the personal qualities of someone in a key position may be such as to secure conformity with his wishes. It might be objected that this is introducing the element of historical accident in a field in which anthropologists are hoping to establish general propositions. Yet Schapera is surely right in making the two points, that individuals are responsible for the local aspects of general policy, and that remote entities such as a church or a colonial government are perceived by their converts or subjects primarily in terms of their local representatives. This is in no way inconsistent with the appearance of movements of rejection of European civilization as such, to which Malinowski points as invalidating his position.

Radcliffe-Brown further asserts that what is happening in an African tribe 'can only be described by recognizing that the tribe has been incorporated into a wide political and economic structural system' (1952, p. 202). Here, if he means anything beyond the truisms to be found in all writings on 'modern diffusion', including those of Malinowski, it is less easy to follow him. The large number of descriptive studies of social change that have been published in the last twenty years have not been found inadequate because they do not explicitly describe the external structural relations of the communities investigated. The question what a study of this kind should take as its universe of discourse is, however, a significant one. Malinowski himself, looking at the problem in his own cultural-functional terms, insisted that the modern ethnographer must be 'acquainted with the sociology of western enterprise, political, economic and educational', 'must know the home foundations of European institutions and movements', and must check his knowledge 'by field-work on Europeans in Africa'. 'It is not legitimate', he wrote (1938a, p. xxxv), 'to choose one side and to forget that the process consists in the constant interaction of both sides.' In a footnote (p. xvii) he

236

indicated that 'a dozen or so of books on native policies, education, economics, and on missionary programmes' would provide sufficient background. It may be that modern anthropologists, faced as they are with a constantly increasing flow of publications both on theory and ethnography, do read these dozen books. Field-work on Europeans in Africa, however, is still confined to the type recommended by Fortes and Schapera, in which the local representatives of European culture are observed as 'integrally part of the community'—that is to say, as persons in daily interaction with them, whose presence and activities are taken for granted. Although Malinowski criticized this approach as if its exponents had asserted that the locally resident Europeans were 'well integrated' into the African community, it remains the only practicable way in which a field study can follow his own principles.

Given the limitations of time and human powers, it is an open question how much knowledge an anthropologist should seek to acquire, or to utilize in presenting his data. Once he goes beyond the superficial general information of the intelligent reader of newspapers, he finds that serious inquiry into either the economic, political, or ideological forces affecting the society he is to study is a full-time occupation. It could even be argued that the most satisfactory study of the impact of these forces would be one in which they were viewed solely as they appear to the persons subjected to their pressure. Certainly inadequately informed assertions about the aims and methods of the emissaries of western culture do nothing to enhance the value of a field-work report. The reactions provoked by their intervention depend on their actions, not on their motives, and it would be perfectly possible to analyse them in the same way as one could analyse the reaction to a natural disaster such as famine or earthquake.

The interpretation of social change in purely structural terms would mean that, instead of seeing the process as one of changes in behaviour, one saw it as the creation of situations in which individuals were invited or forced to enter into new social relationships. This adequately describes the process by which Africans become the employees of Europeans, are subjected to the criminal jurisdiction of chiefs who had no such authority in virtue of the indigenous structure, or elect representatives to legislatures. It is not so immediately applicable to the type of technical change involved in the substitution of the plough for the hoe or the adoption of the bicycle as a means of transport. These are cultural changes which bring changes of structure in their train. In fact, important as is the concept of structure, that of culture cannot be completely rejected unless the definition of structure is extended to cover the whole social field and so lose its significance. The concept of values, that is of qualitative judgements which are socially approved, is also significant here. It may be said that social change comes about when it is recognized that accepted values are in conflict or when

LUCY MAIR

opportunities are offered of realizing accepted values in new ways: and change is resisted when an innovation is alien to accepted values (cf. R. Firth, 1951a, pp. 83 ff.).

Recent Work in this Field

Colson makes an interesting point on the relation of cultural to structural changes in her study of the Makah Indians, who have retained their sense of separate identity while almost completely abandoning all the cultural features which previously distinguished them from white Americans. She finds the reason in the creation by the American government of a separate status for them which is now self-perpetuating. American policy has transformed 'a difference in status due to a difference in cultural background into a structural difference within the American social system. . . . The difference in status will undoubtedly result, as it already has, in differences in culture; for culture is responsive to the situations in which people find themselves' (Colson, 1953, p. 145).

Among the pupils of Malinowski, Nadel and Godfrey and Monica Wilson have discussed the possibility of formulating laws of social change. None of these has linked his generalizations at all closely with the results of field observation. Nadel (1951, p. 101) suggests that the type of social change on which study has been concentrated is in fact exceptional. It has actually proved possible in recent years to observe the reaction of one or two small-scale societies to disturbances not directly connected with colonial rule or the techniques of industrialization, such as famine or volcanic eruption, but even here the responses open to the people affected were limited by the existence of a colonial authority. It would seem to follow that whatever generalizations can be developed must refer to the modern situation, which, exceptional as it may be in the total history of *homo sapiens*, is at any rate universal in the world in which the process of social change is open to study by anthropological methods.

To the Wilsons (1945, pp. 125 ff.) there were two possible reasons for social change—the deliberate preference for new 'ways of action, thought and expression' or the existence of 'intolerable oppositions between groups and categories of people', which were also described as 'the forces of disequilibrium'. Any change which affects only one aspect of a society produces disequilibrium till the necessary concomitant changes have been made; the Wilsons suggest that if these changes were made at sufficiently wide intervals they would be, as it were, digested one by one, but not that social change has ever taken this form.

Nadel takes a line consistent with his view that the essential instrument of the social sciences is the study of concomitant variations. The ideal field for the observation of such variations is that of institutional change within a single society. Hence, if there are any laws of change, they can be none other than 'the sort of laws we can hope to arrive at by any kind of social inquiry'. There is, he says, no difference in principle between changes which arise in an apparently undisturbed culture and those provoked by 'culture contact' except that the latter are greater and are often brought about by compulsion. He also suggests the possibility that radical change in itself may have 'a peculiar shock-like effect' on the group experiencing it, and that the extent of this effect would depend on the degree of habituation to change of the group concerned. Accordingly, it might be possible by comparing 'different societies which are exposed to the same kind of change' to formulate 'laws bearing on some invariant relation between the relative stability of cultural situations and their sensitiveness to change' (1951, p. 103). Comparisons in these terms have not been made, and there might be some difficulty in finding pairs of societies whose experiences were sufficiently parallel and their background at the same time sufficiently different.

It is generally held today that, even if the available data for the study of social change are predominantly drawn from the processes of industrialization and colonial expansion, all societies must have experienced change. In so far as Malinowski took this view into account, he would have said, as Godfrey Wilson almost did say, that the more gradual changes in primitive societies, exposed to forces no stronger than those of the environment and their neighbours, were able to be digested without creating the maladjustments, or as Wilson called them 'radical oppositions', characteristic of societies in a state of rapid change today. Malinowski described his own functional method as having been worked out with the purpose of describing and analysing 'one culture, and a culture at that, which through age-long historical development has reached a state of well-balanced equilibrium' (1938a, p. xxxvi). Such a statement implies not only the teleological conception of culture which he avowedly held towards the end of his life, but the kind of judgement in terms of the health or sickness of an organism which has been made at one time or another by most observers of colonial and comparable societies. It involves two assumptions: that small-scale societies, before they were disturbed by industrialization with or without political domination, were in a state of 'equilibrium', and that since that time they have been in a less satisfactory condition, for which terms are used such as 'maladjustment' or 'disintegration'.

There has been much discussion about the meaning to be attached to these concepts in relation to society. It is now thought probable that a perfect correspondence of means to ends or of institutions to needs has not been realized in any society, and that opposition is inherent in the structure of most. Indeed, at the time when functional interpretations implying such correspondence were at their height, Fortune's *Sorcerers of Dobu* (1932) emphasized those socially disruptive effects of witchcraft beliefs which are now well recognized by anthropologists, who also recognize their significance as a means of social control. Other writers who have developed this theme are Evans-Pritchard (1937), Fortes (1945), Leach (1954b) and Gluckman (1956b). Such terms as 'equilibrium' have been defined in various ways, and much more frequently used without definition.

Radcliffe-Brown has formulated the opposition between the desired and the undesirable state of affairs in terms of the Greek words *eunomia* and *dysnomia*; he holds that *dysnomia* is 'a condition of functional disunity or inconsistency', and that societies in such a condition 'continue to struggle towards some sort of eunomia', perhaps with the result of changing their structural type. He indicates that the colonial field provides opportunities for the study of such situations. He adds that the one kind of social change which is open to observation is disintegration, but that movements towards reintegration can be seen in such phenomena as the appearance of new religions (1952, pp. 182 ff.). One may suggest that in this argument 'society' is hypostatized as much as 'culture' was by Malinowski. The formulation suggests that the nature of change is of no interest for its own sake, but only in so far as it is in the direction of disintegration or reintegration. Fortunately anthropologists have not in practice limited the study of social change so narrowly.

The Significance of History

Malinowski's well-known position on the value of history for anthropological studies was originally taken up in opposition to that of Rivers, in whose *History of Melanesian Society* a whole series of past events were assumed to have occurred to account for contemporary social organization, and of other writers who explained apparently anomalous features of contemporary societies as survivals from an earlier stage of development postulated in order to explain them. In rejecting 'conjectural history' he was in full agreement with Radcliffe-Brown, who, however, said that he did so 'not because it was historical but because it was conjectural' (1952, p. 50). Both were referring, not to the kind of inference from records that all historians must make, but to purely hypothetical pictures of past events. They were using the word in a much more specific sense than that in which Evans-Pritchard (1950, p. 198), and Forde (1950, p. 254) in agreement with him, have asserted that 'all history is conjectural'. They were in agreement too in seeking the explanation of similarities in the institutions of different societies in their relation to other institutions, and in looking for generalizations on the nature of society rather than explanations of unique phenomena. But whereas Radcliffe-Brown recognized that the peculiar characteristics of any institution must be the resultant of its historical development, Malinowski sometimes appeared to argue that no past event was of interest to anthropologists.

His attitude to the study of history in relation to social change was complicated by his preoccupation with policy. The main reason that he gave for discounting the value of reconstructions of the past was that they could be of no value in planning the future; what was important in his view was to forecast future trends, and he does not appear to have given much consideration to the possibility that parallels might be drawn between observed events at one time or place and recorded events at others. He admitted, of course, the relevance of any aspect of past tradition that was still cherished in African memory and so might influence action. His position is illustrated by a reference to the appropriate treatment by colonial authorities of the marriage payment: 'the practical question is not what this type of legal contract looked like a few generations ago but whether it is still an effective social force and what are the prospects of its further development and readjustment'. And again: 'It is the history surviving either in live tradition or in institutional working which is important. . . . Only what still lives can be of any relevance to those who have to control a Native society' (1945, p. 37).

He did, indeed, remark that there was no real contradiction between the functional and historical points of view, since the former, being concerned with processes, must take the time element into account. But in fact the time covered by a functional study as he understood it would extend at most as far back as the remembered experience of living informants. Though he expressly stated that historical data were useful in drawing comparisons, he firmly denied their value for the study of change in one society, partly because of the unreliable character of oral tradition, but even more because of his conviction that the main purpose of the study of social change was to enable governments to control it.

At a late stage in the development of his 'three-column' analytical scheme he suggested adding two further columns, one for the 'reconstructed past' and one for 'new forces of spontaneous African reaction'. Of the specimen charts which are published in *The Dynamics of Culture Change* only that on warfare contains entries under both these heads, and his comment on the reconstruction of the past is that, though of interest for the comparative study of warfare, it is 'of no relevance whatever' for the application of anthropology.

His criticism in this context, however, is based on quite other arguments than those of his earlier attack on 'conjectural history'. His warning that oral tradition must be considered, not as an objective record, but as a factor in the contemporary social situation, of the same order as myth even though it is concerned with historical events, would be recognized as valid by those anthropologists who have been most interested in the historical background of the societies they have studied.

Some interesting studies of traditional 'history' from this point of view have been made in Central Africa (Barnes, 1951; Cunnison, 1951). The process by which genealogical records are deliberately falsified so as to validate the contemporary social structure has also been illuminatingly described (L. Bohannan, 1952).

In discussing this subject Malinowski was concerned entirely with such historical data as can be obtained in the field, by questioning informants on their own memories and on what they accept as the tradition of a yet further past. Some anthropologists in America have claimed that their training in the checking of information enables them to obtain a correct picture from statements of this kind. A good deal depends on the type of problem under investigation. An admirable reconstruction of the political structure of the Ngoni in the period before their defeat by the British in 1898 has been made by Barnes (1954), applying the technique of structural analysis to records of the founding of village groups and their relationship obtained from informants by early residents in the area as well as by himself. By relying on oral tradition only for the record of critical events, and by interpreting it in the light of comparative knowledge of African social structures, he has established the nature and relationships of the political units which were utilized by the British as the lowest level in a new hierarchy, and thus transformed in a process to which the word 'borrowing' has little relevance. Although he had to deal with conflicting accounts of particular events, he did not have to rely on the type of generalization about the behaviour appropriate to different positions in the structure which is most likely to be coloured by the informant's own position and his inclination to idealize or denigrate the past.

Malinowski did not discuss the value of those historical data which are obtained from documents—the records of travellers, missionary bodies, officials and so on. When they are concerned with the nature of non-European societies they are of course no less prone to errors based on prejudice than are the oral traditions of these societies. They have the merit of being contemporary; they show how these societies appeared to a stranger at a given date, and sometimes include eye-witness accounts of actual scenes. For the study of social changes deliberately introduced, the records of governments, missionary societies and sometimes commercial organizations are the one authentic source of information on their aims and intentions. Examples of studies which have made use of them are those of Firth on the Maori (1929), Keesing on the Menomini (1939), Evans-Pritchard on the Sanusi (1939), and Schapera on the Tswana (1943).

As the scope of anthropological studies extends, and more and more work is done in parts of the world which have a long recorded history, the question of the relevance of history takes a new form. No historian has covered the total documentation of China, Turkey, Spain, Norway or London, and the study of history must be secondary to an anthropologist's main work. So we must ask, not, *Is* history relevant? but *What* history is relevant? The answer will not be so far from Malinowski's dictum that the past is significant in so far as it lives in the present. Those recorded events of the past which can be shown to have bearing on the phenomena under investigation are significant. The knowledge of earlier social forms is relevant only if they are still invoked in validation of current norms, or if the behaviour dictated by them is still practised. There is a third condition, which Malinowski did not envisage; historical record may show that a tradition which is living in his sense is not true to historical fact.

Colson's study of the Makah (1953), already quoted, deals with tradition in a manner fully in accordance with Malinowski's view. The theme of this book is not the process of social change, but the present relationship of the Makah to the rest of the American nation and the forces making for and against that total assimilation which was the aim of United States policy for a long period. This policy has been successful to such a point that no distinctively Indian customs are now practised; yet the memory of them is preserved as part of an ideology representing the whites as despoilers of the Indians, which is an important factor in preserving their consciousness of their separate identity as a people.

Contemporary Interest in the Problems

The main source of interest at the present time in social change as a separate study comes, as indeed Malinowski believed it should, from persons with practical aims—from the increasing number who are concerned, as agents of development programmes, with the improvement of productive techniques in peasant societies, and who constantly find themselves faced with unexplained resistance and turn to anthropologists for help. Although there is now a flourishing school of 'applied anthropology' in America, most British anthropologists would now say with Firth (1949) that they are 'interested in understanding social process, not directing it', and with Nadel that although the changes brought about by the impact of industrialization on peasant societies are unusually dramatic, they are to be regarded as one type of social process rather than as a unique field of study.

There has also been a change in the selection of problems for investigation due in part to this shift of emphasis, in part to the final rejection of the notion of culture or the interaction of cultures as the central problem, and in part to the much greater volume of data obtained by modern field-workers employing literate assistants and using sampling techniques. Many recent monographs do not discuss the totality of change in a given society but the development of a particular institution—government, marriage, land rights—or the reaction to a particular intrusive element such as the immigration of members of alien tribes or the demand for wage-labour. At the same time a new type of historical study has been made possible by the return of the same or a second investigator to a field which was studied in detail a generation ago. Such return visits have been made by original investigators to Manus (Mead, in 1953), Chan Kom (Redfield, in 1948) and Tikopia (Firth, in 1952), and by later students to Tepoztlán (O. Lewis, in 1943) and the Trobriands (Powell, in 1950). Some of these peoples had been through dramatic changes in the interim. But no cataclysm is necessary to make a return visit worth while; the recognition that all societies experience development, however gradual, is sufficient to justify the re-examination at a generation's distance of as many as resources permit.

Anthropology as Public Service and Malinowski's Contribution to it

H. IAN HOGBIN

IN physics, chemistry, and biology the distinction between pure and applied science is immediately obvious. The body of knowledge derived from experiment and analysis is used, on the one hand, for further exploration in the realm of theory and, on the other, for the achievement of specific technical ends. While the academic physicist is probing more deeply into the structure of matter, the civil engineer, designing bridges and viaducts, is utilizing the existing data on the behaviour of stone and metal under conditions of stress; and while the academic biologist strives to find out more concerning the principles of heredity and the mutation of genes, the plant breeder can proceed on established facts to develop strains of seed suitable for areas of low rainfall or great extremes of temperature.

Anthropology presents a somewhat different picture. The term 'applied anthropology', it is true, has been current for at least a generation,[1] and anthropologists, in this context sometimes referred to as 'social engineers', have at different times advised on native administration, factory management, and propaganda for broadcasting to foreign nations. But they have never been able to achieve any specific end or promise any specific device. In anthropology, as in the other social sciences, the material studied is not amenable to controlled experiment; and prediction, in the sense of being able to say with absolute confidence that, if the conditions are exactly reproduced, something which has happened once will happen again, is seldom possible. The conditions of social life do not usually reproduce themselves, especially today, now

---

[1] Various workers had written earlier of 'applying' anthropology or of its 'practical application' (e.g. Chinnery, 1919; Boas, 1928, p. 210; R. Firth, 1929, pp. 29, 32); and Pitt-Rivers (1929, p. 498) had even referred to the 'applied science of culture'. But the first use of the actual expression 'applied anthropology' that I have been able to discover is in the title of the paper by Radcliffe-Brown (1930).

that we have begun to undertake planned changes. The anthropologist when he talks about the future is accordingly obliged to lay due emphasis on various qualifications. He is thus less like an engineer constructing a bridge than a meteorologist forecasting tomorrow's weather. The meteorologist tells us whether to expect sunshine or rain but always on the assumption that the pressure systems, which are outside his control and subject to influences beyond his present understanding, will continue to travel at their accustomed rate along the usual paths.

The boundary between pure and applied anthropology is also more blurred than that between pure and applied natural science. The body of knowledge is for a number of reasons smaller, and the anthropologist interested in practical affairs cannot normally rely upon theories and methods worked out by others. On the contrary, he usually finds that he is confronted with issues which present new problems of theory and method. He is therefore forced to carry out research himself—research, moreover, which often differs not at all from that undertaken by those of his colleagues who are concerned rather with confirming or expanding some general hypothesis. Schapera's *Migrant Labour and Tribal Life* (1947) provides an illustration. The government of Bechuanaland had become alarmed about certain features of the labour situation and requested Schapera's help. He devotes the final 23 pages of the book to recommendations; but 193 pages are taken up with the analysis which had first to be made of such matters as how many natives seek employment; the methods of recruitment; the incentives for going away from home; what is done with the earnings; and the effect on the family life of those left behind.

Lay attitudes to the natural sciences and to the social sciences account for further differences when their respective conclusions come to be applied. The average citizen freely admits that civil engineers or plant breeders know more within their special fields than he does himself, and if he wants to bridge a river or find a new type of seed he asks the appropriate expert to do the job for him. He does not always regard anthropologists as more qualified to speak on the solution of certain social problems; indeed, he often claims that his own deductions from previous experience are equally valid. Again we may make a comparison, this time between the anthropologist and the art critic. Many members of the public hold that good taste comes naturally and requires no cultivation, and they are therefore wont to assume that they do not need help to discover whether a contemporary painting has merit.

The analogy might be pressed further. The small minority willing to respect the critic's judgement include a few who, to his embarrassment, regard it as infallible; and the handful prepared to seek out the anthropologist for advice also comprise some who bewilder him by their exaggerated notions of what he can accomplish. It is vain to expect him to prepare schemes for securing social benefits without any accompanying disadvantages. Every cultural innovation leads sooner or later to the disturbance of institutions which were not at first affected, and, at least for a time, some degree of social maladjustment is almost inevitable. Where a colonial administration has decided, for example, to raise native cash incomes by teaching the people to grow a crop for export, the result has also been serious disputes about land ownership and use, or the lessening of loyalties to kinsfolk, or the loss of authority by the traditional leaders and the emergence of a new power structure based on money. The anthropologist, called in beforehand, might foretell which of these difficulties is likely to arise; he might even suggest ways of mitigating some of the worst evils. But he could not ensure that there were no unwelcome changes. It is a safe maxim that in social life everything must be paid for, and social wisdom probably consists in the main of seeking only those things which are worth their price. The anthropologist can indicate what the cost is likely to be and, sometimes, how it may be reduced. Neither he nor anyone else is able to demonstrate a way of avoiding payment.

The application of the findings of the social sciences also causes frequent conflicts of opinion. We know exactly what we want the applied natural scientist to do for us when we consult him and on most occasions are in agreement about the desirability of the result. The new bridge will facilitate transport, the new seed will permit the spread of farming to marginal areas, the new drug will cure a painful disease, and the new machine will cut running costs. Certainly there have been times when those whose vested interests were likely to be adversely affected have sought to discredit the scientist, and at times, too, sections of the community have objected violently to proposed innovations. Social questions, however, are practically always political or administrative, and views on applying the social sciences, far from being unanimous, are generally irreconcilable. It follows that an attempt to introduce measures based on scientific investigation conducted by a disinterested anthropologist—or failure to do anything at all—no matter how popular it may be in some quarters, generally arouses suspicion and anger in other quarters.

The Work of Malinowski

Two kinds of applied anthropology have been distinguished, indirect and direct. In the former the anthropologist is 'teaching those concerned with primitive folk the principles and facts of his subject, with perhaps some special reference to their particular problems'; in the latter the anthropologist himself goes to the field to investigate 'those aspects of primitive life which he is requested to study by an administration, answering specific problems put before him by a colonial official who may or may not use the data in formulating his policy towards native life' (Herskovits, 1936). Indirect applied anthropology is much the older.

The notion that a course of training might be of value to colonial administrative officers was appreciated even before 1900, and in the first decades of the century a large number were attending classes at the universities. Here and there, too, men with the necessary aptitudes were seconded from other duties to collect information on local customs for the benefit of their fellow officials.[1] The authorities had already come to realize that running the affairs of a backward territory demands special preparation. In European countries the members of the civil service are citizens of the society and hence as familiar as everyone else with its organization, traditions, and values. But in the outposts of Empire the white officer is a stranger, dissociated from the life going on around him. Without study he remains ignorant of the most elementary facts about the peoples whom he serves and rules.

Till about 1920, however, a crude theory of evolution held the field, and social history was conceived as essentially a uniform unilinear development from the stage of savagery through barbarism to eventual civilization. Administrators were convinced that native tribes, if they did not die out in the process, would in any event go forward under their own momentum and that with a modicum of help the pace could be accelerated. Unpleasant and absurd practices had to be eliminated, of course, but only a few positive reforms inaugurated. The anthropologists, too, had little to offer that was of practical relevance either to the framers of policy or to the men on the spot who were implementing it. They were still largely devoting their energies to plotting possible early migrations and seeking evidence of previous forms of society. They picked out what they alleged to be survivals, such as matrilineal descent and the custom of couvade, and then described these without any reference to the present cultural context.

This was the situation when in 1922 Malinowski published a paper on 'Ethnology and the Study of Society' (1922b) which the general public must have found revolutionary. He put forward a theory of culture as an integrated whole and stressed that if any part was tampered with a general collapse might follow. No institution, he declared, should be condemned merely because it differs from our own. An attempt should be made to explain it, to investigate its function and find out what biological needs it fulfils. This meant, in effect, going a long way towards justifying it.[2]

[1] See *Applied Anthropology in Government* (E. A. Kennard and G. Macgregor, 'United States', D. Forde, 'British Africa', and C. J. Held, 'The Netherlands'), in Kroeber (1953, pp. 832-79).
[2] The notion of culture as an integrated whole was implied, though not explicitly formulated, by W. H. R. Rivers in a paper published in the same year (1922, pp. 107-9).

248

Malinowski's field-work was carried out in Melanesia, but this was almost the only occasion, when dealing with native administrative problems, that he referred to Pacific peoples (cf. p. 214). Although his statements were phrased in the broadest terms, he was primarily concerned with the application of anthropology in Africa. He began by considering depopulation, at that time a major anxiety throughout Oceania. This evil, he insisted, was 'mainly caused by the destruction of all vital interest to the native, by taking away from him all that was dear and vital to him, of all that gave him the joy of living. All that would appear to the convention-bound, parochial, middle-class mind as "disgusting", "silly", "immoral", was simply destroyed with the stroke of the pen, and, worse, with rifles and bayonets. And yet to a deeper knowledge, based on real human sympathy and on conscientious scientific research, many of these "savage" customs are revealed as containing the very essence of the tribal life to a people as something indispensable to their existence as a race. Imagine well meaning, perhaps, but rigid and conceited bureaucrats sitting in judgement over British civilization. They would see thousands of youths and men "wasting their time" over "silly" games, like golf, cricket, and football, in "immoral" betting, in "disgusting" boxing and fox-hunting. "These forms of sport are *streng verboten*" would be their verdict! . . . Yet anyone looking from an ethnological point of view on this problem would soon see that to wipe out sport, or even undermine its influence, would be a crime.'

The stamping out of warfare is an example of such a mistake. 'It would be good to make it quite clear to ourselves that it is sheer hypocrisy and humbug to pretend that the prohibition on fighting is done for the good of the natives.' Native warfare causes little damage and has the merit of providing 'a wide field of physical exercise, the development of personal courage, cunning, and initiative, and the sort of dramatic and romantic interest, the wider vision of possibilities and ideals, which probably nothing can replace'. 'In the Trobriand Islands . . . in a big war, where a couple of thousand warriors took part, the total casualties might amount to half a dozen killed and a dozen wounded. . . . And such a war afforded excellent amusement, exercise, and development of personal qualities to a large number of men for several weeks. . . . Thus, the establishment of peace and safety is by no means an unmixed blessing, and it is always deeply resented by the natives themselves.' The governments ought to have left the 'milder forms of fighting . . . so as not to unman the natives completely. Perhaps some sportive imitation of warfare might have been permitted without bloodshed, yet allowing the savages to settle their quarrels and satisfy their ambitions in this manner.' Instead, all the war canoes were destroyed, and the building of club-houses, associated with headhunting but fulfilling other purposes besides, was prevented.

'Everywhere the same fanatical zeal to prune, uproot, and make an *auto-da-fé* of all that shocks our moral, hygienic, or parochial susceptibilities, the same ignorant and stupid lack of comprehension of the fact that every item of culture, every custom and belief, represents a value, fulfils a social function, has a positive biological significance. For tradition is a fabric in which all the strands are so closely woven that the destruction of one unmakes the whole. The tradition is, biologically speaking, a form of collective adaptation of a community to its surroundings. Destroy tradition, and you will deprive the collective organism of its protective shell and give it over to the slow inevitable process of dying out.'

It was valuable for the administrative officials of the day to be told about cultural integration and the interrelationship of institutions— useful also for them to learn that every custom has a meaning for the person who practises it. They might have been pardoned, however, for dismissing the advice as unreal in that it implied complete non-interference. No colonial government can condone warfare, any more than it can permit the strangling of widows, cannibalism, or headhunting—though doubtless here, too, something might be said in extenuation, and in terms of values which we ourselves recognize. Again, despite the fact that it is undeniable that certain losses follow once fighting ceases, it is equally true that there are also gains, which the people themselves, once the older generation has disappeared, are the first to appreciate. They are glad to be secure and seize upon the new opportunities to travel. Trade flourishes, and not only goods but ideas also are exchanged. Further, despite the gloomy prophecy, almost the only groups which actually died out were those deliberately killed off by gunfire and poison, as in south-eastern Australia and Tasmania, and those living in extreme isolation too far away for regular medical patrols to be carried out. Elsewhere, now that the initial susceptibility to introduced diseases has been overcome and adequate health services are operating, the numbers usually show signs of increasing. Some Pacific dependencies, indeed, are likely in the near future to be troubled by over-population.

Neither in 1922, when this paper appeared, nor at any subsequent date did Malinowski work out a satisfactory theory of social change. Cultures, in the words of Bartlett (1943, p. 12), have hard and soft parts which respectively resist and yield to change. Armed with a thorough knowledge of the community concerned, anthropologists can say which is which; but they still lack any comprehensive hypothesis applicable to all cases. Under the influence of outside contact certain old customs and beliefs have everywhere vanished without leaving a trace, others have persisted despite efforts to suppress them, and still others have been transformed. Thus the natives of New Guinea have themselves kept 'the milder forms of fighting' under the guise of football (Hogbin, 1938, p. 228).

In 1926 came the foundation of the International African Institute for the express purpose of promoting 'the closer association of scientific knowledge and research with practical affairs' (Lugard, 1928, p. 2). The prime movers, significantly enough, were not scientists but mission leaders like Edwin Smith and J. H. Oldham. This marked the real beginning of the direct type of applied anthropology.

Malinowski's paper 'Practical Anthropology' followed shortly afterwards (1929d). He first demonstrated field techniques for the benefit of administrative officers and urged them to say where they needed help, but on this occasion he addressed his remarks chiefly to anthropologists. Three years before, in a letter to *Nature*, he had reproved them for their 'curio-hunting sensation-mongering' interest (1926d), and he now pleaded with them to give up antiquarianism and concentrate on what was taking place in native societies before their eyes. Above all, he advocated that they should deal with problems which were perplexing the practical man in the colonies and thus qualify themselves for giving him advice.

Anthropologists, said Malinowski, 'must move towards a direct study of institutions as they now exist and work. [They] must also become more concerned in the anthropology of the changing African, and in the anthropology of white and coloured, of European culture and primitive tribal life.' No one had at that period, he pointed out, taken up in Africa any first-hand study of 'primitive economics, primitive jurisprudence, questions of land tenure, of indigenous financial systems and taxation, a correct understanding of African indigenous education, [or the] wider problems of population, hygiene, and changing outlook'. A knowledge of the principles behind African political systems which have a centralized kingship, information which only anthropologists were trained to supply, would have been of immense importance to administrators. The subject of kingship had not been ignored, but investigation had been confined to such matters as 'the ritual aspects of savage monarchies, the dim quaint superstitions about the king's vitality, connections between this and magical potentialities'. As to such questions as the way in which primitive politics work, 'what forms underlie the obedience to the king, to his ministers; the mere description and analytical study of what might be called the political constitution of native tribes, of these things we are largely ignorant'. Primitive law had also been neglected; and social organization largely meant 'explanations of such customs as couvade, the avoidance of the mother-in-law, the disposal of the afterbirth, and the quaint usages associated with the relation between cousins. . . . We know more about the so-called anomalous forms of marriage or classificatory exaggerations of kinship than we know about the organization of the family.'

Malinowski again and again repeated this attack on the older kind of anthropology, and he and Radcliffe-Brown share the credit for its eventual disappearance in Britain and the Dominions. Today no British social anthropologist could be accused of antiquarianism—nobody seeks for survivals or reconstructs the imaginary sequences of conjectural history (cf. Richards, 1941). The study is concerned with native peoples as they are here and now, subject everywhere to the influences of western civilization.[1] Malinowski's was also the stimulus which initiated detailed observation of the day-to-day workings of society, the interconnections between the institutions, and the way in which these are becoming modified. Anthropology could never be applied, so he argued (1930c), unless material of this kind was ready to hand. With it as a background, however, anthropologists might both provide colonial officers with a really adequate training and reveal to them the various issues which every administrative decision raises. In a paper published not long before his death he described himself as the advocate of 'practical anthropology', which he defined as 'the study of vital, relevant, and fundamental problems' (relevant, that is, to adminstrative situations). 'That a question does not become less scientific because it is vital and relevant,' he concluded, 'will only be denied by one who imagines that academic pursuits begin where reality ends' (1939a, pp. 38–40).

Since that date significant developments have also occurred in the application of anthropology to the problems of civilized societies, and in the United States numbers of anthropologists are engaged in giving advice on the reorganization of industry and on factory management. Industrial anthropology is said to have been inspired by the personal influence of Malinowski and Radcliffe-Brown (Chapple, 1953, p. 819). But, as Malinowski wrote nothing directly on the subject—though he constantly stressed the value of anthropological study as a means of acquiring a better understanding of our own society (1922b, pp. 215, 218–19; 1938c)—I shall confine myself in the following pages to applied anthropology in native administration.

Applying Anthropology

Debate turns nowadays not on what anthropologists should study but on whether they ought themselves to take the initiative in applying their findings or leave the task to others. Some of the opposition to their personal intervention is based on arguments of expediency. Thus Evans-Pritchard has issued a warning lest 'the pressure of political and administrative interests [should] draw away so many of our small band from the investigation of purely scientific problems that the advance of the science may be seriously retarded'. 'It often happens in the develop-

[1] M. J. Herskovits (1938, p. 124) suggests that British anthropologists might with advantage pay some attention also to the investigation of the way in which native peoples influence one another.

ment of a science', he writes, 'that the problems which are of the greatest scientific interest to a student, and the solution to which prove to be of greatest benefit to mankind, are precisely those which appear at the time to be of little or no importance to the man of affairs. If, therefore, we allow his interests to decide the direction of our research we shall not only do our science a disservice but do him an injury as well. Settlement schemes, land tenure difficulties, labour migration and such like problems interest administrators; kinship systems, ritual, and mythology do not. But, apart from the fact . . . that in primitive societies the one set of problems can seldom be investigated without investigations into the other, it would be deplorable if such fundamental problems as anthropologists have always concerned themselves with, like religion and magic, were to be neglected because enquiry into them does not promise an immediate dividend' (1946, p. 94; and also 1951a, p. 120). The effective answer is contained in the last sentence—the one set of problems can seldom be investigated without investigations into the other. The interests of theoretical and applied anthropology do diverge, but, as Malinowski reiterated, many matters, such as political organization, land tenure, and law, are of equal concern to both.

Other writers point out that if anthropologists agree to assist colonial governments anthropology itself may become identified with policies which prove to be unpopular. The danger is real; moreover, as has been mentioned, few policies meet with universal approval. More significant, however, is the risk of the anthropologist becoming the instrument of a policy with which, on purely scientific grounds, he disagrees. If he feels that he is being forced to misapply his skills he can only give his reasons and withdraw. The projects for which his aid has been sought may in his considered opinion be unsuitable or impracticable, or he may think that the ends have not been envisaged with sufficient clarity. Many persons who talk about 'native development' do not define their terms or work out the implications of what they are advocating; those who support educational reform, for instance, are sometimes blind to the need for complementary changes in the political organization and the economy (Malinowski—1936c, p. 517—made this point). Yet the anthropologist has no right to assume that governments ought always to act upon his advice. Administrative staffs in the colonies are as anxious as he is to see that the native peoples in their charge get a square deal, as Evans-Pritchard points out. What they want to know from him is how a square deal can best be accommodated to administrative requirements and imperial policy (1946, pp. 97–8). The recommendations may have to be rejected as too costly, or contrary to the defence needs of the country, or as prejudicial to what is held to be the proper administration of justice.

Some anthropologists also argue that, as any serious attempt on their part to apply their knowledge is bound to be futile or, at best, reduced to palliatives, it is wiser to keep clear of direct participation. Herskovits was at one time a strong supporter of this view. The administrator, he said, was there solely to maintain law and order, to see that a supply of labour was available, and to preserve the colonial market for goods produced by the mother country; the missionary to preach his own narrow version of the truth; and the education officer to change the traditional patterns of behaviour. The anthropologist could not hope to combat all the powerful vested interests (1936, pp. 221–2). Nadel deprecates this defeatism, and he speaks for others besides himself when he asserts, 'whether we like it or not, compromise, concessions, palliatives are the very essence of social life everywhere' (1953, p. 11).

Cultural Relativism

The theory of relativism, with which Herskovits's name is closely associated, deserves our consideration here, for if pressed to its conclusion it would mean that the application of anthropology, whether by anthropologists or anyone else, would have no justification. The argument proceeds from the differences of custom, a fact of which everyone is aware, to the complete relativity of moral systems. Values are a cultural product, Herskovits insists, and no objective moral order exists. Cross-cultural judgements are without any rational basis, and the person who praises or condemns the practices of other societies is guilty of applying the values developed by his own group to circumstances where they can have no meaning. Each culture is a closed world, and a common ethical measure cannot be found.

'Judgements are based on experience, and experience is interpreted by each individual in terms of his own enculturation,' Herskovits writes (1948, chap. 5; and also 1947, p. 539). 'Even the facts of the physical world are discerned through an enculturative screen so that the perception of time, distance, weight, size, and other "realities" is mediated by the conventions of any given group.' Evaluations are accordingly relative to the background out of which they arise. 'It is essential, in considering cultural relativism, that we differentiate absolutes from universals. Absolutes are fixed . . . and are not admitted to have variation, to differ from culture to culture, from epoch to epoch. Universals, on the other hand, are those least common denominators to be extracted . . . from comprehension of the range of variations which all phenomena of the natural or cultural world manifest. . . . To say that there is no absolute criterion of value or morals, or even, psychologically, of time or space, does not mean that such criteria, in differing forms, do not comprise universals in human culture. . . . Certain values in human life are everywhere afforded recognition, even though the institutions of no two cultures can be identical in form. Morality is universal, and so is enjoyment of beauty, and some standard of truth. The many forms these concepts take are but products of the historical experience of the societies that manifest them.' Each person should, in the interests of social discipline, abide by the code of his own society; and he ought also to respect the right of others to conform to their code. If this doctrine is difficult to accept, that is only because we have been reared in a community which has stressed the validity of his own system. Everyone, admittedly, is ethnocentric in that he is convinced that the way of life of his own society is the best. Such an attitude is actually commendable if linked with tolerance: it becomes reprehensible only if it leads to an attempt to alter or 'improve' the members of neighbouring communities. Europeans, because they have embraced the dogma of progress, are the worst offenders. We must learn to abandon our bias and transcend our ethnocentrism in the name of cultural relativism.

Redfield and others have pointed out that the two parts of the theory are not logically interdependent. 'The first part says that people are brought up to see the value in things that their local experience has suggested. The second part says that we should respect all cultures,' he remarks. 'But there is no true "therefore" between these two parts. It cannot be proved, from the proposition that values are relative, that we ought to respect all systems of values. We might just as well hate them all' (1953, p. 147).[1]

Herskovits no longer believes that the efforts of applied anthropologists are foredoomed to failure, and in another section of the work from which I have been quoting he urges that they should endeavour to help native peoples to adjust themselves to increasing contact with the West (1948, chap. 38). It is difficult to see how, in the light of the criticism of his theory, he could continue to hold that they have such a duty. If morals were in fact wholly relative, and nobody was obliged to respect any system other than his own, there would be no means of judging between the ethics of Jesus Christ and of Hitler and no reason for assisting foreigners. American citizens and British subjects might disapprove of slavery and of persecuting Jews, but they could not argue that these things were wrong in any absolute sense or that it was their business to try to stop them.

The results could be especially unfortunate if colonial governments were to adopt the relativity theory. The rulers might then assign the subjects to a separate moral universe and subsequently base their

[1] See also Bidney (1953, pp. 682-98). Bidney states that Herskovits is so concerned about respecting differences that he fails to appreciate the polar requirement of a common core of cultural values. 'There can be no mutual respect for differences where there is no community of values also.' 'The fact of cultural relativism in historic cultures does not logically imply the absolute value of cultural differences and the obligation to respect them. The "is" of cultural relativism does not imply the "ought".'

actions on superior power. 'Relativism', in the words of one writer, 'is the preamble to a totalitarian conception of law and right and, if consistently embraced, must lead to it' (McAuley, 1953). Most colonial legal systems, however, accept the traditional doctrine of natural law and, on this ground, forbid practices which are 'repugnant to the general principles of humanity' (the phrase used in the New Guinea Ordinance), such as warfare or cannibalism. Thus, instead of accepting relativism, the civilized peoples of the world have taken it for granted that certain basic principles, derived from truths which are apparent to unprejudiced reason, are deserving of respect by all men irrespective of their cultural background.

The issue as the relativist sees it, Bidney (1953) points out, turns on opposite alternatives, either a doctrine of fixed absolute values or else a denial of objective norms. He suggests that these are but two possibilities and himself puts forward a third. Natural scientists do not argue that objective truth has no existence when, as their knowledge increases, they find themselves forced to modify earlier theories. On the contrary, it is just because they believe in the objective order of nature amenable to gradual human discovery that they are prepared to question their assumptions and generalizations. Similarly, it is unreasonable to reject objective moral norms because some of those which have seemed to be objective turn out to have only subjective value within a given culture. It may well be that a cumulative increment in our knowledge of moral ideals will take place comparable to the growth of the awareness of truth in the natural sciences. Respect for human life and property are already concrete ethnological universals despite the fact that different cultures display variations in the field of their application.

This third possibility, or something closely akin to it, had already been foreshadowed by Malinowski. Relativity, although it is derived from the work of Westermarck and Boas, did not come to the fore in anthropology till after his death, but readers familiar only with his earlier theoretical works might conclude that he would have subscribed to it. They could be misled by his hostility to the evolutionists, though here he had in mind only those of the older school and their unilinear concept of progress; and they would also note that he implied, but did not explicitly say, that the only absolute value is that of survival. All the others, he appeared at this stage to have believed, are a means to this end. In his last book, published posthumously (1947), however, he postulates freedom as an absolute value, which thus might serve as a means of comparing and grading social systems. Primitive groups permit little of it, but in civilized communities, though it may be arbitrarily limited by those in power at the time, the potentialities are far greater. The more freedom individuals enjoy, the better, or more advanced, is the society to which they belong.

ANTHROPOLOGY AS PUBLIC SERVICE

Anthropologists and Administrators

Colonial administrators have in the past expressed some dissatisfaction with anthropological monographs and complained that the material is seldom presented in a form in which it could be of practical use. Sir Philip Mitchell, although he is here more than usually bitter, has summed up the reaction as follows: 'Anthropologists, asserting that they only were gifted with understanding, busied themselves with enthusiasm about all the minutiae of obscure tribal and personal practices, especially if they were agreeably associated with sex or flavoured with obscenity. There resulted a large number of painstaking and often accurate records of interesting habits and practices, of such length that no one had time to read them and often, in any case, irrelevant, by the time they became available, to the day-to-day business of government.'[1]

We can agree that the practical man is frequently obliged to deal with events as they occur and with opportunities that are momentary. On such occasions he has no time for research or to arrange for experiments. He depends upon present information, and if he calls in an expert he wants the opinion at once. Then, with the fragments of knowledge ready to hand, he makes his irrevocable decision. If he is judging between the rival claimants for a chiefdom, he asks the expert to tell him in a dozen words what are the normal rules of succession; if giving a verdict concerning a disputed strip of territory, he asks for a brief summary of the rules of land tenure; and if reckoning compensation for damage done to a crop by a domestic pig, he asks for a statement on the rules relating to the responsibility for fencing gardens. For such a short-term view general anthropological reports are rarely of much help. Native customary law allows a range of variations, and the formulation of such precise rules as our impersonal legislation demands would be an over-simplification.

But the practical man has at times to take the long-range view, as, for example, when he is assessing the effects of past regulations or thinking of framing new ones. Here the position is better, for any literature which interprets one set of cultural values in terms of another is likely to be helpful. Yet the form and bulk of the average anthropological work on particular tribes may still prove to be forbidding.

The blame, if it is to be sheeted home, must rest with the

[1] P. Mitchell (1951), p. 57. (The same volume contains a reply by Schapera.) Mitchell (1930) also criticized Malinowski ('The Anthropologist and the Practical Man'); Malinowski (1930c) replied with 'The Rationalization of Anthropology and Administration'. Yet Mitchell was not opposed to anthropologists as such. He collaborated in an anthropological experiment early in his career (see C. G. Brown and A. M. Hutt, 1935), and during the Pacific war, when he held the office of High Commissioner for the Western Pacific, he invited my help in planning the rehabilitation of the natives of the Solomon Islands.

governments themselves. They have too rarely appointed anthropologists to the permanent staff. The man on the spot all the time, and only he, can be in close touch with the administration and know its real needs.

'It is important that the anthropologist who acts as an adviser, or consultant, to an administration should be a full member of it,' says Evans-Pritchard. 'He cannot advise the administration on the bearing of the legal, educational, economic, and other social programmes . . . unless he knows the bureaucratic machinery from the inside, has full access to all government documents, and meets the heads of departments around the same conference table as an equal. Otherwise he will not be able to see the problems in their full anthropological context, to translate an administrative problem into anthropological terms and vice versa, and to speak as one who shares the full responsibility for the actions and policy of the administration. Administrators naturally resent advice from outsiders but will gladly accept it from one who has the same loyalty to the administration as themselves and who can, moreover, speak about some of its problems with special knowledge they lack' (1946, p. 97).

Problems in which Anthropology has been Applied

Anthropologists have concerned themselves, nevertheless, with trying to find solutions for a large number of practical problems. They have proposed schemes for the establishment of local councils and courts in order to give native peoples a greater share in their own administration, worked out plans for native taxation, suggested methods for strengthening, or in some cases for lessening, the powers of chiefs, recommended forms for the reorganization of native political systems so that these might be more efficient in preserving law and order, counselled on native education and the sort of schools which might prove attractive, dealt with difficulties arising from the determination of the administration to raise native income by introducing cash crops or to prevent soil erosion by reducing the size of native herds, and advised on whether the alleged low status of woman might be raised, or the stability of marriage increased, by imposing a rule of monogamy.

Two examples may be quoted at greater length. Raymond Firth (1936, chap. 12) discussed a population problem a generation before it occurred. Tikopia is a small island in the Solomon group, and in earlier days the natives kept the balance between numbers and resources by allowing only the elder sons of the family to marry (without imposing chastity on the younger sons), by practising infanticide, by encouraging adventurous sea-voyaging (in which many were drowned), and by engaging in warfare and driving the defeated out of the community. Today everyone is permitted to marry, the killing of infants is punished or reprobated, sea-voyaging occurs more seldom, and warfare is forbidden. The population has therefore risen rapidly, and food supplies are no longer adequate. Firth outlined three possible ways of averting famine and gave an account of the difficulties which each would raise—introducing new crops and improving agricultural methods, transferring whole groups to another island, and teaching efficient modes of birth control. (Some of these points were illustrated by a famine in 1952–3, following a hurricane—Firth, personal communication.)

Schapera's work on labour migration in Bechuanaland (1947) was mentioned earlier. The administration wanted to know whether further harm to the tribes could be avoided if a limit was set on the number of men allowed to leave the reservations. In the final chapter, where the recommendations are set out, Schapera begins by listing the most serious effects on tribal life, including the desertion of wives and children, the reduction in the birth rate brought about by the postponement of marriage and the absence of husbands, the spread of disease by the men on their return, the deterioration of agriculture and animal husbandry, and the shortage of labour for the regiments, which carry out all the public works. He then goes on to say that there is thus a *prima facie* case both for reducing the number of migrants and for shortening the period of their absence. But some of the evils could be counterbalanced by other measures, such as improving cultural standards, raising the level of education and of health, and arranging to have public works carried out by some other method than through the regiments, which are at best inefficient. He also points out that migration brings certain advantages. It is a valuable source of income and, in addition, serves as a beneficial experience for men with some education and enables a few to acquire skills which are useful to the community at large. His discussion ends with three suggestions—the application and enforcement of a quota system, the removal of some of the causes which make the men leave home, and a combination of the two policies. These he treats at length, and, again, the difficulties are indicated.

These examples can be separated into two categories. In the first we could place the taxation plans, the schemes for handling chieftainship and political organization, and the reports on the status of women and on marriage. These are almost wholly anthropological matters, and the recommendations are limited in scope, calling for simple executive action. Into the other category would go the introduction of new crops, birth control, resettlement, labour migration, local courts, and schooling. These latter are more complicated: they call for radical changes of policy and are concerned not only with anthropology but also with agriculture, public health, economics, the law, or education. The anthropologist is entitled to expect that his statements about society, of which he is the specialist, will be given due attention, but on other subjects his views carry no more weight than that of the ordinary citizen. When his advice has a bearing on methods of farming, the prevention of diseases, the limitation of the movements of labourers, the administration of justice, or the revision of curricula in the schools, it must be considered in conjunction with that of experts in these fields. The government of the Solomon islands, for instance, would be unwise to act on Firth's suggestion to improve the Tikopia food supply without first having an investigation made of the soil and climate: possibly the natives are already cultivating the only crops which will grow there.

A proposal which finds favour with some of the senior officers of the administrations of the south-western Pacific—to introduce individual titles to land—may be referred to here. By such means, they contend, maximum production might be assured. This is a question on which the anthropologist would have something useful to say. He could point out the resistances which would be encountered, indicate the sort of persuasion required to overcome them, and foretell some of the social consequences of individualization. But he could never give the whole answer. Technical information would have to be sought also from agriculturalists and economists.

Powers and Limitations

Godfrey Wilson (1940), in his full and detailed treatment of the rôle of the anthropolgist, distinguishes between prescribing techniques and prescribing values. Anthropologists, he says, are competent to attempt only the former; and then they are under an obligation to ensure that the advice shall be both objective and disinterested. Executive action involving policy, and policy itself, are solely for authority to decide, and when anthropologists criticize and recommend they must confine themselves to the technical side.

'The social anthropologist cannot, as a scientist, judge good and evil but only of objective social fact and its implications,' Wilson emphasizes (p. 45). If he is faced with such a question as what ought to be done about native marriage or chieftainship he can only say that concepts of human welfare are matters of opinion not of science. When the query is posed in a different form, however, he may be able to give an answer. He can explain the exact state of the marriage laws and say what effects these have in a given area at a given time and tell why certain chiefs have lost the respect of their followers.

Wilson disapproves of anthropologists talking about the future of marriage in general terms because to do so would be tantamount to laying down the kind of relationship between the sexes at which the administration should be aiming. He believes that they have no qualifications to perform such a task. But anthropologists can say why divorce occurs frequently and how its incidence might be reduced, and they can also give an account of the status of women, and, if females are in fact at a disadvantage, indicate methods for overcoming the difficulty. All arguments about the merits of stable marriage or of polygamy are thus avoided. (It is scarcely conceivable that an anthropologist would regard stable marriage and equality for women as undesirable; if he did, he would say why. There is some probability, however, that, if asked to make a plan for equitable taxation, he might think that the native population ought not to be taxed; he would then show how poor they were.)

'Human societies . . . have a hard material reality which cannot be mastered without patient and objective study,' Wilson continues (p. 46). 'It is the scientists' business to undertake that patient and objective study, it is the business of government and industry to make use of their results in fashioning out of the present whatever future they desire. The scientists must make it their boast that both governments and oppositions can trust them equally because they say nothing which they cannot prove, because they are always pedestrian and never leave the facts.'

But the anthropologist has more to offer than bare information: he claims to be able to explain the facts that he describes. He may therefore be led into technical (as distinct from political) criticisms of policy. He can never either approve or condemn policy as such but is often in a position to see whether it is possible of application in given conditions. If it is not, he may also be able to suggest changes.

Doubts have been cast on whether anthropological advice can ever be quite as free from value judgements as Wilson insists that it should. Ginsberg (1953) has remarked that the fact that anthropologists are now employed as consultants makes it difficult for them to live up to the doctrine of ethical neutrality. In helping to shape policy, he says, they cannot confine themselves to a cold estimate of the consequences likely to follow from the various lines of action. Ends and means are so closely related that it is unreasonable to hope for a division of labour which would leave the former to the statesman and the latter to the scientist.

The position of the anthropologist is different from that of natural scientists. The latter have no difficulty in contemplating the object of their work without the intrusion of moral feelings, whether of approval or indignation. He ought perhaps to be like them; and certainly he can investigate customs involving infanticide, senicide, slavery, or ritual murder, if not quite with the laboratory spirit, at least with less emotion than the public at large. But he observes living persons, not inert matter, and his task is therefore much harder. 'In me, man and anthropologist do not separate themselves sharply,' Redfield writes (1953a, p. 165). 'I used to think I could bring about that separation in scientific work about humanity. Now I have come to confess that I have not effected it, and, indeed, to think that it is not possible to do so. All the rules of objectivity I should maintain: the marshalling of evidence that may be confirmed by others, the persistent doubting and testing of all important descriptive formulations that I make, the humility before the facts, and the willingness to confess oneself wrong and begin over. I hope I may always strive to obey these rules. But I think now that what I see men do, and understand that human beings do, is seen often with a valuing of it. I like or dislike as I go. This is how I reach understanding of it.'

Redfield follows a similar line of argument to Malinowski's in *Freedom and Civilization*. He, too, believes in moral development and adopts a theory first expounded by Kroeber (1948, pp. 298–304) and since elaborated by Ginsberg.[1] Certain aspects of some moral systems are better than the corresponding aspects of others, he maintains, in that they give greater scope for human dignity, sympathy, and freedom. Civilized societies, despite recent notorious lapses, are from this point of view more advanced than primitive societies, and it is idle for the anthropologist to deny this when making his investigations or giving his recommendations.

Nadel (1953, pp. 16–20) makes the point even more strongly. Value judgements, he says, are entailed in the anthropologist's universe of discourse. The anthropologist deals with society and with culture. By society we mean a body of persons bound together in unity, acting in an integrated manner, and possessed of some degree of permanence and stability. Integration, regularity, stability, and permanence are all requirements of society as we conceive it. Thus in analysing society we assess its capacity to achieve stability and continuity and to function smoothly as an integrated unit. Again, individuals satisfy their needs in the matrix of conduct we call culture; and culture implies selection and restriction of possible ways of acting, the stimulation of certain desires, and the exclusion of others. Thus culture connotes the co-existence of gratifications and constraints, of satisfactions and frustrations. In analysing culture we assess one against the other to evaluate the adequacy of cultural life. Such judgements are continually being made in anthropological literature, which is full of such terms as 'adjustment', 'maladjustment', 'function', and 'dysfunction'. These imply that the student of society is placing societies and cultures on a scale of 'good' and 'bad' solutions of the problem of existence.

Nadel also urges that anthropologists should go further than offering purely technical criticisms of policy. He admits that they can restrict themselves to studies of given situations without making moral evaluations, hinting at desirable features, or recommending programmes of action; or they can if they wish indicate the likely consequences of various courses of action and leave others to make the choice. But in that case they delude themselves if they think that they are remaining unbiased observers and avoiding all responsibility for the eventual

---

[1] Ginsberg's paper is of special interest because he offers an explanation for the differences in moral systems.

policy. 'The anthropologist working for governments or other employees . . . must in some measure share their responsibility; and this is true if he provides "factual" information, since it may well be through this information that the policies will be rendered practicable or successful. . . . Nothing can alter our responsibility as scientists to carry out our investigations as objectively as is humanly possible and present the results as truly as we can. The question is if our moral responsibility ends there. I [suggest] that it does not' (pp. 12–14).

So far Nadel is speaking specifically of the anthropologist inside a government or comparable institution. Later he fails to make it clear whether he is continuing the argument directly or has switched over to the anthropologist on the outside, working perhaps at a university. 'Since knowledge about societies is capable of being applied, let the anthropologist be the one to apply it,' he writes here (pp. 15–16). 'And let him apply it not as a mere technician who serves ends decreed by others, but as one claiming the right to judge the worthiness of the ends. That is, he must recommend, advise, criticize, and pronounce on the rights and wrongs of policies. The "defeatist" argument that anthropological advice cannot change policy seems to me to be just that; policies are not sacrosanct and have been known to give way before just (and courageous) criticism. That the criticism should be just is the responsibility of the anthropologist. So is the honesty of his approach, in the sense that he must at every step make explicit the premises and reasoning that guide him. . . . And if . . . this means that the anthropologist must enter the arena with politicians, business men, moralists, or that popular hero "the practical man", he has nothing to be ashamed or frightened of; his armoury is strong and his weapons respectable.'

It is highly improbable that if Nadel was thinking of the anthropologist as a full- or part-time civil servant he will ever have his dream fulfilled.

The general view, I believe, would be that anthropologists are not qualified, and still less alone qualified, to dictate policy.[1] Any such statement as, 'Because I am an anthropologist I know what ought to be done', would, I am sure, be condemned as much as the claims of the physicists to decide, because they make atom bombs, when these should be used. The majority of anthropologists see themselves, as Wilson did,

---

[1] This was Malinowski's attitude: cf. 1939a, p. 38 ('Scientific field-work on contact and change is not in any way made dependent on practical issues, advice, or influence. It studies impartially, numerically, and concretely. . . . The practical conclusions can then be drawn by the administrator, entrepreneur, or constructive statesman'), and 1945, p. 161 ('The ethnographer . . . has the right and duty to formulate his conclusions in a manner in which they can be seriously considered by those who frame policies and those who carry them out. . . . But he can go no further. Decisions and the practical handling of affairs are outside his competence.') See also Mair, 1936, pp. 284–6, and 1950; R. Firth, 1938, chap. 7; and Schapera, 1949.

as consultants on the execution of policy. If an anthropologist genuinely believes that the aims of a government are bad he can say so and avoid entanglement; but if he approves of the intentions, and this he can usually do, he is fully entitled to say, 'Because I am an anthropologist I can tell you what is happening and what is likely to happen.' On occasions he may also be able to add, 'Your present methods are not achieving your professed desire to foster native welfare, and for the following reasons.'

The anthropologist satisfied with this modest rôle still does not face an easy assignment. One difficulty is that he so often finds himself expected to provide a simple formula for achieving aims which have already been determined. But society is far from simple, and the aims may be capable of being reached in a number of different ways. Each method of attack, too, will inevitably lead to widespread repercussions, for introducing a social innovation is like throwing a stone into a pond—just as the ripples extend outwards until they ultimately lap against the bank, so one institution after another becomes disturbed until the remote edges of the culture have been reached. So small a modification as the substitution of steel axes for those made from stone on the mission stations of northern Australia, while it lightened the work of the aborigines, has also brought about the abandonment of the old tribal gatherings, caused prostitution among the women, dealt a blow at the unity of the totemic clans, and introduced confusion into the status and kinship systems (Sharp, 1952). In a sense, no perfect solution for a social problem can ever be found. A physician, if the patient consults him in time, can sometimes conquer an infection by administering one of several possible sets of drugs. The anthropologist is not so fortunate. It is as though he were confronted with having to tell the relatives that their kinsman can be saved if they will consent to the amputation of an arm or of a leg, but that one limb must certainly be sacrificed. He enumerates the feasible courses of action—this, this, this, or that—but is obliged to point out that the perhaps uncertain gains must in each case be balanced against assured losses. This is where the value judgements intrude. He can hardly describe the results which he expects in neutral terms and avoid showing which he would himself prefer.

Again, anthropological research has so far neglected the study of factors making for social reintegration. If integration has been destroyed, as it may have been in some parts of the colonial world, the anthropologist cannot give advice on how to re-create it. He must admit that, in the light of our present knowledge, the problem is insoluble. In these circumstances he resembles the physician called in to a patient when the disease is too far advanced for any treatment. The moral is there for those who can read it—that symptoms of social disintegration should be recognized early and help sought in the initial stages.

Selected Bibliography

This bibliography is divided for convenience into three sections:
i. Works by Malinowski (including those cited in the text);
ii. works about Malinowski or dealing largely with his views;
iii. other works cited in the text.

The bibliography under section i is not intended to be complete, but to include all his most significant work. (It has not been possible to check item 1914.)

Abbreviations: AA—American Anthropologist.
JRAI—Journal Royal Anthropological Institute.

i. *Works by Malinowski (including those cited in the text)*

1912a. 'The Economic Aspect of the Intichiuma Ceremonies'. *Festskrift tillegnad Edvard Westermarck* i anledning av hans femtiårsdag den 20 November 1912 [in homage on his fiftieth birthday], pp. 81–108. Helsingfors.

1912b. 'Plemienne związki mężczyzn w Australii' (Tribal Associations of Males in Australia). *Sprawozdania z Czynności i Posiedzen Akademii Umiejętności w Krakowie, Wydziału Historyczno-Filozoficznego* (Bulletin of the Academy of Sciences of Cracow, Historical-Philosophical Section), April–May–June, pp. 56–63. Cracow.

1913a. *The Family among the Australian Aborigines: A Sociological Study*, pp. xv + 326. London.

1913b. Review of: Durkheim, E., *Les Formes Élémentaires de la Vie Religieuse. Folk-lore*, Vol. 24, pp. 525–31. London.

1913c. 'Stosunek wierzeń pierwotnych do form organizacji społecznej. Teoria totemizmu.' (The Relationship of Primitive Beliefs to Forms of Social Organization. The Theory of Totemism.) *Sprawozdania z Czynnosci i Posiedzen Akademii Umiejętności w Krakowie, Wydziału Historyczno-Filozoficznego* (Bulletin of the Academy of Sciences of Cracow, Historial-Philosophical Section), pp. 9–18. Cracow.

1914. 'Sociologie der Famile'. *Die Geisteswissenschaften*. Hft. 32, pp. 883–886; Hft. 33, pp. 911–14, 1080–2.

1915a. 'The Natives of Mailu: Preliminary Results of the Robert Mond Research Work in British New Guinea'. *Transactions and Proceedings of the Royal Society of South Australia*, Vol. XXXIX, pp. 494–706. Plates xxvi–xliii. Adelaide.

1915b. *Wierzenia pierwotne i formy ustroju społecznego. Pogląd na genezę religii ze szczególnym uwzględnieniem totemizmu. (Primitive Beliefs and Forms of Social Organization. A View on the Genesis of Religion with especial respect to Totemism.)* Polish Academy of Science, pp. vii–356, Cracow.

1916. 'Baloma: Spirits of the Dead in the Trobriand Islands'. *JRAI*, Vol. XLVI, pp. 353–430. Reprinted 1948. London.

1918a. (Evidence by Bronislaw Malinowski, 27 October, 1916, on Pacific labour conditions.) Parliament of the Commonwealth of Australia. *British and Australian Trade in the South Pacific. Report*, no. 66. F. 13489. Melbourne.

1918b. 'Fishing in the Trobriand Islands'. *Man*, no. 53. London.

1920a. 'Kula: The Circulating .Exchanges of Valuables in the Archipelagoes of Eastern New Guinea'. *Man*, no. 51. London.

1920b. 'Classificatory Particles in the Language of Kiriwina'. *Bulletin School of Oriental [and African] Studies*, Vol. I, pt. 4, pp. 33–78. London.

1920c. 'War and Weapons among the Natives of the Trobriand Islands'. *Man*, no. 5. London.

1921. 'The Primitive Economics of the Trobriand Islanders'. *The Economic Journal*. Vol. XXXI, pp. 1–16. London.

1922a. *Argonauts of the Western Pacific*, An Account of Native Enterprise and Adventure in the Archipelagoes of Melanesian New Guinea. With a Preface by Sir James George Frazer, F.B.A., F.R.S., with 5 maps, 65 illustrations and 2 figures. Studies in Economics and Political Science, no. 65, pp. xxxi + 527. London.

1922b. 'Ethnology and the Study of Society'. *Economica*, Vol. II, pp. 208–19. London.

1923a. 'The Problem of Meaning in Primitive Languages', in *The Meaning of Meaning*, by Ogden, C. K., and Richards, A. I. International Library of Psychology, Philosophy and Scientific Method, pp. 451–510. London.

1923b. 'Science and Superstition of Primitive Mankind' (review of Frazer, J. G., *The Golden Bough*). *Nature*, Vol. 111, pp. 658–62.

1923c. 'Psychoanalysis and Anthropology' (letter to Editor). *Nature*, Vol. 112, pp. 650–1.

1923d. 'The Psychology of Sex and the Foundations of Kinship in Primitive Societies'. *Psyche*, Vol. IV (October), pp. 98–128 (embodied in 1929a).

1924a. 'Psychoanalysis and Anthropology'. *Psyche*, Vol. IV (April), pp. 293–332 (embodied in 1927a, and issued also as 1924b).

1924b. 'Mutterrechtliche Familie und Ödipus-Komplex. Eine psychoanalytische Studie'. *Imago*, Vol. X, Hft. 2/3 (Ethnologisches Heft). (Also issued separately, with cover ... '... Eine ethnologisch-psychoanalytische Studie' by Internationaler Psychoanalytischer Verlag. Leipzig, Wien and Zurich.)

1925a. 'Magic, Science and Religion' in *Science, Religion and Reality*, ed. Needham, J. A., pp. 20–84. London. (Reprinted in 1948.)

1925b. 'Labour and Primitive Economics' (review of *Primitive Labour* by L. H. Dudley Buxton). *Nature*, Vol. 116, pp. 926–30 (reprint, pp. 1–12). London.

1925c. 'Complex and Myth in Mother-Right'. *Psyche*, Vol. V (January), pp. 194–216 (embodied in 1927a).

1925*d*. 'Forschungen in einer mutterrechtlichen Gemeinschaft auf den Trobriand-Inseln, östlich von Neu-Guinea, Südsee'. *Zeitschrift fur Völkerpsychologie und Soziologie*, Vol. I, pp. 45-53, 278-84. Leipzig (embodied in 1929*a*).

1925*e*. 'The Forces of Law and Order in a Primitive Community'. *Royal Institution of Great Britain*, Weekly Evening Meeting, Friday, February 13, 1925, pp. 1-19. London.

1925*f*. 'Primitive Law' (review of *Primitive Law* by E. Sidney Hartland). *Nature*, Vol. 116, pp. 230-35. London.

1925*g*. 'The Unity of Social Science'. *Nature*, Vol. 116, pp. 38-41. London.

1926*a*. 'Anthropology'. In *Encyclopaedia Britannica*, 13th ed. [14th ed., 1929].

1926*b*. *Crime and Custom in Savage Society*. International Library of Psychology, Philosophy and Scientific Method, pp. xii + 132. London and New York.

1926*c*. *Myth in Primitive Psychology*. Psyche Miniatures, gen. ser. no. 6. pp. 128. London.

1926*d*. 'Anthropology and Administration' (letter to Editor). *Nature*, Vol. 128, p. 768. London.

1926*e*. 'Primitive Law and Order'. Supplement to *Nature*, Vol. 117, pp. 9-16 (expansion and recasting of 1925*e*).

1926*f*. 'Address on Anthropology and Social Hygiene'. *Foundations of Social Hygiene*. Issued by The British Social Hygiene Council, Inc., pp. 54-84. London.

1926*g*. 'The Life of Culture'. *Forum*, Vol. 76, pp. 178-85 (see also 1926*i*, and 1928*a*).

1926*h*. 'The Role of Myth in Life'. *Psyche*, Vol. VI (April), pp. 29-39. London.

1926*i*. 'The Life of Culture'. *Psyche*, Vol. VII, pp. 37-44. London (see 1928*a*) (with portrait).

1927*a*. *Sex and Repression in Savage Society*. International Library of Psychology, Philosophy and Scientific Method, pp. xv + 285. London and New York (includes 1924*a*, 1925*c*).

1927*b*. *The Father in Primitive Psychology*. Psyche Miniatures, gen. ser. no. 8, pp. 93. London (reissued, with some alteration and expansion, as chap. I, sect. 1, and chap. VII of 1929*a*).

1927*c*. Review of S. H. Ray, *A Comparative Study of the Melanesian Island Languages*, *Man*, no. 99. London.

1927*d*. 'Prenuptial Intercourse between the Sexes in the Trobriand Islands, N.W. Melanesia'. *The Psychoanalytic Review*, Vol. XIV, pp. 20-35 (embodied, with minor alteration, as chap. III in 1929*a*).

1927*e*. 'Lunar and Seasonal Calendar in the Trobriands'. *JRAI*, Vol. LVII, pp. 203-15. London.

SELECTED BIBLIOGRAPHY

1927f. 'Useful and Useless Anthropology' (review of Pittard, E., *Race and History*). *The New Republic*, Vol. L, no. 641 (October), pt. 2, pp. 109–11. New York.

1928a. 'The Life of Culture' in *Culture—The Diffusion Controversy* by G. Elliot Smith, B. Malinowski, H. J. Spinden, A. Goldenweiser. Psyche Miniatures, gen. ser. no. 18, pp. 23–42. London.

1928b. 'The Anthropological Study of Sex'. *Verhandlungen des I. Internationalen Kongresses für Sexualforschung*. Berlin and Köln. 5th vol., pp. 92–108.

1929a. *The Sexual Life of Savages in North-Western Melanesia*. An Ethnographic Account of Courtship, Marriage and Family Life among the Natives of the Trobriand Islands, British New Guinea. With a Preface by Havelock Ellis, pp. xxiv + 506. London. (Third ed. with Special Foreword, v. 1932a.)

1929b. 'Kinship' in *Encyclopaedia Britannica*, 14th ed. London.

1929c. 'Marriage' in *Encyclopaedia Britannica*, 14th ed. London.

1929d. 'Practical Anthropology', *Africa*, Vol. II, pp. 23–39. London.

1929e. 'Social Anthropology', *Encyclopaedia Britannica*, 14th ed. (revision of 1926a).

1929f. 'Spirit Hunting in the South Seas'. *Realist*, Vol. II, pp. 398–417. London.

1930a. 'Parenthood the Basis of Social Structure' in *The New Generation*, ed. Calverton, V. F., and Schmalhausen, S. D., pp. 113–68. London.

1930b. 'Kinship'. *Man*, Vol. XXX, no. 17. London.

1930c. 'The Rationalization of Anthropology and Administration'. *Africa*, Vol. III, pp. 405–29. London.

1930d. 'Science and Religion—V'. *The Listener*, Vol. IV, October 29, pp. 683–4, 716, 717. London (reissued as 1931b).

1930e. 'Is Humanism Dead?' (review of Frazer, J. G., *Publii Ovidii Nasonis Fastorum Libri Sexi: The Fasti of Ovid*). *Nature*, Vol. 125, pp. 847–9. London.

1930f. 'Race and Labour'. *The Listener*, Vol. IV, supp. no. 8. London.

1931a. 'Culture'. *Encyclopaedia of the Social Sciences*, Vol. iv, pp. 621–46. New York.

1931b. Chapter V in *Science and Religion—A Symposium*, pp. 65–81. London (see 1930d).

1931c. 'The Relations between the Sexes in Tribal Life' in *The Making of Man*, ed. Calverton, F. V., pp. 565–85. New York.

1931d. 'Zagadnienie pokrewieństwa w swietle najnowszych badań.' (The Problem of Kinship in the Light of New Research). *Przegląd socjologiczny* (Sociological Review). Vol. I, April 1930–March 1931, pp. 17–31. Poznan.

1932a. *The Sexual Life of Savages* with 'Special Foreword to the Third Edition', pp. xix–xliv. London.

268

1932*b*. 'Pigs, Papuans and Police Court Perspective'. *Man*, Vol. XXXII, no. 44, London.

1932*c*. 'Introduction' to Fortune, Reo, *Sorcerers of Dobu*, pp. xv–xxviii. London.

1932*d*. 'Introduction' to Richards, A. I., *Hunger and Work in a Savage Tribe. A Functional Study of Nutrition among the Southern Bantu*, pp. ix–xvi. London.

1933. 'The Work and Magic of Prosperity in the Trobriand Islands' in *Mensch en Maatschappij: Steinmetznummer*, pp. 154–74. Groningen (reissued as chap. VII of 1935, Vol. I).

1934*a*. 'Introduction' to Hogbin, H. Ian, *Law and Order in Polynesia*, pp. xvii–lxxii. London.

1934*b*. 'Stone Implements in Eastern New Guinea' in *Essays Presented to C. G. Seligman*, ed. Evans-Pritchard, E. E., et. al., pp. 189–96. London.

1935. *Coral Gardens and Their Magic*. A Study of the Methods of Tilling the Soil and of Agricultural Rites in the Trobriand Islands, with 3 maps, 116 illustrations and 24 figures. Volume One, The Description of Gardening. Volume Two, The Language of Magic and Gardening, pp. xxxv + 500; xxxii + 350. London.

1936*a*. 'Preface' to Firth, Raymond, *We, The Tikopia: A Sociological Study of Kinship in Primitive Polynesia*, pp. vii–xi. London.

1936*b*. *The Foundations of Faith and Morals:* An Anthropological Analysis of Primitive Beliefs and Conduct with Special Reference to the Fundamental Problems of Religion and Ethics. Riddell Memorial Lectures, seventh series, 1934–5. University of Durham, pp. xi + 62. London.

1936*c*. 'Native Education and Culture Contact'. *International Reivew of Missions*, Vol. XXV, pp. 480–517. London.

1936*d*. 'Culture as a Determinant of Behaviour'. *Scientific Monthly*, Vol. 43, pp. 440–9. London.

1936*e*. 'The Deadly Issue'. *Atlantic Monthly*. December, pp. 659–69. Boston.

1937*a*. 'Foreword' to Ashley-Montagu, M. F., *Coming into Being Among the Australian Aborigines*, pp. xix–xxxv. London.

1937*b*. 'Culture as a Determinant of Behavior' in *Factors Determining Human Behavior*, Adrian, E. D., et al., pp. 133–68. Cambridge, Mass. (see also 1938*b*).

1938*a*. 'Introductory Essay on The Anthropology of Changing African Cultures'. *Methods of Study of Culture Contact in Africa*. International Institute of African Languages and Cultures Memorandum XV [reprinted from *Africa*, Vols. VII, VIII and IX], pp. vii–xxxviii. London.

1938*b*. 'Anthropology as the Basis of Social Science'. *Human Affairs*, ed. Cattell, R. B., Cohen, J., and Travers, R. M. W., chap. XII, pp. 199–252. London (substantially same as 1937*b*).

1938c. 'Culture Change in Theory and Practice'. Essay No. 19 in *Oxford University Summer School on Colonial Administration Second Session,* 27 June–8 July, 1938, at Lady Margaret Hall, pp. 71–5. Oxford University Press.

1938d. 'Anthropology'. *Encyclopaedia Britannica Book of the Year,* pp. 46–7.

1938e. 'Frazer on Totemism' (review of Frazer, J. G., *Totemica, A Supplement to Totemism and Exogamy). Nature,* Vol. 141, pp. 489–91. London.

1938f. 'A Nation-wide Intelligence Service' in *First Year's Work 1937–38* by Mass Observation, ed. Madge, Charles, and Harrisson, Tom, pp. 81–121. London.

1938g. 'Introduction' to Kenyatta, Jomo. *Facing Mount Kenya,* pp. vii–xiv. London.

1939a. 'The Present State of Studies in Culture Contact: Some Comments on an American Approach'. *Africa,* Vol. XII, pp. 27–47. London.

1939b. 'The Group and the Individual in Functional Analysis'. *American Journal of Sociology,* Vol. XLIV, pp. 938–64.

1939c. 'The Dynamics of Contemporary Diffusion'. A summary. (*Congrès International des Sciences Anthropologiques et Ethnologiques*), pp. 357–60. Copenhagen.

1940a. 'The Scientific Basis of Applied Anthropology'. *Atti dell' VIII Convegno*—'Volta'—4–11 October 1938, *Reale Accademia d'Italia,* pp. 5–24. Rome.

1940b. 'Modern Anthropology and European Rule in Africa'. *Atti dell' VIII Convegno*—'Volta'—4–11 October 1938. *Reale Accademia d'Italia,* Vol. XVIII, pp. 6–26. Rome.

1940c. 'La 'transculturación, su vocablo y su concepto'. *Revista Bimestre Cubana,* Vol. 46, pp. 220–8. Havana.

1941a. 'An Anthropological Analysis of War'. *American Journal of Sociology,* Vol. XLVI, pp. 521–50.

1941b. 'Introduction' to Schapera, I., *Married Life in an African Tribe,* pp. i–xvii. New York.

1941c. 'Man's Culture and Man's Behavior' (pt. 1). *Sigma Xi Quarterly,* Autumn issue, Vol. 29, pp. 182–96.

1941d. 'War—Past, Present and Future' in Clarkson, Jesse D., and Cochran, Thomas C., *War as a Social Institution: The Historian's Perspective,* pp. 21–31. New York.

1942a. 'A New Instrument for the Interpretation of Law—Especially Primitive'. *Yale Law Journal,* Vol. 51, pp. 1237–54 (review of Llewellyn, K. N., and Hoebel, E. A., *The Cheyenne Way: Conflict and Case Law in Primitive Jurisprudence;* first appeared in the *National Lawyers' Guild Review* for May, 1942).

1942b. 'Man's Culture and Man's Behavior' (pt. 2). *Sigma Xi Quarterly,* Winter issue, Vol. 30, pp. 66–78.

1942*c*. 'The Scientific Approach to the Study of Man' in *Science and Man*, ed. Anshen, Ruth N., pp. 207–42. New York.

1943. 'The Pan-African Problem of Culture-Contact'. *American Journal of Sociology*. Vol. XLVIII.

1944. *A Scientific Theory of Culture* [and Other Essays]. With a Preface by Huntington Cairns, pp. vii + 228. Chapel Hill, N. Carolina.

1945. *The Dynamics of Culture Change*. An Inquiry into Race Relations in Africa, ed. by Phyllis M. Kaberry, pp. xvi + 171. New Haven and London.

1947. *Freedom and Civilization* (with preface by Valetta Malinowska), pp. xiv + 338. London.

1948. *Magic, Science and Religion and Other Essays* [Selected, and with an Introduction by Robert Redfield], pp. xii + 327. Glencoe, Ill. (contains: 1916, 1923, 1925*a*, 1926*c* and 1941*a*).

ii. *Some publications devoted largely to Malinowski, to his work or to Trobriand culture*

Association of Polish Professors and Lecturers in Great Britain. 1943. *Professor Bronislaw Malinowski, An Account of the Memorial Meeting held at the Royal Institution in London on July 13th, 1942*. Oxford University Press: Humphrey Milford. London.

Austen, L. 1934. 'Procreation among the Trobriand Islanders'. *Oceania*, Vol. V (1934–5), pp. 102–13. Sydney.

Austen, L. 1938. 'The Seasonal Gardening Calendar of Kiriwina, Trobriand Islands.' *Oceania*, Vol. IX (1938–9), pp. 237–53. Sydney.

Austen, L. 1945*a*. 'Native Handicrafts in the Trobriand Islands'. *Mankind*, Vol. III, no. 7, pp. 193–8. Sydney.

Austen, L. 1945*b*. 'Cultural Changes in Kiriwina'. *Oceania*, Vol. XVI (1945–6), pp. 15–60. *Sydney.*

Cairns, Huntington. 1944. 'Preface' to *A Scientific Theory of Culture and Other Essays* by Bronislaw Malinowski, pp. v–vii. Chapel Hill.

de Jong, J. P. B., and de Josselin. 1947. 'Herdenking van Bronislaw Kaspar Malinowski' (7 April, 1884–16 Mei, 1942). *Jaarboek der Koninklijke Nederlandsche Akademie van Wetenschappen*, 1946–1947, pp. 1–11.

Firth, Raymond. 1942. 'Obituary: Prof. B. Malinowski'. *Nature*, Vol. 149, p. 661. London.

Gluckman, M. 1947*a*. 'Malinowski's "Functional" Analysis of Social Change'. *African Studies*. 1947*b*. 'Malinowski's Contribution to Social Anthropology'. *Africa* (reprinted together, 1949, as 'Malinowski's Sociological Theories'. *The Rhodes-Livingstone Papers*, no. 16. Oxford).

SELECTED BIBLIOGRAPHY

Hoebel, E. A. 1954. 'The Trobriand Islanders: Primitive Law as seen by Bronislaw Malinowski'. Chap. 8 of *The Law of Primitive Man*, pp. 177–210. Cambridge, Mass.

Kluckhohn, Clyde. 1943. 'Bronislaw Malinowski, 1884–1942'. *Journal American Folk-lore*, Vol. 56, pp. 208–19.

Lasswell, H. 1931. 'A Hypothesis Rooted in the Preconceptions of a Single Civilization Tested by Bronislaw Malinowski'. Analysis 34 in *Methods in Social Science: A Case Book*. ed. Rice, Stuart A., pp. 480–8. Chicago.

Leach, E. R. 1954a. 'A Trobriand Medusa?' *Man*, no. 158. London.

Leach, E. R. 1950. 'Primitive Calendars'. *Oceania*. Vol. XX, pp. 245–62. Sydney, N.S.W.

Lee, Dorothy. 1940. 'A Primitive System of Values'. *Philosophy of Science*. Vol. VII, pp. 355–78. Baltimore.

Murdock, G. P. 1943. 'Malinowski, Bronislaw'. *AA*, Vol. XLV, pp. 441–451. Menasha, Wis. (with extensive bibliography).

Powell, H. A. 1957. An Analysis of Present-Day Social Structure in the Trobriand Islands. (Ph.D. thesis, University of London).

Redfield, Robert. 1948. 'Introduction' to *Magic, Science and Religion and Other Essays* by Bronislaw Malinowski, pp. vii–xi. Glencoe, Ill.

Richards, Audrey. 1943. 'Bronislaw Kaspar Malinowski'. *Man*, no. 1 (with plate). London.

Seagle, W. 1937. 'Primitive Law and Professor Malinowski.' *AA*, Vol. XXXIX, pp. 275–90. Menasha, Wis.

Not specifically dealing with Malinowski or his work, though giving some account of the Trobrianders, are:

Austen, L. 1939. 'Megalithic Structures in the Trobriand Islands'. *Oceania*, Vol. X (1939–40), pp. 30–53. Sydney.

Austen, L. 1940. 'Botabalu': A Trobriand Chieftainess.' *Mankind*, Vol. II, no. 8, pp. 270–3. Sydney.

Baldwin, G. 1945. 'Usituma! Song of Heaven'. *Oceania*, Vol. XV, pp. 201–38. Sydney, N.S.W.

Baldwin, G. 1950. 'Kadaguwai: Songs of the Trobriand Sunset Isles'. *Oceania*, Vol. XX, pp. 263–85. Sydney, N.S.W.

Seligman, C. G. 1910. *The Melanesians of British New Guinea*, chap. xlix–liv. Cambridge.

Silas, Ellis. 1925. 'An Artist on a Tropic Isle'. *The Wide World Magazine*, pp. 120–8. London.

iii. *Other Works referred to in the Text*

Allen, C. K. 1951. *Law in the Making*. 5th ed. Oxford.

Armstrong, W. E. 1928. *Rossel Island*. Cambridge.

Ashley-Montagu, M. F. 1950. *On Being Human*. New York.

SELECTED BIBLIOGRAPHY

Bales, R. F. 1950. *Interaction Process Analysis: A Method for the Study of Small Groups*. Cambridge, Mass.

Barnes, J. A. 1951. 'History in a Changing Society'. *Human Problems in British Central Africa*, Vol. XI, pp. 1–9. Lusaka, N.R.

Barnes, J. A. 1954. *Politics in a Changing Society*. Oxford University Press.

Bartlett, F. C. 1943. 'Anthropology in Reconstruction'. *JRAI*, Vol. LXXIII, pp. 9–16. London.

Barton, R. F., 1919. 'Ifugao Law'. *University of California Publications in American Archaeology and Ethnology*, Vol. XV. Berkeley, Cal.

Bateson, G. 1936. *Naven: A Survey of the Problems Presented by a Composite Picture of the Culture of a New Guinea Tribe drawn from Three Points of View*. Cambridge.

Bernard, L. L. 1925. *Instinct: A Study in Social Psychology*. London.

Bidney, D. 1953a. *Theoretical Anthropology*, New York.

Bidney, D. 1953b. 'The Concept of Value in Modern Anthropology' in Kroeber, A. L. (ed.), pp. 682–98. Chicago.

Boas, F. 1928. *Anthropology and Modern Life*. New York.

Bohannan, L. 1952. 'A Genealogical Charter'. *Africa*, Vol. XXII, pp. 301–15. London.

Bohannan, P. 1955. 'Some Principles of Exchange and Investment among the Tiv'. *AA*, Vol. LVII, pp. 60–70. Menasha, Wis.

Brown, C. G., and Hutt, A. M. 1935. *Anthropology in Action*. Oxford.

Cairns, H. 1931. 'Law and Anthropology' in *The Making of Man: an Outline of Anthropology* (ed. Calverton, V. F.), pp. 331–62. New York.

Cairns, H. 1935. *Law and the Social Sciences*. London and New York.

Callaway, H. 1868–70. *The Religious System of the Amazulu*. Springvale, Natal (1884, London).

Chapple, Eliot D. 1953. 'Applied Anthropology in Industry', in Kroeber, A. L. (ed.), pp. 819–31. Chicago.

Childe, V. G. 1944. *Progress and Archaeology*. London.

Childe, V. G. 1950. *Magic, Craftsmanship and Science* (Frazer Lecture, 1949). Liverpool.

Chinnery, E. W. P. 1919. 'The Application of Anthropological Methods to Tribal Development in New Guinea'. *JRAI*, Vol. XLIV, pp. 36–41. London.

Codrington, R. H. 1891. *The Melanesians*. London.

Colson, Elizabeth. 1953. *The Makah Indians*. Manchester.

Cunnison, I. G. 1951. 'History on the Luapula'. *Rhodes-Livingstone Papers*, no. 21. Oxford.

Diamond, A. S. 1935. *Primitive Law*. London.

Dundas, C. 1915. 'The Organization and Laws of some Bantu Tribes in East Africa'. *JRAI*, Vol. XLV, pp. 234–306. London.

Dundas, C. 1921. 'Native Laws of some Bantu Tribes of East Africa'. *JRAI*, Vol. LI, pp. 217–78. London.

Durkheim, E. 1938. *The Rules of Sociological Method*, 8th ed., trans. Solovay, Sarah A., and Mueller, John H., ed. Catlin, G. E. G. Glencoe, Ill. (reprinted 1950).

Eggan, F. 1954. 'Social Anthropology and the Method of Controlled Comparison'. *AA*, Vol. LVI, pp. 743–63. Menasha, Wis.

Einzig, P. 1949. *Primitive Money*. London.

Evans-Pritchard, E. E. 1929. 'The Study of Kinship in Primitive Societies'. *Man*, no. 148. London.

Evans-Pritchard, E. E. 1937. *Witchcraft, Oracles and Magic among the Azande*. Oxford.

Evans-Pritchard, E. E. 1940*a*. *The Nuer*. Oxford.

Evans-Pritchard, E. E. 1940*b*. 'The Political Structure of the Nandi-speaking Peoples of Kenya'. *Africa*, Vol. XIII, pp. 250–67. London.

Evans-Pritchard, E. E. 1946. 'Applied Anthropology'. *Africa*, Vol. XVI, pp. 92–8. London.

Evans-Pritchard, E. E. 1949. *The Sanusi of Cyrenaica*. Oxford.

Evans-Pritchard, E. E. 1950. 'Social Anthropology: Past and Present. The Marett Lecture 1950'. *Man*, no. 198. London.

Evans-Pritchard, E. E. 1951*a*. *Social Anthropology*. London.

Evans-Pritchard, E. E. 1951*b*. *Kinship and Marriage among the Nuer*. Oxford.

Firth, J. R. 1930. *Speech*. London.

Firth, J. R. 1937. *The Tongues of Men*. London.

Firth, J. R. 1946. 'The English School of Phonetics', *Trans. Philological Society*, pp. 92–132. London.

Firth, J. R. 1950. 'Personality and Language in Society'. *Sociological Review*, Vol. XLII, sect. II, pp. 8–14. Ledbury.

Firth, J. R. 1951*a*. 'General Linguistics and Descriptive Grammar'. *Trans. Philological Society*, pp. 69–87.

Firth, J. R. 1951*b*. 'Modes of Meaning'. *Essays and Studies* (The English Association), pp. 118–49. London.

Firth, Raymond. 1929. *Primitive Economics of the New Zealand Maori*. London.

Firth, Raymond. 1936. *We, The Tikopia: A Sociological Study of Kinship in Primitive Polynesia*. London.

Firth, Raymond. 1938. *Human Types*. London.

Firth, Raymond. 1939. *Primitive Polynesian Economy*. London.

Firth, Raymond. 1946. *Malay Fishermen: Their Peasant Economy*. London.

Firth, Raymond. 1949. 'Anthropology and Colonial Affairs'. *Man*, no. 179. London.

Firth, Raymond. 1951a. *Elements of Social Organization*. London.

Firth, Raymond. 1951b. 'Contemporary British Social Anthropology', *AA*, Vol. LIII, pp. 474–89. Menasha, Wis.

Firth, Raymond. 1953. 'The Study of Values by Social Anthropologists: The Marett Lecture 1953'. *Man*, no. 231, London.

Firth, Raymond. 1954. 'Social Organization and Social Change'. *JRAI*, Vol. LXXXIV, pp. 1–20. London.

Forde, C. D. 1950. 'Anthropology, Science and History'. *Man*, no. 254. London.

Fortes, M. 1937. 'Kinship, Incest and Exogamy of the Northern Territories of the Gold Coast' in *Custom is King: Essays presented to R. R. Marett*, ed. Dudley Buxton, L. H., pp. 239–56. London.

Fortes, M. 1938. 'Culture Contact as a Dynamic Process' in *Methods of Study of Culture Contact in Africa* (see Malinowski, 1938a), pp. 60–91. London.

Fortes, M. 1945. *The Dynamics of Clanship among the Tallensi*. Oxford University Press.

Fortes, M. 1949a, *The Web of Kinship among the Tallensi*. Oxford University Press.

. Fortes, M. 1949b. 'Time and Social Structure: An Ashanti Case Study' in *Social Structure: Studies Presented to A. R. Radcliffe-Brown*, pp. 54–84. Oxford.

Fortes, M. 1950. 'Kinship and Marriage among the Ashanti' in *African Systems of Kinship and Marriage* (ed. Radcliffe-Brown, A. R., and Forde, D.), pp. 252–84. Oxford.

Fortes, M. 1953a. 'The Structure of Unilineal Descent Groups'. *AA*, Vol. LV, pp. 17–41. Menasha, Wis.

Fortes, M. 1953b. 'Analysis and Description in Social Anthropology', *The Advancement of Science*, Vol. X, pp. 190–201. London.

Fortes, M. 1955. 'Radcliffe-Brown's Contributions to the Study of Social Organization', *British Journal of Sociology*, Vol. VI, pp. 16–30. London.

Fortune, R. F. 1932. *Sorcerers of Dobu*. London.

Freud, S. 1910. *The Interpretation of Dreams*. London.

Freud, S. 1924–50. *Collected Papers*. 5 vols. New York and London.

Gallie, W. B. 1952. *Peirce and Pragmatism*. London.

Gardiner, A. H. 1932. *The Theory of Speech and Language*. Oxford.

Geddes, W. R. 1953. Review of Firth, Raymond, *Elements of Social Organization* in *Journal of the Polynesian Society*, Vol. LXIV, pp. 415–18. Wellington.

Gerth, H., and Mills, S. 1954. *Character and Social Structure: The Psychology of Social Institutions*. London.

Ginsberg, M. 1921. *The Psychology of Society*. London.

Ginsberg, M. 1953. 'On the Diversity of Morals'. *JRAI*. Vol. LXXXIII, pp. 117–35. London.

Gluckman, M. 1947*a* and *b*. See Bib. ii.

Gluckman, M. 1955*a*. *The Judicial Process among the Barotse*. Manchester.

Gluckman, M. 1955*b*. *Custom and Conflict in Africa*. Oxford.

Goodfellow, D. M. 1939. *Principles of Economic Sociology*. London.

Greenberg, J. H. 1954. 'Concerning Inferences from Linguistic to Non-Linguistic Data' in *Language in Culture* (see Hoijer, H.), pp. 3–19.

Gregg, Dorothy, and Williams, E. 1948. 'The Dismal Science of Functionalism', *AA*, Vol. L, pp. 594–611. Menasha, Wis.

Gutmann, B. 1926. *Das Recht der Dschagga*. München.

Halbwachs, M. 1940–8. 'Mémoire et Société'. *L'année Sociologique*, 3e Serie, Tome I, pp. 11–177. Paris. Republished as *La Mémoire Collective*, 1950, pp. 1–167. Paris.

Hankins, F. H. 1935. *An Introduction to the Study of Society*, revised ed. New York.

Harris, Z. S. 1951. *Methods in Structural Linguistics*. Chicago.

Hartland, S. 1924. *Primitive Law*. London.

Herskovits, M. J. 1936. 'Applied Anthropology and the American Anthropologist', *Science*, Vol. LXXXIII, pp. 215–22.

Herskovits, M. J. 1938. *Acculturation: The Study of Culture Contact*. New York.

Herskovits, M. J. 1948. *Man and His Works: The Science of Cultural Anthropology*. New York.

Herskovits, M. J. 1952. *Economic Anthropology*. New York.

Herskovits, M. J., et al. 1947. 'Statement on Human Rights' submitted to the Commission on Human Rights, U.N., by the Executive Board, American Anthropological Association. *AA*, Vol. XLIX, pp. 539–43. Menasha, Wis.

Hobhouse, L. T. 1912. 'Morals' in *Notes and Queries in Anthropology*, 4th ed., pp. 175–6. London.

Hobhouse, L. T. 1915. *Morals in Evolution*. London.

Hobhouse, L. T. 1924. *Social Development*. London.

Hockett, C. F. 1954. 'Chinese versus English: An Exploration of the Whorfian Theses', see Hoijer, H., pp. 106–23.

Hockett, C. F. 1954. Discussion on 'The Problem of the Whorf Hypothesis' in Hoijer, H. p. 225.

Hoebel, E. A. 1954. *The Law of Primitive Man*. Cambridge, Mass.

Hogbin, H. I. 1938. 'Social Reaction to Crime: Law and Morals in the Schouten Islands, New Guinea'. *JRAI*, Vol. LXVIII, pp. 223–62. London.

Hoijer, H. (ed.). 1954. *Language in Culture: Proceedings of a Conference on the Interrelations of Language and Other Aspects of Culture*. American Anthropological Association memoir no. 79. Menasha, Wis.

Huxley, A. 1932. *Brave New World*. London.

Jakobson, R. 1953. Chapter Two in 'Results of the Conference of Anthropologists and Linguists', Supplement to *International Journal of American Linguistics*, Vol. 19, no. 2 (Memoir no. 8), pp. 11–21. Baltimore.

Jespersen, J. O. H., 1922. *Language: Its Nature, Development and Origin*. London.

Kaberry, Phyllis M. 1939. *Aboriginal Woman Sacred and Profane*. London.

Keesing, F. M. 1939. *The Menomini Indians of Wisconsin: A Study of Three Centuries of Cultural Contact and Change*. Memoirs American Philosophical Society, Vol. X. Philadelphia.

Kelsen, H. 1945. *General Theory of Law and State*. (trans. by Wedberg, A.). Cambridge, Mass.

Kluckhohn, C., and Mowrer, O. H. 1944. 'Culture and Personality: A Conceptual Scheme', *AA*, Vol. XLVI, pp. 1–29. Menasha, Wis.

Kluckhohn, C. 1951. 'Values and Value-Orientations in the Theory of Action: An Exploration in Definition and Classification' in *Toward a General Theory of Action*, ed. Parsons, T., and Shils, E. Harvard.

Kroeber, A. L. 1948. *Anthropology*. London.

Kroeber, A. L., and Kluckhohn, C. 1952. *Culture* (Papers Peabody Museum of Harvard, Vol. XLVII, no. 1). Harvard.

Kroeber, A. L. 1953. (ed.) *Anthropology Today*. Chicago.

Labouret, H. 1953. 'L'Echange et le Commerce dans les Archipels du Pacifique et en Afrique Tropicale'. Livre i of Tome III in *L'Histoire du Commerce* (ed. J. Lacour-Gavet), pp. 9–125, Paris.

Lasswell, H., and associates. 1949. *The Language of Politics*. New York.

Leach, E. R. 1951. 'The Structural Implications of Matrilateral Cross-Cousin Marriage', *JRAI*, Vol. LXXXI, pp. 23–55. London.

Leach, E. R. 1954a (see Bib. ii).

Leach, E. R. 1954b. *Political Systems of Highland Burma*. London.

Lee, Dorothy. 1948. 'Are Basic Needs Ultimate?' *Journal of Abnormal and Social Psychology*, Vol. 43, pp. 391–5.

Lenoir, Raymond. 1924. 'Les Expéditions Maritimes, Institution Sociale en Mélanesie Occidentale'. *L'Anthropologie*, Tome 34, pp. 387–410. Paris.

Lévi-Strauss, C. 1949. *Les Structures Elémentaires de la Parenté*. Paris.

Lévi-Strauss, C. 1950. 'Introduction a l'Œuvre de Marcel Mauss' in *Sociologie et Anthropologie par Marcel Mauss*, pp. ix–lii. Paris.

Lévi-Strauss, C. 1953a. 'Social Structure' in Kroeber, A. L. (1953), pp. 524–53. Chicago.

Lévi-Strauss, C. 1953b. Chapter One in 'Results of the Conference of Anthropologists and Linguists' Supplement to *International Journal of American Linguistics*, Vol. 19, no. 2 (Memoir no. 8). Baltimore, pp. 1–10.

Lewis, O. 1951. *Life in a Mexican Village: Tepoztlan Restudied.* Urbana, Ill.

Lienhardt, G. 1954. 'Modes of Thought' in *The Institutions of Primitive Society.* Evans-Pritchard, E. E., and others, pp. 95–107. London.

Linton, R. 1939. Foreword to Kardiner, A. *The Individual and His Society: The Psychodynamics of Primitive Social Organization,* pp. v–xviii. New York.

Llewellyn, K. N., and Hoebel, E. A. 1941. *The Cheyenne Way: Conflict and Case Law in Primitive Jurisprudence.* Norman.

Lowie, R. H. 1920. *Primitive Society.* New York.

Lowie, R. H. 1927. 'Anthropology and Law' in *The Social Sciences* (ed. Ogburn, H. F., and Goldenweiser, A.), pp. 50–7. New York.

Lowie, R. H. 1948. *Social Organization.* New York.

Lugard, F. D. 1928. 'The International Institute of African Languages and Cultures'. *Africa,* Vol. I, pp. 1–14. London.

McAuley, J. P. 1953. 'Anthropologists and Administration'. *South Pacific,* Vol. VI, pp. 518–22. Sydney, N.S.W.

McDougall, W. 1908. *An Introduction to Social Psychology.* London.

MacIver, R. M. 1921. *The Elements of Social Science.* London.

MacIver, R. M. 1926. *The Modern State.* Oxford.

MacIver, R. M. 1937. *Society: A Textbook of Sociology.* London.

MacLean, J. 1858. *A Compendium of Kafir Laws and Customs.* Mount Coke, S.A.

Mair, L. P. 1936. *Native Policies in Africa.* London.

Mair, L. P. 1950. 'The Role of the Anthropologist in Non-Autonomous Territories' in *Principles and Methods of Colonial Administration,* pp. 178–92. London.

Marett, R. R. 1912. *Anthropology.* London.

Mauss, M. 1925. 'Essai sur le Don', *L'Année Sociologique,* n.s., Vol. I, 1923–4, pp. 30–186 (reissued in 1950 in *Sociologie et Anthropologie,* by Marcel Mauss, ed. Lévi-Strauss, C., pp. 143–279. Paris; transl. as *The Gift.* Cunnison, I. 1954. London).

[Mauss, M.] Hubert, H., and Mauss, M. 1903. 'Esquisse d'une Théorie Générale de la Magie'. *L'Année Sociologique,* Vol. VII, 1902–3, pp. 1–146 (reissued in *Sociologie et Anthropologie,* by Marcel Mauss, ed. Lévi-Strauss, C., pp. 1–141. Paris).

Meillet, A. 1926. *Linguistique Historique et Linguistique Generale* (La Société de Linguistique de Paris). Paris.

Mitchell, P. 1930. 'The Anthropologist and the Practical Man'. *Africa,* Vol. III, pp. 217–23. London.

Mitchell, P. 1951. Review of *Native Administration in the British Territories in Africa* by Lord Hailey in *Journal of African Administration.* Vol. III, pp. 55–65. London.

SELECTED BIBLIOGRAPHY

Mitchell, T. F. 1952. 'The Active Participle in an Arabic Dialect of Cyrenaica'. *Bulletin School of Oriental and African Studies*, Vol. XIV, pt. 1, pp. 11–33. London.

Mitchell, T. F. 1953. 'Particle-Noun Complexes in a Berber Dialect'. *Bulletin School of Oriental and African Studies*, Vol. XV, pt. 2, pp. 375–90. London.

Murdock, G. P. 1949. *Social Structure*. New York.

Nadel, S. F. 1942. *A Black Byzantium*. London.

Nadel, S. F. 1947. *The Nuba: An Anthropological Study of the Hill Tribes in Kordofan*. Oxford.

Nadel, S. F. 1950. 'Dual Descent in the Nuba Hills' in *African Systems of Kinship and Marriage*, ed. Radcliffe-Brown, A. R., and Forde, D., pp. 333–59. Oxford.

Nadel, S. F. 1951. *The Foundations of Social Anthropology*. London.

Nadel, S. F. 1953. *Anthropology and Modern Life*. Canberra.

Needham, J. 1954. *Science and Civilization in China*, Vol. 1. *Introductory Orientations*. Cambridge.

Oldham, J. H. 1929. *Report on Closer Union of the Territories in East and Central Africa*. H.M.S.O. Cmd. 2324. London.

Parsons, T. 1951. *The Social System*. Glencoe, Ill.

Parsons, T., and Shils, E. A. (eds.). 1951. *Toward a General Theory of Action*. Harvard University Press.

Parsons, T., Bales, R. F., and Shils, E. A. 1953. *Working Papers in the Theory of Action*. Glencoe, Ill.

Parsons, T. 1954. 'Psychology and Sociology' in *Toward a Science of Social Man*, ed. Gillin, J. L., pp. 67–101. New York.

Parsons, T., and Bales, R. F. 1955. *Family, Socialization and Interaction Process*. Glencoe, Ill.

Paton, G. W. 1951. *A Textbook of Jurisprudence*, 2nd ed. Oxford.

Pavlov, I. P. 1927. *Conditioned Reflexes* (trans. Anrep, G. V.). London.

Piddington, R. O'R. 1950. *An Introduction to Social Anthropology*, Vol. I. Edinburgh and London.

Pitt-Rivers, G. H. L.-F. 1924. 'Some Problems in Mental Anthropology and the Problem of Civilization'. *Australasian Association for the Advancement of Science*. Wellington Meeting (1923), pp. 497–517. Wellington.

Pitt-Rivers, G. H. L.-F. 1927. *The Clash of Cultures and Contact of Races*. London.

Post, A. H. 1887. *Afrikanische Jurisprudenz: Ethnologisch-juristische Beiträge zur Kenntnis der einheimischen Rechte Afrikas*. Oldenburg.

Postan, M. M. 1939. *The Historical Method in Social Science*. Cambridge University Press.

Pound, Roscoe. 1936. Introduction to Ehrlich, E., *Fundamental Principles of the Sociology of Law*, pp. xxix–xxxvi. Harvard University Press.

SELECTED BIBLIOGRAPHY

Radcliffe-Brown, A. R. 1913. 'Three Tribes of Western Australia', *JRAI*, Vol. XLIII, pp. 143-94. London.

Radcliffe-Brown, A. R. 1914. Review of *The Family among the Australian Aborigines* by B. Malinowski. *Man*, no. 16. London.

Radcliffe-Brown, A. R. 1929. 'A Further Note on Ambrym', *Man*, no. 35. London.

Radcliffe-Brown, A. R. 1930. 'Applied Anthropology'. *Proceedings Australian and New Zealand Association for the Advancement of Science*, pp. 267-80. Brisbane.

Radcliffe-Brown, A. R. 1931. *The Social Organization of Australian Tribes* (Oceania Monograph, no. 1). Sydney.

Radcliffe-Brown, A. R. 1933. *The Andaman Islanders*. 2nd ed. (1st ed. 1922). Cambridge.

Radcliffe-Brown, A. R. 1935. 'On the Concept of Function in Social Science', *AA*, Vol. XXXVII, pp. 394-402 (reprinted in 1952 in *Structure and Function in Primitive Society*, pp. 178-87). Oxford.

Radcliffe-Brown, A. R. 1941. 'The Study of Kinship Systems', *JRAI*, Vol. LXXI, pp. 1-18 (reprinted in 1952, *Structure and Function in Primitive Society*, pp. 49-89). London.

Radcliffe-Brown, A. R. 1949. 'White's View of the Science of Culture', *AA*, Vol. LI, pp. 503-12. Menasha, Wis.

Radcliffe-Brown, A. R., and Forde, D. (eds.). 1950. *African Systems of Kinship and Marriage*. Oxford University Press.

Radcliffe-Brown, A. R. 1952. *Structure and Function in Primitive Society*. London.

Rattray, R. S., 1929. *Ashanti Law and Constitution*. Oxford.

Redfield, R. 1950. *A Village that Chose Progress: Chan Kom Revisited*. Chicago.

Redfield, R. 1953*a*. *The Primitive World and its Transformations*. New York.

Redfield, R. 1953*b*. 'Relations of Anthropology to the Social Sciences and to the Humanities' in Kroeber, A. L. (1953), pp. 728-38. Chicago.

Richards, Audrey I. 1932. *Hunger and Work in a Savage Tribe*. London.

Richards, Audrey I. 1934. 'Mother-right among the Central Bantu' in *Essays Presented to C. G. Seligman*, ed. Evans-Pritchard et al., pp. 267-80. London.

Richards, Audrey I. 1935. 'The Village Census in the Study of Culture Contact'. *Africa*, Vol. VIII, pp. 20-33. London.

Richards, Audrey I. 1939. 'The Development of Field Work Methods in Social Anthropology' in *The Study of Society*, ed. Bartlett, F. C., et al., pp. 272-316. London.

Richards, Audrey I. 1944. 'Practical Anthropology in the Life-time of the African Institute'. *Africa*, Vol. XIV, pp. 289-300. Oxford.

Richards, Audrey I. 1950*a*. 'Some Types of Family Structure Amongst the Central Bantu' in *African Systems of Kinship and Marriage*, ed. Radcliffe-Brown, A. R., and Forde, D., pp. 205-51. Oxford.

Richards, Audrey I. 1950*b*. 'Huts and Hut-Building among the Bemba: Part I'. *Man*, no. 134. London.

Richards, Audrey I. 1956. *Chisungu: A Girl's Initiation Ceremony among the Bemba of Northern Rhodesia*. London.

Rivers, W. H. R. 1904. Chapters II, III, IX in *Sociology, Magic and Religion of the Western Islanders* (*Reports of the Torres Straits Expedition*, Vol. 5). Cambridge.

Rivers, W. H. R. 1906. *The Todas*. London.

Rivers, W. H. R. 1913. *Kinship and Social Organization*. London.

Rivers, W. H. R. 1914. *The History of Melanesian Society*. 2 vols. Cambridge.

Rivers, W. H. R. 1922. 'The Psychological Factor' in *Essays on the Depopulation of Melanesia*, pp. 84–113. Cambridge.

Robins, R. H. 1953. 'Formal Divisions in Sundanese'. *Transactions of the Philological Society*, pp. 109–42.

Robson, W. A. 1935. *Civilization and the Growth of Law*. London.

Royal Anthropological Institute. 1912. *Notes and Queries in Anthropology*. 4th ed. (5th ed., 1929). London.

Schapera, I. 1938*a*. *A Handbook of Tswana Law and Custom* (2nd ed., 1955). Oxford University Press.

Schapera, I. 1938*b*. 'Contact between European and Native in South Africa. 2. In Bechuanaland' in *Methods of Study of Culture Contact in Africa* (see Malinowski, 1938*a*), pp. 25–37. London.

Schapera, I. 1940. *Married Life in an African Tribe*. London.

Schapera, I. 1943. *Native Land Tenure in the Bechuanaland Protectorate*. Lovedale.

Schapera, I. 1947. *Migrant Labour in Tribal Life*. Oxford University Press.

Schapera, I. 1949*a*. 'The Tswana Conception of Incest' in *Social Structure: Studies Presented to A. R. Radcliffe-Brown* (ed. Fortes, M.), pp. 104–20. Oxford.

Schapera, I. 1949*b*. 'Some Problems of Anthropological Research in Kenya Colony'. *Memorandum International African Institute*, no. 23. London.

Schapera, I. 1953. 'Some Comments on Comparative Method in Social Anthropology'. *AA*, Vol. LV, pp. 353–61. Menasha, Wis.

Seagle, W. 1937 (see Bib. ii).

Seagle, W. 1941. *The Quest for Law*. New York.

Seligman, B. Z. 1929. 'Incest and Descent: Their Influence on Social Organization'. *JRAI*, Vol. LIX, pp. 231–72. London.

Seligman, B. Z. 1950. 'The Problem of Incest and Exogamy: A Restatement'. *AA*, Vol. LII, pp. 305–16. Menasha, Wis.

Seligman, C. G. 1910. *The Melanesians of British New Guinea*. Cambridge.

Shand, F. A. 1920. *The Foundations of Character: being a Study of the Tendencies of the Emotions and Sentiments*. London.

SELECTED BIBLIOGRAPHY

Sharp, L. 1952. 'Steel Axes for Stone Age Australians' in *Human Problems in Technological Change*, ed. Spicer, E. H., pp. 69–90. New York.

Simpson, S. P., and Stone, J. 1948. *Law and Society in Evolution*. (Vol. I of *Cases and Readings on Law and Society*, 3 vols.) St. Paul, Minn.

Smith, E. W. 1926. *The Golden Stool*. London.

Spencer, B., and Gillen, F. 1899. *The Native Tribes of Central Australia*. London.

Stebbing, Susan. 1945. *A Modern Introduction to Logic*. London.

Steinmetz, S. R. 1903. *Rechtsverhältnisse von Eingeborenen Völkern in Afrika und Ozeanien*. Berlin.

Tead, O. 1918. *Instincts in Industry: A Study of Working-Class Psychology*. Boston, Mass.

Temple, R. 1899*a*. 'A Theory of Universal Grammar, as Applied to Savage Languages'. *The Indian Antiquary*, Vol. XXVIII, pp. 197–208, 225–35. Bombay.

Temple, R. 1899*b*. 'The Skeleton of a Theory of Universal Grammar'. *Journal Royal Asiatic Society*, pp. 597–604. London.

Thomson, G. 1949. *Studies in Ancient Greek Society*. Vol. 1: *The Prehistoric Aegean*. London.

Timasheff, N. S. 1939. *An Introduction to the Sociology of Law*. Cambridge, Mass.

Titiev, M. 1954. *The Science of Man*. New York.

Tylor, E. B. 1881. *Anthropology*. London.

Vidich, A. J. 1954. Review of Gerth, H., and Mills, C. *Character and Social Structure. Man*, no. 185. London.

Vierkandt, A. 1935. 'Wundt'. *Encyclopaedia of the Social Sciences*, Vol. XV, p. 506. New York.

Viljoen, S. 1936. *The Economics of Primitive Peoples*. London.

Vinogradoff, P. 1913. *Common Sense in Law*. London and New York.

Voegelin, C. F., Yegerlehner, J. F., and Robinett, Florence M. 1954. 'Shawnee Laws: Perceptual Statements for the Language and for the Content' in *Language in Culture* (see Hoijer, H.), pp. 32–46. Menasha, Wis.

Voegelin, E. 1952. *The New Science of Politics*. Chicago.

Wallas, G. 1921. *Our Social Heritage*. London.

Warner, W. L. 1952. *Structure of American Life*. Edinburgh.

Watson, J. B. 1919. *Psychology from the Standpoint of a Behaviorist*. Philadelphia.

Watson, J. B. 1924. *Behaviourism*. London.

Weber, M. 1947. *The Theory of Social and Economic Organization* (trans. Henderson, A. R., and Parsons, T.; revised and ed., with introd. Parsons, T.). London, Edinburgh and Glasgow.

Wegener, P. 1885. *Untersuchungen ueber die Grundfragen des Sprachlebens*. Halle.

SELECTED BIBLIOGRAPHY

Westermarck, E. 1913. Review of *The Family Among the Australian Aborigines: A Sociological Study* by Malinowski, B. *Folk-Lore*, Vol. 24, pp. 406-8. London.

White, L. A. 1948. 'Definition and Prohibition of Incest'. *AA*, Vol. L, pp. 416-35. Menasha, Wis.

Wilson, G. 1937. 'Introduction to Nyakyusa Law'. *Africa*, Vol. X, pp. 16-36. Oxford.

Wilson, G. 1940. 'Anthropology as a Public Service'. *Africa*, Vol. XIII, pp. 43-61. Oxford.

Wilson, G., and Wilson, Monica. 1945. *The Analysis of Social Change Based on Observations in Central Africa*. Cambridge.

Wissler, C. 1923. *Man and Culture*. London.

Wittgenstein, L. 1953. *Philosophical Investigations*. Oxford.

ADDENDA

i. *Works by Malinowski*

1911-13. 'Totemizm i egzogamia' (Totemism and Exogamy). *Lud*. Vol. XVII, pp. 31-56; XVIII, pp. 14-57; XIX, pp. 153-71. Lwow. (A critical review of Frazer's book, in the form of three articles.)

1931*e*. 'Marriage Past and Present. *The Listener*. Vol. V, Jan. 7th-Feb. 11th (six issues). London. (Reissued as 1956).

1937*c*. 'Kultura jako wyznacznik zachowania się.' (Culture as a Decisive Factor of Behaviour). *Ruch prawniczy, ekonomiczny, socjologiczny* (Mouvement juridique, economique, et sociologique). Vol. 17. pp. 101-27. Pozhan. (v. 1937*b*.)

1956. *Marriage Past and Present*. A Debate between Robert Briffault and Bronisław Malinowski. Edited with an introduction by M. F. Ashley Montagu, pp. 90. Boston. (Reissue of 1931*e*.)

1957. (With Julio de la Fuente). 'La Economía de un Sistema de Mercados en México.' Un Ensayo de Etnografia Contemporánea y Cambio Social en un Valle Mexicano. *Acta Anthropologica*. Epoca 2. Vol. I, no. 2. pp. 187. Mexico, D. F.

SELECTED BIBLIOGRAPHY

ii. *Works about Malinowski.*

Ashley Montagu, M.F. 1942. 'Bronisław Malinowski 1884-1942.' *Isis.* Vol. 34, pt. 2, no. 98. Autumn, pp. 146-60. Harvard.

Lynch, Frank., S.J. 1955. 'Trobriand Kinship by Compass and Rule'. *Anthropology Tomorrow* (Anthropology Club, University of Chicago), Vol. 4, no. 1, pp. 59-66.

Okinski, Wladyslaw. 1935. Review of Malinowski's *Sex and Repression in Savage Society. Przegląd socjologiczny* (Sociological Review). Vol. III, pp. 316–22. Poznan.

Peter, Prince of Greece and Denmark. 1953. 'Wspomnienie o Bronisławie Malinowskim' (Bronisław Malinowski—a Memoir). trans. by Jan Fryling. *Wiadomości.* 21 June. Year VIII, no. 25 (377). London.

Symmons-Symonolewicz, Konstantin. 1958. 'Bronisław Malinowski: An Intellectual Profile'. *The Polish Review*, Vol. III, no. 4, pp. 1-22. (reprint).

iii. *Other Works referrred to in the Text*

Warnotte, D. 1927. *Les Origines Sociologiques de l'Obligation Contractuelle.* (Institut Solvay). Brussels.

Index

INDEX

INDEX

Function, vii, 1, 6, 16, 17, 19, 48, 58, 59, 60, 62, 63, 75, 76, 81, 82, 83, 94, 98, 101, 106, 111, 112, 115, 118, 123, 124, 128, 129, 131, 132, 150, 162, 172, 189, 196, 197, 201, 203, 205, 206, 215, 225, 240, 250

Functional theory, 10, 11, 20, 21, 26, 29, 30, 51, 54, 55, 56, 64, 65, 66, 69, 70, 72, 76, 81, 100, 101, 119, 122, 123, 124, 125, 127, 129, 136, 137, 142, 157, 159, 163, 164, 170, 174, 232, 234, 239, 241

Gallie, W. B., 122, 127
Gardiner, H., 7, 96, 102, 111
Geddes, W. R., 33n., 49
Genealogical method, 6, 73-4, 75, 77, 78, 162, 178, 242
Gerth, H., 136
Gift, 134, 181, 182, 183, 184, 188, 199, 201, 218, 221-2
Gillen, F., 73, 166
Ginsberg, M., 4, 8n., 153, 262
Gluckman, M., 21, 23n., 24, 26n., 28, 30, 48, 70n., 87, 151, 153n., 240
Golson, J., 33n.
Goodfellow, D. M., 218
Graebner, F., 7
Greenberg, J. H., 114n.
Gregg, Dorothy, 42
Gregory, R., 7
Grierson, G., 97
Grosse, E., 7
Gutmann, B., 145, 151

Haddon, A. C., 2n., 6, 72, 73, 74, 76, 80n., 96, 160
Hahn, E., 7, 209
Halbwachs, M., 207
Hankins, F. H., 151
Harris, Z. S., 108n.
Hartland, S., 127, 145, 147, 148, 149, 150
Held, C. J., 248n.
Herskovits, M. J., 33, 154n., 225, 248, 252n., 254, 255
Hill, A. A., 114n.
History, 7, 20, 21, 25, 26, 50, 75, 86, 88n., 89, 90, 91, 100, 125-6, 163, 168, 204, 205, 207, 209, 210, 226, 236, 239, 240-3, 248, 255
Hobhouse, L. T., 7, 121, 145, 148, 150, 213
Hocart, A. M., 74n.
Hockett, C. F., 117

Hoebel, E. A., 151, 153n., 154, 155
Hogbin, H. I., 14n., 88, 126n., 142, 143, 144, 145, 153, 162n., 245-64
Hubert, H., 73
Humboldt, W. von, 94
Hunter, Monica, see Wilson, Monica
Hutchinson, Constance, 3
Hutt, A. M., 257n.
Huxley, Aldous, 22n., 46
Huxley, Julian, 7

Imperatives, 24, 36, 64, 65, 66, 68; Instrumental, 24, 142; Integrative, 33, 37, 39, 43, 45
Incest, 28, 135, 145, 158, 165, 166, 168, 169, 170, 172, 173, 174, 176, 177, 178, 179, 186, 187
Industrialization, 226, 229, 234, 237, 238, 239, 243
Inheritance, 140, 183, 184, 185
Instinct, 22, 23, 48, 67, 169, 170, 204; see also Drive
Institution, 18, 19, 21, 22, 26, 27, 28, 29, 30, 41, 43, 45, 49, 57, 62, 66, 69, 72, 75, 76, 80, 81, 82, 83, 96, 126, 141, 150, 152, 162, 163, 168, 171, 178, 179, 185, 212, 230, 232, 233, 234, 235, 238, 240, 243, 247, 251; analysis, 25; classification, 60; definition, 24, 58-9, 136-7
Integration, 17, 18, 19, 20, 51, 56, 60, 68, 75
International African Institute, 7, 8n., 230, 231, 251
International Council for Philosophy and Humanistic Studies, 115
Intichiuma, 18, 210, 211, 212

Jakobson, R., 116
James, William, 121-3, 127, 131
Jespersen, J. O. H., 94, 99
Joking relationship, 167
Jones, E., 172
Junod, H., 73
Jural relations, 137, 164, 165, 175, 176, 177, 178, 179, 180, 181, 182, 184, 185, 187
Jurasz, A., 8n.
Jurisprudence, 50, 139, 144, 145, 146, 151n., 251

Kaberry, Phyllis, 71-91, 213, 231
Kardiner, A., 67
Keesing, F. M., 242
Kelsen, H., 149

INDEX

89, 90, 130, 133n., 134, 135, 136, 147, 162, 163, 166, 171, 172, 175, 176, 177, 178, 180, 183, 185, 194, 201, 205, 207, 210, 212, 213, 219, 229, 236, 237, 239, 242

Social system, 38, 53–70; *see also* Social organization, Social structure

Sociology, 3, 4, 24, 30, 53, 60, 69, 74, 84, 95, 112, 119, 121, 131, 134, 136, 158, 160, 165, 168, 187, 202, 209, 226

Soprabolzano, *see* Oberbozen

Sorcery, *see* Magic, Witchcraft

Spell, 105, 106, 110, 132, 190, 191, 196, 197

Spencer, B., 72, 73, 166

Spencer, Herbert, 54

Status, 38, 41, 60, 84, 88, 143, 183, 215, 220, 224, 227, 238, 264

Steinmetz S. R., 7, 145

Stone, J., 149

Strachey, Lytton, 88n., 91

Structural approach, 1, 101, 163, 185, 188

Structure, linguistic, *see* Linguistic structure

Structure, social, *see* Social structure

Stuart, Mrs. Walker, viii

Suicide, 141, 146, 178

Survivals, 55, 127, 252

Swann, Valetta, *see* Brante, Mrs. A. V.

Swazi, 4

Sweet, H., 93, 94, 99

Swift, M. G., 209n.

Symbolism, 30, 36, 37, 38, 41, 45, 61, 89, 90, 122, 131, 132, 133, 135, 171, 197, 199, 206, 219, 223, 224, 227

Taboo, 130, 140, 141, 145, 146, 148, 153, 154, 171, 172, 178, 186, 187, 189, 196, 198, 199, 204, 216, 223

Tallensi, 87, 88n., 179

Tamaris, 4

Teacher, Malinowski as, 2, 8–10, 18, 23, 24, 25, 33, 70, 136, 157, 231, 232, 234, 238

Tead, O., 22

Technology, 16n., 20, 24, 26, 27, 36, 37, 39, 49n., 71, 77, 78, 79, 84, 85, 127, 143, 198, 216, 218, 226, 235, 237, 264; Malinowski as technologist, 6, 15n.

Temple, R., 97, 98, 105

Tenerife, 4

Tepoztlan, 244

Thomas, W. I., 70

Thomson, G., 158

Thurnwald, R., 7, 209

Tikopia, 10, 74n., 161, 163, 177, 244, 258, 260

Timasheff, N. S., 148, 151, 152

Titief, M., 154n.

Tiv, 87

Todas, 74, 159

Torres Straits, 159

Totemism, 73, 75, 76, 158, 162, 179, 189, 195, 212, 264

Trade, *see* Exchange

Tradition, 37, 65, 68, 147, 148, 201, 206, 232, 241, 243, 250

Translation, 93, 94, 96, 106–108, 110, 114, 115; *see also* Linguistics

Trevor, J. C., 33n.

Trobriand Islands, 75, 76, 77–86, 120, 124, 158, 161, 229, 244, 249; islanders, 3, 6, 8, 10, 17, 18, 19, 21, 23, 24, 33, 54, 70, 71, 112, 119, 125, 126, 129, 134, 135, 146, 153n., 154, 160, 161, 164, 168, 169, 176–8, 188, 190, 210, 214–26; language, 96, 98, 105–13, 115

Tswana, 242

Tucson, Arizona, 4

Tylor, E. B., 16, 49, 50, 54, 72, 80n., 125, 128, 148, 199

Tyrol, 4, 10

Urigubu, 84, 85, 180, 181, 182, 215, 219, 226

Value, economic, 212, 217, 218, 219–221, 225; orientation, 45, 47

Values, 30, 34, 37, 38, 39, 41, 42, 59, 62, 65, 82, 83, 90, 107, 111, 123, 125, 132, 186, 199, 201, 205, 213, 234, 237, 238, 248, 254, 255, 256, 257, 260–4

Van Gennep, A., 7

Veddas, 74

Vidich, A. J., 136

Vierkandt, A., 121n.

Viljoen, S., 216

Vinogradoff, P., 146, 147

Voegelin, C. F., 108n.

Voegelin, E., 114n.

Wagner, G., 87

Wallas, Graham, 22

INDEX